Reader's Digest

THE EXPERTS TELL YOU

MORE THAN

1,500

INSIDERS' TIPS

TO SAVE YOU TIME, MONEY AND TROUBLE

EXPERT
CONSULTANTS

Simon Arron

Ruth Binney

Gill Chilton

Graham Dixon

Simon Gilham

Fiona Hunter BSc Hons (Nutrition) Dip. Dietetics

Daphne Ledward

Jonquil Lowe BSc(Econ)

Susannah Marriott

Pamela Mason BSc MSc Ph.D MRPharmS

Sheena Meredith MB BS M.Phil

Tony Rilett

Paula-Jane Rothermel FRSA AFBPsS

Helen Spence

Carrie Stockton FCIPD

Andrew Turvil

You've thought it a thousand times – if I'd only known the full story, the hidden facts, the way the system really works, I could have saved my hard-earned cash. I could have made far better use of my time. I could have used my energy for something much more important or enjoyable.

The fact is, we've all been victims of either misinformation or information withheld, which has ultimately cost us money, time and energy. Call it the silence of the experts. It's usually not that they are downright lying, or even consciously deceiving. But sometimes they know precious information that could really help us – and they simply don't tell. They may be bored or lazy. They may assume that we know, or worse, that telling us could cost them a sale. And yes, sometimes experts fail to disclose information for the worst of reasons – to make a quick profit out of our ignorance. Whatever the reason, commercial forces that obscure or blur the real truth are a sad reality, touching every aspect of our lives.

MORE THAN
1,500 WAYS TO WIN!

SECRETS THE EXPERTS WON'T TELL YOU

Oh, to be a mind reader! Wouldn't you love to know what's really going through the mechanic's mind when he inspects your engine? Or the dark secrets your bank may hide from you when you sign up for a loan?

A CORNUCOPIA OF INSIDER SECRETS If the answers to those questions are 'yes', then you are about to be delighted. For months, we have been tracking down and interrogating experts and have searched out as many insider secrets as we could find, which are not only guaranteed to look after your interests but will also make you feel like a genius.

In the pages ahead you'll find little-known hints and tips from top-notch professionals with a wide cross-section of expertise that will give you the upper hand at home, at work, in high-street stores, on the road and on holiday, anywhere, anytime, even at the races. They range from food-industry secrets, which can boost your health and slash your supermarket bills, to crucial appliance-care instructions that should be in every owner's manual.

These are secrets that tell you what corporations and marketers don't want you to know, from the pharmaceutical company that would never highlight the best drug-free treatment for depression to the websites that slide hidden spyware onto your home computer. *Secrets the Experts Won't Tell You* gives you the facts that will make you the smartest, sharpest consumer on the block. Over and over again, we've uncovered highly effective ways to outwit unscrupulous professionals and beat them at their own game.

Each of the pieces of 'forbidden' advice in this book comes straight from the mouth of knowledgeable insiders. Here are just some of the things that you'll discover:

⊙ Cunning ways the slim and trim get – and stay – that way
⊙ Games that supermarkets play to persuade you to buy the priciest product
⊙ Scary chemicals that sneak into your home in household fresheners and cleaning products
⊙ Price-slashing strategies for buying clothes
⊙ Rarely revealed car sales tactics that you'll be able to resist

- ◉ £££-an-hour scams that some repair people use and common, quick fixes you can easily do yourself
- ◉ Tricks that insurance companies may hide up their sleeves
- ◉ Unspoken rules that HR and office managers actually follow
- ◉ Corner-cutting tips from seasoned travellers that will enhance your holidays around the globe

You'll be amazed at how surprisingly enlightening and straighforward many of these expert remedies and professional solutions are.

UNRIGGING THE GAME Of course, you're no fool. You probably already knew – or strongly suspected – that the game might be rigged. And by 'the game' we mean absolutely everything around you – repair people, credit cards, supermarkets, clothing stores, car dealers, hotels, airlines, restaurants, medical care, insurance, your job, the educational system.

Because it is a fact of life: mixed in undetected among the many honest professionals is the occasional cowboy who's laid a trap that's ready to snap closed on your money. It's a complex world, getting more and more confusing all the time. And, no matter how hard the average person tries, it seems at times to be almost impossible to keep up with all the spin and gobbledegook aimed our way by people who want our money. Which is precisely why everyone needs *Secrets the Experts Won't Tell You* – the book you're about to read.

YOUR WELL-BEING part **1**

AROUND THE HOUSE part **2**

EVERYDAY LIVING

part 3

FAMILY AND FUN part 4

YOUR WELL

CONFIDENTIAL

BEING

secrets of
YOUR FOOD

70

PSST! We've got a lot of secrets to share about matters that affect you personally.

WANT TO KNOW WHICH simple vitamin can help to regulate your cholesterol levels? Or which **delicious treat** can also soothe a persistent cough? Why a dog can boost happiness and which tasty fruit juice can help to build up your muscle strength? And how to **tell instantly** if a packaged food is healthy?

OR WHY YOU SHOULD buy herbs and spices at health-food stores and use them in a variety of sweet and savoury dishes? How to enjoy **food for free** from the countryside and why buying fresh produce locally can boost the health and wealth of your community?

HOW ABOUT AN EASY TRICK that the best cooks use to add **richness and zest** to gravies, sauces and stews?

IT'S HERE ... All this and much, much more.

secrets of
HEALTHCARE

All the things your doctor
doesn't tell you

SAVING YOUR SKIN

7 SIMPLE TRICKS for preventing and treating common skin problems

● **Repel insects with vitamin B**
A mosquito bite can be more than an itchy nuisance; in tropical and subtropical countries it could also involve the transmission of a deadly disease such as malaria or Dengue fever. When visiting such places, always consult a doctor first; the usual precautions are a prescribed course of anti-malaria pills. To avoid getting bitten in the first place, pack the insect repellant and don't forget to use it. Or try the old hunter's trick of taking a daily dose of 100mg vitamin B_1 or 300mg brewer's yeast, which some people find helps to ward off mosquitoes and other flying pests. You should notice the benefits after a week, and they'll continue as long as you take the vitamin.

● **Neutralise that sting** A bee or wasp sting can ruin a summer picnic. But not if you carry a small spray bottle of white vinegar and a little container of bicarbonate of soda when you venture into the great outdoors. Bee sting venom is acidic, so applying an alkaline paste, made by mixing the bicarbonate of soda with a little water, will soothe away the pain. Wasp stings, on the other hand, are alkaline, so applying some of the acidic vinegar will deactivate them. And if you're lucky enough to be lying on an exotic beach, but have the bad luck to get stung by a jellyfish, a quick spray of vinegar will soothe that, too.

● **Dab yoghurt on cold sores** Why is it that you develop a nasty cold sore just when you have an important event coming up, such as your daughter's wedding? Probably because most cold sores are caused by the common herpes virus. This will live quietly in your body until you experience something stressful, which activates it and triggers the cold sore. Don't despair. Get rid of it quickly by smearing a teaspoon of cultured yoghurt over it, two or three times a day. The active micro-organisms in the yoghurt will attack the virus, reducing the itching and helping the cold sore to heal faster.

● **Glue that splinter** Your child has been running around barefoot and picked up a large splinter. The screaming starts as you sterilise the needle you'll use to lift it out; it's as if you were offering amputation as a cure. But there's no need for tears. A quick and pain-free way to solve the problem is to put a large blob of PVA glue over the splinter site. Let it dry, then quickly peel it off – the splinter should come away too. Children who are still suspicious, may feel happier pulling the glue blob off themselves.

se cret weapon

VEGETABLE OIL
The rash caused by eczema is not only unsightly, it can be irritatingly itchy, and scratching it only seems to make matters worse. The solution is close to hand – in your kitchen. Just smear some of the vegetable oil you might use for cooking over the rash, then cover it with cling film. But be sure to test this treatment on a small patch of skin first and wait 24 hours to check for any allergic reaction.

● Banish bruises with an onion

You've just fallen and an unsightly bruise is taking shape on your knee. Quickly take a slice of onion and hold it against the bruise for 15 minutes. The substance in onions that makes your eyes water – allicin – will also help to flush away the excess blood in the damaged tissues that leads to bruising.

But remember that this 'cure' only works if the onion is applied almost immediately after an injury. If you're too late to try it or it just isn't working for you, dab on some witch-hazel (available at chemists and health-food stores) instead. Then hold an ice-pack, or some ice wrapped in a clean cloth, over the bruise for 5 minutes. This will constrict the blood vessels, reducing bleeding into the tissues and speeding up healing.

● Beat athlete's foot with bicarb

Dry your feet thoroughly after a bath, then take that box of bicarbonate of soda from the kitchen cupboard and sprinkle some on your feet and between your toes. The bicarb absorbs moisture, so it helps to combat the fungus that can develop into itchy, unsightly athlete's foot if the skin is wet or sweaty. It will also help to freshen up and deodorise your feet.

If athlete's foot has already taken hold, try using garlic, which contains ajoene, a powerful antifungal agent. Stir 6 crushed cloves into 2 tablespoons of olive oil, then cover and leave for a few days. Strain the oil and apply it to the infected area once a day.

● Avoid that itch – use nail polish

You've found a pair of jeans that fit perfectly. But there is one problem: after wearing them for just a few hours, you have a red rash around your waist that you can't stop scratching. Before you donate those jeans to the local charity shop, try applying a thin coating of clear nail polish to the backs of the studs. This will stop them irritating your skin by providing a barrier between the offending metal and your flesh.

HAIR & NAIL CARE

4 SECRETS for keeping your hair and nails healthy and strong, and looking fabulous

● Fight dandruff with Listerine

Yes, that antiseptic mouthwash in your bathroom cabinet is not just for keeping your gums in good order and your breadth smelling sweet, it can also work wonders for your hair. Combine one part mouthwash with nine parts water and apply this mixture to your scalp after shampooing. Leave it on for 5 to 10 minutes, then rinse thoroughly. Do this regularly and your dandruff will soon start to become a faint memory – and you can also be confident that your hair will always smell clean.

● Try a mint rinse

Listerene may cure your dandruff problem, but the antiseptic smell may not be the aroma you would choose for your silky locks. A mint rinse might be just what you need. Crush a handful of fresh or dried leaves in a bowl, then pour over enough vodka to cover them. Leave for a day – no tasting – then strain. Now add about ¼ teaspoon of water at a time to the mixture until it becomes cloudy. Apply to the scalp after shampooing and leave on for at least 5 minutes before rinsing thoroughly. You should see results by the second use and, if not, you can always drink the stuff – the vodka and mint mix, not the shampoo.

● Take biotin for strong nails

The secret that vets have long kept under wraps is that biotin (also known as vitamin B_7) helps to strengthen horses' hoofs, which are made from the same substance as human fingernails – keratin. A team of Swiss researchers confirmed this by giving a daily biotin supplement to a group of people with brittle nails. After six months their nails were on average 25 per cent stronger and thicker. But biotin should not be taken in very large doses. About 250mcg, three times a day, should be enough to markedly improve the condition of your nails.

● Freeze-dry your nails

Using a quick-drying nail polish may seem like a good idea, but what you won't know is that such products often contain large amounts of alcohol and formaldehyde, which can cause your nails to dry up and split. So stick with 'slow' varieties and try this fast-dry solution. Empty a tray of ice cubes into a bowl, add enough cold water to cover, then dip your freshly painted nails in for 1 to 2 minutes after applying each coat.

STIFLING THE SNIFFLES

6 SOLUTIONS for dealing with colds, allergies and other respiratory problems

● Ward off hay fever with honey

It is spring, and while everybody else is outside enjoying the warmer weather, you're stuck at home without even an open window to let the new season in. That's because you're so allergic to pollen that just a few grains make your eyes start watering and your nose start running. Raw honey may be the answer to your problems. It contains traces of pollen, so eating a few tablespoons a day, perhaps spread on toast or stirred into your tea, may help to accustom your immune system to pollen and stop it from triggering hay fever every time you are exposed to it. Make sure the honey you use is raw and try to buy it from a source close to home so that it contains pollen from your area. Raw, local honey is often sold at farmers' markets and roadside stalls.

● Take algae for allergies

Here's another trick for controlling those seasonal sniffles: try drinks or supplements that contain spirulina, a blue-green algae. This is a powerful anti-inflammatory agent and can help to quell an over-reactive response of the immune system to triggers such as pollen. In a study that involved giving a group of hay-fever sufferers a daily dose of 2,000mg spirulina, researchers found an approximately 32 per cent reduction

Ward off hay fever with honey

in the severity of hay-fever symptoms. According to a review in the *Journal of Laryngology and Otology*, this and other studies give good evidence that spirulina has positive effects in relieving hay-fever symptoms.

● **Avoid colds with yoghurt** You may have heard of 'friendly' bacteria – the type that keeps your body in good working order and stops the 'bad' bacteria from taking over. Well, yoghurt is packed with these health-giving micro-organisms and it has been shown that eating two 150g servings a day may help you to avoid the misery of colds this winter. Swedish researchers discovered this when they gave a group of factory workers a drink enriched with *Lactobacilli reuteri*, the bacteria found in yoghurt, daily for two and a half months. Just 11 per cent of these people took a day off work because of a cold or flu during the study, compared with 23 per cent of their co-workers. And yoghurt itself may also help. In another study, people who ate a small bowl of it every day had 25 per cent fewer colds than non-yoghurt eaters – regardless of whether the yoghurt contained live bacteria or had been pasteurised. If you plan on embarking on a yoghurt-eating regime, start in summer. Doing so will give your immune system plenty of time to build up resistance to viruses before the cold and flu season sets in.

● **Gargle away colds** You may remember your grandmother telling you that gargling every morning with warm salt water would keep colds and flu at bay. But if just thinking about the taste of such a solution makes you feel nauseous, then skip the salt. A study published in the *American Journal of Preventive Medicine* in 2005 showed that gargling with plain water works just as well. In fact, it appears that you are likely to have far more resistance to cold and flu viruses if you use water straight from the tap for your daily gargle.

● **Ask for a CRP for sinusitis** You've a sore throat and inflamed sinuses, but don't just swallow the antibiotics your doctor prescribes. Ask for a CRP test first. This inexpensive blood test measures the level of an inflammatory marker that rises when you have an infection. High levels suggest that you have a bacterial infection, in which case antibiotics should help. But low levels mean your infection is viral and only time will clear it up. A Danish study found that doctors

HIDDEN TRUTHS What your health authority won't tell you about COMPLEMENTARY THERAPIES

You're suffering, and conventional medicine hasn't brought much relief. You've heard that acupuncture or chiropractic might provide the answer, but worry whether you'll be able to afford it. Did you know that the NHS funds some complementary therapies? Your GP decides whether to refer you and the local health trust must also be willing to fund a course of treatment. About 40 per cent of GPs now refer patients – usually for herbal medicine, acupuncture, homeopathy, osteopathy or chiropractic – and about 20 per cent offer some therapies within their surgery. If your GP doesn't know it, direct him or her towards the NHS directory of complementary practitioners: www.nhsdirectory.org/ and ask for a referral. If you have any problems, write to the Patient Advice and Liaison (PAL) co-ordinator of your local Primary Care Trust.

Try chocolate for a cough ... a delicious solution

who use the CRP test for sinusitis wrote about 20 per cent fewer prescriptions for antibiotics than those who didn't.

● **Try chocolate for a cough**

A persistant cough is one of the most common reasons for a visit to the doctor. But there is usually little on offer in the way of effective medicines, so here's a tip you won't get from your GP – try taking a regular dose of dark chocolate. Researchers in London and Budapest have proved that an ingredient in chocolate – theobromine – is highly effective in inhibiting laboratory-induced coughs in volunteers. It's a delicious solution and – who knows – it might just work for you.

STAYING HEART-HEALTHY

9 LITTLE-KNOWN WAYS to help to prevent
heart-related disorders

● **Ask about niacin** You've had your blood cholesterol measured and the result shows raised levels of LDL (low-density lipoprotein) – the so-called 'bad' – cholesterol. Your doctor prescribes statins, drugs to help your body to flush out the excess LDL. But your LDL level is only half the story. The amount of HDL (high-density lipoprotein) or 'good' cholesterol in your blood is just as important, if not more important, in predicting your risk of a heart attack. Talk to your doctor about adding a dose of the B vitamin niacin to your prescription. According to Dr Anthony Wierzbicki of St. Thomas' Hospital, London, niacin has been shown to be highly effective in boosting levels of HDL cholesterol, which play a crucial role is sweeping the harmful LDL kind out of your system. Niacin can be taken on its own or alongside statins. Indeed, a European Consensus Panel recently recommended that niacin should be combined with statins as standard treatment in some high-risk patients, such as those with diabetes. Don't be put off by any negative talk about hot flushes as a side effect of niacin. New slow-release formulas offer all the benefits of this vitamin without the red face. You can buy niacin in health-food stores, under the brand names Niaspan and Niacor, but to treat high cholesterol you need a larger dose than is found in most over-the-counter supplements.

● **Eat chocolate** Although it may seem to contradict all the nutritional advice you were ever given, it appears that dark chocolate is actually good for you. It is full of essential, health-giving ingredients, such as monounsaturated fat, fibre, antioxidants and magnesium, and some studies have shown that it can help to regulate your blood pressure, too. Scientists who fed 100g dark chocolate to people with raised blood pressure every day for two weeks found that their blood pressure dropped by a significant amount. And according to researchers at Ninewells Hospital in Dundee, chocolate lowers the risk of 'platelet aggregation', which can result in the formation of blood clots that are potentially life-threatening. But only dark chocolate offers these benefits – white and milk chocolate merely pile on the calories. Evidence suggests that this is due to compounds called flavonoids that are concentrated in the high cocoa content of dark chocolate.

● **Substitute avocado for butter**
Dairy farmers won't be delighted with this tip, but avocados are a tasty and satisfying substitute for butter and cream, which are both crammed with the major cause of heart and circulation problems – saturated fat. When you mash them, avocados take on the same creamy texture as butter. As well as being a delicious spread, they can be used to enrich soups and sauces or make mashed potatoes creamier. Avocados are one of the only two fruits (along with olives) that are high in fat – but it's the heart-healthy, monounsaturated kind.

● **Check your blood pressure**
When was the last time your doctor took your blood pressure? Although it is well known as a major risk factor for heart disease and stroke – in fact, it's the UK's third biggest killer – high blood pressure (hypertension) often remains undetected and untreated. According to the Stroke Association, nearly a quarter of the UK population has undiagnosed high blood pressure. No wonder it is sometimes called 'the silent killer'.
'Every 5 minutes someone in the UK has a stroke – that's 150,000 strokes every year. But over 40 per cent of those strokes could be prevented by the control of high blood pressure', says Stroke Association spokesman Joe Korner. 'There is no doubt that blood pressure testing really can save lives.' So next time you see your GP for any reason, ask for a blood pressure check. It's quick and painless – and it could mean that you avoid a life-threatening stroke or heart attack.

● **Hold back on statins** So your GP has told you that you have raised cholesterol and is advising a course of statins – cholesterol-lowering drugs. These are notorious for their 'poor patient compliance', which means the side-effects are often so bad that patients stop taking them. Several studies have also shown that statins often fail to be as effective for women as they are for men. So, if you're female, a few simple changes in your general lifestyle, such as cutting down on the amount of saturated fat in your diet, could be more effective than statins. Your doctor may even be relieved – a recent poll in the *British Medical Journal* revealed that 81 per cent of medical practitioners didn't believe that statins should be offered at all to women whose cholesterol levels indicate only a slightly increased risk of having a heart attack.

● **Avoid clots with horse chestnut**
Flying economy class is probably the nearest you'll ever come to feeling like a sardine. And if it's a long-haul flight, you could be stuck in a cramped position for a very long time, which can lead to circulation problems. Airlines, in fact, recommend that you exercise, or get up and walk around whenever possible, during a flight to help to prevent DVT (deep-vein thrombosis) – blood clots forming in the legs that can

... rubbing horse-chestnut cream into

travel to the lungs, where they are potentially fatal. Another tip, if you are preparing for a long flight, is to take twice the standard dose of horse-chestnut extract before heading off to the airport. This can help to avoid or reduce leg swelling during your trip, therefore minimising your risk of blood clots. Virgin Holidays also suggests rubbing horse-chestnut cream into your legs during long-haul flights to improve circulation. But remember that horse chestnut can aggravate certain medical conditions and may conflict with other medications you're taking, so check first with your doctor before using it.

● **Watch your waistline** Putting on weight around your waist poses problems more serious than having to let out clothes or buy new ones. It's a sign that you're at high risk of a heart attack (or developing diabetes). Abdominal fat is more inflammatory than fat on your rear or hips, and those inflammatory chemicals it puts out can wreak havoc with your coronary arteries.

Measuring your waist is a simple way to gauge your risk of heart disease. Yet when the World Health Federation surveyed groups of doctors and other health practitioners in 26 countries, it found that 62 per cent of them stated that they hardly ever measured their patients' waistlines to check for levels of excess weight and obesity.

Elsewhere, 95 per cent of women patients, who were known to be at risk of heart disease, reported that their doctors never measured their waist and 71 per cent said that their doctors never told them that excess weight, could be a key factor in boosting their risk of heart disease. Dr Ian Campbell, president of Britain's National Obesity Forum says this is deplorable: 'We are facing a public health time-bomb and can't

---

> ## EXPERT ADVICE
> ### GREAT TIPS FROM THE PROFESSIONALS
>
> #### A test your doctor won't suggest – yet
>
> If you've been relying on the assessment of a traditional risk factor, such as a high cholesterol, to judge your likelihood of having a heart attack, you're missing the boat. Half of all heart attacks occur in people with no recognised risk factors, according to Dr Paul Jenkins of St Bartholomew's Hospital in London. Instead, he recommends a simple, 10-minute test called an electron beam computed tomograph, or EBCT. By showing the level of potentially clogging calcium in your coronary arteries, this type of scan offers a far more accurate picture of your heart-disease risk. It is able to detect the very earliest signs of a blockage, many years before it progresses enough to cause symptoms. Increased calcium in the coronary arteries is associated with a 10- to 20-fold greater risk of major heart problems developing in the future. It's not yet possible to have an EBCT carried out on the NHS, but a few centres do offer the test privately – see: http://www.heartscan.co.uk

afford to be complacent about waist size.' So grab a tape measure and put it around your waist, midway between the top of your hip bone and the bottom of your rib cage. Relax and breathe out, then take a reading. If your waist is no more than 89cm for women or 101cm for men, you're okay. Any larger and you should exercise more and cut down on fattening foods and excess alcohol.

● **Get a flatmate** And no, in this case, a cat doesn't count. Given the latest research from scientists in Denmark, it appears that it's worth giving up a bit of privacy and learning to share the kitchen shelves and bathroom with another human being. The Danish study found that people who lived alone were almost twice as likely to develop

your legs during long-haul flights to improve circulation

serious heart disease than those who shared their living space. If you want to try it but can't find a flatmate, you could begin your search by scanning the 'Accommodation Wanted' section of your local newspaper or click onto http://www.spareroom.co.uk/ or http://www.flatmateclick.co.uk

● **Stay at work** You're two years away from collecting your pension and no longer find your job stimulating. And your boss keeps piling on the pressure.

You're feeling stressed and bored and would love to be offered the chance to take early retirement. You even daydream about quitting your job or getting yourself fired. But perhaps you should try to stick it out. A study published in the *British Medical Journal* of employees who worked for the petrochemical company Shell showed that those who retired early – at 55 or 60 – developed more health problems and on average died younger than those who kept working until they reached the age of 65.

SECRETS OF **GOOD SLEEP**

7 RARELY DISCLOSED WAYS to make the most of your slumber time

● **Refresh your memory** Poor sleep patterns are generally obvious, but another clear sign that you may not be getting a solid 8 or so hours of good-quality rest a night is increasing forgetfulness. If you go to your doctor complaining that you frequently fail to remember the cat's name and have twice forgotten your dental appointment, such symptoms might well be attributed to the general ageing process. You're unlikely to be asked how well you're sleeping, which could be a serious oversight, as research has shown that the amount and quality of sleep you get significantly affects your memory, particularly the type that helps you to recall facts and events.

So raise the possibility of poor sleep patterns being at the root of your memory loss. Your doctor may be able to offer you some sound advice that will help you to get a better night's rest.

● **Go herbal** Ever wondered why some GPs are so quick to whip out the prescription pad when you consult them about insomnia? Because they often have just 10 minutes for each patient and it's a quick and easy fix that works – but only temporarily. All sleeping pills have side-effects, many causing dependency, so that you find it impossible to sleep without them and need increasingly higher doses to get results. They may also leave you in a 'fog' next morning – rather than feeling refreshed, which is the main point of getting a decent night's sleep in the first place.

Brew up some lettuce ... this infusion works

So say no to the prescription pills and try some of the gentler herbal solutions that are on the market instead. Look out for supplements containing the herb valerian, such as Kalms and Nytol. Valerian is a traditional remedy for helping you to relax and improving sleep patterns, but it is unlikely to offer an 'instant' solution to your problems and you may have to take it for up to three weeks before noticing any effect. You could also try chamomile tea as a bedtime drink. Chamomile, like valerian, has been used for centuries to calm the nerves and promote restful sleep, as has lavender. Try sprinkling some dried or fresh flowerheads or a few drops of the essential oil under your pillow, or add some to your bedtime bathwater.

● **Brew up some lettuce** This may be more time consuming and a little messier than making a cup of herbal tea, but it can be worth the effort. Simmer three or four large lettuce leaves in approximately 200ml water for 15 minutes. Remove from the heat, add two sprigs of mint, leave for a few minutes, then strain off the liquid. Sip this just before getting into bed. Note that any kind of lettuce can be used in this brew, so go for the cheapest and most readily available, such as iceberg. This infusion works because lettuce contains a substance called lectucarium, which acts on the brain in a similar way to opium (which would be a little trickier to obtain).

● **Try turkey – or a banana** Have some turkey or chicken for supper. Both meats contain high levels of tryptophan, a compound that promotes drowsiness – which is one of the reasons you might feel sleepy after a big Christmas dinner. Bananas are also full of tryptophan, so are ideal for a late evening snack.

HIDDEN TRUTHS What the drug companies don't want you to know about **SLEEP**

The *British Medical Journal's* 'Best Treatments' site advises that, while sleeping tablets may help with severe insomnia, they don't treat its cause – and they have side-effects. Most people can in fact help themselves to better sleep, just by making a few changes to their routine. Tips include keeping the bedroom cool and well aired and making sure it's as dark as possible, perhaps by using blackout blinds. It's a good idea to avoid large meals and caffeine too close to bedtime. Try to eat at least 3 hours before you turn in. Don't lie in if you've had a bad night; get on with the day and, if you need a nap, limit it to no more than 30 minutes.

● **Check your medications** Doctors are always supposed to ask you which medications you're taking, when you consult them – or to know by looking at your notes – but may be so pressed for time that they forget to do so. If you go to them complaining of insomnia, they may not think to connect your sleeplessness with one of your current medicines. Yet many drugs can interfere with sleep. These include beta blockers, thyroid medication, decongestants, some antidepressants, corticosteroids and medicines containing caffeine, such as many of the over-the-counter painkillers and cough and cold 'cures'. So if you're seeing your doctor about insomnia, take along a list of everything you're using or have recently used and their dosages – including all over-the-counter medications and herbal and nutritional supplements.

● **Take a vitamin** You regularly go to bed, worn out and ready for a solid 8 hours' slumber. But just as you're drifting off, your legs jerk and suddenly you're wide awake again, and this continues on and off throughout the night. If so, you could be suffering from restless legs syndrome and the answer to your poor sleep pattern could be as simple as taking a vitamin supplement. In one study, researchers found that women who frequently experienced restless legs syndrome, were often deficient in folic acid, a form of vitamin B_9 that is essential for proper brain and nerve function. Symptoms improved when these women were given a dose of folic acid. So try taking a supplement of between 400 to 800mcg folic acid a day, along with 50mg vitamin B-complex in order to avoid upsetting your body's vitamin B balance.

● **Exercise at the right time** It has been shown time and again that even mild exercise, such as 30 minutes of walking, can be the route to sounder sleep. But when you take your exercise is also important. Exercise is stimulating; it's not something you should do just before getting into bed. Instead, plan to do some in the early evening – about 4 to 6 hours before bedtime. This is how long it takes for your body's metabolism and temperature to drop after exercising, so that you'll be better primed for sleep.

LIFTING **DEPRESSION**

6 SECRETS for banishing those dark thoughts and raising your spirits

● **Find a new friend** Research shows that fewer people have close friends than they did 30 years ago. Surveys also reveal that there has been a considerable increase in the number of people suffering from clinical depression over the same period; in 2,000, doctors issued more than 20 million prescriptions for antidepressants in the UK alone. While there's no clear-cut evidence that the two factors are linked, they probably are. That's because there's so much to show that supportive relationships – whether with friends or family – can protect you against major depression. Since family members can often be the cause of emotional problems too, finding new friends may be the best path to a brighter life. But how do you make new friends, especially when you're an older adult? Signing up for a committee or an evening class may be a good way to start. Or try inviting a colleague to join you for lunch or a drink after work.

● **Get a dog** Walking the dog could be the key to happiness, according to a team of researchers at the University of Portsmouth. They conducted a survey of 65 dog-owners and found that they nearly always felt obliged to take their pet for a walk, even if they were feeling low and it was freezing cold or raining heavily. Once they had stepped outside, they usually felt much better. Being made to exercise also kept them physically fit and improved their social contact with like-minded people, which clearly played a part in helping to ward off any feelings of isolation and worthlessness they may have had.

● **Eat fish** The reason why so many of us complain about being depressed could be that we're not eating enough fish. That's what a growing body of evidence indicates. The link, researchers say, is related to omega-3 fatty acids. These 'good' fats help nerve cells, such as those in the brain, to communicate with one another more effectively. Among the many studies into the links between fish consumption and mood, several found that people who ate a healthy diet which included fatty fish, such as salmon and tuna, two or three times a week for five years, had significantly fewer feelings of depression and hostility than a similar group who rarely consumed such fish. So elevate your mood with a daily dose of omega-3. If you don't like fish, try taking 2 tablespoons of flaxseed oil or up to three 1g capsules of fish oil a day.

● **Seek out the sun** If you live in the UK, you know that February is actually the longest, not the shortest, month – at least, that's how it feels. By this point in winter, poor weather, lack of sunshine, grey skies by day and the seemingly endless dark nights all

EXPERT ADVICE
GREAT TIPS FROM THE PROFESSIONALS

What the pharmaceutical industry would rather you didn't know about therapy

Cognitive behaviour therapy (CBT), a form of therapy that can help to change a patient's view of the world, has been shown to be at least as effective as drugs when it comes to treating depression. It has the additional benefits of costing less and having no side effects. In fact, it has proved so successful that, to allow it to be used more widely, the Institute of Psychiatry at King's College in London has devised a computerised CBT programme called 'Beating the Blues'. This has been recommended, in preference to drugs, by the National Institute of Health and Clinical Excellence (NICE) for NHS use to treat people with mild to moderate depression. Results have shown again and again that the CBT programme alleviates anxiety and depression quicker, with longer-lasting results, than any of the usual prescription pills.

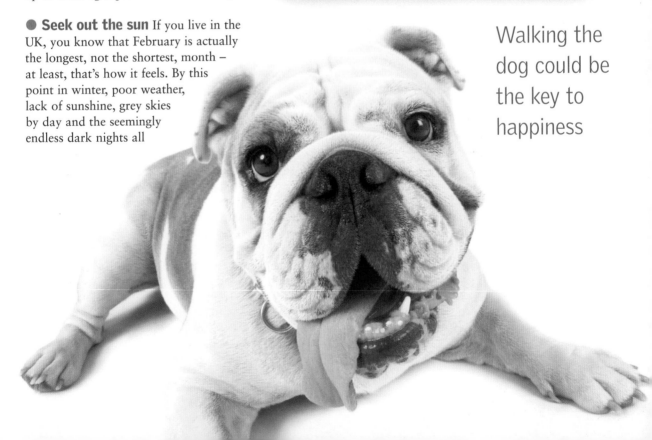

Walking the dog could be the key to happiness

conspire to create a sense of gloom. A trip to sunnier climes will give you a powerful dose of natural light, which can help to lift your mood. You don't have to be wealthy – look at web sites such as www.lastminute.com which often has good bargains. Just make sure you get some sunshine. When you get back, you'll not only be refreshed and revitalised, you'll only have a few weeks left until spring arrives.

● **Stay awake** If you struggle with depression, here's a surprising finding that might make you feel better. Researchers have discovered that skipping an entire night of sleep can

quell depression for as long as a month. No one is sure why this works, but speculation is that depriving yourself of sleep 'resets' your internal clock and this enables someone who is depressed to relax and sleep better.

● **Indulge yourself** You're always economising and doing things on the cheap. Someday, you say, you'll buy cashmere, and splurge out on other luxuries. Don't wait too long. There is evidence that constantly denying yourself life's little pleasures can lead to a serious sense of regret as you get older. Over time, the regret gets worse, while the guilt over indulgence quickly fades.

ALLEVIATING **ANXIETY**

12 LITTLE-KNOWN WAYS to deal with anxiety and avoid the damaging effects of stress

Beat stress by adding some extra exercise to your life

● **Get involved in sport** Beat stress by adding some extra exercise to your life. According to a study conducted by Bristol and Cardiff universities, men who participated in high-intensity sports, such as running or football, were less likely to get depressed or anxious than men who were less active. Researchers speculate that this may be due to the mood-elevating chemicals produced in the brain when you exercise. Or it could be that by participating in a fast-moving sport, you become much fitter. And that means you look better, which boosts your self-esteem.

● **Be more truthful** Every time you tell a lie, your stress hormone levels

shoot up. If this happens on a regular basis, it can over time affect not just your mental health, but cause lasting physical damage as well. You may find that surprising, but think about how polygraph lie-detector tests work. They pick up on changes to your skin texture and increases in blood pressure, heart rate and breathing that are triggered by the unease, or anxiety, you feel when you tell a lie. In fact, the body's reaction to all forms of anxiety or stress is usually so marked that a 'sniffer test' is being devised that can detect changes in your stress hormone levels simply by monitoring your breath.

● **Cut down on caffeine** If you're the sort of person who is prone to worry and anxiety, then giving up drinks that contain large quantities of caffeine, such as coffee and cola, or at least cutting down on them, may help. Caffeine blocks the action of the brain chemical adenosine, which helps to promote a sense of serenity and calm. And you don't have to drink large amounts of strong coffee in a single sitting for this to happen. One study found that drinking the equivalent of 2 cups of coffee over a period of 5 hours could make you just as jittery and anxious as if you'd downed 2 cups in quick succession.

● **Learn breath control** You may have noticed that when you're really worried about something, your heartbeat starts to race and often you can't seem to get enough air into your lungs. The harder you try to return to normal, the worse things become. In such situations, forget the old breathe-in-a-paper-bag trick to calm yourself down and help you to catch your breath. Instead, try one of the following:

✚ Lie on the floor – somewhere quiet, if possible. Place a hand on your chest and press down gently to limit the amount of up-and-down movement, while attempting to breathe normally. Do this for at least 5 minutes, all the time using your hand to control the rate at which you draw breath. You're aiming to keep your chest movements as small as possible, while encouraging other parts of your body, such as your diaphragm, to handle the rate at which you breathe in and out.

✚ If you can, move away from the source of your anxiety. Then try to imagine yourself in a relaxing situation, such as when you're curled up on the sofa reading a book or watching television, or enjoying a warm bath. Think hard about how you would breathe under such circumstances. Remain focused on this non-stressed style of breathing and

secret weapon

BASIL TEA
If you're feeling rattled, rankled, and wound up, relief could be as close as your nearest supermarket, or perhaps your own herb garden. Basil tea is a calming concoction for many people. Just put three fresh basil leaves into a mug of water that has just come off the boil and leave to infuse for about 5 to 10 minutes. Then strain off the liquid and drink it.

you should soon start to recover your breath and be back in control.

● **Keep pen and paper by the bed** People who are under stress often lie awake at night worrying. So follow the advice of Dr Roger Henderson, a family doctor and author of *Stressbeaters: 100 Proven Ways To Manage Stress*. He suggests noting down all your concerns and any possible solutions, which should allow you to set such disturbing thoughts to one side so that you can get back to sleep. Keeping pen and paper on your bedside table will make this much quicker and easier to do. By morning, many problems may seem less bad, or irrelevant, or your subconscious may have come up with some answers.

● **Munch sunflower seeds** You've got a big speech to deliver tomorrow and already you can feel your palms sweating and your heart racing. Here's some advice: munch on sunflower seeds for a few hours before the presentation. Why? Because anxiety depletes your body of magnesium and low levels of magnesium, in turn, contribute to anxiety. But magnesium-rich sunflower seeds can break this vicious cycle. And before you go to bed tonight and first thing in the morning, take a 200mg supplement of this valuable mineral.

How they do it . . .
controlling anger

'As soon as you realise that you are about to express anger over a situation, be quiet,' says Mick Quinn, the author of *Power and Grace: The Wisdom of Awakening*. 'This was the position Gandhi took, and note what he achieved.'

Mick's advice is to pay careful attention to all the feelings of anger or anxiety that arise in your dealings with others. Always ask yourself how much you care about the person who is irritating you. This may clarify how much someone means to you and how much you value their friendship.

Be prepared for the sometimes overwhelming need to express negative thoughts or emotions without regard for the consequences. Then 'discern, decide, and disregard': 'discern' what thoughts could potentially destroy your relationship, 'decide' not to express them, and through introspection and selective silence, 'disregard' them.

● **Watch some funny films** Build up a collection of your favourite comedy films or television shows on video or DVD. Then you'll always have a stock of something funny to watch whenever you need cheering up. Laughter is one of the best ways to reduce the levels of cortisol and other stress hormones in your body and it also appears to act as an 'internal massage'. Research shows that when we laugh, we exercise our upper body, relax muscle tension, massage our lungs and gently expand our circulation. And laughter can also stop us from taking ourselves or our problems too seriously.

● **Beat a drum** Research has shown that beating on a drum with a group of other people is a great way to relieve stress. One study compared the blood chemistry of 50 people, including some who participated in a drumming circle and others who just sat and listened to drumming. They found that the drummers had much lower levels of the stress hormone cortisol and much higher levels of natural immunity. The John Radcliffe Hospital in Oxford has introduced drumming sessions for their staff, as a way to relieve the pressures of their working day.

● **Create a space to relax** If you've got a spare room, paint the walls in a calming shade of light blue or green, install a dimmer switch to control the lights and add a comfortable chair with some soft, plump cushions. You now have a special space where you can relax completely – away from the stresses and strains of daily life. Retreat there after work, light a candle, scented with a soothing essential oil, such as lavender and let the problems and demands of the day just float away.

● **Become an art lover** You could start by visiting local galleries or attending art auctions or simply framing and hanging your children's pictures on your walls. Regardless of their quality, studies show that viewing works of art can reduce the level of stress hormones in your body. Your could even try making your own art. Any kind of creative activity, such as painting or drawing, can help you to relax.

● **Ask for a prescription** You know the feeling – your heart pounds, you feel sick, you can hardly breathe and the knot in your stomach is tightening by the second. Despite the fact that you've only got a 2 minute presentation to give, you're panicking. You feel as though you've had 6 cups of strong coffee and run two miles chased by an alligator. It never occurred to you to ask your GP for help in tackling your severe stage fright, but consider it next time you have such an ordeal. There are drugs, called beta blockers, that can relieve the sort of short-term 'situational' anxiety you are experiencing. They counteract the effects of the stress hormone adrenaline, and so reduce the physical symptoms of acute anxiety, such as a racing heart and trembling. But they're only available on prescription, and should never be taken long term or if you have any type of heart problem or asthma.

● **Just say 'no'** Repeat: 'No, I can't serve on the committee for the village fete.' 'No, I do not want to spend nearly every night and most of my weekends driving vast distances to ferry my son to football tournaments.' 'No, I can't lend you the money for a new car ... or allow you to move back home ... or take on the work of a colleague who has just been made redundant ...'. It may sound simple, but most of us haven't got a clue how to say the 'n' word without feeling wracked with guilt, which can stress you out just as much as taking on the extra

responsibility or added duties involved in saying 'yes'. Susan Newman, a social psychologist provides this handy five-step plan to help you to assert yourself:

✛ Count the number of times in the past week that you've agreed to take on something you really don't have time for. Try to keep a record. It will shock you.

✛ For one week, note down how you spend every hour of your time and who you're with. You may discover one friend is monopolising you or one family member is being over demanding.

✛ Look at the records you've kept and see if you can find ways of managing your time better. Decide who has your first priority for attention: your spouse, your child or your boss. Ask where you fit in.

✛ Carefully assess your limits. How long can you go on listening to your friend repeat their sad story, without starting to lose sympathy? How many more pointless meetings can you sit through without screaming?

✛ Pick one chore a week to delegate. Maybe it's making dinner, doing the washing or ironing or cutting the grass. Remember that it doesn't have to be a perfect job, so maybe your teenage son or daughter could do it.

bad toothache ... clove oil can work wonders

DENTAL SECRETS

8 SIMPLE TRICKS you can use to keep tooth problems at bay

● **Use a plant extract** You have such bad toothache that you're almost ready to tie one end of a piece of string around the offending tooth and the other end around a doorknob and slam the door shut. But hang on. Before you take such drastic action, put a few of drops of oil

of clove on a ball of cotton wool, then apply this to the sore tooth, bite down hard and hold for 3 to 4 minutes. Then spit out the cotton ball and rinse your mouth with a tumbler of water mixed with a generous pinch of salt and several drops of the clove oil.

Clove oil can work wonders when it comes to toothache – it doesn't just deaden the pain, it also kills any bacteria that could make it even worse. Vanilla extract has a similar effect and can be used instead. But remember that this remedy is temporary. You should still make an appointment with your dentist to see what's causing the pain.

● **Chew gum to prevent cavities**
Chewing gum used to cause cavities, but these days it can actually prevent them. Just make sure your gum is sweetened with xylitol, not sugar. Gum chewing helps to maintain a good flow of saliva that will flush away bacteria and, as several studies show, also makes it less likely that bacteria will stick to your teeth, causing decay. But it is advisable to avoid gum altogether if you have bridges, crowns, veneers or other reconstructive dental work as chewing can loosen them.

● **Brew a pot of tea** Tea often gets a bad press when it comes to teeth, because the tannins in it can stain. Yet it contains fluoride and other substances that help to reduce cavities, protect tooth enamel and inhibit the growth of bacteria. Rinsing with green tea after brushing can reduce overall plaque and the risk of gum disease. Studies have shown that tea drinkers tend to have have fewer dental problems.

● **Floss and floss again** You tell your dentist that you floss regularly, but you know that unopened pack of dental floss has been gathering dust on your bathroom shelf for at least three years. Did you also know that flossing prevents gum disease and that study after study confirms that gum disease not only increases your risk of losing a tooth, it can also lead to heart problems? This is because sore gums release high levels of compounds that can cause inflammation anywhere in the body. So floss after every meal and before bed.

● **Try this new way to floss** Would it make you more enthusiastic about flossing if you discovered a tool that's much easier to use and works better than regular dental floss at reducing plaque and gum inflammation? Well, BrushPicks are now on the market, although they're only available in the UK via the internet. Researchers at the University of Pennsylvania School of Dental Medicine compared flossing with BrushPicks – which have a narrow, three-sided blade at one end and a probe with six bristles at the other end – to using regular dental floss and found that they did a far superior job.

● **Avoid hidden sugar** You choose apples over apple pie, carrots over sticky toffees and water over fizzy drinks, but what about avoiding the hidden sugar? It lurks everywhere, including in antacid tablets, cough syrups and vitamin pills. The sugar content of some children's medicines is particularly high and research shows it contributes to dental cavities. So brush your teeth after taking medications, just as you'd do after that piece of cake or chocolate.

● **Swallow your vitamins** Many chewable vitamin supplements contain high levels of sugar, which can really attack your tooth enamel as you bite into them. So buy the kind of vitamins that you have to swallow whole instead.

● **Use an electric toothbrush** Put some spin into your daily routine with an electric toothbrush. Endless studies over nearly 40 years have shown that people who used one have less plaque and gum disease and far cleaner teeth than those who use a manual brush.

Chewing gum used to cause cavities, but these days it can actually prevent them

EYE CARE

4 SECRET WAYS to prevent difficulties with your vision

● **Serve fish** How much oily fish have you been eating lately? None? Very little? Do you also find yourself rubbing your eyes a lot and needing eye drops to soothe them? Then the two – lack of fish and dry eyes – could be related. Oily fish is rich in omega-3 fatty acids, which means oilier tears that will keep your eyes well lubricated – and also help to reduce any inflammation. So for clear, healthy eyes, either eat a fatty fish, such as salmon or mackerel two or three times a week, or take a daily supplement of 3g fish oil.

● **Try acupuncture** Numerous studies have shown that this ancient Chinese treatment can significantly increase eye moisture – although, as with many alternative remedies, researchers are not sure why. And don't worry: the needles don't have to go anywhere near your eye and if you're still afraid of them, many acupuncturists can achieve just as good a result using acupressure.

● **Eat spinach for eye nutrients** Thanks to Popeye, many people eat spinach believing that it will make them stronger. In fact, spinach is not as good a muscle-builder as the cartoons suggest, but if you do include plenty of it in your diet – along with similar leafy greens such as kale – you're far less likely to have sight problems as you age. Spinach is rich in carotenoids, such as lutein and zeaxanthin, which can help to prevent any degeneration of the retina that may lead to partial blindness. You will need to cook it a little to fully release the carotenoids, so boil, steam or try sautéing spinach in 2 tablespoons olive oil and a garlic clove until it begins to wilt, then serve. You could also try chopping it up and stirring in a finely chopped fresh chilli, then serve as a vegetable or on pasta with a topping of grated Parmesan cheese.

● **Munch some bilberries** Did you know that some RAF pilots, during the Second World War ate large quantities of bilberry jam before setting off on missions, in order to improve their night vision. They knew then what science is only just beginning to discover – that bilberries can help to keep your eyes in good condition. Research shows that these tiny black berries are crammed full of antioxidants that benefit the retina. If you can't get hold of the fresh fruit or don't want to eat too much jam, take a 160mg bilberry supplement twice a day.

se**cret** weapon

SUNGLASSES

You wear sunscreen to protect your skin, don't you? Well, you need the equivalent for your eyes too. In fact, sun exposure is one of the leading contributors to potentially blinding diseases such as age-related degeneration of the retina and cataracts. But not just any pair of sunglasses will do, You need glasses that transmit no more than 1 per cent each of ultraviolet A and ultraviolet B (UVA and UVB), with a wraparound design to prevent sunlight from leaking in from the sides. Go for grey lenses too, because they offer the best protection. You can also get contact lenses with ultraviolet light protection, but since these don't cover the entire eye, it's best to wear proper sunglasses as well in strong sunlight.

CARING FOR YOUR EARS

6 LITTLE-KNOWN TRICKS for staving off hearing problems

● **Get plenty of exercise** Now, this is something we suspect your doctor doesn't know – the more physically active you are, the better your hearing is likely to be. This is because aerobic activities, such as biking and walking, bring more oxygen into your lungs, which increases blood-flow throughout your entire body, including your ears. And that, according to several studies appears to improve your hearing.

● **Eat avocado** The creamy flesh of this tropical fruit is rich in magnesium, a mineral that helps to protect you from noise-related hearing loss. Just make sure the fruit is uniformly dark when you buy it and yields slightly – but not too much – when you press on it. You can store a ripe avocado in the fridge for two or three days.

● **Have a glass or two of wine** When was the last time your doctor told you to drink? Probably never, even though it is well known that a little wine is good for your heart. But did you know that it can also help to keep your ears healthy. Just one to three small glasses of wine or beer a day could protect you against age-related hearing loss. But don't drink more; four or more servings of alcohol may adversely affect your hearing loss – and possibly your general health.

● **Take care of your teeth** The more teeth you keep as you age, it seems, the better your hearing will remain too. That's what researchers found when they compared dental health and hearing loss in more than 1,000 people. Apparently, every tooth lost more than doubles the risk of hearing loss. Scientists aren't sure why, but suspect it has something to do with the changes in the position of the jaw or maybe lack of muscle activity, that affects the auditory tube.

● **Sort out your partner's snoring** While you may know about the harmful effects of noise, such as loud rock music, or that from road drills or electric sanders, you may never have heard about the potentially dangerous effects that snoring can have on your hearing. Research has revealed that the sound produced by snoring can be louder decibel-wise than that of average levels of city traffic. Over time, repeated exposure to any loud noise will damage your ears. After proving to your partner that, he or she does indeed snore – a tape recorder may help – suggest a visit to your GP. You will be helping your partner as well as yourself – snoring can be a sign of sleep apnoea, a breathing disorder that can lead to heart disease.

se**cret** weapon

EARPLUGS

You don't have to have spent your entire youth at rock concerts to damage your hearing with loud noise. The sounds of everyday life – lawnmowers, screaming babies, traffic or having an iPod constantly plugged into your ears – can be more than enough. So get a few pairs of earplugs, scatter them around the house and in your car and bag, and use them occasionally to turn down the volume of your world.

● **Take ginkgo biloba** Very few GPs would recommend herbal supplements as part of a healthy life but research suggests pretty conclusively that some work very well. For instance, ginkgo biloba is a traditional treatment for hearing problems and several European studies have shown that this herb can, indeed, radically improve hearing and even help to restore it. One compared ginkgo biloba to the drug pentoxifylline, which is used to increase blood flow in cases of sudden hearing loss. It was found that the herb worked better than the drug. Try taking between 12 to 120mg, twice a day, depending on the severity of your problem.

CLEAN OUT YOUR OWN EARS

If your ears are blocked with wax, but you're certain you have no other problems, such as an infection, you may not need to visit your GP. You can clean out the wax yourself. Go to the chemist and buy a small bottle of 3 per cent hydrogen peroxide and a medicine dropper. Mix no more than 1 teaspoon peroxide with 2½ tablespoons warm water and suck up some of this mixture into the dropper. Tilt your head sideways and release the solution, drop by drop, into the opening of your blocked ear – never stick the end of the dropper into your ear. You'll feel and hear bubbling, but don't worry. Those bubbles help to loosen the earwax as the warm liquid softens it. In a few seconds, the bubbling will stop. Then turn your head the other way to drain out the liquid along with the troublesome wax.

DEALING WITH THE NHS
6 WAYS of getting the best from your doctor

● **Go early** Why is it that doctors so often leave you hanging around in the waiting room for an hour or more past your scheduled appointment? One way to avoid this is to make sure you book the first appointment of the day, or the first appointment after lunch. Your doctor could still be delayed by some medical emergency, but it's less likely, and both of you will probably feel more refreshed and less rushed.

● **Do your homework** The days of trusting what your doctor says implicitly are over. You're more likely to get the best treatment if you play an active role in your healthcare. And that means learning a little about your condition. Thanks to the internet, health information and national guidelines

for treating many conditions, based on the latest scientific evidence, are just a few mouse clicks away.

Consult reputable sites, such as those of the NHS National Library for Health (www.library.nhs.uk) or the National Institute for Health and Clinical Excellence (www.nice.org.uk/) or Patient UK (www.patient.co.uk). You will then be equipped to ask about tests and procedures that could help you, but which your doctor might not mention, because your local health trust is not keen on funding them. Even if you have private health cover, some insurers are known to have asked their specialists to avoid offering patients some high-cost treatments. The remedy is to be an informed patient, so that you can always suggest and discuss alternatives.

● Ask for hormone treatment

Until recently, younger women with breast cancer also had to face infertility and an early menopause, as a result of chemotherapy treatment. But for women with certain types of tumours, drugs called LHRH agonists that stop the ovaries producing oestrogen can be just as effective as chemotherapy, without the undesirable side-effects. That is according to a trial analysis by Cancer Research UK. This means that some women 'with hormone-receptor positive, low-risk breast cancer' could be considered for treatment with LHRH agonists rather than having to face the terrible consequences of chemotherapy, according to Professor Jack Cuzick, who headed the study.

● Go for a mammogram

The NHS Breast Screening Programme offers a free mammogram test – a type of X-ray of the breast – every three years to all women aged 50 and over. But only women aged between 50 and 70 are routinely invited to have such a test, because this is the age group in which breast cancer is most common – about half of all cases. But about a quarter of all breast cancers occur in women over 70 and the other quarter in women under 50. So if you're over 70 and you haven't had a mammogram in the past three years, ask your GP about having one – you're entitled to it, but you won't get an automatic invitation to attend for a screening. In fact, regardless of your age, if you're worried about a breast problem at any time, you should consult your GP, who is likely to refer you to a hospital breast clinic where you may be offered a mammogram. This service is not part of the national screening programme, although the same investigative techniques are used.

● Get the low-down on prescription charges

Most prescriptions in the UK are dispensed without any charge. If you are under 16 (or under 19 and still in full-time education) or over 60, you don't have to pay. People on low incomes or receiving certain state benefits also get their prescriptions free, and some others can get a certificate exempting them from prescription charges. This includes pregnant women and those who have had a child in the past year, and people with certain medical conditions. Ask your GP if you qualify. But if you don't, there are still several ways to cut the cost of those necessary medicines.

HIDDEN TRUTHS What drug companies don't want you to know about FUNDING

Many patient websites and consumer health organisations are heavily funded by drug companies. Some campaigns that raise awareness about a particular disease depend on cash from companies that make the drugs for treating the condition they are highlighting. It has even been suggested that some manufacturers actually create 'diseases' – and anxiety about them – in order to promote their products. For example, it was alleged in the *British Medical Journal* that 'female sexual dysfunction' was defined as a disorder – supposedly affecting 43 per cent of women – by 'experts' who were sponsored by the companies offering a 'cure' for it. So check websites for fund sources and be aware of messages steering you towards a particular drug or diagnosis.

If you know you are likely to need a lot of medicines in the coming months, it will probably work out cheaper to buy a Prescription Prepayment Certificate. This is like a season ticket – you pre-pay to cover the cost of all your prescriptions during a particular period. Your doctor's surgery or local pharmacist will supply you with a form to apply for a Prepayment Certificate, or you could download a form from the Prescription Pricing Authority on www.ppa.org.uk You should also check if there are any cheaper, over-the-counter alternatives to what your doctor has prescribed for you. Sometimes your pharmacist will advise you if there are when you hand in your prescription. You could consider asking your doctor to prescribe your medicines in larger quantities, so that they last longer. Sometimes a GP will do this, although many health trusts limit the amount of a single drug that can be prescribed to one person at once.

Lastly as an extreme measure, you could move to Wales. From April 2007, prescription charges have been abolished altogether for patients who are registered with a Welsh GP.

● **Time your smear** Before you make an appointment for a cervical screening, check your calendar carefully. The NHS Cervical Screening Programme advises that the best time to have a smear screening is at the mid-point of your menstrual cycle, usually around 14 days after the first day of your last period. That's because cervical mucus is at its thinnest at this time and so it is far easier to obtain a good, clear sample for examination. Also, the lining of the cervix is at its thickest then, which means that the sample taken is far more likely to include the full range of the different cell types that are found in the cervical region. All this greatly improves the accuracy of your screening results.

HOSPITAL SAVVY

6 SURPRISING TIPS for making hospital stays as brief and as safe as possible

● **Stay away in August** During their junior years, most doctors change jobs at intervals of between six months and two years. The peak changeover period, when they all seem to switch jobs at once, is in August. This is the month when most newly qualified doctors – those who were mere medical students a few months before and those moving up to higher grades or to a different specialty – take on their new roles. Apparently, it's also the month in which the highest number of medical errors usually occur. Mistakes in writing out prescriptions are especially common at this time. 'Starting a new job is always stressful, particularly your first professional post. Unsurprisingly,

10 tips to help you to AVOID medical errors

YOU ARE MORE LIKELY TO DIE FROM A MEDICAL ERROR than from cancer or a car crash. Even the Department of Health's estimates suggest that there are a staggering 850,000 medical accidents each year in English hospitals. Healthcare officials are working to reduce these figures, but there are also ways you, as a patient, can help. **Here are the top ten recommendations, based on the National Patient Safety Agency's 'Top 10 tips for Safer Patients'.**

1 **FIND OUT** all you can about your treatment. Ask questions and gather information from patient groups and the internet. Research shows that people who are involved with their care tend to get better results.

2 **ASK YOUR DOCTOR** to explain all the options for treatment that are open to you, including any potential risks.

3 **IF YOU'RE NOT** quite sure what a doctor or nurse is saying, ask them to repeat it. If you don't understand, ask them to explain any medical terms in everyday language.

4 **IF YOU'RE ALLERGIC** to anything or have reacted badly to a medicine or an anaesthetic in the past, make sure you tell everyone who's treating you: doctors, nurses, the anaesthetist – if you're having an operation – and the pharmacist.

5 **IF YOU** or your child are going to have an operation, check that all the details on the consent form are correct before you sign it.

6 **ALWAYS READ** the instructions on medicines. Check that you understand why you're taking something, how to take it and for how long. Note any possible side effects and what to do if they occur. Ask if it is safe to take with other medicines or dietary supplements and what foods or activities to avoid.

7 **IF A FAMILY** member or friend needs treatment and has difficulty communicating or understanding what is happening, go along too, to help to explain and ask questions.

8 **WHEN IN HOSPITAL,** make sure that every member of your healthcare team has accurate information about you, the medicines you are taking and the treatment or operation you're in for.

9 **IF YOU'RE PREGNANT,** or think you might be, make sure you tell the doctor, nurse or radiographer before you have an X-ray, scan or any radiation treatment.

10 **ALWAYS ASK DOCTORS,** nurses, ward staff, porters and anyone else who is about to touch you or any equipment you're using, if they've washed their hands.

prescription and therapeutic errors are more likely to occur at these times,' says Nigel Langford and Anthony Cox, both pharmacists working at the West Midlands Centre for Adverse Drug Reaction Reporting. Some hospital pharmacists make an effort to provide a seasonal safety net for patients, by being on high alert for medication errors whenever they know that a large number of new doctors are on duty. And many hospitals have systems in place to help those who have only just taken up their posts. But if you can wait until September for that much-needed hip replacement, you might be better off.

● **Avoid weekends** Unless it's really an emergency – if you're just having tests or elective surgery – try to avoid being admitted to hospital at the weekend or on a public holiday. A survey by the Dr Foster Unit at Imperial College, London, showed that mortality rates in hospitals generally rise steadily from their lowest level on Tuesdays to their highest point on Sundays, before dropping back sharply on Mondays. 'We found that death rates for elective and emergency admissions increased by 7 per cent over the weekend,' said Professor Sir Brian Jarman, who led the research. He strongly suspects that the lower staffing levels at weekends and at holiday times are the underlying cause of these variations.

● **Check for clean hands** The nurses change the soiled dressings of the patient in the next bed, then come straight over to deal with yours. If they didn't take the time to stop and wash their hands before approaching you, ask them to do so. Hand-washing before and after contact with a patient is the main recommended method for reducing the spread of infections in hospitals. Yet a study carried out at the University of Hertfordshire found that 88 per cent of hospital staff frequently didn't bother. A quarter of them didn't even clean their hands properly after they had been handling human waste. No wonder the UK has high rates of hospital-borne infections, such as the MRSA 'superbug'. Not washing your hands 'is the clinical equivalent of drink driving. It maims and kills,' according to Sir John Oldham, a government adviser on primary healthcare. So don't feel nervous or embarrassed about asking nurses, doctors and other hospital staff to wash their hands before they touch you – it could save your life. One study revealed that when patients took the trouble to check whether healthcare workers washed their hands before treating them, the workers began to wash their hands more often as a matter of course and they used more soap or hand sanitiser. As a precaution, you could also take your own bottle of antiseptic gel into hospital with you to keep by your bed – the hospital should provide one, but not all do.

● **Don't worry about the fumes** You are about to go under the knife, when you notice a strong smell of alcohol emanating from members of your surgical team. Don't panic. When his father reported such an experience, Dr Matt Morgan, a junior doctor at the Royal Gwent Hospital in Newport, Wales, was a little concerned – until someone accused him of smelling of alcohol too. A quick test of the hand sanitiser at the foot of his father's bed revealed that the cleanser, which is alcohol-based, was the source of his father's concerns and that the staff who had operated on him were far from inebriated but simply practising essential good hygiene.

● Ask for a different catheter

One of the most humiliating and painful parts of being in hospital can be having to have a catheter inserted in order to drain away urine. About a quarter of all hospital patients in the UK need one, at least for a short time – and about 7 per cent get a nasty urinary tract infection as a result. If you're a man, there may now be an alternative. When you only need a catheter for a limited amount of time, ask if an external or condom catheter, also known as a urinary or penile sheath, would suit your needs. This is a rubber latex pouch that fits neatly on the penis, rather than having to be inserted into it like a standard catheter. It is connected to a tube that collects urine in a bag attached to it. The first-ever study to compare the two different types of catheter found that the condom catheter reduced the risk of urinary tract infections by nearly 80 per cent. It is also far more pleasant, easier to use and it could also mean a shorter stay in hospital, not to mention a much quicker recovery.

● Learn to avoid blood clots

Around one in ten of all hospital deaths in Britain are thought to be caused by pulmonary embolism – blood clots on the lungs. Clots often form in the lower legs when a patient has to lie still in bed for long periods. This is known as deep vein thrombosis or DVT – the same problem that can arise when flying long distances in the cramped conditions of economy class. These clots can break away and travel in the bloodstream to the lungs, causing a fatal blockage. People over 40, and those having surgery on the abdomen, hips or legs, are especially at risk. Yet drugs that 'thin' the blood and mechanical aids, such as special compression socks that can stop blood from pooling in the legs, could prevent as many as 60 per cent of DVT cases, saving thousands of lives every year. Lifeblood, the thrombosis charity, offers information about DVT and advises anyone who is about to go into hospital to speak to their medical team about the risk of blood clots and measures they can take to avoid them.

USING MEDICINES
EFFECTIVELY

6 SECRETS you should know about taking prescription and over-the-counter drugs

● Check your medicines

Before you leave the chemist's counter, check the medicine you've been given and, if you have any doubts about it being correct, ask: 'Is this what my doctor prescribed?' One study involving 23 doctors in three general practices found that 7.46 per cent of prescriptions contained an error. Mistakes were most common in those that were handwritten rather than computer-generated.

● Read ingredients lists

If your child has the sniffles, you may be tempted to use all manner of over-the-counter treatments to provide comfort.

But you could be putting your child's health at risk, unless you bother to read the medicine label carefully. Make sure especially that you aren't inadvertently harming your child by handing out too much of one particular ingredient. You might administer the recommended dose of paracetamol tablets, for instance, but not notice that the cough medicine you're also providing contains the same drug. Too much paracetamol can cause liver damage. So always check the small print on the packaging of medications.

● **Take penicillin with live yoghurt**
Your doctor may not tell you when handing you a prescription for antibiotics, but such drugs can have annoying side effects, including diarrhoea and Candida infections (thrush). The easy way to avoid these is by eating at least 2 pots of live yoghurt a day while you are taking the antibiotics. The 'good' bacteria in the yoghurt will restore any wiped out by your medicine, helping to maintain a healthy balance in your intestines. If you're a woman who is prone to vaginal thrush infections, ask your doctor to prescribe an appropriate medicine at the same time as the antibiotics.

● **Measure medicines accurately**
Surveys have discovered that many people don't know how to measure liquid medicines properly. Too often, they use a normal teaspoon, which doesn't deliver the full 5ml of liquid. So save that teaspoon for stirring hot drinks and use a medicine spoon or syringe instead.

● **Quit the Pill and quit smoking**
You're female, you've tried the patch, the gum and the inhaler, but nothing seems to work. You're still smoking half a packet a day. If you're on the Pill, try

WATER
It may be the elixir of life, but did you know that research has shown that by drinking at least 5 glasses of water a day, particularly if you're over 65, you can reduce your risk of falls, constipation, coronary heart disease and even bladder cancer (in men)? In fact, one study found that nearly half of older adults admitted to hospital from accident and emergency departments were dehydrated – and hadn't a clue that they were. A good way to get enough water is to fill about a third of a large jug with water and keep it in your fridge, ready to refill a glass at regular intervals throughout the day. Try to have emptied the jug by the time you go to bed.

switching to a non-chemical method of contraception, such as an IUD or a diaphragm, instead. Women apparently not only metabolise nicotine faster than men, but the effects are even more pronounced in those who take oral contraceptives. Researchers say this sex difference may be one reason women seem to have a harder time quitting smoking than men.

● **Keep taking the tablets** A report that analysed 21 studies found that people who take their medicine as prescribed have a lower risk of dying within a specified time period than those who don't take it or take it irregularly. Don't rely on doctors to remind you how important it is to follow their prescriptions. Many surveys have shown medical practitioners are notoriously bad when it comes to counselling their patients. They hardly ever mention the most important point about any prescribed drug – that if you don't take it, it definitely won't do you any good.

ALLEVIATING PAIN

8 RARELY MENTIONED TIPS about coping with aches and pains

Stop arthritic pain with chillies

● **Skip paracetamol** Does your doctor still recommend paracetamol to numb the pain of arthritis? Then ask for an alternative, such as ibuprofen, or maybe cut out the drugs and try some form of exercise. A major study published in the *Archives of Internal Medicine* has found that paracetamol, an ingredient in many painkillers, often worked no better than a placebo, or dummy pill. Plus, in large doses it can cause kidney and liver damage.

● **Don't mix painkillers** You're taking ibuprofen for your arthritis and paracetamol for your headache and an over-the-counter flu remedy that you don't realise also contains paracetamol. Do you know how much strain all this is putting on your liver? So before you take another pill, check the label to make sure you're not getting too heavy a dose of any single ingredient.

● **Cut down your dosage** You start the day by taking ibuprofen for your bad back. A few hours later, your back still aches, so, unthinkingly, you shake a couple of aspirin from the bottle in your bag. Later on, you take another proprietary medicine for a headache. If you regularly take pills to soothe your way through life, you're putting yourself at increased risk of developing high blood pressure. Research has shown this again and again. If you take a lot of pills, try to keep a medication diary so

that you are fully aware of all the different drugs you're taking in – the quantity and range might just surprise and shock you enough to make you reduce your self-medication.

● **Go for content and price** Even though many over-the-counter medicines tout their 'specialty' by claiming to be specifically for colds or headaches, they often contain the same basic ingredients – aspirin, paracetamol or ibuprofen – regardless of the type of pain they're claiming to address. So check the labels of whatever you're interested in, note the amount of active ingredient in each dose, then pick up the cheapest generic (non-branded) product and save yourself some money.

● **Stop arthritic pain with chillies** Since no drug company is going to be marketing them to your doctor, you may never hear about chilli peppers being effective for relieving arthritic pain. The active ingredient in chillies, capsaicin, is usually applied in a cream to the affected area. In the UK, this is available on prescription as Zacin, although some capsaicin preparations, such as Fiery Jack or Tiger Balm, can be bought over the counter and on the internet. You have to apply capsaicin four times a day for several days before it kicks in, but the relief will be worth it.

● **Take fish oil** More than 25 million prescriptions for nonsteroidal anti-inflammatory drugs (NSAIDs) are written in the UK each year. These drugs reduce inflammation and pain – but at a cost. Some 12,000 people are admitted to hospital in the UK annually with NSAID-related side-effects, and 2,600 people die each year as a result. Imagine if there were a completely natural compound that would not only relieve your pain, but provide additional health benefits too. Well, there is – fish oil supplements. When researchers asked 125 people with back and neck pain who were already taking NSAIDs to add 2,400mg a day of omega-3 fatty acids for two weeks, followed by 1,200mg per day thereafter, 59 per cent said they completely stopped their NSAID medication after two weeks and were pain-free, and 60 per cent of the rest, who continued taking NSAIDs said their overall level of pain had improved when they added the fish oil.

● **Warm away pain** Drug companies aren't going to advertise this, but you can get more pain relief from a muscle-warming wrap than from paracetamol or ibuprofen. At least, that's what one study of people with lower back pain discovered. Successful pain relief was reported by 57 per cent of patients using heat-wrap therapy, compared with 26 per cent of those taking paracetamol and 18 per cent of those on ibuprofen. The results were so impressive that economists analysing the study suggest that heat-wraps should be used by the NHS to treat lower back pain. Plus, if you wear the wrap overnight, you'll have less pain over the next two days – even without using it. Why not try it? It certainly isn't going to increase your risk of liver, kidney and heart problems in the way that some pills do. Heat wraps are widely available from chemists.

● **Relieve headache without drugs**
Got a headache? Before you fork out your hard-earned cash at the chemist, try this. From a standing position, bend forward from the hips and rest your forehead on the padded back of a sofa or armchair. Relax in this position for 30 seconds, then sit down on the chair or sofa, spread your fingers, slide them into your hair and make a fist. Pull your hair very gently away from your scalp, hold for 3 seconds, and release. This relieves tension in the connective tissues underlying your scalp. Continue grabbing handfuls of hair and pulling gently, working from the top of your head to the sides and finally to the back. With your scalp more relaxed, you should feel refreshed and free of pain.

HIDDEN TRUTHS What doctors don't want you to know about **SURGERY**

Surprisingly, there is little or no clinical evidence to prove that many operations are effective and some show no more benefit than 'placebo', or sham, surgery. That's because no regulatory body has to 'approve' surgical procedures in the way that formal evidence is required to demonstrate the safety and effectiveness of medicines before they can be prescribed. Back surgery merits particular caution. Although it has been used for nearly 90 years and is still often recommended for chronic back pain, spinal fusion surgery may be no more effective than an intense regime of exercise and rehabilitation. That's the conclusion of the Medical Research Council's Spine Stabilisation Trial, led by Jeremy Fairbank, a consultant orthopaedic surgeon. So if a doctor recommends surgery for a chronic condition, particularly back pain, try to get a second and even a third opinion, and don't go under the knife until you have explored and exhausted all other options.

8 useful things to know about SUPPLEMENTS

THERE'S A WHOLE NEW ARSENAL OF SUPPLEMENTS now available over the counter. Taking them can make a huge difference to your health and general well-being. But there are pitfalls to avoid when taking them. **Here are eight tips to make sure your supplements live up to their promise:**

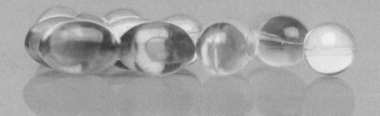

1 TAKE WITH FOOD Taking your multivitamin at any old time is about as effective as trying to put out a fire with a watering can. If your body can't absorb the vitamins and minerals in that horse-size pill, it's not doing you any good. To maximise absorption, most vitamins and minerals are best taken with food (but check individual labels).

2 DON'T TAKE WITH COFFEE You could be missing out on important benefits. It seems that caffeine interferes with your body's ability to absorb calcium, manganese, zinc and copper, as well as vitamins A, B and C. NHS Direct advises that you don't drink tea or coffee for 15 minutes before or after taking supplements. Instead, take supplements with water at room temperature.

3 TAKE CHILDREN'S VITAMINS if you have a swallowing problem. Pastille or liquid vitamins for children are a godsend for anyone who has problems swallowing tablets. So look for brands like Bassets Jelly Babies Soft & Chewy Vitamins – but make sure you check the label and increase the dose to your usual adult amount.

4 **TAKE VITAMIN D** Also called the sunshine vitamin, because it's produced in the skin on exposure to light, vitamin D can protect against more than a dozen types of cancer, help to maintain strong bones, reduce the risk of developing type 2 diabetes and multiple sclerosis, and improve immunity and brain function, among other benefits, according to research. So those who don't get enough sunlight (most of us in the winter months) should get an extra 1,000 IU per day from food (including vitamin D-fortified milk or orange juice) or supplements. The rest of us should aim for at least 400 IU a day.

Peppermint for indigestion ...
It's a traditional remedy and it works

5 **CHECK YOUR CALCIUM SOURCE** We need around 700mg a day of elemental calcium from food or supplements. When taking supplements, choose calcium citrate as it is better absorbed than calcium carbonate. But as calcium citrate contains less elemental calcium, you may need to take more.

6 **PEPPERMINT FOR INDIGESTION** It's a traditional remedy and it works for all kinds of intestinal disturbances, from indigestion to flatulence. Peppermint oil stimulates secretion of digestive juices and improves the flow of bile, so helping the body to digest fats. But don't take it if you have heartburn or reflux disease – by relaxing the sphincter that controls flow from the gullet into the stomach, it could make symptoms worse.

7 **STAY AWAY FROM SEX-ENHANCEMENT DRUGS** It's dangerous to go on-line to buy herbs and other supplements to increase your sexual prowess. Numerous on-line sexual enhancement products contain drugs, herbs and other products that aren't listed on the labels. These could be dangerous, potentially interacting with other drugs you're taking or triggering a life-threatening allergy. Specific ones to watch out for are Zimaxx, Libidus, Neophase, Nasutra, Vigor-25, Actra-Rx, or 4EVERON. If you have a persistent problem with erections, talk to your GP – in about 70 per cent of cases, an underlying medical problem, such as clogged arteries or diabetes is really to blame.

8 **BEWARE OF CONTAMINANTS** We're accustomed to assuming that anything sold in a chemist's or health-food store is safe. So it never occurs to us that some remedies could contain dangerous levels of heavy metals. But cases of lead, arsenic and mercury poisoning have been reported from the use of Indian herbal remedies. Symptoms range from headaches and joint and muscle pain to sickness, confusion and memory loss. A survey of Ayurvedic herbal medicines, made in South Asia, has shown that a significant proportion had potentially harmful levels of heavy metals.

secrets for a
FIT BODY

Clever ways that the
slim and trim get their edge

HEALTHY FOOD CHOICES

11 SECRETS for selecting foods that make meals more nutritious

● **Start with vegetables** To ensure that you and your family get all the vitamins, minerals, fibre and protective compounds that these foods supply, start a meal with a hearty vegetable soup in winter and, in summer, a cold soup, such as refreshing, vitamin-rich gazpacho, or a small salad. Vegetables don't pile on the calories and you'll find you eat less of the main course.

● **Opt for cleaned, bagged veggies**
If you avoid vegetables because you're in a hurry or can't be bothered to peel and chop them, choose ready-prepared and bagged ones instead. Most supermarkets sell a wide selection of washed salad leaves as well as green beans, carrots, baby sweetcorn, mangetout, chopped cabbage, cauliflower, broccoli and much more, ready to pop straight into the pan.

● **Stock up on frozen vegetables**
Supermarkets and greengrocers may not want you to know this but frozen vegetables, which are often cheaper, can be more nutritious than fresh. This is because they're flash-frozen within hours of picking, whereas some 'fresh' vegetables – particularly out-of-season varieties – have travelled hundreds or thousands of miles.

In a winter survey, Austrian researchers tested a selection of frozen peas, cauliflower, beans, sweetcorn and carrots and discovered that their vitamin content was significantly higher than fresh vegetables imported from Italy, Spain, Turkey and Israel, tested at the same time. The fresh vegetables also had higher levels of lead, cadmium and pesticides than the frozen vegetables.

● **Try something new** Green soya beans (or edamame), now available frozen in most supermarkets, are nutritious, low in fat, high in protein and much easier and quicker to prepare than dried soya beans. A small 80g helping counts as one of your daily vegetable portions. They can be used like peas in risottos or stir-fries, or as a tasty vegetable accompaniment.

● **Make sweet potato chips**
If you can't resist chips, use sweet potatoes, which are richer in many essential vitamins and minerals (see page 52) than plain white potatoes. Scrub a large sweet potato and cut into 2.5cm strips. Arrange on a baking tray, sprinkle

HIDDEN TRUTHS What your supermarket doesn't want you to know about **STORE AISLES**

In many supermarkets, 'real' foods – fresh meat, fish and vegetables (which are usually much cheaper when bought loose and in season) – can be found on the outer aisles. If you stick to these – only venturing into the heart of the shop for essentials such as spices, flour, olive oil and vinegar – you're more likely to reach the checkout with a trolley of healthy foods. Avoiding cakes, biscuits, sweets, crisps and ready-meals will save you money as well. Identify the foods you really need by writing out a weekly meal plan and a shopping list based on it. Go armed with this list and stick to it. If you still can't resist temptation, try shopping online.

over 1 teaspoon of rapeseed oil, then bake in a preheated oven at 220°C (gas 7) for about 10 minutes, turning until well browned and crisp. Dust with chilli or curry powder if you like spicy food.

● **Buy wholegrain bread** Make sure you get the real thing by checking the ingredients list for the word 'wholegrain' or 'wholewheat'. If it says 'multigrain', 'seven-grain', 'cracked wheat', 'stone-ground wheat' or 'enriched wheat', it is not a wholegrain product and will lack some of the nutrients, including fibre, present in whole grains.

● **Liven up salads** A good dressing can turn a boring salad into a treat. Use flavoured olive oils, such as those infused with herbs, lemon, chilli or garlic, or perhaps a dash of balsamic vinegar, to give dressings an extra kick. Use a mister or oil spray to keep the calorie and fat content low.

● **An apple a day to keep fractures at bay** Did you know that the more fresh fruit and vegetables you eat, the higher your bone-mineral content is likely to be, according to a study by the Medical Research Council? This means that you will develop stronger teeth and bones, offering you more protection against fractures and the risk of developing osteoporosis as you get older.

● **Eat more mushrooms** Research has shown that mushrooms contain useful amounts of B vitamins as well as disease-fighting antioxidants. Shiitake mushrooms in particular are known to contain chemicals that can help to strengthen the immune system.

● **Eat chocolate – the right kind** A little dark chocolate is a healthy treat. As well as being delicious, it is a good source of antioxidants and minerals, such as magnesium.

● **Add spices for flavour** Stock up on a range of spices to lift your cooking and provide the basis for many tasty sauces and marinades. You'll be less likely to smother dishes in salt, fatty mayonnaise or creamy dressings when they arrive at the table. When buying ready-made sauces and stocks, choose low-salt or sugar-free varieties, as many brands are packed with salt and sugar.

BETTER **BREAKFASTS**
6 SIMPLE STRATEGIES for a healthy start to the day

● **Drink tomato juice for breakfast** Instead of orange juice, have a glass of low-salt tomato juice. It's more filling, less likely to raise your blood sugar, and supplies more nutrients and fibre.

● **Try a smoothie** What about drinking your fruit instead of eating it? Just toss a handful of berries – strawberries, blueberries, raspberries – a chopped banana and a sliced (but not peeled) apple, peach or pear into your blender. Add some skimmed milk and a pot of low-fat yoghurt and blend them until smooth. For a dairy-free version, replace the milk and yoghurt with soya milk or blend the fruit with some fresh fruit juice.

● **Mix your cereals half and half**
Eating some high-fibre, wholegrain cereals can seem like munching on cardboard. So try mixing those hearty grains with something a little lighter. Even stirring a tablespoon of whole grains into your children's favourite cereal is a good idea, as it may help to gradually wean them off the sugary stuff. Or choose a commercial fibre-rich breakfast cereal, such as All-Bran.

● **Add a dash of cinnamon** Several studies suggest that small amounts of cinnamon, taken daily, can help to keep blood sugar at a healthy level and lower cholesterol by as much as 30 per cent. Sprinkle about ½ teaspoon of ground cinnamon over your daily cereal or on top of your morning coffee, or stir a generous pinch into your nutritious breakfast smoothie.

● **Sprinkle blueberries on your cereal** Studies show that these tiny purple berries are loaded with valuable antioxidants that can slow down brain ageing and protect your memory. Or try mashing them with low-fat, soft cheese to spread on your toast instead of jam or marmalade.

● **Choose eggs** If you're watching your weight, eggs – poached, scrambled or boiled – are a great choice for breakfast. Research has shown that on days when people ate eggs for breakfast, their overall calorie intake was lower.

If you have raised cholesterol levels, ask your doctor how many eggs you can eat a week.

COOKING TECHNIQUES

5 TRICKS for making your dishes healthier

● **Spray on the oil** Buy a non-aerosol oil mist sprayer and fill it with your favourite cooking oil. Use it for coating pans, grills and woks, or for spraying directly onto bread or over salad leaves. It's economical and you'll find that you can cut down radically on the amount of fat you use for cooking without affecting the taste.

● **Replace the cream in sauces**
When you're making beef stroganoff or a creamy pasta sauce, use Greek yoghurt or fromage frais instead of cream. Both of these options will provide the same rich taste for far fewer calories and much less fat.

● **Sneak in the fruit and vegetables** Here are two easy ways to increase your and your family's fruit and vegetable intake:
❋ Purée a few handfuls of lightly sautéed mixed vegetables, such as onions, celery, red peppers, cauliflower or carrots. Then stir this into sauces, stews and soups to add extra flavour, along with a healthy dose of vitamins and antioxidants.
❋ Replace half the fat in cake recipes with apple or prune purée. Allow about 5 tablespoons of water for every 100g cooked apples or soaked, pitted prunes, and blend to make the purée. Or, to create a quick dessert, simply add the purée to yoghurt.

**Make ice lollies ...
with freshly squeezed juice**

● **Try potato variations** Avoid serving potatoes mashed with cream and butter. Try these instead:
✳ Blend some puréed cauliflower into your mash. You'll taste little difference, but get less starch and more fibre. Also, cut down on the butter you add and blend in skimmed milk instead.
✳ For a simple change, pep up mash by stirring in a teaspoon of grainy mustard.
✳ As an alternative to roast potatoes, serve roasted pumpkin or celeriac – both richer in nutrients than plain potatoes.

● **Eat a little fat** Your doctor may not tell you this, but – because some vitamins are fat-soluble – you need fat in your diet in order to absorb them. But this doesn't always mean adding extra fat to your food. A steak, for example, provides enough fat to make use of the nutrients in the vegetables served with it.

EXPERT ADVICE
GREAT TIPS FROM THE PROFESSIONALS

4 guilt-free ways to enjoy cheese

1 Choose hard, dense cheeses Parmesan, pecarino and Grana Padano are strong cheeses, so a little goes a long way. Two tablespoons of either, grated, will flavour a sauce yet contain less than 4g of fat.
2 Grate it When preparing an omelette or salad, grate the cheese, instead of adding slices or chunks. It will look more, but you'll find that gram for gram you use far less, cutting down on both calories and fat.
3 Go for soft cheeses Ricotta, soft goat cheeses and even creamy Brie are lower in fat than many harder cheeses, such as Cheddar.
4 Go for flavour Just a tiny morsel of a strongly flavoured cheese, such as one of the blue-veined varieties like Stilton, can transform a salad without helping to expand your waistline.

YOU KNOW THAT YOU'RE SUPPOSED TO EAT AT LEAST five servings of fruit and vegetables every day, but you don't find all that healthy food appealing and you're struggling to fit them into your diet. Yet, a single serving is not very big and with a few minor adjustments to your eating habits, you'll soon be meeting your quota of daily nutrients without even noticing. **Here are some easy ways to get your five in one day:**

1 ADD SOME FRUIT Spread a mashed banana on your toast in the morning instead of jam or marmalade. If you prefer cereal for breakfast, toss in a few chopped apricots (fresh or the dried, ready-to-eat variety out of season) or some fresh berries. Dried apricots or prunes also make a great addition to casseroles and salads.

10 ways to get FIVE SERVINGS without even trying

2 **MAKE A SUPER SALAD FOR LUNCH** A cereal bowl of salad leaves makes up one serving. Add a sliced tomato, a chopped-up apple and 2 tablespoons of raisins, and you will have four servings in one bowl. And, if you top your salad with some cooked chicken or sliced, hard-boiled egg for protein, you've got lunch.

3 **DIP 'EM** For a pre-dinner snack, dip slices of raw carrot, red pepper and radishes into tzatiki or a fresh tomato salsa. For a special after-dinner treat, dip whole strawberries, or chunks of pineapple or banana into melted, dark chocolate, then place in the fridge to set.

4 **DRINK 'EM** Did you know that just one small glass (about 150ml) of fruit or vegetable juice counts as a single serving?

5 **ROAST 'EM** Nothing brings out the natural sweetness of vegetables like roasting. You can roast almost anything, but carrots, onions, beetroot, turnips, swedes and even Brussels sprouts are very good. Just cut into chunks, mix with enough rapeseed or olive oil to lightly coat, sprinkle with a little salt, and spread in a single layer in an ovenproof dish or roasting pan. Roast at 230°C (gas 8) until well browned and tender.

6 **MAKE ICE LOLLIES AND JELLIES** Offering your children such tempting treats – made with freshly squeezed juice – is a great way to ensure that they receive their essential daily nutrients.

8 **PILE ON TO PIZZA** Add an extra vegetable topping to your pizza. Try chopped peppers, sweetcorn, young spinach leaves, sliced artichoke hearts and mushrooms.

7 **SERVE COLD MEATS WITH A FRESH, SPICY SALSA** Prepare the salsa by mixing finely chopped red onion, chilli and tomato with avocado. For a fruity salsa, mix onion, chilli, mango and cucumber.

9 **GRATE SOME VEG INTO YOUR SANDWICH** Hummus mixed with grated carrot makes a tasty and satisfying filling for sandwiches. Red pepper hummus is also good. Roast the peppers first, then peel off the charred skin and purée with the hummus in a blender or food processor.

10 **SERVE FRUIT PURÉE** As a topping to ice cream. or as an alternative to custard, make a raspberry purée. Just blend 225g fresh or frozen raspberries with 4 tablespoons of orange juice in a blender or food processor. Pass the purée through a fine sieve, then sweeten to taste, if necessary, with a little icing sugar.

TRACKING
EATING HABITS

4 SIMPLE TRICKS for creating a revealing record of your food intake

● **Keep a food diary** Buy a notebook and use it to record what you eat, each day for two weeks. Write down everything, especially snacks, and note when, where you were, what else you were doing at the time and how you felt. You will soon have a clear picture of your eating habits, which may help you to plan ways of balancing your food intake better. You may sometimes feel genuinely hungry, but often we eat to satisfy an emotional need. Your food diary will reveal your 'danger' times and the conditions that trigger your urge to reach for that chocolate bar or biscuit.
.

● **Create a photo record** Here's a new way of keeping a food diary – and a number of studies have shown that it really can help with weight loss. Instead of creating a written record of what you eat, snap a picture of it with your mobile phone or digital camera. Download the image on to your computer and at the end of each day, have a look at what you have consumed. Seeing your high-calorie, nutritional mistakes can be a far more effective incentive to change your ways than just reading about them.

● **Check your weight every day** Careful monitoring of your diet and what you weigh can help you to lose weight. One study of 40 obese people found that those who followed this tracking advice lost nearly twice as much as those who didn't. Other studies have found that those who check their weight daily, lose more and keep it off better than those who don't.

● **Give yourself a star** It might sound silly, but just try it. Buy a packet of shiny, metallic star stickers. Then stick one in your food diary against every day when you meet a fitness or nutritional goal, such as taking a brisk walk or preparing a healthy meal instead of ordering a take-away or grabbing a calorific snack. A row of shiny stars can be encouraging. It's tangible proof of how well you're doing.

HIDDEN TRUTHS What Weight Watchers and Atkins don't want you to know about **DIETS**

What's most important when it comes to losing weight is following the diet, no matter which weight-loss programme you choose. That's what a study by American scientists found. Researchers compared the effectiveness of Weight Watchers, which limits calories and portions; Atkins, which limits carbohydrate intake; the Zone, which moderates foods based on balancing protein and carbohydrate intake to control blood sugar levels; and extremely low-fat diets.

The scientists found that sticking with the plan is far more important than the plan itself. But researchers also found that regardless of the diet, none of the participants stuck with it long term, Around 21 per cent gave up within two months and 42 per cent quit in the first six months.

HIDDEN TRUTHS

TRIMMING SUGAR & SALT

5 SIMPLE TRICKS for cutting your and your family's intake of these ingredients

● **Crack the sugar code**
Manufacturers quite deliberately make many products temptingly sweet. So sugar gets hidden in surprising places, including cough medicine, canned vegetables and even meat products and some prescription medicines. The word 'sugar' may not appear on the ingredient list but you can be sure that it's there if you see the following names: corn syrup, dextrin, dextrose, fructose, fruit juice concentrate, galactose, glucose, honey, hydrogenated starch, lactose, mannitol, maple syrup, maltose, molasses, polyols, sorghum, sucrose, sorbitol and xylitol.

● **Go for fruit** If you have a sweet tooth, you can satisfy your cravings for sweets, cakes and biscuits just as well with fruit. Reach for a juicy peach next time you crave a Mars bar and see if it doesn't meet your needs. Keep a small packet of dried apricots in your bag, desk or the glove compartment of your car, so that when you need a sweet fix, you've always got something healthy to hand.

● **Choose 'no added sugar/salt' varieties** If you can't find these, rinsing thoroughly before use will help to remove some salt. Salt is the prime culprit for loading our diet with sodium, but it's not the only one. Look out for monosodium glutamate (MSG), baking powder and bicarbonate of soda on food labels. They are also forms of sodium.

● **Break the salt habit gradually**
Don't expect to be able to cut your salt consumption overnight. It takes around four weeks for your taste buds to adjust and start to recognise the subtle flavours masked by salt.

● **Make it yourself** Ready-meals and canned soups usually contain a lot of salt and sugar. By preparing more food yourself, you'll cut your intake of both radically. And use herbs, spices, a drop of lemon juice, mustard or grated horseradish, instead of salt, to give your meals a lift.

Reach for a juicy peach next time you crave a Mars bar

YOUR EATING MIND-SET

5 WAYS you can psyche yourself up and triumph in the battle of the bulge

● **Learn what *your* body needs** It's not what the weight-loss and exercise industries want you to do, but if you simply stop trying to remake your body and accept it for the way it is, you're more likely to eat better and may even lose weight unintentionally, according to researchers at Ohio State University. They carried out studies on the eating habits of more than 500 female students and discovered that those who were broadly happy with their body shape, were more likely to choose a diet that was well balanced and in tune with their nutritional needs, than the ones who were unhappy with their looks.

● **Hypnotise yourself** Several studies have shown that adding self-hypnosis to weight-loss programmes improves the results. Every night, just before falling asleep, repeat four or five times out loud, 'I am in the process of becoming thinner and thinner'. Repeat for 30 consecutive nights and it will become your automatic subconscious thought and you should soon begin to see results.

● **Go interactive** If you're going to follow a diet, choose one that offers you weekly advice from a counsellor or therapist. Studies show that dieters who received some direct, on-going advice lost three times as much weight over six months as those who took a more passive approach to information on weight loss and had no real feedback.

Programmes with staged targets, based on individual performance offer you more encouragement to succeed. While face-to-face advice is best for some, you could try one of a number of interactive diet programmes available via the internet; research suggests that, for many people, they can be just as effective.

● **No-nibble cooking** About an hour before you start to prepare the evening meal, sit down and have a small healthy snack – a pot of low-fat yoghurt or some raw vegetable crudités. Many people consume as many calories while making the evening meal as they do eating it. If you're hungry and tired before you start cooking, you are far more likely to nibble on what you're preparing. You may also find that sucking a mint or chewing gum before you start to cook stops you from nibbling.

● **Get ready for bed straight after dinner** You don't have to change into pyjamas but you should brush your teeth and have a wash. Once you're fresh and clean, you might think twice about eating chocolate and losing that minty-fresh taste, or dipping your hands into a bag of greasy crisps or peanuts.

SUBVERSIVE HABITS

4 SURPRISING CHANGES in everyday behaviour that can help you to lose weight

● **Turn off the television** There's probably no simpler way to lose weight than to stop watching so much TV. One US study involving 486 people in Boston, two-thirds of whom were overweight or obese, found that every

hour of television viewing was associated with 144 fewer steps walked. Researchers have estimated that the ideal level of daily activity is around 10,000 steps a day, measured with a pedometer. So, for each hour of

... a solid 7 or 8 hours a night can help to prevent obesity

television the study participants watched, they were 16 per cent less likely to achieve the 10,000-steps goal. And, because watching TV encourages snacking, you'll probably consume far fewer calories if you limit your viewing.

● **Limit your hours at work** Your boss might not encourage this, but the fact is, if you work more than 9 hours a day (and lunch is included, whether you work through it or not) you are more likely to be overweight and will often be less productive. You might think of looking for a less stressful job, as studies have shown that the more stressful your job, the more likely you are to snack and pile on the pounds.

● **Take a walk before dinner** Going for a short walk does more than burn calories. Like most exercise, it also lessens your appetite. And if you do it just before your evening meal, you won't want to eat as much as you usually do.

In a study of ten excessively overweight women conducted at Glasgow University, 20 minutes of walking reduced appetite and increased the sensations of fullness as effectively as eating a light meal.

● **Get a solid 8 hours of sleep** There is compelling evidence that getting a solid 7 or 8 hours a night can help to prevent obesity. Researchers from the University of Warwick, reviewed the cases of more than 15,000 adults and found that sleep deprivation is associated with almost twice the risk of being obese. They also found that the less you sleep, the more your body mass index and waist size increase over time. This is probably due to hormonal changes produced by sleep deprivation. Other studies show that lack of sleep increases the production of ghrelin, a hormone that stimulates the appetite, and reduces the production of leptin, a hormone that suppresses the appetite.

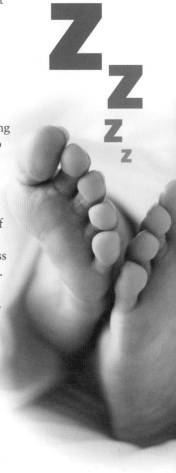

CUTTING **CALORIES**

7 SECRETS for reducing the temptations that compel you to eat more than you need

● **Clear out all tempting foods** You can't eat what you don't have. So go through every cupboard, the fridge and the freezer and throw out all the high-fat, calorie-packed foods that you don't trust yourself to be within reach of. Putting them in the bin is almost certainly going to be better for you than putting them in your mouth. If you want to keep biscuits or cakes in reserve for guests or family, devise a special hiding place and summon up your will-power.

● **Pay extra for smaller packs** It may not make good financial sense – as weight for weight, small packs cost more than larger ones – but it can help you to lose weight. Studies show that people will eat less of something when it comes in smaller amounts. This is partly because smaller packs provide obvious stopping points for you to consider whether you want to keep eating. And the higher cost might just persuade you to be more frugal with your snacks.

continued on page 54 ➤➤

10 FRUIT & VEGETABLES
to enhance your meals

YOU MAY NOT BE FAMILIAR with all the foods listed here and you probably don't know how good they are for your health. All of them are both delicious and rich in useful nutrients. **Try them. We've also added some recipe ideas:**

1 GARLIC We don't recommend doing this alone. Find someone you love to share the experience with. Remove the loose papery outer layers from a whole head of garlic, then slice a thin piece off the top, drizzle lightly with olive oil, wrap in foil, and bake in a preheated oven at (180°C, gas 4) for about an hour. Then squeeze the creamy paste out of the softened garlic cloves and spread on warm toast. The result is not only delicious, it will also provide you with a large dose of thioallyls, a plant nutrient that can lower blood cholesterol levels, as well as prevent blood from becoming sticky and clumping into heart-damaging clots. Scientists believe you can lower your total cholesterol by about 9 per cent by just eating a few cloves of fresh garlic daily for up to six months.

Avocados ... yes, they are high in fat but it's 'good' fat

2 AVOCADOS Yes, they are high in fat, but it's 'good' fat – the monounsaturated kind that helps to lower cholesterol. Try mashing a ripe avocado with a bit of lemon juice, chopped onion and chopped tomato as a topping for baked potatoes or spreading over oatcakes.

3 FENNEL Also known as sweet anise, fennel has a sweet, mild liquorice flavour. The feathery fronds can be used as a herb to flavour soups and stews. The broad, bulbous base is served as a vegetable and can be eaten raw or sliced and diced for stews, soups and stuffing. Fennel aids digestion and goes particularly well with fish.

4 PAK CHOI An Oriental cabbage, pak choi is a cruciferous vegetable, a type associated with many health benefits, including cancer-fighting properties. It has a light, delicate flavour and retains some of its crunch when cooked. Serve it chopped and stir-fried in a splash of groundnut oil and soy sauce. Or chop and toss into a hearty vegetable soup.

5 **SWEET POTATO** Just one sweet potato can supply your entire recommended daily dosage of vitamin E and you'll get a hefty helping of vitamins A and C, along with a good quantity of other vitamins and minerals. Sweet potatoes aren't related in any way to ordinary potatoes, but they can be used in similar ways. Bake them in their skins or mash the soft flesh with a little butter and a sprinkling of freshly ground cinnamon.

6 **WATERCRESS** The ancient Romans and Egyptians ate this peppery green vegetable to boost their brain-power and energy levels. Watercress is rich in vitamin C and iron, and also has a high level of antioxidants and useful quantities of magnesium and potassium. Toss it into a salad, stir into a stew or purée with cooked potatoes and seasoning to make a tasty soup.

7 **KOHLRABI** Another member of the cruciferous family and sometimes known as a cabbage turnip, kohlrabi is sweeter and juicier than an ordinary turnip. The cooked leaves have a strong cabbage-like flavour. Trim and pare the bulb to remove all traces of the fibrous layer just beneath the skin. Then boil, steam or sauté, or toss into your casseroles. Also try it raw, grated into a salad.

8 **ENDIVE** These white, bullet-shaped heads are packed tight with thick, juicy leaves that have a mild, slightly bitter taste. Endive is a great source of iron, potassium and fibre. Add to salads and use the long, stiff leaves for scooping up vegetable dips.

9 **MANGO** This luscious fruit is one of the best sources of fibre and the essential daily vitamins – A, C and E. Its succulent, honeyed flesh is also an excellent source of powerful antioxidants, which are thought to help to combat heart disease, cancer and the ravages of old age. Mangoes are particularly rich in potassium, which is known to reduce the risk of developing high blood pressure. Add the flesh to smoothies, dice it into fruit salads and salsas, and purée it to create a fabulous sauce for fish or chicken.

10 **PRUNES** The dried fruit of a few particular species of plum, prunes contain a special kind of soluble fibre called pectin, which forms a gel in your intestines when ingested. This will absorb any excess cholesterol, sweeping it from your body. In a scientific study, 41 men with slightly raised cholesterol levels added 12 prunes a day to their diets for four weeks. Their blood cholesterol levels dropped dramatically. Blend soaked prunes with a little water into a soft purée and use this to replace some of the oils and fats you normally use when making cakes, muffins, pies and biscuits. Prunes will also lend a delicious tangy sweetness to your stews and salads.

● **Find lower-calorie alternatives to the foods you crave** You will quickly lose pounds without feeling deprived if you find reasonable substitutes for the high-calorie foods you crave. We're suggesting baked potato crisps instead of the usual, deep-fried variety and reduced-fat ice cream rather than full-fat Häagen-Dazs.

● **Hide the biscuit tin and sweet jar** If you can't resist munching when you're at work, here's some advice that will not only cut back on the calories but could also save you some money. Keep the sweet stuff out of your line of vision, or put it in an opaque dish; better still, get it as far away from your desk as possible. One four-week study looked at how much chocolate 40 secretaries ate and discovered that they consumed an average of 2.2 more chocolates each day when they had a clear view of them – for example, when they were stored in a clear glass or plastic container – and 1.8 more again if the chocolates were on their desks. Which strongly suggests that keeping temptation out of sight and reach is key to controlling it.

● **Crack your own nuts** Try to avoid buying shelled nuts. If you have to go to the trouble of shelling them, you'll eat far less. In addition, the nutritional value of nuts drops quite considerably when they have been processed in any way. So, a little effort with the nutcracker not only helps to limit the amount you consume, but also provides a fresher, tastier nut, delivers more health-giving vitamins and minerals, and even burns a few calories.

● **Munch on fruit** Between meals, enjoy a pear, apple or a handful of fresh strawberries. The snack-food industry wouldn't want you to know this, but each of these fruits contains 1.5g of fibre. Getting just that much extra fibre a day – although more is better – is enough to reduce your risk of becoming overweight. Not only does fibre fill you up without filling you out – because its calories are not absorbed – but it boosts the secretion of hormones into the bloodstream that send an 'I'm full' message straight to your brain.

● **Control portion size with frozen ready-meals** In some cases frozen can do more for your weight-loss efforts than fresh food. That's what scientists from the University of Illinois discovered when they compared the regimes followed by two groups of

---

EXPERT ADVICE
GREAT TIPS FROM THE PROFESSIONALS

Five of the best foods to include in your diet

1 Fish supply high-quality protein that is low in saturated fat and cholesterol. Oily fish (mackerel, salmon and tuna) are full of healthy omega-3 fatty acids. Try to eat two portions of fresh fish a week, one of them being of the omega-3-rich variety.

2 Beans are the richest source of vegetable protein. They're low in fat and calories, a good source of iron for vegetarians, and packed with fibre – especially soluble fibre, which helps to lower cholesterol.

3 Fruit of all types is good for you and it's much better to eat fruits whole, rather than as processed juices. Some, including blueberries, kiwis and strawberries are particularly rich in antioxidants and fibre.

4 Porridge oats Studies find that people who eat porridge regularly keep a stable weight and a healthy cholesterol level. That's because oats provides a high-fibre, high-protein source of magnesium and selenium.

5 Sweet potatoes contain beta carotene, which produces the antioxidant vitamin A. They're rich in vitamin C and B$_6$, and are also packed with fibre.

similarly obese men. One group ate two frozen ready-meals a day, plus other foods. The other group prepared their own meals from fresh ingredients. Both followed established nutritional guidelines and limited their daily intake to 1,700 calories. All the participants lost weight, but those who got their food from the freezer lost, on average, 5lb (2.25kg) more than those individuals who cooked their own food. Another study showed a similar pattern of results for overweight women. And the main reason for this difference between the two groups? It could clearly be attributed to the automatic control imposed on portion size by the use of frozen, pre-prepared meals.

SNACK CONTROL
3 STRATEGIES for limiting the damage caused by the urge to nibble

● **Don't be duped by 'energy' bars** In food-industry language, 'energy' means calories. And that's what 'energy bars' are packed with. Manufacturers use the imagery of hard-driven athletes who need a quick dose of calories to supply their muscles with enough energy to run a marathon. But there aren't enough marathon runners around to keep all those energy-bar producers in profit. So most of their goods are bought by armchair athletes, who eat them instead of lunch, or just as a snack. Researchers say that while the majority of bars do contain ingredients that are good for you – nuts, fruit and oats, for example – these are usually held together by a sugary goo. As a lunch, energy bars are better than crisps and a fizzy drink, but not as good for you as an apple and a salad. If you think you need them when exercising, just be sure you're burning more calories during your workout than you're getting from the bar. And if you are eating these bars because you really do need a shot of energy, then experts advise eating them slowly – one bite every 10 minutes.

● **Choose plain crisps** Crisp manufacturers go to great lengths to entice you with new flavours, backed up with glitzy advertising campaigns and fancy packaging. What they don't tell you is that such flavourings often come with hefty doses of added salt. And excessive salt can lead to high blood pressure, heart and kidney problems, and bone disorders. If you do snack on crisps, choose plain ones – preferably those with the choice of optional salt.

● **Don't buy it ... don't eat it** Are you engaged in a constant struggle to resist tempting calorific junk foods in your fridge or larder. Here's a simple secret: just say 'no' at the supermarket or grocery store. Again and again, research shows that among the many factors that contribute to our unfortunate tendency to overstuff ourselves and get fat is proximity. If food is easy to get, you're more likely to eat too much of it. If you're trying to cut down on specific foods, or certain kinds of food, a good first step is to make an effort to keep them out of your house.

Choose plain crisps ... flavourings often come with hefty doses of added salt

BURNING CALORIES

5 TRICKS for losing fat by increasing your metabolism and your daily level of activity

● **Drink iced water** Here's a simple fact that you rarely get to hear. Not only does pure water have zero calories, but when you drink it chilled, you will burn calories warming it up and absorbing it. German scientists measured the metabolic rate (how fast you burn up calories) of a group of people before and after drinking a large glass of iced water. Within 40 minutes of drinking the water, they found that the volunteers' metabolic rates had risen by 30 per cent. Such an increase would burn off around 35,000 calories a year (or about 10lb (4.5kg) of fat).

● **Quench your thirst** Place a glass of iced water next to you and sip from it continually throughout the day, refilling it when it gets warm or you finish the glass, and you'll never get dehydrated. Why should you care? Well, according to research carried out at the University of California, if you're really thirsty, your metabolism slows down. Even being slightly dehydrated can result in you burning approximately 45 fewer calories a day. That might not sound very much, but it adds up to nearly 5lb (2.25kg) extra body weight in one year.

● **Hot-up your metabolism** Don't pity the vendors of those 'miracle' weight-loss products when you hear this. While they're enticing you to shell out large sums of money, scientists have identified a simple and inexpensive food that can help to turbocharge your weight-loss programme. Chillies will not only liven up a meal, but some studies show that very spicy foods can temporarily increase your metabolism.

So spice up that lunchtime omelette by sprinkling a few chopped chillies over the top or fire up that beef stew you're preparing for dinner by dicing and deseeding a small red or green chilli and tossing it in.

Scientific studies carried out in the Netherlands have discovered that when a group of men and women were given a glass of tomato juice, spiced up with a dash of chilli-hot Tabasco sauce, about 30 minutes before a meal, they consumed 16 per cent fewer calories than when they were given unspiced juice. Further research indicates that chillies may be stimulating nerves in the mouth and stomach, so that you start to feel fuller much quicker.

● **Walk up and down stairs** Just 4 minutes of stair-climbing a day can lead to a 4lb (1.8kg) drop in weight in one year. A person weighing around 11½st (73kg) will burn about 50 calories climbing upstairs for 4 minutes (and down for 1 minute). By doing this five days a week, for a year, he or she will burn about 12,700 calories (the equivalent of nearly 4lb (1.8kg) fat).

● **Keep moving** You've heard the statistics: most people regain not only the weight they lost, but a few extra pounds, very soon after they finish dieting. Well, you're not a statistic and you can avoid becoming one if you spend just 30 minutes, four days a week, walking, swimming or cycling during and after your diet. That's because such low-intensity exercise can halt the sharp, sudden drop in calorie-burning that often occurs when a diet ends.

Drink iced water ... Not only does pure water have

EATING OUT

7 TRICKS for avoiding overconsumption when you eat out at a restaurant

● **Avoid romantic restaurants** It's not something restaurateurs are going to admit, but one reason they keep the lights low and play soft music is that they know this atmosphere encourages you to eat slower for a longer length of time. It also makes you more likely to order dessert and another drink. How do they know? Research proves it.

● **Skip the alcohol** What's the first thing the waiter wants to bring you in a restaurant? A cocktail or a glass of wine or beer, of course. Waiters know that people who have an alcoholic drink before dinner tend to eat more. A study found that men who drank a glass of beer half an hour before a meal ate more during the meal than those who drank a non-alcoholic beverage. Those who drank alcohol also ate more fatty and salty foods and felt hungrier after the meal than men who didn't have alcohol. So if you're trying to control your weight, order a jug of water to drink while you wait for your food to arrive.

● **Cut the bread basket** Don't fill up on bread while waiting for dinner to be served. If you know you won't be able to resist, ask the waiter to remove the bread from the table.

● **Double up on starters** Before ordering, look around at what others are eating. If portions look huge, why not go for two starters rather than a main course. You'll cut back on both calories and cost. This is a particularly good idea if the restaurant has a good selection of low-fat, nutrient-rich seafood and vegetable starters.

● **Stick to the basics** When you're choosing salad from a serve-yourself bar, avoid extras such as cheese, salami, ham, croutons and rich, mayonnaise-based dressings. All add extra calories and fat. And don't be afraid to ask if you want something special. If you want your vegetables without butter or your fish without sauce, just order it that way. Most restaurants are happy to oblige.

● **Check fast-food calories** Many of the highly hyped meals at fast-food restaurants are little more than a helping of fat and calories. This isn't something you'll find out by reading the menu, of course. But, if you enjoy the convenience of fast food and also want to keep your arteries clear, this is a useful way to find the most healthy options: go to the internet and find out the typical fat, protein, sugar and other nutrient content of the type of fast-foods you are thinking of ordering. You'll quickly discover that chips and other deep-fried foods, burgers, pizzas and many sauces are a shocking nutritional minefield. You'll soon see the wisdom of ordering smaller portions or heart-healthy salads and sandwiches.

● **Keep coffee simple** That pricey coffee shop wants you to order your brew in as fancy a form as possible. Not only does this drive up the price of each visit, but it also piles on hundreds of calories – in the form of whipped cream, sugar and flavoured syrups. A regular coffee made from good-quality beans and with a dash of skimmed milk can be just as satisfying, so protect your wallet and arteries by keeping things simple.

zero calories, but when you drink it chilled, you will burn calories

AT THE **TABLE**

7 **SECRETS** for reducing your food intake when you sit down to eat

● **Limit your choices** Nutritionists call it the 'smorgasbord effect', which means that the wider the variety of food you are offered at a meal, the more you are likely to eat. Researchers at the University of Pennsylvania discovered this when they offered a group of people a single flavour of yoghurt or a choice of three different flavours. Those with the choice ate an average of 23 per cent more. So limit the range of dishes you bring to the dinner table.

● **Cut the company** It's a drastic solution but you could try eating alone; it might just save you unwanted weight.

Research has revealed that meals eaten with just one other person are on average a third larger than those you eat on your own, and the amount increases in direct proportion to the number of your fellow diners. By the time you sit down to eat with six people, you could consume as much as 72 per cent more than if you had dined alone.

● **Avoid distractions** You won't find this on Weight Watchers' list of tips, but looking at the TV, reading or watching sporting events while you eat can distract you from your meal and make you eat more. So no more meals on automatic pilot. Declare a media blackout, sit down at a table and start to focus a little more on what you are putting into your mouth.

● **Serve smaller helpings** Scientists at Cornell University in America held an ice-cream party to test whether oversized bowls and extra-large ice-cream scoops led to overeating. They found that doubling the size of the serving bowls increased the amount eaten by participants by 31 per cent. So, keep bowls and portions small.

● **Divide and serve** When you're serving delicious but fattening foods, such as roast potatoes, don't put them on the table in one large serving dish; split them between two bowls and people will tend to eat less of them. That's what was discovered when a group of university students were invited to a party. They were offered food from a table with a large dish of snacks on it, and from another with two smaller bowls that, together, contained the same

---

EXPERT ADVICE
GREAT TIPS FROM THE PROFESSIONALS

Medicines that may help you to lose weight

If you're seriously overweight, you might ask your doctor to consider prescribing a drug to help you to shed those stubborn pounds and – better still – keep them off. Sibutramine and orlistat are two drugs that have been approved for assisting weight loss. Research has also shown that the antidepressant bupropion (also used to help smokers to quit) can help people to lose weight when combined with a strict diet and exercise, and was more effective than diet and exercise alone. Bupropion is not an officially approved treatment for obesity, but an individual doctor can prescribe it 'off-label' if he or she thinks it might be useful.

A doctor should discuss any side-effects with you and should be fully aware of your medical history, including other medicines you might be taking. If sibutramine is prescribed, your blood pressure must be carefully monitored while taking it.

Use chopsticks for all your food … you're likely to eat much less

amount as the large bowl. Students who helped themselves from the large bowl ate 56 per cent more than those snacking from the two smaller ones.

● **Use chopsticks for all your food**
You may find them fiddly, but by using chopsticks instead of a knife and fork, you're likely to eat much less. When a group who dined regularly in Chinese restaurants were monitored, it was revealed that those who were overweight were less likely to favour chopsticks.

● **Go for blue** Designers of fast-food restaurants tend to avoid using the colour blue and they do this for a very good reason: blue is believed to suppress the appetite. So, to give yourself one more weapon in the war against a bulging waistline, you could try using blue dinner plates, covering the dinner table with a blue tablecloth, and wearing something blue as well. You might also avoid using red, yellow and orange in your dining room. These colours are thought to encourage eating.

EXERCISE MOTIVATION

7 SURPRISING WAYS to focus your mind on getting active and keeping fit

● **Make your fitness goals known**
Tell your family, friends and colleagues about the fitness goals you are setting yourself and encourage them to ask you how you're doing whenever you see them. It will be rewarding to report your successes. And knowing that everyone is watching you will give you the motivation to stick to your goals.

● **Talk to your doctor** Time-pressed GPs are more likely to want to discuss immediate ailments than ways to improve your general health, so it may be up to you to take the initiative and ask for advice about general fitness. But, as the NHS now actively encourages GPs to promote patients' well-being, they should be able to help and it is well worth a try. Surveys have shown that just 3 hours of counselling by GPs or other healthcare professionals over a period of two years can help to transform the physical health of many former couch-potatoes.

● **Hire a personal trainer** In addition to giving you the workout you need, the trainer will also set your fitness goals. A study by researchers at McMaster University in Ontario, Canada, found that if you're new to exercising, you'll do better if you have a professional expert who determines your goals rather than trying to work them out for yourself. That means, for example, setting the weights on machines to match your abilities, your health, your build and your age. Or, perhaps, determining how long you should walk or run on a treadmill or the newer elliptical trainer, which works both arms and legs and minimises the impact on your joints. But why would you see better results? Partly it's the self-confidence you can get when an expert believes in you and thinks you can reach a certain goal. You only need to hire the trainer for an hour to get your goals set but, if you want to continue, that's good too.

● **Bring fitness into daily life** Of course, the exercise industry makes more money if everyone thinks of fitness solely in terms of formal workouts at the gym. But, as you'll probably only spend 3 hours or so a week there, what about the other 100-plus waking hours in your week? The truth is that really fit people go through their entire day living in a high-energy way. Not only do ongoing spurts of everyday activity make life more exciting and fun, they can also add up to a huge difference when it comes to your well-being and level of general health. So how do you go about living in a fitter way?

Here are a few easy examples:

✳ Stand up and walk around whenever you are on the phone.

✳ Always take the stairs, not the escalator or lift.

✳ And when you take the stairs, try striding up two steps at a time.

✳ Stand up and move around during every television commercial.

✳ Routinely stretch your arms, legs and back at intervals during the day.

✳ Carry more things, more often – garden plants and supplies, groceries, washing. But be careful not to lift too much and strain your muscles.

● **Exercise with a friend** Many people find it much easier to exercise in company, rather than alone. It's often more fun and you can support each other and offer mutual encouragement. You could run, walk, cycle or go to the gym, or a dance or yoga class together. The important thing is that it becomes a regular commitment you both want to make. For extra incentive, you could give it a charitable edge – for instance, you could donate a sum of money for every mile you walk or cycle in a week.

● **Measure what's important** There are so many ways to measure fitness that it's hard to decide what matters. Is it weight? Body mass index? Pulse? Is it mileage covered, pounds lifted, calories burned or minutes of activity? For maximum motivation, focus on what concerns you most: do you feel better than you used to? Do you look better than you used to? Do your clothes feel less tight? Can you see a difference? Are others noticing your improvements?

● **Fly to your next race** Sign up for a charity walk or race that requires taking a plane journey to get there. Book your flight when you sign up for the event, even if it's six months away. The thought of what it will cost if you chicken out and cancel your flight may keep you more motivated to press on than any personal coach ever could.

se cret weapon

A PERSONAL TRAINER'S TOOL KIT

If these tools work for personal trainers and nutritionists, they can work for you:

● A digital, easy-to-read scale to monitor your weight, so that you can see it dropping as you burn more calories.

● A tape measure, to check out how many inches you are losing (or gaining).

● A camera, to take a 'before' photo to remind you how much better you look when you exercise regularly.

● A workout chart, for monitoring increases in strength.

● A heart rate monitor, so that you can check how close you are to your target heart rate during aerobic exercise.

● Body composition calipers, for comparing your levels of body fat to leaner tissue.

ESSENTIAL **WARM-UP**

WARMING UP BEFORE EXERCISE is an important first step that is sometimes ignored. It prepares your body for the demands of activity as muscles and joints will not respond as easily while cold

You're not always told this but warming up – before you stretch or do any other exercise – should be an integral part of your routine. It increases blood flow, bringing oxygen and nutrients to the working muscles and joints, and makes them looser, more pliable and less susceptible to injury. It also prepares your mind and body for activity.

Impatient people don't like to spend the time but this routine should take no more than 5 minutes and, if you're in a hurry, you can pick just a few of the exercises. When you have time, complete the routine, then start your chosen activity at a slow pace, building up gradually to your normal tempo.

1 **SIDE STEP** Bring your feet together. As you sway to your right, step your right leg to the side and allow your left leg to follow, so that you are standing with your feet together again. Repeat the movement over to your left side, with your left leg stepping and your right leg following. Continue stepping in this way for at least 1–2 minutes.

2 **ANKLE CIRCLES** Lift your right foot and place your toes against the floor. Using your toes as a pivot, circle your ankle ten times in a clockwise direction and ten times in an anti-clockwise direction. Then, repeat the exercise using your left foot.

3 **KNEE CIRCLES** Bring your feet together, bend slightly forward and gently place your hands just above your knees. Bend your knees a little and slowly circle the knees ten times in one direction, using your hands for support. Repeat ten times in the opposite direction.

4 **HIP CIRCLES** Place your hands on your hips. Keeping your knees slightly bent gently circle your hips ten times to the right and then ten times to the left. Imagine you are slowly twirling a large hula-hoop around your waist.

5 **ARM RAISE AND TWIST** Stand with your feet together, your arms down in front of you and your fingers interlocked. Inhale and raise your arms above your head, turning your palms upwards. Twist your torso smoothly from the waist to face to the right. Take three or four normal breaths before twisting to the left.

6 **SHAKE** Gently shake your hands, keeping your wrists and fingers loose. Do this about 20 times. Then, keeping your hands, elbows and shoulders relaxed, shake your whole arms about 20 times. Finally, let your whole body bounce up and down around 20 times, keeping the limbs loose and relaxed.

Arm raise and twist ...

WORKING OUT

6 TRICKS for making the most of your exercise time

● **Increase intensity, not time**
Forget those hour-long workouts or the 5 mile (8km) runs. A study carried out by exercise gurus at McMaster University in Ontario, Canada found that as little as 6 minutes of intense exercise a week could provide the same physical benefits as longer periods of more moderate exercise. The 6 minutes were spread over three exercise sessions that also included some recovery time. The researchers compared two groups – 'sprinters', who did between four and seven 30-second bursts of all-out cycling on exercise bikes, three times a week for two weeks, with 'moderates' who did 4 minutes of regular cycling, three times a week over the same period. All-in-all, the 'sprinters' achieved similar results to the 'moderates' but spent around 20 per cent less time exercising to achieve it (about 1¼ hours compared with 5¼ hours).

● **Do it in the morning** Don't think about it. Just roll out of bed, brush your teeth, get dressed and go. Extensive research has shown that you're far more likely to get your workout in if you do it first thing. Later in the day, say after work, exercise may be over-stimulating and you may find it harder to sleep.

● **Weigh into the free weights**
People trying to sell expensive multi-exercise machines hope you don't catch on to this idea: inexpensive free weights actually offer a number of advantages in terms of fitness and convenience. When you use free weights, you can exercise each side of your body separately, eliminating imbalances in muscle tone. Only a few exercise machines allow you to do that. Also, if you have a slight build, the typical exercise machine – designed for men – may not fit you, no matter how much you adjust the settings. The machines are also too big for most homes, whereas dumbbells are compact, inexpensive and easy to use.

● **Power up with cherry juice** Who would think that a glass of red juice could make a difference to muscle tone and strength? Researchers at the University of Vermont in the USA asked 14 volunteers to drink either fresh cherry juice blended with apple juice or a juice

How they do it . . .
losing weight

When Dan Collins graduated from university in 1984, he was 21, just under 5ft 11in (180cm) tall and weighed 17st (108kg). He was also suffering from alarmingly high blood pressure. His GP was concerned enough to suggest that Dan should come in for a check-up every month. It was enough to make the overweight young man take his condition seriously.

Dan had tried many other ways of losing weight including the 'sleep diet' – 'I slept as long as I could – the logic being that if you're asleep, you're not eating'.

But this time, his GP's scrutiny kept him in line. He stopped night eating – the bane of many food addicts – and gradually lost weight. He'd never liked exercise but as he started to feel fitter, he wanted something that would help him to keep the weight off and signed up for a class that intrigued him called 'Fencing for Beginners'. 'I felt good enough about myself at that time to dare to don the very unforgiving whites,' he laughs. And 20 years later, Dan still enjoys fencing, stays fit and weighs a healthy 13½st (86kg).

mix with no cherry juice, twice a day for three days before exercise and for four days afterwards. The cherry-juice drinkers lost far less muscle strength in the days after their workouts than those drinking the cherry-free mixture. They also suffered far less pain after working out than the other group. Plus, the cherry-juice drinkers said their pain peaked at about 24 hours after exercising, while it lasted twice as long for those getting the cherry-less drink. The researchers suspect that the high levels of anti-inflammatory and anti-oxidant compounds found in fresh cherry juice are behind its benefits.

● **Stick to water** The television ads may feature elite athletes downing sports drinks to replenish their energy levels and so enhance their performance, but this has little relevance for most people. Research shows that top athletes need higher levels of sodium and far more liquid than less active people. Sports

drinks fill that need – they're rich in salt, which provides the much-needed sodium and also keeps the athlete thirsty. But most people don't need that extra salt. Unless you're testing yourself to the limit for extended periods, plain water should quench your thirst nicely.

● **Use music to pump up the pace** Programme your iPod or other portable music player to start with slow-moving music, then something a little faster and more vibrant, gradually building up to a burst of rapid-fire dance music. Studies show that this can help you to work harder and for longer than if you listen to either fast or slow music, or if you move from a fast piece to something slower paced.

And here's another use for your favourite toy: tune into it when you're out walking. Research has revealed that listening to music while strolling along can also help people to cover more miles in a given time-span.

> Research has revealed that listening to music while strolling ... helps people to cover more miles

WOMEN'S
EXERCISE CONCERNS

5 **THINGS** every woman should know to get more out of her workouts

● **Time your exercise to your menstrual cycle** It's not the sort of thing you'd want to shout about in your local gym but, if you're in the latter part of your menstrual cycle, that's an excellent reason for an energetic work-out on the step machines. A study from the University of Adelaide in Australia found that women who exercise at this time of the month, when levels of

oestrogen and progesterone are at their highest, burn more fat for energy, which leads to weight loss and less exercise-related fatigue.

● **Check your iron levels** A study from Cornell University in the USA found that women with low levels of iron in their blood – but not low enough to be classified as anaemic – find it more

10 secrets for CHOOSING a health club

FIND THE GYM THAT SUITS YOU – advice from Steven Nance, performance director at Pure Sports Medicine, a specialist sports medicine clinic in London.

1 HEALTH CLUBS CAN ALWAYS WAIVE THE ENROLMENT FEE That fee is just a way for them to get more money out of you. If you don't want to pay it, just tell the sales rep that you're going to join somewhere else. In most cases, you're pretty much guaranteed to have the fee waived.

2 MAKE SURE YOU CAN CANCEL AT ANY TIME And set it down in writing. You might even have to write on your contract that 'as agreed with [salesperson's name], I can cancel this membership at any time with no fees.' Ask the salesperson to sign and date it or, even better, ask the manager to sign and date it in case there's a staff turnover and your salesperson no longer works there.

3 FIND OUT WHEN THE GYM IS BUSIEST and make sure that works for you. If you prefer to work out during a quiet time but the only time that you can get to the gym is after work when the machines are mobbed, you should look for somewhere else.

4 ASK FOR A ONE-WEEK TRIAL and bring a friend. Your friend might be able to spot problems you didn't see.

5 INSIST ON A FREE personal training session if you join. If they already provide one, ask for two.

6

ASK HOW OFTEN the equipment is serviced and cleaned. Cleaning should be done daily; servicing at least once a month.

7

WHEN YOU GET A TOUR OF THE FACILITY, look at its general state of repair, check for outdated cardio equipment, and inspect the cleanliness of the locker and shower areas.

8

IF THE SALES REP IS WOOING YOU with visions of Pilates and yoga classes, ask about additional fees. Many make you pay more for such classes.

9

FITNESS CLUBS OVERSELL MEMBERSHIPS in the hope that people won't go. If just 20 per cent of the members turned up at one time, most clubs would not have enough space or equipment to support them. Ask when the busiest times are, and pay a visit then to see if the place is too crowded for your taste.

10

PERSONAL TRAINERS AT GYMS are on commission plus a small hourly rate. So beware of trainers who hound you to sign up for sessions – they're possibly under pressure to make a sales target. You should also ask trainers what qualifications they hold and talk to others who have worked with them.

difficult to maintain an exercise regime than women with normal levels. If you suspect that is why you tire so easily, go and see your GP, who may prescribe a daily supplement of 100mg of iron, which can double the exercise endurance level of women who are slightly deficient in iron. But note that this is prescription-strength iron, which should only be taken in consultation with a doctor. In addition, good sources of dietary iron include red meat and eggs. Drinking citrus juice with meals will also improve absorption from iron-rich foods such as beans and green leafy vegetables.

● **Ignore the mirrors at gyms** The designers of fitness clubs often install mirrors in exercise rooms, thinking that you want to watch yourself work out. It may be useful to monitor your technique but looking at yourself can also work against you. One study found that women who exercised in front of a mirror felt less calm and more tired after 30 minutes of working out than those who exercised without mirrors.

● **Avoid celebrity exercise videos** If you've ever bought an exercise video or DVD, did you choose one featuring a celebrity? Experts think that the super-slim, super-toned models in such videos can actually sap your motivation, making you feel less confident about achieving any fitness goals. Why? Because they seem to reinforce the seemingly unbridgeable gap between exercise divas and 'real' women.

If you want a motivating exercise video or class, you should look for a teacher with whom you feel relaxed. Find someone with a fitness background who, like the rest of us, looks as though they need to exercise to look their best.

● **You can be both healthy and heavy** Many women think they are too heavy to benefit from exercising; others get discouraged when they don't see significant weight loss after weeks of exercise. But the most important benefit of exercise is keeping your heart healthy. And research shows that the amount of activity you get, not your weight, is the chief predictor of heart disease.

SECRET WORKOUTS

8 EASY WAYS to sneak some beneficial exercises into your daily routine

● **Squeeze hard** Your gluteus maximus is the biggest of the three gluteal muscles in your buttocks. Exercise it. Whether you're standing or sitting, an invisible buttock squeeze (tighten, hold for 2 seconds, release) repeated 10 to 15 times, one to three times a day, tightens the muscle and burns calories.

● **Practise proper posture** By making an effort to stand 'tall', you contract dozens of muscles from your legs up to your neck. This burns calories and builds muscle. Whether you're ironing, doing dishes or queuing at the bank, concentrate on keeping a solid foot stance, a slight bend in your knees, an open chest, with shoulders depressed and head up. Another secret workout: imagine you're squeezing a pencil between your shoulder blades and you have to hold the muscles tight so that the pencil doesn't fall. It doesn't take long before the muscles in your back start to tire. Every time you realign your posture, sit or stand a bit taller, you're exercising your back and core muscles.

● **Exercise while washing** Whether you're waiting for the cycle to end or folding clothes, fit in some leg work. Try performing ten or so plié squats (think ballerina). Place your heels just shoulder width apart and rotate your toes out to a 45° angle. Drop into a squat, keeping your knees in line with your toes and make sure your head, shoulders and hips are aligned. Return to the starting position, squeezing the muscles in your buttocks as you stand tall.

● **Play games with your children** Instead of always watching your kids play sports, join them. Chasing and catching games can be great fun; your children will love it and you'll burn plenty of calories. And something like rounders is a game that youngsters and most fit adults will enjoy.

● **Do isometric exercises** You may not know the term. Isometric exercises, are exercises in which muscles are tensed without movement. For example, pushing as hard as you can against a brick wall is an isometric exercise, because neither you nor the wall moves. Research has shown that isometric exercises can be extremely helpful, particularly for people who have a limited range of motion. And you can do them any time, anywhere. The basic rule is to hold the tension for 5 to

10 seconds, then relax for a few seconds. Repeat five to eight times. Here are some simple isometric exercises to try:

※ Tense your abdominal muscles.

※ Hold your hands in front of you, as if praying, and press firmly together.

※ Stand with your legs apart about a foot from a wall. Push against the wall with your hands as if you were trying to move it.

※ Stand inside a doorway and, with your arms straight down and by your sides, put the backs of your hands against each door frame. Push your hands against the doorway as hard as you can, as if trying to widen the space.

※ While still inside the doorway, push your palms against the frame above you, as if you were trying to lift the building.

※ Sit down in a chair, feet flat on the ground. Push your legs into the ground as hard as you can.

● **Get outdoors** Ever noticed how much of the equipment at the gym – treadmills, stationary bikes, rowing machines – merely replicates what you would be doing if you were outside? One of the best indications of a fit lifestyle is how much time you spend outdoors. Even if you are just walking, gardening or washing the car, you are likely to be more active than you would be indoors.

So step outside for at least 3 hours every weekend. Best of all, once you get used to spending time outdoors, you'll soon be hankering after more active pursuits.

● **Lengthen and speed up your stride while walking** Not just occasionally – but all the time. Become a high-energy walker – fast, confident, with good posture and healthy arm swinging. Just this small adjustment will burn extra calories and give you stronger legs and a shapelier behind.

● **Make cooking into a workout** By adjusting your equipment, storage and cooking style, you can make every meal healthier to create:

※ **Use a cleaver** It's heavier than an basic cooking knife, giving your arms and hands a workout as you chop.

※ **Use cast-iron pans** Again, they are much heavier to lift.

※ **Buy drinks in larger containers** Pouring then becomes an exercise.

※ **Store utensils you use most often either very high or very low** Stretch slowly and deliberately as you reach up or squat down for them.

※ **Toss food** It takes more effort to pick up a pan and toss the contents to turn them, than to mix them with a spoon, and it looks impressive too.

Get outside ... for at least 3 hours every weekend

WALKING

7 SECRET WAYS to make the most of this healthy, no-cost activity

● **Walk to control your body weight** You may not think such a mild level of activity can help. But, in one significant study, a group of sedentary people were given a daily goal of 10,000 steps of brisk activity, as measured by their pedometers. They improved their fitness levels just as much as a group that followed a traditional gym-based aerobic routine. Overall, studies find that getting 8,000 to 10,000 steps a day (about five miles or 8km) helps you to lose weight, while adding to that another 2,000 steps (an extra one mile or 1.6km a day), helps you to maintain your current weight and stop gaining weight.

● **Walk for entertainment one day a week** Instead of walking around your neighbourhood, walk around a zoo, an art museum, or a shopping centre. You could even try walking around them twice – first at a brisk pace and then more slowly to take in the sights.

● **Walk in the prettiest neighbourhood** Pleasant surroundings make all the difference. Just circling the same streets can become very boring. So do what one of our exercise advisers does: get in the car and drive to a new neighbourhood. And make it a nice one. When researchers from the University of Wollongong in New South Wales, Australia, surveyed walkers about their walking habits, they found that men who found their neighbourhoods attractive were much more likely to walk around them. Other research finds that neighbourhoods which have well-maintained pavements and safe and well-lit walking areas encourage walking more than neighbourhoods which don't. Also, people who live in neighbourhoods where they feel safe and comfortable, walk an average of 70 more minutes each week than people who live in less attractive areas.

● **Walk faster nearer the start of your walk** If you want to increase the amount of fat you burn during a walk, add some bursts of faster walking towards the beginning of your walk. Many walkers wait until the end of the walk to speed up, treating their faster walking as a finishing flourish. Yet a study published in the *European Journal of Applied Physiology* found that exercisers burned more fat and felt less tired when they inserted their faster segments towards the beginning of a workout rather than closer to the end.

secret weapon

PEDOMETER

The manager at your local gym will hate you, because once you figure out the benefits of this palm-size gadget, your days on the treadmill are history. You wear pedometers on your waist. The device senses your body motion and counts your footsteps, then converts the count into distance based on the length of your stride. But don't skimp on quality when you buy a pedometer. A study published in the on-line edition of the *British Journal of Sports Medicine* found that cheap pedometers are not only less likely to accurately measure steps taken, but most overestimated participants' steps, which could lead to a false sense of accomplishment.

Doing this works because it speeds up your heart rate early on and keeps it elevated for the rest of your walk.

● **Walk when you shop** Online shopping is great in terms of selection and convenience, but it is pretty useless when it comes to burning calories. But, making the effort to go out shopping, walking to the shops if they're close enough and carrying your shopping back home, can burn about 200 calories an hour, which is much more than what you'd burn sitting at your desk surfing the internet. You can increase the effectiveness of your walk by doing a lap around the shopping centre between store visits.

● **Walk to fund-raise for a cause** It's always better and often much more fun to walk for a charitable cause. In the UK, many charities including the Samaritans and Marie Curie Cancer Care, regularly stage fundraising walks. You'll need to find sponsors but you'll take pride in the fact that you're walking for something beyond yourself, which will motivate you to go longer and faster. After every walk, mark the amount you've raised on a chart: it will encourage you to do more.

● **Walk around the office or house** Are you stuck at your desk working all day, practically chained to your computer screen? Get up and walk around for 5 minutes every 2 hours at least. A brisk 5 minute walk every 2 hours adds up to an extra 20 minutes walking by the end of the working day. And getting a break will make you less likely to eat compulsively at your desk. It's also a good idea to get up and walk around for a few minutes every hour or so if you are sitting for long periods of time at home reading, watching TV or pursuing any other sedentary hobby.

secrets of
YOUR FOOD

Vital facts the food industry would
rather keep under wraps

FOOD LABELS

10 INSIDER TIPS to help you to decipher the information given on packaged foods

● **Don't believe the hype** Think twice about claims like 'no cholesterol' and '90 per cent fat free'. Cholesterol is a fat that occurs only in animal products – meat, fish, eggs and milk. So why do many plant-derived products, such as cereals, bother to have 'no cholesterol' on their label? Because food companies know that people are concerned about their cholesterol levels and that few realise that plants don't contain any.

If a food is labelled '90 per fat free', it means it is still 10 per cent fat. Some brands of snacks, crisps and cakes use this form of labelling to make you believe their product is better for you, but in many cases they contain no less fat that other similar products.

Don't be misled by labels that make claims like 'no artificial colours', as they may tell only half the story. The food in question may still contain other additives. Check the ingredients list, as all additives must be listed there by law.

● **Look for short ingredient lists** Whenever you take a packaged food off the supermarket shelf, glance at the list of ingredients. A long list often means the product is highly processed and crammed with additives. Some of these additives will have plus points. Preservatives, for example, help to keep food safe by preventing the growth of bacteria that can cause food poisoning. Without emulsifiers and stabilisers, products such as reduced and low-fat spreads would not be feasible. But some food additives, particularly artificial colourings, have been linked to health problems, such as hyperactivity, allergies and asthma.

● **Learn about additives** In Europe, stringent tests must be carried out on all food additives before they are approved for use. But you still need to be wary of the following, as they have been known to cause problems for some people:

✲ **Coal tar and azo dyes** These include E102 (tartrazine) E104, E110, E122, E123, E124, E127, E128, E129, E131, E132, E133, E151, E154, E155, E120 (cochineal) and E160b (anatto)

✲ **Benzoate and sulphide preservatives** These are E210, E211 and E220–288.

✲ **Synthetic antioxidants** These are E310, E311, E320, E321.

Concerns about artificial colourings have led some food manufacturers to stop using them altogether. But that

---

HIDDEN TRUTHS What the food industry doesn't want you to know about **FOOD POLITICS**

The food industry would have you believe that buying food is all about price and convenience – and to some degree, it is. But more importantly, buying food is about the health of you and your family, and it's also about agriculture, the environment and your local economy, to name just a few of the issues involved. Think of your purchases as votes. By choosing or refusing to buy certain products, you can vote for or against the use of pesticides, chemical fertilisers, preservatives and antibiotics; you can vote for food that is locally produced or food that has been transported hundreds or even thousands of miles; you can vote for or against the humane treatment of animals.

What you really want to see on a loaf of bread or packet of cereal

doesn't mean that they don't add colour to their products to make them more appealing – they use natural colourings instead. These include E100, a yellow dye derived from turmeric, and E162 (betanin), a red dye extracted from beetroot. Adverse reactions to these are rare, but they still occur, so it's worth trying to avoid foods that contain such unnecessary additives.

● **Learn what 'organic' means**
There's considerable confusion about the meaning of the term 'organic'. Broadly speaking, farming organically means not using chemical fertilisers and pesticides, irradiation and genetically modified seeds. Livestock must be reared only on organic food, without any by-products from other animals, and cannot be given hormones or antibiotics.

Manufacturers of organic products are allowed to include up to 5 per cent non-organic ingredients in their foods. If organic ingredients make up only 70 to 95 per cent, a product cannot be labelled 'organic', but organic constituents will be clearly marked as such on the label.

There's no clear evidence to show that organic food is better for you. But as pesticides are widely used on fruit and vegetables, a way to avoid traces of them in your food is to buy organic. If you're on a tight budget, it's worth knowing that the amount of chemicals used on different crops varies greatly, so concentrate your resources on buying organic apples, pears, potatoes, carrots, spinach, lettuce and soft fruits, but don't worry too much about eating bananas, broccoli, cauliflowers, onions, peas or oranges that are not organically grown.

● **Be wary of 'natural' products**
Use of words like 'natural', 'homemade', 'pure', 'fresh' and 'traditional' on labels is a much looser affair than marking a

product as 'organic'. There's no set of official rules for applying any of these adjectives to foodstuffs, but if they are used, some explanation for doing so must be given. If, for example, meat is claimed to be 'natural' because the animal was not fed any antibiotics or hormones, the label must state that too. But food producers that use the 'natural' label are not subject to inspections. You just have to take their word for it.

● **Don't compare by 'serving'**
Food labelling regulations stipulate that quantities of vitamins, minerals and other nutrients must be given per 100g or 100ml, although many manufacturers also give the amount per serving. So it's worth remembering that a producer's idea of what 'a serving' is and your own may be quite different. If you want to compare the nutritional value of two similar products – to find out which has the most fibre or least salt, for example – remember to compare figures per 100g or 100ml, rather than per serving.

● **Get the 'whole' story** Marketing departments know that shoppers are keen on wholegrain products these days. But don't think that's what you're getting when you buy something labeled 'wheatmeal'. What you really want to see on a loaf of bread or packet of cereal is 'wholewheat' or 'wholegrain'.

● **Check cereal labels** If you want a healthy breakfast cereal and not one that just claims to be, always take a close look at what's in it. There should only be a few basic constituents, without a long list of additives. Look for a whole grain as the main ingredient and make sure there's no mention of added sugar. Then scan the nutrition label. A good cereal should contain at least 3g fibre per recommended serving.

is 'wholewheat' or 'wholegrain'

● **Beware of added water** While you might expect a can of soup to contain a fair amount of added water, you'd be less likely to think that water would be a key ingredient in chicken. Yet, a Food Standards Agency (FSA) survey, carried out in the UK in 2003, revealed that some chicken pieces contained as much as 55 per cent added water. In 2007, a number of chicken products imported from the Netherlands were discovered to have a water content as high as 35 per cent, even though the meat content was described as 80 per cent. The water is pumped into the meat to add weight and so bulk up the price – a practice which is not illegal – but under European Union rules, products treated in this way must be clearly labelled 'with water'. Because such products are often aimed at the catering trade, restaurant customers seldom see such labels and are unlikely ever to know what they are eating or paying for.

● **Scan the can for MSG** Look carefully down that ingredient list for MSG (monosodium glutamate). It's sometimes listed under another name: hydrolysed soy protein, autolysed yeast or sodium caseinate. MSG is a synthetic version of umami, as it is known in Japan, a savoury flavouring that occurs naturally in some foods, including soy sauce, mushrooms and Parmesan cheese. MSG was widely used in Asian cooking, but went out of favour after it was linked with the onset of headaches and other unpleasant symptoms. Now many Asian restaurants proudly state 'No MSG' on their menus, but the food industry still likes to sneak some in.

BUYING PRODUCE

6 CANNY STRATEGIES for getting the best-tasting and most nutritious fruit and vegetables

● **Be sceptical about 'fresh' food** Don't be fooled. The produce you're buying has probably spent at least a week being picked, transported, packed, hauled, transferred, unpacked, displayed, arranged and rearranged. Some fruits and vegetables are picked before they are really ripe so they won't spoil during the time lag. Some have been treated with gases, washed, cut and bagged. Even then, they may sit in your fridge for several days before you use them. All the while, they're losing taste and nutritional value. If vegetables and fruit had to be labelled with a country of origin, that might offer a clue as to how long they'd been on the road – although many are air-freighted for speed. But the food industry has resisted any such requirement for years. Individual shops may state where their produce comes from, so that customers can draw their own conclusions about its freshness, but in most cases it's less clear.

Let common sense be your guide. If your supermarket has strawberries or asparagus in February, you can be pretty sure they've come a long way. Also, go by looks. If the lettuce is limp, it's been around too long. But fruit and veg that are too shiny may also be stale. Some produce is waxed to preserve it and that healthy sheen may be no more than skin deep. Even something labelled as 'local'

EXPERT ADVICE
GREAT TIPS FROM THE PROFESSIONALS

Don't be fooled by 'superfoods'

So-called 'superfoods', such as goji and acaci berries, have been getting a great deal of press, but don't believe the marketing hype, says nutritionist Fiona Hunter. 'There's no legal definition of "superfood", so it's a term that's open to abuse,' she warns. 'Eat goji berries if you like the taste, but don't expect them to change your life and don't think they'll turn a bad diet into a good one. Strictly speaking, all fruit and vegetables are "superfoods", because they all provide important vitamins, minerals and phytochemicals that help to keep us healthy. Some, such as blueberries and broccoli, contain such large amounts of these health-promoting substances that it is a good idea to include as much of them as possible in your diet. This doesn't mean that you should stop eating more commonplace produce , such as apples and bananas. When it comes to fruit and veg, variety is the thing.'

may not be as fresh as you think, because it will have had to travel to a central packing and distribution centre before being transported back to your supermarket's shelves.

● **Buy frozen** If you have any doubts about the freshness of the produce in your supermarket, here's an insider tip: Sometimes frozen fruit and vegetables are fresher than what you'll find in the 'fresh' produce section. That's because frozen fruit and vegetables are picked when they're fully ripe – and frozen on the same day. Freezing does change the texture somewhat, but very little nutritional value is lost in the process. In fact, in many cases, frozen vegetables contain more vitamins than fresh ones that have been sitting around in the supermarket and in your kitchen.

In a study carried out by scientists from Unilever Research in Bedfordshire, levels of vitamin C and other key nutrients in fresh vegetables at various stages of distribution and storage were compared, with the same vegetables that had been commercially frozen and kept in the deep-freeze for up to 12 months. They found that the nutrient status of frozen peas and broccoli was superior to any that had been bought fresh and stored in a vegetable rack for several days.

● **Pick your own** If you can't grow your own produce, then do the next best thing. Many farms offer a wide range of fruit and vegetables, including apples, beans, pears, pumpkins and seasonal berries and you pay less if you pick them yourself. You'll get the freshest food possible, more cheaply than in the supermarket or greengrocer – and you'll get some exercise as well. Look out for advertisements in the local press for pick-your-own farms or for signs by the roadside directing you to them. Many do their best advertising by word of mouth.

● **Get a box delivered** Why not buy your fruit and veg from a company that runs a box-scheme? It will offer you a good mix of the best local produce, usually delivered to your door. And it will often be cheaper than the same food bought in a supermarket, although the main reason to try this arrangement is that what you get will be really fresh. Abel and Cole (www.abel-cole.co.uk) run a good nationwide box-scheme in the UK, but you also can track down one on www.localfoodworks.org Unless you make a specific request, your box will contain a mix of whatever is currently available. As you may not know exactly what you're going to get, buying in this way could help to expand the range of fruit and vegetables you eat.

EAT FOR FREE

SOME OF THE MOST NUTRITIOUS fruits and vegetables await you just outside your door.

DANDELION This common plant – often regarded as a weed – is found almost everywhere in spring and summer. The dark green leaves can be eaten cooked, in soups or as a vegetable, or raw in salads. They have a slightly bitter, peppery taste and are rich in vitamins A and C, as well as iron. The flowers make good wine or delicious jam. Ground, roasted dandelion root can be used as a coffee substitute. Dandelion 'coffee' is said to aid digestion.

SAMPHIRE Resembling miniature cacti, samphire is sometimes sold in fishmongers, but by far the best way to get hold of this hardy, coastal plant is to pick your own at low tide. It is in season from June to September. Samphire is usually boiled and served warm, topped with a few knobs of butter. Because it doesn't keep well, it's often pickled. Try it as pre-dinner snack or as an accompaniment to fish.

BLACKBERRIES These dark, juicy berries are a common sight in hedgerows throughout late summer and autumn. The brambles on which they grow are covered in sharp thorns, so it is advisable to wear clothing that covers the arms and legs when gathering them. Pick them when they're deep purple, but still slightly firm, if you are going to serve them as a soft fruit, topped with whipped cream, yoghurt or ice cream. Slightly unripe berries make good jams and jellies. They are rich in vitamin C and also contain compounds called anthocyanins, which evidence suggests can help to slow down the growth of cancerous cells.

ELDERFLOWERS AND BERRIES In June, the large, flat, white flowerheads appear, scenting the surrounding air for about three weeks. Pick them and use immediately to make a delicious, refreshing cordial. Rinse about 20 heads thoroughly to remove all insects and debris and place in a large pan with a slice of lemon, a few teaspoons of lemon juice and about 1.5kg sugar. Pour over about 4 litres boiling water and stir until the sugar dissolves. Cover and leave for three to five days, stirring twice a day. Serve diluted with still or sparkling water and some ice. The tiny, dark berries appear in autumn. They are very good mixed with apples in a pie, but should always be cooked – raw elderberries, along with the leaves, are slightly poisonous.

MUSHROOMS Gathering mushrooms is becoming more popular, but a novice should always go on organised forays with an expert, or make sure anything they gather is checked by an expert before eating. There's a lot of information about wild mushrooms on www.bbc.co.uk and also on the website of the British Mycological Society (www.britmycolsoc.org.uk). The nutritional value of mushrooms varies with type, but generally they are rich in B-complex vitamins, especially vitamin B_2 (riboflavin) and are a good source of minerals, particularly potassium. They are also low in salt, fat and calories.

IMPORTANT WARNINGS Beware of gathering wild plants in any area where herbicides or other poisons have been sprayed on crops and, if you're uncertain as to whether a plant is edible, don't touch it. Buy a good field guide, such as *A Field Guide to Edible Wild Plants* by Lee Allen Peterson (Houghton Mifflin, 2000), to help you. It is always best is to consult an expert if you are thinking of going on a mushroom-gathering expedition.

Ground, roasted dandelion root can be used as a coffee substitute

● **Ripen fruit in a paper bag** You rarely get fruit that is fully ripe from the supermarket. If it was picked at its peak, it would spoil during the time it takes to move it from the grower to you. You may have heard that putting fruit in a paper bag concentrates the ethylene gas ripening fruit gives off and so speeds up the process. To make it ripen even quicker, put some fully ripe fruit, such as a banana, into the bag with it. The ripe fruit gives off more ethylene, which the unripe fruit can use. Don't use plastic bags or the fruit will just spoil. The paper bag trick only works with fruits that continue to ripen after they've been picked, such as apples, avocados, bananas, blueberries, kiwi fruit, mangoes, peaches, pears and plums. It therefore pays to know which fruits won't ripen after picking. These include citrus fruits, cherries, grapes, honeydew melons, pineapples, raspberries and strawberries.

● **Go steady with the juice** Drinks manufacturers have done a great job of persuading people that fruit juice is good for them and that the sooner children get started on it the better. Well, there's some truth in that. Fresh orange juice, with plenty of pulp, provides vitamins, fibre and some minerals – and it tastes great. But there's no need to drink so much of it. A 150ml glass will supply about 60mg vitamin C, well above the daily recommendation of 40mg for adults. And do note what you don't hear so much about – the calories. Every 250ml orange juice contains about 90 calories, only a little less than the 103 offered by the same amount of cola.

TOMATO TRICKS

5 SURPRISING WAYS to make the most of this popular food

Grow your own or buy the best available

● **Keep out of the fridge**
Ripe, freshly picked tomatoes have a vibrant taste, which isn't improved by refrigeration. So keep them in a cool place, in a basket or ventilated container, so that air can circulate around them. To help to develop the flavour of slightly under-ripe tomatoes, put them in a paper bag with an apple. Prick the bag with a fork to make a few air holes and leave at room temperature for one to two days.

● **Hold on to the flavour** Tomatoes freeze well, so it's well worth preserving some for future use, when they're at their peak. Grow your own or buy the best available from a farmers' market or farm stand. Simply cut out the tough core, leaving the rest whole, and arrange on a baking tray. Place in the freezer and, when frozen, transfer to a plastic bag and return to the freezer. They can be thawed and used for sauces, soups and casseroles. The skin will peel off easily if they are left to thaw until they're beginning to soften on the outside. Or you can run warm tap water over them and then peel off the skin.

● **Dry them** Another good way to enjoy the tastiest tomatoes, out of season, is to dry them. Cut into quarters and remove and discard the seeds. Pat the flesh dry with kitchen paper, then place, cut side up, on a large baking tray. Drizzle over a little olive oil, sprinkle with sea salt and freshly ground black pepper – together with some chopped herbs or garlic, if you wish – and place in the oven, set at around 150°C, for 1 hour. Allow to cool, then pack the dried tomatoes in a plastic container. Keep in the fridge for up to two weeks.

● Avoid chopped tinned tomatoes

They're convenient and can be very tasty, but it is always advisable to choose tinned *whole* tomatoes. That way, you can drain off the accompanying sauce that tends to be rather watery and often has a slightly metallic after-taste. For most recipes you won't need to chop the tomatoes; you can simply break them up with your hands as you add them to a sauce or casserole. In fact, good canned tomatoes may have a better flavour than fresh ones, especially some of the fresh plum tomatoes on the market, which can be quite tasteless.

● Make tomato sauce quicker

A tomato sauce that simmers away gently for several hours may taste wonderful, but one that takes only a fraction of the time to cook can be equally delicious – especially when it's made with locally grown tomatoes at the peak of their flavour. Heat 2 tablespoons of olive oil in a large pan over a medium heat, then add 2 finely chopped garlic cloves and cook for 3–4 minutes until they are golden brown. Stir in about 1kg tomatoes – really ripes ones that have been peeled, deseeded and chopped, or use two 400g cans of top quality tomatoes, that have been drained and chopped. Season the sauce to taste with salt and freshly ground black pepper,

then lower the heat and leave to simmer for 15–20 minutes, until it is thick. Tear 8–10 fresh basil leaves into small pieces and stir them in – herbs such as basil, chives and mint help to bring out the sweetness of the tomatoes. This sauce may lack the complexity of its long-simmered cousin, but it's quick and easy, and still makes a mouthwatering meal when stirred into freshly cooked pasta. It is also far superior to any of the sauces found in jars on supermarket shelves.

The seeds and skin contribute to a tomato's flavour, so some people prefer to make a coarser textured sauce that includes them. This can be made a little smoother by processing for a minute or two in a blender or food processor.

EXPERT ADVICE
GREAT TIPS FROM THE PROFESSIONALS

Make your own salad dressings

A dressing can make the difference between a pleasant salad and an outstanding one. Bottled salad dressings are also a good source of profit for the companies that make them. But ready-made dressings often contain cheap, bland ingredients and are packed with artificial flavourings and preservatives. Instead, make your own – it's quick, easy and much cheaper, even when using far superior ingredients. For a basic vinaigrette, mix three parts olive oil with one part vinegar – wine, cider or balsamic – then season to taste with salt and pepper. Keep a jar, ready to use, in the fridge. You can then vary the flavour as you wish. If you want a blue cheese dressing, blend in some softened blue cheese; if you want a tarragon dressing, stir in a handful of the chopped, fresh herb; for a garlic dressing, add a crushed garlic clove. Quantities need not be precise; just keep adding and tasting until you get something you like. Flavoured oils, infused with spices, fresh herbs, lemon, chilli and garlic, can also be used in dressings but, as some have quite a strong taste, they are best used mixed with plain olive oil.

12 reasons to buy LOCAL FOODS

INTEREST IN LOCAL PRODUCE IS GROWING as consumers recognise that seasonal, organic food is often tastier and more nutritious than fresh foods shipped from faraway places. It's not what big supermarkets want you to know but **here are a dozen key points that may make you reconsider your weekly grocery shop.**

1 IT SUPPORTS LOCAL FARMERS
By buying directly from farm shops or farmers' markets, you cut out the middlemen. That means more of the money you spend on food goes into the pockets of the producers, which helps them to stay in business and make a decent profit.

2 THE LOCAL ECONOMY IS GIVEN A BOOST
Money you spend on locally grown food can help to increase the financial stability of your community. If local farms get more business, they may well need to employ more staff. The creation of new jobs in your area and having more people in employment will also mean that other local businesses are more likely to prosper.

3 IT CUTS 'FOOD MILES'
Look at the labels on packaged fruit and vegetables in the supermarket. Sometimes the country of origin is given, in which case, you will probably discover that a great deal of the produce on offer comes from all corners of the globe. In most cases it will have been transported by air so that it can reach the shelves while it is still fresh, which adds up to an enormous amount of greenhouse gas emissions. Research shows that choosing to buy locally produced food, from a farmers' market or farm shop, can cut the carbon dioxide emissions linked to food distribution by up to 99.8 per cent.

4 IT REDUCES WASTE

A proportion of the food grown for supermarkets is rejected, because it's the 'wrong' size or shape, or not quite the 'right' colour. All of this perfectly good food goes to waste. Farmers selling their own produce directly will offer you a variety of shapes and sizes – just as nature intended.

6 FOOD WILL BE TASTIER

Try peas straight from the pod ... or visit a farmer's shop and buy sweetcorn, freshly picked from the field a few hours earlier. These vegetables will often be so sweet and tender that you could almost eat them raw. From the moment food is picked, any natural sugars begin to turn into starch. So the farther produce has to travel and the longer it takes to reach you, the less tasty it is likely to be.

5 YOU HAVE MORE CHOICE

When farmers cultivate produce specifically for supermarkets, they may restrict themselves to the most popular fruit and veg varieties – which often means the most bland. If they can sell directly, farmers can cater for the tastes of individual customers and offer a wider range of produce. Which means that you get a larger selection of flavours to enjoy.

7 YOU EAT PRODUCE IN SEASON

Buying direct from the farm and farmers' markets puts you in touch with the seasons, when specific produce will be at its best and most abundant – and therefore cheaper. The best chefs know that to create great dishes you must use only the finest ingredients. This is why many of them are big fans of farmers' markets and farm shops.

9 IT'S MORE SOCIABLE

When you buy locally from farms and farmers' markets, you are likely to meet some of the people, who grew or reared your food. Apart from being a more sociable way to buy, this contact helps to develop a stronger sense of community.

8 IT'S A FAMILY OUTING

Buying a punnet of strawberries from the supermarket may be quick and easy, but if you want to taste the freshest and the sweetest, and have an inexpensive, fun day out as well, go to a farm where you can pick your own produce. You'll pay less and gain an insight into what goes into getting food onto your table.

10 IT'S MORE INTERESTING

Whether you buy at a farm or a farmers' market, you may be able to talk to the farmer and learn a little more about local agriculture. You could ask which vegetables and fruit grow best on local soil – with perhaps a view to growing your own.

11 IT PRESERVES THE COUNTRYSIDE

The layout and condition of fields or woodland near you will have been fashioned over the centuries by the style of farming to which they are probably best suited. By buying directly from local farmers whenever you can, you are helping to preserve farming traditions that are more likely to be in harmony with the local countryside and that will help to keep it looking its best.

12 IT STIMULATES TOURISM

When you travel, do you try to eat the local foods and doesn't that help to make your holiday more memorable? It's the same at home. If you buy from local sources, you are helping these businesses to thrive. This means that they're going to be there for visitors too, adding to the character and interest of your area. For information on where you can buy at source – either near where you live or when travelling around the country – visit these websites: www.farma.org.uk, www.farmshopping.com and www.farmersmarkets.net or contact a local tourist office for details of nearby farm shops and markets.

EGG SECRETS

9 THINGS you should know about buying, cooking, and storing this versatile and nutritious food

Storing eggs in their carton will help to stop them from losing moisture ...

stroke. A medium-sized egg may contain about 12 times more cholesterol than 25g Cheddar cheese, but the cheese is more likely to add to the cholesterol in your blood because it contains almost seven times as much saturated fat as the egg.

Eggs, far from being bad for us, have a lot to offer. They're one of the few dietary sources of vitamin D and also provide good amounts of vitamins A, E, B_2 and B_{12}. They're also rich in choline, which research suggests may play a key role in brain function. Several animal experiments show that choline boosts memory and learning skills.

A paper published in the *Journal of the American Medical Association*, which compared the diets of more than 100,000 men and women living in the USA, over a 14 year period, found that those people who ate one egg a day had no increased risk of heart disease or stroke. The official advice from the British Dietetic Association and the American Heart Association is that eating an egg a day is unlikely to have any effect on blood-cholesterol levels, provided that the amount of saturated fat in your diet remains low.

● **Buy omega-3 enriched eggs**
They're more expensive, but they're so much better for you. In study after study, omega-3 fatty acids, have been shown to benefit everything – from your mental health (by improving your memory and reducing the risk of depression) to the workings of your heart. The recommended daily intake of omega-3 fats for good general health is around 450mg. Research has shown that many people don't get even half of this in their diet. If you eat less than one serving of oily fish, such as salmon or mackerel, once a week, it's very hard to get an adequate supply of omega-3 fat. So using eggs enriched with this essential nutrient will go a long way to helping you to reach the ideal target.

● **Don't worry about cholesterol**
Eggs do contain a lot of cholesterol. But it's the amount of saturated fat in a food – not the amount of cholesterol – that has the most impact on raising blood-cholesterol levels and therefore increasing the risk of a heart attack or

● **Ignore the hype** White eggs are just as good for you as brown eggs. The colour of the shell is determined by the breed of hen. It bears no relationship to an egg's nutritional value.

● **Test for freshness** To check whether an egg is still fit to eat, place it in a jug or bowl of salted cold water: if it sinks, it's fresh, so enjoy it; if it floats, throw it away.

● **Make shelling easy** Pricking eggs before you hard-boil them will make it much easier to remove the shell once they're cooked. To do this, take a pin and insert it about 1cm into the broader end of the egg. This will let in enough air to break the seal between the shell membrane and the egg white that's clinging to it.

This tip is especially useful if you need to keep hard-boiled eggs whole, so that they slice up neatly for use as a garnish or as part of a salad, or if you want to stuff and serve them as a snack or starter.

● **Freeze whites individually** How many times have you used only the yolks in a recipe and stored the left-over whites, all together, in a container in the fridge. Then when you need to use them, you can't remember how many whites you have or how long they've been there. Here's a better way of saving egg whites. Pour each spare white into one compartment of a clean ice-cube tray and freeze them. Then transfer the frozen cubes to a plastic freezer bag, seal and clearly label with the date you placed the bag in your freezer. It's then obvious how many egg whites you have stored and how old they are. Thaw out as many as you need overnight in the refrigerator before using. To lighten an omelette, add several whites to the whole eggs you use. Whites that have been frozen will still make a good meringue or whisked sponge, although they won't whisk up to quite such a large volume as fresh ones.

● **Keep in the box** Storing eggs in the box that they came in will help to stop them from losing moisture and absorbing odours from other foods in your fridge. Always store eggs broad-end up – it helps to keep them fresher.

● **Warm before whisking** Eggs separate more easily straight from the fridge – when they are chilled. But if you're then going to whisk up the whites until stiff, say for a meringue or a mousse, you'll get a much bigger volume if you leave them to stand on your kitchen work surface for at least 30 minutes – to come to room temperature – before you beat them.

● **Salt away spills** You've dropped an egg on the floor and are finding it difficult to mop up the slippery mess with a damp cloth – it just seems to spread it out more. Stop dabbing it. Instead, sprinkle over a generous amount of salt, then leave for about 5 minutes. You should then be able to scoop up the entire mess quite easily with a damp paper towel.

EXPERT ADVICE
GREAT TIPS FROM THE PROFESSIONALS

And another great source of omega-3s

Fish is one of the best sources of omega-3 fatty acids. But buying top-quality fish can be tricky. You need to know what's going on behind the scenes.

'Wild' fish have become scarcer as automated fishing fleets have enabled increasing numbers to be caught. This overfishing has driven some species, such as Atlantic cod, to the verge of extinction. Fish farming is often used to boost stocks but it can sometimes introduce diseases into wild populations and also pollute the water.

So how do you make sure that you get the very best fish – only from sustainable sources? The answer is to look out for the distinctive blue MSC label. This is awarded to fish taken from fisheries that meet a set of rigorous, environment-friendly standards laid down by the Marine Stewardship Council. Consult its website – www.msc.org – for a list of all current MSC-approved products and details of where to buy them.

SERVING MEAT

7 KEY METHODS for achieving tasty, healthy results when buying, cooking and serving meat

● **Do it yourself** Even 'extra-lean' mince is around 10 per cent fat. A much healthier option is to buy lean cuts of meat, such as steak, and mince it up yourself using a food processor or hand-cranked mincer. That way you'll know exactly what you're getting.

● **Freeze first** It will be much easier to slice up meat thinly, for dishes such as stir-fries, if you pop it into the freezer. Leave it to chill for about 30 minutes before trying to cut it.

SOMETHING DIFFERENT

Don't be afraid of the exotic or unusual. Some butchers and many large supermarkets stock rabbit and venison. Less common meats, such as ostrich, kangaroo and buffalo are often available at farmers' markets or by mail order.
Rabbit The pale flesh has a delicate flavour. Joints can be roasted or used in stews. Doe meat is considered the best.
Hare The meat is similar to rabbit, but hare has stronger-tasting, darker flesh. A whole hare can be stuffed and roasted, or joints can be used in casseroles.
Venison This versatile meat is very low in fat and has twice as much iron as beef. It is also full of flavour. The leg and saddle are good roasted. Lean steaks are suitable for pan-frying or grilling and diced venison is delicious in stews and pies. Minced venison makes great burgers.
Wild boar This richer form of pork is best when marinated before cooking. This helps to keep it moist and mellows down the rather strong taste.
Ostrich Most ostrich is imported, although some is now farmed in the UK. It is low in fat and high in protein.
Kangaroo A protected species, kangaroo is farmed under strict regulations. The lean, tender meat tastes like hare and is an excellent source of iron and zinc.
Buffalo Another low-fat meat. Try the fillet, marinated in wine and herbs, then roasted, or sliced up and pan fried.

● **Avoid commercial tenderisers** These often contain MSG or salt which will extract some of the meat's natural juices. Use fresh papaya instead. Papaya contains an enyzme called papin, which helps to break down protein. Purée some fresh papaya and rub it into the surface of the meat. Scrape off the purée and pat dry with kitchen paper before cooking.

● **Hang it** Hanging meat helps to improve its flavour, but supermarkets aren't keen on doing this. According to top UK chef Heston Blumenthal, the reasons are purely commercial. Put simply, if you hang meat for any length of time, your stock will take longer to reach the shops and start making a profit; also meat loses water while it hangs and, although this intensifies the flavour, it leaves the retailer with less in weight. Blumenthal says that any piece of meat that's a little on the tough side is likely to be lacking not in quality, but in hanging time. But there's a solution – hang it yourself. In most cases, a rib of beef or even a piece of steak, fresh from the supermarket, would benefit from extra ageing. To do this, Blumenthal suggests you take a sealable container and punch about five holes, around 0.5cm in diameter, in each side; don't make any holes in the base or blood from the meat placed in it will leak out when it's in the fridge. Put your meat in the container, replace the lid and leave it in the fridge for up to a week – but not beyond the 'use-by date'. As the meat ages, it will darken and shrink, and the outside will start to look leathery. Don't worry – it's not gone off; the texture and flavour have improved beyond measure.

● **Mix up your beef** The meat industry would like you to saw your way through a large slab of steak for dinner. But do your arteries a favour and save the whole-steak approach for special occasions. For day-to-day dining, find ways to cook your steak with other ingredients. For example, slice it up and stir-fry it in a wok with a selection of different vegetables. Thinly sliced pieces of steak can also be flash-fried and added to a salad. Or make shish kebabs by threading cubes of steak, with whole mushrooms and chopped peppers on to skewers and grilling. You almost always eat less meat, and therefore consume less fat, when you prepare it as part of a broader dish. Bulking out mince for a bolognese sauce or shepherd's pie with vegetables or lentils is much healthier.

● **Choose low-fat mince** Whenever you find yourself reaching for a packet of minced beef, move to the poultry section instead and pick up some minced chicken or turkey. These lighter meats are just as good for making meatballs,

meatloaf or a chilli. And they can mean more than 30 per cent less calories and at least half the fat per 100g serving than when using beef. If you are worried about losing the meaty flavour, use a mixture of half poultry and half beef.

● **Roast a chicken breast down** Cooked in the traditional way – breast up – the white meat of a chicken is often completely dried out by the time the dark meat is done. Yet most cookery books omit to mention that roasting a bird breast down and backside up produces meat that is moist and tender throughout. Another way to roast a chicken and keep it moist, favoured by some cooks in the Provence region of France, is to roast it, lying breast down on a densely packed bed of garlic cloves. Some, more modern, recipes suggest simply stuffing about 40 cloves of garlic into the cavity of the bird before putting it into the oven. Either way, cooking gives the garlic a much milder flavour and creamy texture, so that it makes a delicious accompaniment to the meat.

BARBECUE SECRETS

5 CHEF'S TIPS to make your barbecued food taste better – and more fun to prepare and eat

● **Master grilling** Most people never use their barbecue to its full potential, and restaurants and chefs that specialise in barbecued food are rarely keen to divulge their secrets. There's a lot more to it than throwing on a piece of meat and trying not to burn it. The best cooks make good use of the variations in temperature across the cooking area. To produce a perfect steak, they sear it first

on the hottest section, then move it to a medium-hot spot to allow the flavour to develop. They also use different types of charcoal for the distinctive flavours they impart. Oak charcoal, for example, gives food a smoky taste, while mesquite charcoal gives a slightly sweet flavour. Also, mesquite produces a very hot fire, suitable for cooking fish; oak is best for vegetables and meat.

● **Butter it up** Why do the steaks you barbecue at home never taste quite as good as they do when they're cooked by a professional? Here's a simple chef's tip for achieving that elusive flavouring and texture. As soon as your steak is cooked to your liking, remove it from the barbecue. Then scoop up a teaspoon of butter, smear it across the top of the steak and leave it to melt. The meat will seem extra succulent and tasty.

● **Add extra flavour** Sprinkle a handful or two of fresh or dried herbs, such as rosemary, oregano and tarragon over the hot coals just before cooking. The fragrance will make your mouth water and the food will taste wonderful.

● **Turn kebabs with ease** The wooden skewers were supposed to work if you soaked them in water first. But no amount of soaking ever seemed to stop them from catching fire. Metal skewers were an improvement – until your kebabs needed turning. Then every time you flipped the skewer over, the food swung around as well. Flattened skewers were an improvement – they held the food in position – but onions, peppers and especially mushrooms, often split in two when you were attempting to thread them on. Well, the answer to all these problems is to used kebab baskets, available from kitchen shops and some department stores. These ingenious devices consist of a long wire box with a lid and a long handle. You pack your kebab ingredients into them, close the lid to hold the food firmly in place, then arrange on the hot barbecue.

● **Banish bacteria** The germs that cause food poisoning love barbecues because any undercooked food gives them the perfect opportunity to multiply and do their damage. But a little care and attention will keep bugs at bay:
✿ Make sure that the barbecue is really hot before you begin cooking. Charcoal, is ready to use when it is just glowing and covered with an even, pale grey ash. This will take about 30 minutes.
✿ Don't leave raw food out in the sun. Only transfer it from the kitchen to the barbecue when you're ready to cook it.

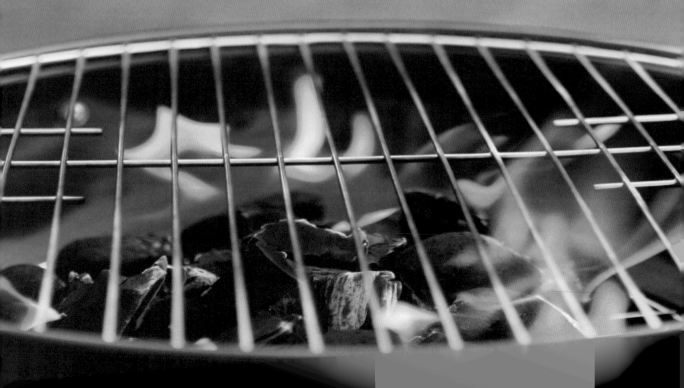

✪ Check that any frozen food you are planning to cook is completely defrosted before you place it on the barbecue.

✪ Never be tempted to rush a barbecue. Make sure that all fish and meat – particularly chicken – is cooked right through. Avoid putting it on the hottest part of the barbecue, where it is likely to char on the outside while remaining raw and pink on the inside. To test whether chicken is cooked sufficiently, insert a skewer into the thickest part of the meat – the juices should run clear and there should be no sign of blood.

✪ Keep raw and cooked food separate. You should use one set of equipment for raw food and a different set for anything that has been cooked. Never keep any left-over marinades if they have been in contact with raw meat. Throw them away and clean out their containers thoroughly before using again.

How they do it . . .
barbecue vegetables

For many people barbecues are about feasting on meat. But, says nutritionist Fiona Hunter, for a healthier meal, try cooking fresh vegetables as well.

To cook corn on the cob, she says, don't remove the outer husk. Place it on a medium-hot part of the grill and turn the ears as they brown. The object of this step is to cook the kernels, and that should take 20 to 25 minutes. Then peel back the husks (leaving them on the cob), remove the silk and sprinkle the golden kernels with a little olive oil and a dash of salt and pepper. Return to the grill and cook for another 4-5 minutes, until nicely browned.

Even lettuce can be cooked on a barbecue. Wash and pat dry some Kos lettuce leaves, cut in half lengthways, sprinkle with olive oil, then a little salt and pepper and cook briefly, over a hot fire, removing when browned. Serve, brushed with a light dressing.

STORING **FOOD**

5 **SMART WAYS** to keep food fresh and revitalise any that is past its best

● **Always read the label** Storage instructions on a food packet or label are always worth reading, even on familiar products. Because of growing concerns about food additives, many producers are beginning to cut down on salt, sugar and other preservatives, so the length of time that a food will remain in good condition may have changed. Jams and pickles, for example, that traditionally would have been packed with sugar or salt, and so would keep well in a cupboard or a larder, now need to be stored in the fridge. If you tend to buy low-sugar, low-salt and preservative-free foods, then it's wise to shop for such products regularly – buying little and often – and take extra care that they are stored correctly.

Most pre-packed food will carry a 'best before' or a 'use by' date, so you should understand exactly what these dates mean. A 'best before' date is concerned with the quality, rather than the safety of the food – it's the date up to and including which the food can be expected to remain in peak condition, if it is properly stored. It will not be dangerous to eat after this date, but it won't taste as good as it did when it was really fresh. 'Use by' dates are given on foods that are highly perishable. Eating any food product after its 'use by' date could make you ill.

● Learn fridge and freezer basics

Even in the chilled environment of your fridge or freezer, food can go off, but it will keep longer if you follow a few simple rules:

❂ **Check the temperature** The best way to do this is to use a fridge/freezer thermometer. These are widely available at kitchen shops. Your fridge should be set between 1°C and 5°C and your freezer at -18°C or lower, to work well. If your fridge is very full or if you're going to be opening and closing the door frequently – when, for example, you're preparing for a party or special dinner – you will probably need to set the temperature closer to 1°C.

❂ **Separate cooked and raw** To avoid cross-contamination, keep raw and cooked foods on separate shelves. Store any raw meat, poultry or fish in a sealed container at the bottom of the fridge, so that it cannot touch or drip on to any cooked or ready-to-eat, chilled foods.

❂ **Store cold** Allow any left-over food to cool down thoroughly before placing it in the fridge or freezer. Do this as quickly as possible. Left-overs shouldn't be left unrefrigerated for longer than 1 hour and should be consumed within two days, if kept in the fridge.

❂ **Never refreeze** Once frozen food has thawed, it should not be returned to the freezer, unless it has been cooked first.

❂ **Empty the tin** Never put open tins of food in the fridge. Transfer the contents to a container, cover and store. Most tinned foods, even if kept in the fridge, should be used within two days.

❂ **Remove packaging** If you buy vegetables or hard fruits, such as apples and pears, wrapped in cling film or in plastic bags, remove the packaging before you put them in the fridge to allow air to circulate around them. Soft fruits, such as strawberries or blueberries are best kept in their packaging to prevent them from becoming damaged. Mushrooms keep best if they are placed in a paper bag.

Fruit and vegetables will keep for longer in the salad drawer of the fridge than they will in a vegetable rack or larder. The cold will also help to preserve their vitamins. But never refrigerate bananas – they will go black.

● Don't bin over-ripe bananas

When bananas get too ripe to be eaten whole, or even to be presentable as slices, they're still fine for cooking. Make some banana bread with them or blend them into a healthy dessert or drink. If you can't use them immediately, peel and slice, then drop the pieces into a freezer bag and place in your freezer. Thaw before using. Partially defrosted bananas are great for smoothies.

● Freeze leftover tomato purée

If you buy a tin of tomato purée and just need to use a tablespoon or two, any that remains will keep well if you freeze it. Drop spoonfuls of the left-over purée on to a sheet of greaseproof paper and put these dollops – paper and all – into the freezer. Once they're frozen, peel them off and transfer the pieces to a freezer bag for long-term storage. Next time you need a little tomato purée, just drop one or two of the frozen chunks into your sauce, soup or stew. There's no need to thaw them first.

● Soften those rock-hard raisins

You can prevent raisins and other dried fruit from getting hard, or at least slow down the process, by storing them in a jar with an airtight lid. But if you've

never refrigerate bananas – they will go black

forgotten to do that and just left them in the packet, then they're probably rock hard and may seem more or less inedible. But don't give up and throw them out; you can still revive them by dropping them into a saucepan and adding cold water until they're all completely submerged. Place the pan over a high heat and bring the water to a boil. Then remove the pan from the cooker and leave it for at least 10 minutes, so that the raisins get a good soaking. Set a large metal colander in the sink, tip the contents of the pan into it and leave, shaking from time to time, until all the water has drained off. Your revived raisins will be soft and ready to eat or use in recipes. If you want to store them, make sure they are really dry, by patting them with some kitchen paper, before packing them into an airtight storage jar.

COOKING **SKILLS**

4 **EASY STEPS** to get you on the road to becoming a fantastic cook

● **Ignore the hype – you can cook**
Cooking isn't an art practised only by the talented few, although there are plenty of high-priced restaurants and supermarkets selling exotic ready-meals that profit by encouraging you to think that is the case. Julia Child, the noted food writer and broadcaster, who introduced the secrets and techniques of French cuisine to the American general public, took issue with the idea of cooking as an elitist pastime. 'If you can read, you can cook,' she wrote.

● **Get a good basic cookbook**
Being told that all you need to do to produce great food is to follow the instructions given in a book, may not be very reassuring if you have no idea where to start reading. There are so many cookery books on the market and often they do little more than intimidate the novice – as do so many of the food programmes on television. So if you want to learn to cook, don't start with one of those hyped-up volumes from the latest 'hot' celebrity chef. Buy yourself a nuts-and-bolts guide – one that will actually explain terms that may be obvious to an experienced cook, such as 'roast', 'sauté or 'braise'. Look for a book that doesn't just cover special dinner party dishes, but one that takes you step-by-step through preparing all the basics – stocks, soups, sauces, pastry and the standard methods of preparing meat, fish and vegetables.

Once you have acquired some skills, expand your range by trying out recipes given in magazines and newspapers. Supermarkets sometimes produce their own collections of recipes or have free recipe cards on offer.

● **Find out what your family likes**
Nothing will boost your confidence in your cooking skills more than having satisfied customers – that is, family members and friends who really seem to be enjoying the food you serve them and who show their appreciation. Ask everyone what their preferred foods are

and try to get them involved in menu planning. Make a note of the dishes family members tend to choose when eating in restaurants. Ask them what they've enjoyed at friends' houses and – where possible – get them to ask whoever cooked the meal to supply a recipe; home cooks love praise and most will be happy to oblige. Or consult your own cookery books and surf the internet for similar recipes, then surprise everyone by serving up their favourite dishes at home.

● **Read through recipes.** Don't start cooking until you've read a recipe from beginning to end and assembled all the ingredients on the kitchen worktop. That may sound obvious, but many dishes fail if you don't do this. You may not be told you need softened butter until the middle of a recipe, when what you have is still rock hard in the fridge. Or you may not have been told to preheat your oven at the outset, so that it is still cold when you're ready to bake your carefully assembled cake.

ADDING FLAVOUR

5 CLEVER POINTERS that will help to give your cooking that professional touch

● **Buy herbs and spices in bulk**
Stop buying dried herbs and spices in those tiny jars and tubs you find in the supermarket. Instead, go to your local health-food store, where they will probably stock them in large jars, from which you can weigh out what you want. You can buy as much or as little as you like and, if you buy in bulk, you'll save money. They're often fresher, too, and many are organically grown.

The aromatic qualities of ground spices tend to fade with storage so if you buy large quantities, go for whole seeds and grind them as you need them. Most spices are best stored in the dark in an airtight container.

● **Grow your own** Keep pots of herbs growing on your kitchen window sill. They'll last longer and taste fresher than cut herbs sold in packets.

Keep pots of herbs growing on your kitchen window sill

EXPERT ADVICE
GREAT TIPS FROM THE PROFESSIONALS

Spice up your life

Spices have been valued throughout history for both their culinary and medicinal properties. Learning to use them in your cooking is a great way to add flavour without adding extra salt or fat.

- **Caraway** The seeds have a delicate aniseed taste. Try adding a pinch of them to potato salad or coleslaw. Or stir a tablespoon into your mixture when making homemade biscuits and bread.
- **Cardamom** Add crushed, whole pods of this pungent spice to rice dishes such as pilafs or rice pudding. A pinch of ground cardamom seed lends an exotic touch to stewed fruit..
- **Chillies** These belong to the same family as red and green peppers. There are hundreds of different varieties of chillies, ranging in heat from mild to very fiery. They contain vitamin C, but they are rarely eaten in large enough quantities to provide useful amounts. Give tomato sauce or salsa a spicy tang by stirring in a finely chopped fresh chilli.
- **Cinnamon** Add a sprinkling of ground cinnamon to stewed fruit or, for a soothing drink when you have a cold, pour hot water over a cinnamon stick and sweeten with a little honey.
- **Cloves** As well as lending a pungent, warming taste to both sweet and savoury dishes, cloves are used for their antiseptic and pain-relieving properties. If you're suffering from toothache, chewing a clove or rubbing a few drops of clove oil around the affected area will help to ease the pain.
- **Coriander** The seeds have a sweet, slightly fruity flavour. Add a pinch of ground coriander seed to meat dishes, casseroles or tomato sauce. Or sprinkle some into biscuit and cake mixtures.
- **Fennel seeds** These have a strong liquorice flavour that is popular in Mediterranean dishes. A few crushed seeds make a delicious and distinctive difference to baked fish dishes and casseroles.
- **Ginger** The Chinese were using ginger as a medicine as early as the 6th century BC. Ginger tea can be made by grating a 1cm piece of fresh root ginger into a mug of boiling water. Leave to stand for 10 minutes, then strain, sweeten with a little honey and sip slowly.
- **Horseradish** Phytochemicals found in horseradish are believed to help fight cancer and have antibacterial properties. A little freshly grated horseradish is good in mashed potato, or mix it with some Greek yoghurt to make an appetising dip.
- **Nutmeg and mace** Nutmeg is the seed of a tropical evergreen tree and mace is the seed's outer coating. Both have a sweet, warming flavour. A little freshly ground nutmeg is excellent in cheese sauces, stewed fruit or rice pudding.
- **Paprika** The flavour and the heat of paprika vary according to the blend of ground red peppers used to make it and its country of origin. Hungarian paprika tends to be hotter than Spanish. Add a pinch to tomato sauce or mix some into egg mayonnaise to give it an added kick.
- **Saffron** Saffron is the dried stigma of the purple-flowering saffron crocus. It takes 1,500 flowers to yield 1g of saffron, which explains why it is so expensive. Fortunately, a few strands are enough to flavour and colour most dishes, such as risottos, paella, cakes and biscuits.
- **Star anise** The warm, aniseed-like flavour works well with sweet or savoury dishes. It is commonly used in Chinese cooking. Use a whole star anise in a tropical fruit salad or sprinkle a pinch of ground star anise over vegetables you plan to roast.
- **Turmeric** This member of the ginger family is a key ingredient in curry powder. A pinch of ground turmeric adds a subtle spicy touch to soups and rice dishes, as well as a rich yellow colouring.

● **Pour in some wine** The celebrated food writer, Elizabeth David, wrote, 'If every kitchen contained a bottle each of red wine, white wine and inexpensive port for cooking, hundreds of store cupboards could be swept clean forever of the cluttering debris of commercial sauce bottles and all the synthetic aids to flavouring.' So if you have wine left over from a party, don't throw it away. Freeze it in an ice-cube tray and you'll always have 'wine-cubes' to hand, ready to add richness to your gravy, sauces and stews.

● **Celebrate celery** This ingredient often appears in soups and casseroles, adding its distinctive burst of flavour. But celery is generally soft and overcooked. It would be better to throw in a few tablespoons of chopped celery at the last minute – so it keeps its crunch and doesn't go soggy. Then it will add both texture and taste. Here's a twist on a traditional accompaniment to pork, using chopped celery to make a lively relish. Add 2 tablespoons finely chopped celery and 1 tablespoon creamed horseradish to 0.5 litre apple sauce, varying the amounts of celery and horseradish, according to taste.

● **Don't avoid butter** We all know that butter is full of saturated fat and that too much saturated fat is bad for you. But healthy eating is less about avoiding one particular food than about your overall diet. If you eat Danish pastries for breakfast and eat chips rather than vegetables, avoiding butter won't improve your health. Good cooks swear by butter to give dishes an extra special finish. So use it – in moderation.

GADGETS & GIZMOS

5 THINGS to think about when buying and using kitchen equipment

● **Buy what you find useful** A lot of producers of kitchen gadgets, would like to convince you that a particular product is essential to your cooking or will transform it. But the truth is that what is a crucial tool to one cook is clutter to another. There are many fine cooks who consistently produce wonderful meals without ever using a food processor or a blender or a microwave or a juicer, or even a coffee maker. Many find it quicker and easier to whip up eggs and cream with an old-fashioned, hand-held beater or a wire whisk. When it comes to gadgets, you should do what suits you – and that will simply be a question of trial and error, and time.

● **Chop on wood ... or plastic** For a long time, experts stated that plastic chopping boards were more hygienic than wooden ones. It was assumed that plastic could be cleaned more easily and more thoroughly than wood. Then, in 1994, researchers declared that wood retained fewer bacteria than plastic. Further studies followed that confused the issue, but the general consensus now is that there isn't much difference. Bacteria can persist on both materials for a long time, so choose whichever you prefer to use and make sure all your chopping boards are washed well in hot soapy water after use.

● **Discover the double-boiler** Here's a kitchen tool that's so old it never gets any hype, so it might as well be new and unknown. Yet chefs and experienced cooks use a double-boiler – also known as a bain-marie – all the time. It's ideal for keeping food, especially sauces and soups, warm without overheating them, and it offers a foolproof way of melting chocolate without burning it. You can improvise a simple double-boiler by setting a heatproof bowl – Pyrex is perfect – over a pan of gently simmering water. Make sure the bowl sits securely on the rim or the pan, so that its base is over the water and not in it.

● **Try the new, but keep the old** Manufacturers often label new gadgets as 'breakthroughs', claiming that they are superior replacements for the older version that's in your kitchen drawer. If you succumb to temptation and buy, hang on to what you already have – at least until you're confident that your new acquisition is doing a better job. The old-fashioned, four-sided box grater, for example, is still the best tool for grating many vegetables and cheeses, such as Cheddar. It will also do a decent job on Parmesan. The newer rasp grater, may be equally good or even better with Parmesan, garlic, nutmeg and chocolate, but it is hopeless with the softer things, such as cucumbers and tomatoes.

● **Strain with coffee filters** Many traditional recipes call for cheesecloth to strain liquids and purées through, but it can sometimes be difficult to find in the shops. Here's a modern alternative – paper coffee filters. Straining through the filters may take a little longer, but they are easier to use and produce a better result. Try them for preparing a crystal clear broth or consommé and to strain pith and seeds from fresh fruit juices. If you're using a cone-shaped filter, set it in a funnel, over a container that is large enough to hold the strained liquid. If you're using a basket-type filter, set it in a sieve, over a jar or bowl.

PICNIC TRICKS

6 LITTLE-KNOWN WAYS to eat well and more safely when you pack your basket

● **Keep it cool with frozen drinks** The night before your picnic, place some cartons of fruit juice or other soft drinks in the freezer. You could try making some lemonade, by stirring the juice of 3 large lemons and 3 heaped tablespoons sugar (or to taste) into about 1 litre freshly boiled water. Allow this to cool, then pour into clean, plastic bottles and freeze. Pack the frozen containers around your picnic food in a cool box. The ice-cold drinks will help to keep the food fresh and they should be thawed enough to drink when you need them.

A slice of watermelon ... the perfect ending to an outdoor meal

● **Make potato salad safer**
No picnic food gets a worse press than potato salad; when it's made with mayonnaise, it can easily harbour bacteria that can lead to food poisoning. But there are many delicious and less risky variations on potato salad that use a vinaigrette, made with oil and vinegar instead. Here's a very simple version: boil the potatoes until they're tender, then drain and dice them. While they're cooking, mix 3 parts olive oil with 1 part white-wine vinegar, a couple of finely chopped spring onions and some salt and pepper to taste. Pour this over the warm potatoes and mix well.

It's always a good idea when choosing picnic food to avoid anything containing ingredients that go off easily. As a general rule, this means no raw or lightly cooked eggs (or homemade mayonnaise that contains them) and no milk, cream or shellfish. Leave all the food you prepare in the fridge until the last possible minute, then pack it into a cool bag. Cover food, whenever possible, to protect it from insects, birds and pets that can spread germs.

secret weapon

A CHECK LIST
Many a picnic has been less than perfect because some essential item was left behind. Make a check list of all the food you're bringing and the equipment that you need to transport and serve it. If you often go on picnics, put together a special basket or box that contains all the basics – plates, bowls, cutlery, cups, paper napkins, a bottle opener and corkscrew, as well as insect repellent, antiseptic cream and plasters. Leave it packed from picnic to picnic. Also include several large bin bags to hold rubbish that you can dispose of when you get home.

● **Think finger foods** You can make a terrific meal with dishes that require only two fingers to eat. Start with healthy nibbles, such as celery and carrot sticks, olives, cheese cubes and cherry tomatoes, served with a selection of simple dips. Next, serve up some homemade appetisers that will be good cold, such as sausages, chicken drumsticks and various cold meats, mini quiches, stuffed mushrooms or tomatoes, or foccacia bread topped with fresh herbs or olives. All are in the no-cutlery category.

● **Keep desserts simple** There's nothing better than fresh fruit on a hot summer's day. A slice of watermelon, a ripe peach or a bowl of strawberries will provide the perfect ending to an outdoor meal and all require little or no preparation. If you have the time, you could also make up a batch of small cakes or some brownies or biscuits to bring along as well – which also require no plates or cutlery. Avoid attempting to serve anything that is delicate or likely to go off, such as a mousse or trifle.

● **Use squeezy bottles** You can buy squeezable, plastic bottles very cheaply at kitchen shops and catering suppliers. They are perfect on a picnic for carrying and serving ketchup, mustard, salad dressings, oils and any other condiments or liquids. They are light, easy to pack and clean to use.

● **Bring hand wipes** Warm water and soap are usually in short supply on picnics, so use the next best thing – hand wipes. They're the perfect hand-cleaning solution, particularly if you are serving finger foods. Many brands contain antibacterial agents that will kill germs instantly. Be sure to have a large packet of them on hand.

EATING ABROAD

5 TIPS to help you to stay healthy, conserve cash and eat well when you're on holiday

● **Check out the food** Make sure that everything you eat is freshly cooked and, if appropriate, piping hot, when dining out in countries where food hygiene may not be as stringent as it is at home. Never eat undercooked or raw meat, fish or shellfish, even if it is a local delicacy. In places where it is customary to inspect the kitchen, take a look, and don't be afraid to walk away if you don't like what you see. By taking extra care when selecting food and drink while abroad, you will reduce your chances significantly of developing 'Delhi belly', 'Montezuma's revenge' or the 'Aztec two-step', to give just a few of the many euphemisms for traveller's diarrhoea.

● **Make a 'forbidden' list** In some countries, no matter how good dishes look or how much the locals enjoy or recommend them to you, it's much safer and wiser to draw up a list of foods to avoid and to make sure that you never eat any of them:

◎ **Dairy products and eggs** Avoid unpasteurised milk and ice creams and yoghurt from uncertain sources. Never eat lightly cooked or raw eggs, which means no mayonnaise, hollandaise sauce, mousses or soft-boiled eggs. And be cautious about omelettes – check that they're not too lightly cooked.

◎ **Fruit and veg** Only eat vegetables that have been cooked and fruit that has been cooked or peeled. Avoid salads and any unpeeled fruit.

◎ **Street food** Don't buy snacks from street and market stalls – however tempting they might look.

◎ **Water** Unless you're 100 per cent certain that the tap water is safe to drink, stick to bottled water – even for brushing your teeth. Always check that the seal on bottled water is intact and, in restaurants, make sure that you see the waiter break the seal, when a bottle is brought to your table. Carbonated water is probably safer than still water, as the bottle can't be re-filled from the tap. Avoid ice in drinks.

● **Follow the crowd** If a restaurant is never full – even at peak times – there is probably a very good reason. Does it look clean? Is the food covered? Ask for recommendations from fellow travellers and tour guides and always follow your own instinct.

● **Go for lunch** If you want to enjoy a special meal at a top-class restaurant when you're travelling, go at lunch time. Many establishments may offer a selection of the same dishes then for far less than they do in the evening.

● **Dine alfresco** Tourist boards and travel companies may encourage you to take all of your meals in restaurants when you're away from home. But you can always extend your travel budget by having a few picnics instead. A trip to the local markets should furnish you with plenty of healthy cheaper food, as well as being an adventure in its own right. Buy a selection of fresh local produce – bread, cheeses, pâtés and fresh fruit (remember to peel it), find a particularly picturesque spot and sit down and enjoy it.

AROUND THE

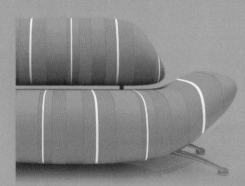

TOP SECRET

HOUSE

chapter **6**

secrets for
**YOUR
WARDROBE**

154

THAT NICE YOUNG REPAIRMAN was charming and chatty. But did you realise that he'd charge you for *all* that time? Discover **simple ways to cut labour costs.**

GARDEN LANDSCAPERS, DECORATORS, ESTATE AGENTS and the people who sell you appliances, clothing and electronics all practise a similar code of silence. Well, we've managed to get a few of them to open up and let you in on **secrets that could save you a mint.**

LEARN ABOUT unnecessary fees and warranties, simple repairs that you can do yourself, low-cost decorating tricks, time and cost-saving garden tips and why it's **dangerous to download** computer screensavers or security software that calls itself 'free'.

secrets of
HOMECARE

From the personal files of the cleverest home experts

DECORATOR SECRETS

3 STRATEGIES professionals use to change a room from faded to fabulous

● **Learn some tricks with colour**
It is always inspiring to see before-and-after photos of a room that has been transformed from dull to dazzling. Designers who achieve such magic are often considered naturally creative. Many, in fact, do have a special knack, but it is usually one that has been nurtured by years of study and hard work – and by learning some fundamental design rules. There is method to the magic – and this is where you come in. You won't have to enrol on a diploma course in interior design, but you will benefit from learning some professional basics and putting them into practice:

Give your ceilings a lift Have you noticed that many traditional, up-market houses have high ceilings? So why not make your rooms look taller with a clever optical illusion. Just stitch a contrasting strip of darker fabric down the sides of your curtains or blinds. If your curtains are beige, add chocolate brown strips; if they are lilac, add deep mauve. Your ceilings will instantly appear much higher.

Add 'architectural' interest
Transform a dull room into something that is handsome and eye-catching by adding a few extra features. Fix a cornice or some moulding along the join between the walls and ceiling, or add a dado rail or a decorative ceiling rose. Then paint these additions – and your doors – a shade or two darker than the walls. If you have sash windows with a deep recess, go for the same darker colour here too and apply an even deeper shade to the actual window frames.

Draw the eye outdoors If you've got french windows – or any another kind of glazed door – leading out on to an attractive patio or garden, paint the frame or wooden part in a dark colour. This will automatically lead the eye to whatever lies beyond. And do make sure that there is something worth looking at out there: a large plant pot containing a substantial shrub should work. Have several and, as each one comes into bloom or its leaves turn a more vibrant hue, move it into a prime viewing position, close to the glass.

● **Avoid predictable seating** Why do you always go for a sofa, a pair of matching armchairs and a coffee table in between? You're not trying to re-create a dentist's waiting room. Instead make your living space somewhere people will want to be, rather than wish they were about to leave. Go for non-matching seating. Making the mix you choose a little less uniform will keep it looking fresh and unique. Shop somewhere you don't normally buy furniture and select a piece that will inject something different into your existing set-up.

● **Make the most of basics** Top designers know that you don't need to spend large sums of money to get a pleasing result. Having to stick to a tight budget often forces people to take chances they might not otherwise take with an expensive piece of furniture or fabric. And it's those chances which can turn into the most successful features in your home. To trigger your imagination, here are some easy suggestions that you might like to try:

Recycle old sofa cushions When you throw out an old sofa, keep the seat cushions, especially if they're large and a regular rectangular shape. Cover them in an attractive fabric and use them on the floor for extra seating. If you choose a material that is suitable for outdoor use, you will be able to use your cushions in the garden too. Stack them away in an understairs cupboard, so that they can be pulled out quickly when your children invite their friends round for a film night or to play computer games.

Make a stylish garden swing Rescue an old garden bench, or pick up a cheap one at a DIY store. Next, cut off the legs. Then attach chains or sturdy ropes and hang it, using metal hooks if necessary, from the front porch of a summerhouse, if it's especially strong, or from something like an old children's climbing frame or the frame of a double swing. You will probably need to put restraining chains on the side, so that it doesn't swing up too high.

Customise off-the-shelf items Take a cheap white lampshade – costing less than £5. Next, glue a handsome red ribbon around the top and bottom edges, and you've got something that is both attractive and unique. The trick here is not to skimp on the cost of the embellishment. Use the best ribbon you can afford. You'll only need about 60cm, so you can achieve a top-quality look for little outlay. Similarly, you could use exquisitely crafted buttons or strips of fine lace. Or, if you have a plain wooden door, you could add interest with a highly decorative door knob. Just remember to keep the 'backdrop' cheap and put the money into the detail.

CLEVER COVER-UPS

6 CANNY TRICKS to transform a room with fabric or wallpaper

● **Create a sofa that flatters** In other words, cover it in a material that would suit you if you were wearing it, instead of a neutral shade that simply blends into the room. If you choose a fabric in your favourite colour, you're unlikely to ever get tired of the sofa and you'll look good sitting on it.

● **Limit bold patterns** A little decorative detail can go a long way, so don't overwhelm. Adding striking touches, for instance on the edge of cushions or a lampshade, is a good way to use expensive fabric without breaking the bank. When you need less than a metre of material, you may find exactly what you need at a greatly reduced price in the remnants section of a shop.

● **Large chair, small print** If you're covering a large chair, like a wingback, choose a fabric with a small-patterned print. The shape and style of these chairs makes them dramatic enough. A small-scale pattern helps to balance the drama and lends a touch of sophistication.

● **Go for child-proof covers** If you have young children, select a 'forgiving' fabric on your sofa and armchairs. You probably already aware that patterns can help to hide spills and crumbs, but did you know that a textured fabric – a cotton velvet or some other textile with a pile – will also work wonders when it comes to masking any mess?

Try it. You'll worry less about your children's sticky fingers and enjoy the time spent with them more.

● Dress up boring windows

Buff-coloured roller blinds are about as dull as it gets, but they're cheap and stop the sunlight from bleaching your furniture. And, for only a few pounds more, you can transform them – and the entire room at the same time – in just one afternoon. Simply glue a bold wallpaper print to the inside of each blind. This works best with blinds that are 68cm wide (the width of a standard roll of wallpaper) or less.

Roll out the blind to its full length, then cut out a sheet of wallpaper to fit the width exactly, but about 5cm longer. Using a clean paint roller, spread some wallpaper adhesive over the inside face of the blind. Lay the cut piece of wallpaper on the glued surface, letting the extra 5cm wrap under the bottom. Press down and smooth out any air bubbles with a rolling pin. Trim away excess wallpaper, if necessary. Because the wallpaper makes the blind stiffer and therefore harder to roll, this trick works best on windows where you don't mind leaving the blinds partially down.

● Make a decorative noticeboard

Large acoustic ceiling tiles – the kind you often see on office ceilings – make good, inexpensive noticeboards. Go to a DIY store and look for a tile-size that appeals to you, but note that larger tiles will be easier to work with, so choose ones that are at least 60cm square, if possible. Wrap them in decorative fabric of your choice, leaving a 10cm overlap and glue this to the back. These can be attached directly to your wall. Or, you could paint a lightweight hollow door and attach the fabric-wrapped tiles to it in neat rows. Lean the door against the wall and you've got an attractive and inexpensive noticeboard.

ORGANISING PAPERS

5 SMART WAYS for keeping papers and photographs from becoming an insurmountable problem

● Get ruthless with paperwork

If you haven't got the time to go through it thoroughly, don't waste your time by half-doing it. Just skimming a pile of mixed letters, bills and scribbled notes takes up time and gets you nowhere. Only open the post when you're near a bin. If your council has a separate collection for recycling paper, keep one bin exclusively for collecting this.

● Be selective

Many people feel obliged to keep every greetings card they've ever received or everything their child ever made. You'll enjoy such items more if you select your favourite pieces and put them in a scrapbook or album, or make a wall decoration with them. If you really can't bear to throw anything away, take a photograph of it and keep that instead. This works really well with

Get ruthless with paperwork

children's things. Arrange everything your child made in one school year on the kitchen table and then snap the lot into one digital frame. You will be able to enlarge the image on your computer screen and see all the detail.

● **Weed out photos** Sort your snaps by person, event or time – for example, 'Summer 2008' or 'David and Jo's Wedding'. Then choose the 20 best pictures from each group and put these in an album. Throw away the rest, or spread the memories by giving them away.

● **Bin old negatives** New pictures can be made directly from prints these days, so clear some space on your shelves and get rid of that pile of negatives you've been storing for years.

● **Organise and prune daily** Spend a few minutes every day picking up and organising household papers. Junk mail and newspapers can build up so fast that clearing them once a week isn't enough. Make special stacks or folders for bills, receipts and bank statements and it'll be quicker to go through everything in one hit, say on a Sunday evening.

CLUTTER CONTROL
5 SECRETS for cutting down

● **Do it like a professional**
Decluttering is big business these days. Professional home organisers know that busy people will shell out for peace of mind, which is why they charge fees of between £30 to £60 per hour. But while many of these professionals do good work, you can easily achieve the same results yourself. And – once you get going – it's surprisingly satisfying, too. Home organiser Karen Lawrence offers these general tips:

▪ **Think time, not money** This is often the hardest idea to take on board when dealing with clutter. Everything you buy is an investment of your time. Clothes must be cleaned and mended. Trinkets have to be dusted. Toys need storing and fixing. So while you think you're

economising every time you bring home another bargain, you are also committing yourself to spending time caring for it. Before you rush to buy, mentally add the 'cost' of maintenance to the purchase price of the new item. It might begin to look more expensive than it appears. Perhaps you'll start to buy less and begin to save some money.

▪ **Set smaller goals** Decluttering one room a week or tackling one shelf or one drawer a day is good, steady progress. If you try to organise your entire house in a weekend, you'll get so discouraged, you may stop altogether.

▪ **Prepare first** Before decluttering, set aside bags and boxes labelled 'Rubbish', 'Charity Shop' and 'Belongs Elsewhere'. You'll break down that big pile of clutter into smaller, more manageable bits.

▪ **Sort like items together** You may discover you have six sleeveless black dresses, four cool-boxes or eight torches. Keep the best and chuck out the rest.

Get focused Define key decluttering activities, such as going through your post, paying bills or mending things, then create 'centres' for them. Fill each centre with the tools for the task and use them to stay on top of the clutter.

● **Balance your wardrobe** Start with a clean-out then, whenever you buy anything new – a winter coat, for example – give away a similar item you no longer wear. Your wardrobe will stay streamlined and be better balanced.

● **Donate regularly to charity** Don't wait for a random request at your door. Keep a box by the ironing basket and you'll be able to throw in old clothes as soon as they've been washed and dried. When the box is full, take it to your local charity shop.

● **Fix it quick or throw it out** Fixing stuff is admirable. But hanging on to broken household items until you find the time to repair them, clutters up your garage or understairs cupboard and burdens you mentally. If you haven't got round to it in a month, you never will.

How they do it ...
decluttering

'To mark her 48th birthday, Sue Kay set herself a challenge – to throw out at least 48 things she no longer used that were taking up valuable space around the house. Sue, a founder member of the Association of Professional Declutterers, felt her birthday was an ideal time to do this, because, of course, it is a time when new things arrive. She gave herself a month to complete her task.

Sue is confident that most of us could find 20, 30 or even 50 things that are lying around gathering dust and decluttering is made much easier by setting well defined goals and deadlines, as she did. Sue kept a record of everything she threw out and, when she looked at this a year later, she realised that she hadn't missed a single thing.

● **Don't have a car boot sale** You may make some money, but you're also likely to be left with a load of surplus items and the delusion that, next time, they will sell. Worse, you may even start stock-piling stuff to sell at a future date.

CONTAINER MAGIC

5 CREATIVE USES for baskets and other containers to help bring order to chaos

● **Use the basket trick** Place a decorative basket or crate in or near the most cluttered room of your house – generally the kitchen or living room. Place items that belong in other rooms in the basket. Anytime you leave the room, take items out of the basket and return them to their rightful place.

● **Sort loose items** Anything that you have more than four of warrants a container to itself. Good examples are batteries, buttons and shoe polishes. Use old sweet tins, washed-out ice-cream cartons and screw-top jars. Label, then store items with a similar use together, in a household maintenance cupboard.

● **Have three laundry baskets** One is for whites, one for coloureds and one for hand-washing. Drop your dirty clothes into the appropriate basket and you won't have to spend time sorting everything out before each wash.

● **Give it a 'home'** Can you never find the remote control? You will if you keep it in a small basket or china dish or a wooden bowl, rather than just on the table. That's because giving an object a 'home' means you know where to find it and where to return it to after use. Pens, notepads and scissors can also be given their own special places too. Make a habit of doing this and you'll find everything faster – and avoid cluttering up tabletops and work surfaces.

● **Crate children's stuff** Go for crates on wheels and, at the end of the day, put all their toys and clutter into them and push it behind the sofa. Use clear plastic crates so that you can see what's inside. If you can't get any, tape a photo of the contents on the lid, so your toddler can work out what's kept where.

HOUSE **CLEANING**

9 SIMPLE PLOYS that can save you time, effort and money when doing housework

● **Use a timer** Decide how long you're going to spend cleaning before you start. Next, divide your time into chunks – 15 minutes to vacuum and perhaps the same again at the sink, and so on. Now you have a timed target, you'll find you work that bit harder. Also, if you absolutely hate a job – cleaning the bathroom, for example – knowing you're going to spend just 10 minutes in there, may make you feel less bothered about tackling it.

● **Avoid concentrated products** This isn't something the manufacturers are going to shout about, but unless you use them sparingly, you're just throwing money away when you choose expensive, high-powered cleansers. Standard-strength products are quite sufficient for most jobs. You actually need very little detergent to clean a dirty kitchen floor – about 2 tablespoons of most standard brands, swished into half a bucket of water. With bleach, adding more doesn't make it more effective, either. Germs die from the time spent in contact with the disinfecting solution, even when it's only at the recommended dilution of 1 part bleach to 30 parts water.

● **Clean your windows for pennies**
Why should glass cleaner, which is mostly water, cost you more per litre than petrol? Because the manufacturers want you to pay for their fancy advertising campaigns. Make your own for much less. Simply pour 4 litres warm water into a bucket. Add 100ml white vinegar and 1 teaspoon washing-up liquid and stir well. If you're cleaning a lot of windows, apply this mixture with a squeegee mop, straight from the bucket. Otherwise, pour it into plastic spray bottles, ready for future use.

● **Give your sink a bath** Abrasive cleaners can scratch your sink. Instead, try a herbal bath. Steep several bunches of rosemary or thyme in hot water for a few hours, then strain. Stop up the sink, pour in the herb solution and let it sit overnight. In the morning, you'll find a glistening, fragrant sink.

● **Fizz your toilet clean** Most toilet cleaners are highly caustic, so try something gentler that will do the job just as well. Once a week, drop two denture tablets into the bowl and leave for at least 20 minutes. Then give the inside of the bowl a quick brushing and flush. The same action that brightens dentures will leave your toilet gleaming.

And you'll save money: a month's supply of denture tablets costs around £1.

● **Oven-clean your grill**
Put away that wire brush and leave that caustic oven cleaner in the cupboard. Here's an effortless, non-toxic way to clean the mess off your grill rack. Simply slide it into your self-cleaning oven, turn the setting up to high (around 250°C) and leave for 45 minutes or so. This will scorch away any greasy remnants from the rack. If your barbecue isn't too big, you can clean its greasy racks in this way, too.

● **Clean your own curtains** Dirty curtains send some homeowners straight to the Yellow Pages. Then they find out that professional cleaners often charge by the inch to clean curtains. And soon you're into triple figures … Here are some tricks to keep curtains in peak condition for longer:

🛋 **Dust them regularly** Don't bother taking them down. Simply run your vacuum cleaner over them – from top to bottom – using the dusting brush or upholstery attachment. Focus on the tops and hems, where most dust gathers. Avoid sucking the fabric into the nozzle by either reducing the vacuum pressure or grasping the bottom and holding the curtains tight. If you don't have the proper attachments, use a feather duster. Dusting prevents dirt build-up and lessens the chances that the curtains will need a major cleaning.

🛋 **Wash if you can** Try to identify the fabric, including any trimmings and linings, and use that information to choose the best cleaning method. If you're unsure about washing, play safe by just wetting an inside turn-up of fabric first to gauge the effect. Even if

To keep curtains in peak condition … dust them regularly

scary **CHEMICALS** that **SNEAK** into your home

MANUFACTURERS OF CLEANSERS, building materials and pesticides tend to focus on their product's benefits; they rarely mention any negative side effects. But many air fresheners give off naphthalene, a suspected carcinogen; ammonia-based cleaners can cause respiratory irritation; and some cleaners contain butyl cellosolve (also known as ethylene glycol monobutyl ether), which is believed to cause nerve damage. **And these are just a few examples of the harmful chemicals that sneak into our homes.**

BAD STUFF

Familiarise yourself with the chemical culprits, scan ingredient labels on all household products, and avoid these substances whenever possible:

BUTYL CELLOSOLVE
CRESOL
FORMALDEHYDE
GLYCOLS
HYDROCHLORIC ACID
HYDROFLUORIC ACID
LYE
NAPHTHALENE
PDCBS
(PARADICHLOROBENZENES)
PERCHLOROETHYLENE
PETROLEUM DISTILLATES
PHENOL
PHOSPHORIC ACID
PROPELLANTS
SULPHURIC ACID
TCE (TRICHLOROETHYLENE)

GOOD STUFF

Keep healthy alternatives around the house. Not only will you reduce indoor pollution, but you'll save money. Here's a list:

BAKING POWDER Many of us have a tub of this inexpensive product somewhere in our kitchen cupboard. As well as its obvious use in baking, it is a mildly abrasive cleaner, with whitening properties. It's also good for removing pet odours from carpets.

ESSENTIAL OILS The boiled-down essences of different plants – peppermint and lavender, for example – these can be used as natural air fresheners and to add a pleasant scent to homemade cleaners. You will find a selection in health-food stores and in some chemists and supermarkets. A bottle of good-quality essence can be expensive, but you'll only need 2 drops to have an effect.

VEGETABLE OIL–BASED LIQUID SOAP This is a biodegradable alternative to petroleum-based detergents. It can be found in most health-food stores.

VINEGAR Because it is highly acidic, vinegar is effective for killing germs, cutting through grease and dissolving mineral deposits, such as limescale. Use it to descale the kettle. Simply pour in the vinegar until the kettle is about a third full, bring to the boil, then empty out. Repeat with water to remove all traces of the vinegar.

WASHING SODA This will make light work of greasy dirt and stains.. It is also a water softener. Look for it next to the washing powders in the supermarket. Be aware, though, that it should only be used for hand-washing; never put it in a washing machine.

Baking powder ... it is a mildly abrasive cleaner, with whitening properties

you know your curtains can be machine washed and tumble dried, remove them from the dryer and hang while still damp. This way, you'll avoid having to iron them.

If washing seems too risky, but you want to freshen your curtains between visits to the dry cleaner, hang them out on the line on a breezy day. You can guarantee they'll will come back fresher.

🖾 **Get them measured** Ask your dry cleaner to measure your curtains before leaving them for cleaning. If they refuse, go elsewhere. The best cleaners will do as you ask because they will be happy to guarantee that your curtains will come back the same length as they started.

● **Buy extra basics** Having at least two sets of sheets means that you can change bedding on a set day, then launder when you have time. You'll also save trips upstairs if you keep a set of cleaning products on each floor. Build a high shelf for them in the bathroom, out of reach of young children.

● **Give wipes the boot** Use your own cloths, spray them with a suitable cleanser and wipe. Then stick them in the washing machine when you've finished and select a hot wash to kill any germs. You won't have to change cloths as often as impregnated wipes, so you'll work faster. And you'll save money.

CLEANING **VALUABLES**

3 CLEVER WAYS to save serious money when cleaning jewellery and other expensive items

● **Keep that sparkle** Jewellers would like to help you to look after the pieces you buy from them – for a price. But while resetting a stone requires specialist skill, care and periodic cleaning don't:

🖾 **Remove jewellery before you swim** Gold and silver can be damaged by repeated exposure to chlorinated water.

🖾 **Avoid the toothpaste trick** You may have been told that gold and silver can be cleaned with toothpaste. But many brands contain harsh abrasives that can scratch and dull the metal's finish.

🖾 **Don't soak stones** Jewellery set with precious stones shouldn't be soaked for more than a few seconds. Water can dissolve glue holding a stone in place.

🖾 **Take care with silver cutlery** Acidic foods, such as mustard and ketchup, and foods containing sulphur, such as eggs

and mayonnaise, can tarnish and damage silver. So if you do use silver or silver-plated cutlery when eating or serving any of these foods, clean it as soon as possible afterwards.

🖾 **Wash gold jewellery** Over time, oils from your skin, and any soaps and lotions you use, will leave a dull film on any gold you wear. To revive it, soak for about 5 minutes in a bowl of warm water mixed with a squirt of mild washing-up liquid. Then scrub gently using a soft toothbrush. Rinse and pat dry with a clean lint-free cloth.

🖾 **Buff silver to a shine** A soft cloth is all you should need to smooth away the dull patina that forms on silver when exposed to air. For more drastic action, drop the silver into a bowl and add a scrunched up ball of aluminium foil.

Pour over hot water and – it's magic – the dirt will transfer from the silver on to the foil over the next 30 minutes.

● **Wipe pearls often** Because pearls are highly sensitive to chemicals, it's important that you wipe them down after wearing them, using a slightly damp, very soft cloth, such as chamois. This removes any perspiration, make-up and perfume that may penetrate the pearls' porous surface. From time to time, clean with lukewarm water mixed with a little mild soap to create light suds. Dip a cloth in the suds and gently wipe the pearls, then rinse with clean water and dry on a soft cloth. Never soak pearls – and never hang them up to dry, since the weight of the water might stretch the string. Any stubborn solids may be removed from the surface using your fingernail. Pearls are as hard or harder than most people's fingernails, so are unlikely to be scratched in this way.

● **Swish grime away** To shift that hard to remove dirt that can get trapped inside decanters and narrow-necked vases, pour in a little vinegar, followed by a few teaspoons of uncooked rice. Swish them around, when you think of it over the next day or so, then pour them away and rinse. The dirt should be gone. The vinegar loosens the stains, while the rice scours the surface. For wine stains, swirl warm water mixed with a few teaspoons each of baking powder and salt. Or fill with warm water, add a denture-cleaning tablet and leave overnight. Then rinse and dry. Drying is another challenge. An easy way is to wrap kitchen towel around the handle of a wooden spoon, so it extends slightly beyond the end. Stick the towel-wrapped handle into the decanter or vase and let it rest on the bottom overnight. By morning, the kitchen towel will have absorbed any moisture and can be pulled out and thrown away.

INSECT PESTS

3 NATURAL WAYS to get rid of annoying bugs in your house without chemicals

> Turn back ants with vinegar ... Unlike insecticides, vinegar is 100 per cent harmless

● **Shoo away flies with basil**
Here's a great way to get rid of flies. Put several basil plants into small pots and place them along your kitchen windowsills. Flies hate basil, so they'll stay away and your kitchen will be filled with the fragrance of summer all year round.

● **Turn back ants with vinegar** Fill a clean spray bottle with a solution made from equal quantites of water and white vinegar. Spray this anywhere you see ants infiltrating your space – along skirting boards, on kitchen worktops or in moist bathrooms, for example. Unlike insecticides, vinegar is 100 per cent harmless, so it's safe to use in areas where you prepare food.

● **Despatch moths with scent** Buy citronella-scented candles from your local garden centre. When you want to keep the windows open on a warm summer evening, light one, place it near the window and moths won't come in.

PERSONAL CARE ITEMS

3 TRICKS to keep brushes, combs and other personal-care items in good order

● **Take it easy on the curlers** If you use harsh cleaners on your hair curlers, you risk transferring those damaging chemicals to your hair. Instead, clean them with shampoo. Soak velcro-style rollers and foam-coated wire sticks in a bowl of warm, sudsy solution, made with a squirt of shampoo. Gently comb out any hair and wipe off caked-on grime with an old flannel. Stubborn stains, such as hardened setting lotion or gel, may need a further soak in 100ml warm water mixed with 1 tablespoon fabric softener. Then rinse and air-dry.

Obviously, you can't soak electric curlers or hair straighteners, so clean these with the fabric softener solution, applied with a cloth or brush. Rinse by wiping with a damp rag, then dry.

● **Clean hairbrushes regularly**
Keep on top of things, by removing hairs that lodge in your brush every day. Then, every few weeks, wash it in this economical and effective cleaning solution – 2 teaspoons shampoo and 60ml vinegar stirred into a bowl of warm water. Soak the brush in this for several minutes, then use a wide-toothed comb to remove any remaining hair stuck in it. The solution will loosen built-up oil and dirt, as well as sticky hair gels and sprays. Scrub the brush clean with a nailbrush. Rinse with warm, running water, then leave to air-dry.

● **Soak razor blades in mineral oil**
Razor manufacturers hope you'll change blades as often as you change shirts. But here's a simple trick to prolong their life. Pour some mineral oil into a shallow dish and soak the blade in it for a few minutes. The oil will halt the corrosion that dulls the blade's cutting edge. When soaking time is up, wipe off excess oil, with a cloth dipped in methylated spirit.

CONTROLLING ODOURS

5 LOW-COST METHODS to prevent and remove offensive smells around the house

● **Banish pet smells from carpets**
You may think that professional cleaning or a new carpet are the only solutions if your pet has a bad accident on the living room floor. Think again. Sprinkle baking powder on the odour-causing stain, leave it overnight, then vacuum it up next day. Repeat until the smell has gone.

● **Skip air fresheners** Chemists are out there in laboratories right now cooking up the next new air-freshener scent, while marketing departments are busy concocting the selling points to get you to give good money for it. But air fresheners don't really freshen the air. They simply mask smells – and evidence

ACTIVATED CHARCOAL

Here's what to do if you are faced with a strong, unpleasant and persistant odour in your fridge or freezer. Go to your local pet shop and buy some fine activated charcoal from the aquarium section. Spread some in a shallow dish and put this on a fridge or freezer shelf. The charcoal won't harm your food, but it will absorb any nasty smell. After 8 hours, the charcoal will need to be reactivated. Do this by heating it in a medium oven for 20 minutes. You can then re-use it. If you can't get any charcoal, try cat litter or fresh (unused) ground coffee instead. They do a similar job, though less well.

shows that some may irritate the lungs. Instead, look out for products that actually kill the bacteria that cause odours – such as Febreeze.

● **Control cooking smells** Bring 50ml vinegar and 200ml water to the boil on the stove, then lower the heat and leave to simmer gently. The rising water vapour will carry particles of odour-neutralising vinegar to the greasy, smoked-covered kitchen surfaces on which you have just cooked dinner.

● **Bleach that bin** Make up a solution of 60ml bleach, 5 litres water and two short squirts of washing-up liquid. Scrub the inside of a smelly bin with this mixture, using a nylon-bristled brush. Make sure you cover all internal surfaces, then tip any remaining solution down the drain and rinse the bin out thoroughly. Leave to dry.

● **Perfume the bathroom** By placing some pot pouri, or even a square of fabric, in a bowl, in your bathroom and sprinkling over a few drops of essential oil, you will fill the space with an inviting perfume. You'll make the smell more intense if you can also add heat to the mix and contain it in some way. So try to keep the bathroom door shut and position your scented container on a shelf above the bathroom radiator or over a heated towel rail.

FURNITURE FIXES

7 EASY TRICKS for giving new life to old furniture

● **Revive your wicker** Cane furniture can be a challenge to clean. But that's no reason to pay a professional to do it. Stephen Berne, a Canadian antique chair restorer offers these insider tips:
🖌 **Use a vacuum cleaner** with a brush attachment to lift dust, dirt and lint from within the woven reeds.
🖌 **Wipe clean** with a cloth moistened with paint thinner (first try a little thinner on an inconspicuous spot to make sure it does not harm the finish). For stubborn stains, rub lightly with a paintbrush moistened with thinner.
🖌 **Bring up the sheen** by applying some furniture wax with a clean, soft cloth.

● **Tighten that sagging seat** Like all seasoned craftsmen, furniture repairers have their tricks. Here's one that will save money the next time your wicker chair seats stretch and droop.

First, make sure the seat is made from rattan or bark – not paper rushing. Then turn the chair upside down and wet the underside of the seat by wiping it with a clean sponge soaked in warm water. Once this is really wet – the top of the seat should remain dry – gently push down on the damp underside and then turn the chair upright. Once it has dried out, the seat will be much tighter.

● **Mask furniture scratches** Avoid restorer's fees by hiding scratches. An easy and cheap way to do this is to match a wax crayon to the colour of the wood and use it to work over the scratch. Then rub lightly to blend in.

● **Keep antiques as they were** Do as little as possible to change the original construction and finish of old furniture. By stripping off a finish and putting on a new one, you could drastically reduce the value of an antique. If a chair is a little loose and creaky or a table's lacquer top is cracking, leave it as it is.

● **Protect without fuss** Contrary to what the makers of those lemon-fresh, spray-on furniture polishes claim, you don't need fancy chemicals to clean and protect wooden chests, desks, tables and chairs. In fact, those products can do more harm than good.

At the National Trust, this minimalist approach is taken to the extreme: to reduce wear and tear, loose surface dust is cleaned off only when it is deemed really necessary. In some instances, that might be just once a year. For the gentlest of treatment, smooth flat surfaces are cleaned with soft cotton dusters folded into a pad. And when it comes to especially prized objects, intervention can be even less frequent. Books may get cleaned once every three to five years, ceramics every five to ten

years and paintings once every 25 years. Fading from exposure to sunlight, and darkening caused by absorbing chemicals and moisture are the major enemies of wooden furniture.

To avoid such problems occurring, experts suggest the following:

🔹 **Protect wood** from moisture by using coasters for drinks and wiping up spills immediately. And try to avoid cleaning with water, if at all possible.

🔹 **Dust regularly** with a soft, dry cloth.

🔹 **Wax once a year** with a product such as Johnson's paste wax – but only if the finish of the wood is intact. A paste wax will protect without penetrating the wood and will stop dust from binding with the surface. Pick a wax that matches the colour of the wood. If the wood is cracked or the finish has rubbed away, skip the paste altogether.

● **Steam out dents** A dent on a wooden surface can often be removed by swelling the compressed wood fibres back to their normal size, using moisture and heat. To do this, prick the varnish finish of the dented area several times with a fine pin, so that any moisture applied will be able to penetrate into the wood below. Then cover the dent with a pad of wet cloth, put a metal bottle cap on top of the pad to spread the heat, and apply a hot iron to it for a few minutes. Be careful not to scorch the finish. Afterwards, when the wood is completely dry, fill the pinholes with a thin coat of fresh varnish.

● **Paint over plastics** Once plastic and furniture has been scratched, there is often little that you can do to remedy it. But one solution is to paint the damaged object. The latest paints cover plastic easily and smoothly, with no need for a primer coat. If you're in a hurry, go for the spray-on kind.

5 secrets for buying MATTRESSES

SAVVY TIPS for getting a good night's sleep

1 BEWARE OF 'COMFORT' GUARANTEES Money-back guarantees are generally a good thing: you can try something out without any financial risk. But do you really want a mattress that someone may have used for several weeks? You should realise that bedding manufacturers would never allow a retailer to return a mattress simply because it didn't feel right. So if a shop offers you the chance to return a mattress after you've given it a test run, it is almost certainly putting any returns back on show and selling them off as new – and this is probably not the mattress you will want to buy.

2 BUY THE SET Divan bases and mattresses that come in sets are built and fitted for each other. If the units are from a separate source it can cause problems. And since the base will absorb up to 50 per cent of the impact placed upon the bed, using a well-fitted one can prolong the life of your mattress.

3 AVOID BOX PLATFORMS Unlike sprung divan bases, these plain box supports, covered with fabric, have no springs. They are usually there just to make a cheap mattress feel firmer. But the reality is that they can actually cause the mattress to break down more quickly. Without box springs, the mattress ticking, padding, and other upholstery can wear out much quicker. Also, don't assume a firm mattress is the best. Studies show that the long-held belief that firmer mattresses are better, especially for people with back pain, may not be true. Chiropractors say your spine should look the same when you're lying down as it does when you're standing. So go for a mattress designed to conform to the spine's natural curves and to keep it in alignment when you lie down. Also, if you sleep on your side, a firm mattress may not have enough 'give' to allow your shoulder and hips to sink into it, so that your body will be unnaturally compressed. A good mattress will distribute pressure evenly across your body.

4 SKIMP ON THE KIDS' MATTRESSES Yes, you did read that correctly. Mattress manufacturers and retailers know how young parents dote on their children. They prey on this to provide 'the best that money can buy' by offering high-priced bedding designed specifically for children. Choosing top-quality goods is fine when it comes to car seats, food and other things directly related to your child's health and safety. But almost any medium-priced bed will offer enough support and a comfortable night's sleep. When you weigh less than 38kg, you aren't putting that much pressure on the mattress. So why buy your toddler such an expensive one, which will probably be too small in a few years time – if it isn't destroyed first by bed-wetting or being used as a trampoline?

5 DON'T BE BLINDED BY LOOKS Manufacturers of beds take great pains to give their products showroom appeal, with luxurious, hand-stitched satin tops. But most of the time, all this loveliness will be covered up by a sheet. But do check how the sides of a mattress are finished. Hand stitching here means your bed will keep its shape for longer – as long as you avoid sitting on the edge. This can distort the shape of a mattress.

Don't assume that a firm mattress is the best

TOOLS & **SUPPLIES**

8 KEY TIPS for using tools to their best advantage and making them last a lifetime

● **Get the right tools for the job**
Many people shy away from doing household repairs because they think they will be too difficult. But with the right tools, daunting tasks often turn out to be easy. If, for example, you need to turn off the outdoor water stopvalve because the indoor one has jammed, you might think of calling in a plumber. But, instead, investing a few pounds in the right type of long stopcock key will take the sweat out of the job. So next time some household maintenance is called for, visit your local DIY store or trade supplier (you will find names and addresses in the Yellow Pages and on the internet) and ask about special tools for the jobs you need to tackle. Even if they seem expensive, they are likely to be far cheaper than calling someone out.

● **Invest in new screwdrivers**
Some types of tools are great to pass on from generation to generation. Slotted screwdrivers are not among them. After prolonged use, their blades grow thin and become rounded at the corners. A worn screwdriver can ruin your woodwork when it slips out and gashes the surface. The wisest move is to keep old, worn screwdrivers only for prising open tins of paint and invest in a new, high-quality set for doing a decent job.

● **Keep paint in jars** Leftover paint is often kept in its original tin. Then, the labels fall off, the tin rusts, air leaks in and the paint is ruined. A better way to store paint is in glass jars. Not only can you see the colour of what's inside, but a jar with a screw-top lid is far more airtight than a tin with a lid that has been removed many times and become

distorted. To tighten the seal further and to ensure the lid won't stick, wrap a few layers of plumber's PTFE tape around the jar threads before sealing.

● **Make brushes last longer** How many times have you thrown away a perfectly good paintbrush because you didn't want to face the mess of cleaning it? If you're using an oil-based paint, such as gloss, and need to pause for a break, you don't have to clean your brush or roller. Just wipe off the excess paint, then wrap tightly in aluminium foil, a plastic bag or some cling film. Exclude as much air as possible, then seal the neck with an elastic band. This will stop any paint left on the brush or roller from drying out.

If you're using a water-based paint, such as emulsion or eggshell, and your brush or roller won't come clean, don't throw it away. Many of today's water-based paints contain resins similar to those used in oil-based paints in order to improve their adhesion and durability. After cleaning and rinsing with water, clean the brush or roller again using paintbrush cleaner that can then be rinsed out with more water.

● **Track pipes and wiring** Devices for locating the position of water pipes, electric cables or timber studs in walls have become cheaper and easier to operate in recent years. So don't ever take chances when you are drilling into a wall that could have cables or pipes buried in it: an inexpensive pipe/cable detector will help you to locate them. And a joist/stud detector will help to find the solid wood studs that you can screw into.

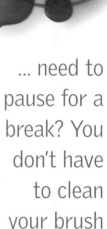

... need to pause for a break? You don't have to clean your brush

7 ESSENTIAL TOOLS
for making DIY easy

A SUPRISINGLY SMALL NUMBER of tools can cope with a wide range of repair and maintenance jobs around the house. Keep these tools together in a lightweight box or bag, in an easily accessible place, and you will save both time and effort whenever something needs fixing.

As with all things, you usually get what you pay for, and DIY tools are no exception. Don't buy the cheapest, as the quality of the materials used is likely to be inferior and there is nothing worse than a crucial piece of equipment letting you down, just when you need it.

1 CLAW HAMMER This is an excellent general-purpose tool, that can be used for a wide range of tasks from knocking in a picture hook to nailing a fence panel or lifting a floorboard. The claw can be used to extract rusty nails from salvaged wood. Choose wood, steel or fibreglass for the hammer shaft, but if heavy use is anticipated, go for a rubber handgrip for comfort and safety.

2 COMBINATION PLIERS There are many different types of pliers on the market. Each one is designed for a specific task, but the most useful are combination pliers. These feature a pair of jaws with both flat and curved teeth for gripping a wide range of objects, as well as sharp-edged cutters for slicing through wire. Pliers are extremely versatile, but it is never wise to use them for removing nuts and bolts, as these can easily be damaged by the plier's serrated jaws.

3 SET OF SCREWDRIVERS A range of good-quality screwdrivers is an essential for any home toolbox. Normally a boxed set will contain a selection with slotted, Phillips and Pozidriv heads in a variety of different sizes, that are suitable for most household tasks. Including a couple with short stubby handles in your collection will allow easy access to areas where space is tight. If room for storing your tools is at a premium, then you could buy one all-purpose screwdriver with a hollow handle for storing the interchangeable driver bits. Such tools are brilliantly compact, but the shape of the handle on these multifunction tools may make them less effective and more difficult to use.

4 ADJUSTABLE SPANNER Your house may contain a wide range of hexagonal nuts and bolts, all in different sizes. A single adjustable spanner can do the same job as a box of conventional spanners and it can be swiftly changed to the required size. It is a good idea to have a pair of these spanners handy, as quite often you need to hold two parts of the threaded item, such as when tightening a compression fitting on a section of your plumbing system.

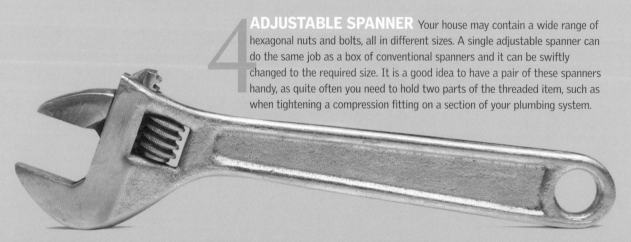

5 **RETRACTABLE TRIMMING KNIFE** This type of knife can cope with most cutting tasks around the house. It will slice neatly through paper, card, vinyl, carpet, leather, cork and many other materials. Go for one that can accept a good range of specialist blades, designed for different purposes, and choose one with a blade that can be retracted back into the handle for safe storage. Always try to keep a supply of fresh blades stored in the handle, ready for a quick change when necessary: as with all cutting tools, a sharp blade is not only more efficient, it is far safer than a blunt one.

6 **JUNIOR HACKSAW** There are various types of saw available, but this small tool is particularly useful. It will not only cut through metal – nails and pipes, for example – but it will also cut through plastic, such as that found in curtain rails and guttering, and small timber mouldings. It uses replaceable blades, so make sure that you buy some spares so that you are ready when the blade wears out or breaks.

7 **CORDLESS DRILL** Whether you need to drill a hole or to insert or remove screws, usually the most effortless and convenient way is with a cordless drill/driver. Powered by rechargeable batteries, the drill can be taken anywhere in the house or garden as it does not need a mains power supply or trailing extension lead – making it safer to use outside or up a ladder. If you choose a model with variable speeds, torque settings and hammer-action, you will be able to tackle most household jobs including drilling into masonry. Also, a keyless chuck allows quick changing of drill or screwdriver bits. Keep a spare battery, charged ready for use.

● **Stock up on tapes** There is a tape for every purpose and keeping just a few types in your tool kit can be a life saver, when you need a quick fix. Here are five of the most useful:

Parcel tape is excellent for sealing up cardboard boxes and large envelopes. If you make up lots of packages, you could buy a tape-dispensing gun with a cut-off blade to speed up the work.

PVC insulation tape is a good general purpose tape. Designed for electricians, it is also ideal when mending a broken object, such as a vase, for holding the pieces together while the adhesive sets.

Masking tape is the decorators' choice. It can be used to mask off areas, such as windows, to protect the glass when you are painting the frames. It peels away cleanly after it has done its job.

Duct tape is weatherproof and strong, with good adhesion. Designed to seal off ducts in heating systems, it can be used for all sorts of repair work, such as temporarily sealing a cracked window.

Double-sided tape has a multitude of uses – from holding carpet down and mirrors up to providing a way of displaying Christmas cards or holding screws and nails whilst working.

● **Unclog your sander** The abrasive used on belt or disc sanders can clog up quickly, especially when sanding through paint or resinous timbers. Every time this happens, the temptation is to throw away the old abrasive belt, pad or disc and replace it with a new one – which can become expensive. Before discarding it, you could try unclogging the old abrasive with an inexpensive cleaning stick available from some DIY stores and professional tool suppliers. Just hold the stick against the moving belt or disc and it will be instantly rejuvenated and ready for action.

● **Prevent rust** Moisture in the air promotes rusting. If dampness gets into your tool box, which may well be stored in a damp shed or garage, it will corrode any steel or iron tools, affecting their appearance and their usefulness. One way to make sure that the inside of your toolbox remains dry is to place some packets of silica gel in it. You can either buy these or save them from the packaging of new products you acquire, such as cameras or electrical goods. You can also try placing a few mothballs in your tool box to help to suck up any excess moisture.

To protect wood-working tools from corrosion, wipe or spray them with a light film of oil before packing them away. This protective layer can be easily wiped off, just before the tool is used. It's also good practice to sharpen any tool after you have used it and to cover the sharp edge in some way to protect it from damage while it is being stored.

HIRING HELP

4 SAVVY STRATEGIES to get the best value for money

● **Use a qualified electrician** You may be considering giving a small wiring job to a general handyman. But before you do, enquire about qualifications. Many electrical jobs, including all new work in kitchens or bathrooms, must now be inspected and approved by the Building Control department of your local council, or be carried out by a competent electrician who can certify that the work has been done correctly.

The National Inspection Council for Electrical Installation Contracting (NICEIC) is the largest trade association representing electricians. It provides details of approved contractors in each area of the UK. You can visit their website (www.niceic.com), put in your postcode and search for approved electrical contractors in your area.

● **Ask for a guarantee** Builders often give no guarantee for their work. When the job is finished, they leave and any chance of getting them to return to fix faults disappears with them. When hiring tradesmen, search out those who come highly recommended by someone you know and trust. Or maybe find a long-established company that is keen to maintain their professional reputation. Before hiring any firm to do a job, ask if it will guarantee its work for up to a year at least. If it will, get the guarantee in writing. If it won't, don't hesitate to take your business elsewhere.

● **Get a plumber, then the fittings** If your plumber is charging you by the hour to install a new bathroom or kitchen, here's an approach that will probably save some money. Ask for a recommendation on what makes of fixtures and fittings to choose. The chances are that well-known, reliable manufacturers will be suggested. If you choose products made by them, you can be fairly certain that they will be installed more efficiently than anything with which your plumber is unfamiliar. Less effort will be spent struggling through detailed instructions about which bit goes where – saving time, money and a lot of hassle. And your plumber is more likely to install a familiar product correctly – which could save on repairs in the long run.

● **Keep it short** Any handyman or repair person who is paid by the hour will happily lounge around your house chatting or watching while you get organised. But with a little forethought and careful planning you can make sure that every minute of a repair visit is totally productive. Here are some rules to follow:

🖾 Inspect the house for all the necessary jobs that could be carried out in a single visit. This will save you money on future call-out charges.

🖾 Discuss all the fine details of the work required over the telephone – while the clock isn't ticking. This will also help to ensure that the worker will arrive equipped with the necessary tools and materials for the job.

🖾 Make sure, in advance of the visit, that the area where the work is to be done is free of clutter and that there is clear access to it. And make sure there's enough light to work by, as well.

🖾 Tell the worker not to worry about cleaning up before leaving. This is hardly ever done to your satisfaction anyway. The worker will be out of your house in the least possible time – and your bill will be kept to the minimum.

HOW-TO SECRETS

4 LITTLE-KNOWN TRICKS that
ensure a successful and cost-effective job

There's no need to employ professional help to silence a door that slams noisily

● **Offer some assistance** A neat electrical installation will generally involve burying unsightly cables so that they are not seen. A professional electrician will 'chase' wires into a masonry wall or run a cable to an outbuilding in a deep trench. You may be able to save money by doing some of the non-electrical work yourself – perhaps digging the trench in the right place and filling it in afterwards or making good the plaster of the masonry wall once the cables are securely in place. Few professional electricians are good plasterers so you may get a better result as well.

● **Silence that door** There's no need to employ professional help to silence a door that slams noisily. Here is a way to

dampen the din. Apply a few dabs of clear silicone sealant along the edge of the door stop where the closing door hits it. Now leave the door propped open for a few hours to make sure the silicone dries out before closing it again. The silicone bead should act as a cushion, reducing the noise of wood striking against wood.

● **Keep pictures level** A decorator might charge you to solve the annoying and recurring problem of pictures that won't stay level. But if you follow this clever trick, you will never have to find out how much. If you have plasterboard walls, tap panel pins into the back of the picture frame, one at each bottom corner, then clip off the heads, leaving about 5mm sticking out of the frame.

MONEY-SAVING
EASY-TO-DO REPAIRS

DON'T RUSH TO THE TELEPHONE and call in the professionals every time a piece of household equipment fails or doesn't seem to be working properly. **With a little know-how, you could probably fix it yourself.**

. . . your shower doesn't perform

If the flow of water from your shower is slower that it was and you live in a hard-water area, the problem may be down to the holes in the spray head being blocked with limescale. There is no need to call out a plumber. All you have to do is to unscrew the spray head and examine the back of the perforated plate for any limescale build-up. This can easily be removed with a strong solution of lemon juice or vinegar or a special proprietary limescale remover, available from many supermarkets and from DIY or hardware stores. Before you re-attach the spray head, run the shower for several minutes to flush away traces of limescale that may be lodged in the piping or hose.

. . . your kitchen or bathroom sealant isn't working

That bead of silicone sealant around the edge of your kitchen sink is starting to deteriorate. Water is slowly seeping beneath the laminate on your worktop and the chipboard underneath is beginning to swell and rot. Soon you'll have to replace the entire worksurface and possibly a cupboard or two. The same can occur in bathrooms. If the sealant around the bath or shower tray fails, water can penetrate and ruin the floor covering, joists and ceilings below. Yet a little easy and inexpensive maintenance could prevent such potentially expensive damage. When silicone sealant starts to break up, it's best to remove it completely. Sometimes you may be able to pull it off but, if not, first use a sharp trimming knife to cut back as much as possible, and then use a silicone sealant remover gel (from DIY stores) to get rid of the remainder. Clean the surface with methylated spirit before applying new sealant containing a fungicide, which will prevent black mould from growing on the surface.

. . . you feel a chilling draught in the bathroom

It may be coming in via the overflow pipe that runs from the toilet cistern through an external wall to the outside – particularly if the pipe faces into the prevailing wind. A simple remedy is to fit a right-angled 'elbow' pipe to the outside end of the overflow, so that it faces down and not directly into the wind. If this doesn't work, try making a flexible tube from a long party balloon. Cut the end off the balloon with scissors, to create a short tube, then fit the neck of the balloon over the outlet. Test the overflow to make sure that it allows water to flow out easily. When the water stops, the balloon should relax, preventing wind from blowing back up the tube.

. . . a door lock or latch bolt won't work

You can't lock a door because the bolt no longer engages cleanly with its striking plate. Rather than calling in a costly locksmith, you may be able to solve it yourself, by moving the plate or enlarging its cut-out with a file. Smear a little shoe polish on the end of the bolt, close the door and operate the lock so that it leaves a mark on the plate. This will indicate how the plate needs to be moved or where to enlarge the cut-out with a file. Simple periodic maintenance could help to solve other door problems:

● Check screws that hold hinges, catches or locks in place as they often become loose over time. Tighten, if necessary, with a screwdriver or cordless drill/driver. If the screws just turn and won't tighten properly, try replacing them with longer or, possibly, slightly larger screws.

● Prevent squeaking and friction by lubricating hinges and locks with a proprietary spray lubricant, using a narrow flexible applicator to apply the spray.

Hang the picture and straighten it with the help of a spirit level. Then gently push the bottom corners so that the pins dig into the wall, securing the frame in place. If your walls are too hard for a pin to penetrate, try using double-sided sticky pads instead of the cut-off pins.

● **Plumb with plastic** You might find it less daunting to do some of your own plumbing if you use plastic rather than copper piping. There are a number of proprietary plastic plumbing systems on the market that are suitable for DIY enthusiasts. Most of them can be used for hot and cold-water systems and for central-heating installations, but you should always use copper for the first length of pipe attached to a boiler.

The main advantages of plastic piping are that it is easy to cut, easy to join (no spanners or hazardous blow lamps), does not corrode, does not support scale build up and is less hot to the touch if carrying hot water. Because plastic pipe is flexible – it can be bent around corners and threaded through holes cut in floor joists – far fewer fittings are needed, which helps to offset the extra cost. Another advantage is that the fittings themselves are very easy to make – they just push together – and allow the pipe to be twisted once in the fitting. This makes aligning the pipe runs a much simpler task. Plastic pipe, though, does need supporting at more regular intervals than copper to avoid unsightly sagging and additional electrical cross-bonding may be needed to earth bathroom fittings.

A full range of fittings is available – including couplers, elbows, tees – and you can get special pipe clips, valves and a support for taking pipe round corners.

BATH & KITCHEN TIPS

5 THINGS TO CONSIDER when upgrading your plumbing and ceramic fittings

● **Stick with white** When you are buying a new bathroom suite, it is very tempting to go for the latest fashion colours – but almost nothing dates a bathroom quicker than the colour of the suite. Many homeowners in the UK wish that their predecessors hadn't decided on the avocado or deep blue so popular some years ago. It's better to stick to plain white for the main items – bath, basin, toilet and bidet – and to use the colours and designs of your choice for the tiles, wall coverings, flooring and curtains. All of these are much easier to alter when the fashion changes.

● **Make maintenance easier**
The flap valve in a siphon unit (the mechanism which flushes the toilet) is made of thin sheet plastic. This will deteriorate over time and have to be replaced periodically, which normallly means turning the water off at the gate valve by the main cold water cistern. This can be avoided if a small in-line 'servicing' valve is fitted in the water pipe leading to the toilet cistern. Alternatively replace the existing siphon mechanism with a three-part siphon which can be repaired without turning the water off at all.

when buying taps ... remember to ask about materials and mechanics

● **Allow for underfloor access**
Many people now choose stone, ceramic, cork or timber floors for their bathroom or kitchen floors. Before you lay any of these options down, you need to establish what is underneath your existing floor. You may find that in the past joints and junction boxes have been installed under the floorboards and if, for example, you have opted for a suspended timber floor, these will no longer be accessible without destroying the new flooring in the process.

The easiest way around this is to re-route the wiring and pipe work, so that there are no connections or joints under the floor. Another, slightly more complicated, alternative is to create removable 'inspection hatches' in the floorboards or chipboard sheet flooring. Matching cut-outs then need to be made in the new flooring directly above the hatches to allow access.

● **Choose a tap that lasts** Most people select kitchen or bathroom taps on design criteria alone. If you want to keep repair bills to a minimum, look beyond the styling and consider the materials used to make it and the mechanism inside, to determine its reliability. Some cheap taps have plastic handles which are more likely to break than the metal equivalent. Top-quality taps are often manufactured from cast brass, which is then plated; chromium plating is probably the most durable. Most modern taps use precision-made ceramic discs instead of the traditional rubber tap washers. The advantage is not only that a quarter-turn of the tap is all that is need to operate the water flow but also that ceramic discs do not wear out over time like rubber and last much longer. So, when buying taps, choose a style that you like, but remember to ask about materials and mechanics as well.

● **Test a tile pattern** Are you having trouble visualising how those stylish tiles will look when they're installed as a splashback over your kitchen worktop? Or are you finding it impossible to decide which pattern of tiling will work best in your bathroom? What looks perfect in the showroom could turn out to be disappointing once it's on your wall. To avoid an expensive disaster, ask for samples of some of the tiles you are considering. Make colour photocopies of them and tape these over the area you wish to cover. You can then reject what doesn't work and rearrange any possible tiles until you get the right look.

SAVING ENERGY

7 CALCULATING WAYS to cut your home's energy usage

● **Calculate and compare** Add up the cost of all the gas, electricity and other fuel used in your home over the past 12 months. Then divide the total by the number of square metres of floor space you have, not including unheated garages and workshops. If you ask friends and neighbours to do the same calculation, you can compare results and find out who is being the most energy efficient. You may also find it helpful to discuss and share ideas for cutting down on fuel consumption and for improving your home insulation.

● **Update your boiler** One way to cut your heating bills is to fit a modern condensing boiler. With any boiler, some of the heat generated passes up the flue and out into the atmosphere. Markedly less heat is lost in this way from a condensing boiler. Although it is likely to be more expensive to buy than other boilers, the savings made through greater energy efficiency should pay back the added investment in as little as two years. So the sooner you upgrade, the sooner you will start to be more energy efficient and to save money.

● **Modernise controls** The efficiency of an existing central-heating system can also be increased by fitting more up-to-date controls. Older systems tend to rely on gravity circulation for the hot water, a boiler thermostat and a simple timer – any addition you make will be an improvement on this. Add a room thermostat to control the temperature of a particular area; a cylinder thermostat to control the temperature of the hot water from the taps; a programmer to switch the heating and hot water on and off at different times; a pump to drive water round the system and motorised valves to control the flow of water.

Modern electronic programmers allow you to control the heating and hot water separately and allow different settings for each day of the week to suit variations in your lifestyle.

● **Go for efficient appliances**
When you replace an appliance, such as a fridge, freezer, oven, tumble dryer, washing machine or dishwasher, look out for the EU Energy Label. These coloured tabs are marked with a letter, ranging from A to G: the most efficient machine having an 'A' and the least a 'G'. The more efficient the product, the less electricity it will consume.

Once you have purchased your new energy-saving machine, how much it costs to run will also depend on how you use it. For example, running your washing machine or dishwasher only when you have a full load and as much as possible on low-temperature and economy settings can also save energy.

● **Stop early bulb burn-out** It's as annoying as it is costly to have a lamp or light fitting that needs a new light bulb every month or two. Light-bulb manufacturers would just as soon you did nothing about it – except keep buying their products. But if you notice that your bulbs are burning out well before the estimated life expectancy

EXPERT ADVICE
GREAT TIPS FROM THE PROFESSIONALS

Four ways to cut your electricity bill

1 Fit energy-saving bulbs in the five most frequently used areas of your home. Around 20 per cent of your electricity bill goes on lighting, so fitting these should make a considerable dent in your bill. If the higher cost of low-energy bulbs puts you off making the switch, remember that they last up to 10 times longer than conventional bulbs and use one-fifth of the electricity.

2 Switch off appliances, such as televisions and computers, rather than leaving them on stand-by mode. If a number of appliances are left on overnight, every night, this adds up to a large amount of wasted energy.

3 Unplug that charger Few people realise what a drain battery chargers are. After using one, switch off and unplug it. Otherwise, it's costing you money.

4 Adjust security floodlights so that they stay on no longer than really necessary. These lamps, activated by infra-red detectors, are designed to light up a dark doorway for the householder and to deter intruders. But once on, they often stay on for quite a long time. Make sure yours do their job, then go out rather than illuminating an empty garden for long periods.

printed on their packaging, you may have a problem. Here are three possible causes of premature burnout, along with quick solutions:

☞ **Poor ventilation** If the insulation in your loft is covering the top of a light fitting set into the ceiling below, that fixture can overheat everytime it is switched on, burning out the bulb much too quickly. Removing the insulation from around the fitting will allow the heat to escape, prolong the life of the bulb and reduce the fire risk.

☞ **Excess wattage** If you're using a high-wattage bulb in a small, enclosed light shade, such as in a globe lamp, the build-up of heat could help to snuff out the bulb's filament faster. So try fitting a lower-wattage bulb or a compact fluorescent one instead.

☞ **The shakes** Vibration, like heat, can make a filament fail sooner than it should. If your lamp or light fitting is near a door that is constantly being slammed or on a ceiling beneath a floor where young children play, then fit a compact fluorescent bulb, which doesn't have a fragile filament.

● **Fit extra insulation** Because heat rises, a good deal of it can be lost through the loft of a house. Even if you have some insulation in the loft, it often pays, especially in older houses, to add a layer. This won't cost a fortune, and it's a job that most homeowners can do themselves, using rolls of mineral wool insulation, available at any DIY store.

Most loft insulation blanket these days is encapsulated – that is, wrapped in an outer plastic layer – so you do not need to wear a protective face mask and gloves to install it. Run the new material over the tops of the joists at right angles to the existing insulation so that you cover up any gaps. Try to avoid burying

electric cables as these can overheat. When adding new rolled insulation, work from near the eaves toward the centre, using a piece of plywood as a platform to kneel on. The insulation material can be cut using heavy-duty scissors. Always remember to keep loft insulation away from the eaves by fitting proprietary plastic ventilator trays, in order to avoid blocking off the air-flow around the roof timbers.

The hatch leading into the loft is often forgotten when it comes to laying insulation and this can can be a major escape route for heat from the room below. So don't forget to attach a piece of insulating material to the upper side of the hatch door and to fit a draught-proofing strip around the edges where the hatch meets the frame.

If you have a cold-water cistern in the loft, don't lay insulation directly underneath it, as here heat rising up from rooms below can play a useful role, preventing it from freezing up in winter. If the cistern is set on a high frame, you could even construct an enclosure around the frame out of fire-retardant polystyrene, to effectively funnel warm air from the house below upwards to the underside of the cistern.

● **Lag water pipes** Protect your piping with insulation of some sort. The split-sleeve foam kind is widely available from DIY stores and plumbers merchants and is simple to fit. For the best protection, go for lagging that is at least 50mm thick. Wrap up gate valves and stopvalves too, so that there are no exposed metal parts which could freeze. Hang a brightly coloured label over a wrapped-up gate valve so that you can find it again and know what it does. Also cover joints with PVC insulation tape, ensuring that there are no gaps.

vibration ... can make a filament fail sooner than it should

WINDOW SECRETS

8 LITTLE KNOWN POINTS to consider if your windows no longer fit properly and are letting in draughts

● **Carry out a health check** Before you think about replacing those rattly old windows, check if they are really beyond repair. Get some expert advice, if necessary, to do this. Some contractors are just as happy to quote for renovating your windows as they are for making and fitting new ones – in fact, there are businesses that specialise in window renovation. (Look for information in *Yellow Pages* and on the internet.)

Sometimes, all that may be required to make your windows more energy efficient – and to stop your boiler from working twice as hard to keep your home warm – is a little routine maintenance. You might even be able to do this yourself. Here are two tips for sealing up those draughty windows and saving some hard-earned cash:

Fill gaps Any gaps around the outside of a window frame can allow moisture to penetrate, causing timber frames to rot. To stop this happening, fill cracks up to 10mm wide with exterior-grade building silicone and seal up any larger gaps with mortar.

Draughtproof Draught-excluding foam and rubber strips come in a variety of different shapes and sizes. The rigid type is sold in standard lengths, the softer flexible kind is sold on a roll. First establish where any draughts are coming in. To help do this, hold a lit candle in front of the offending window, taking care not to set any curtains alight. Move the candle around the frame. The flame should flicker when placed near a spot where a draught is coming in. Decide where the draught-proofing strip will be most effective. Make sure that the surfaces to which the strip is to be attached are really clean; this ensures that it will stick firmly to the window frame. Then, attach the strip according to the manufacturer's instructions.

● **Check energy regulations** If you cannot avoid having to fit replacement windows, check first with your local council as the work is subject to Building Regulations, which stipulate the minimum insulation requirements – measured in U values – that the new windows must have. The lower the U value of a glazed area, the better the level of insulation it provides.

For new windows to meet the standards imposed by Building Regulations, it will usually be necessary to fit some form of low-emissivity glass, in a professionally manufactured, sealed double-glazed unit. Low-emissivity glass has a thin metallic coating that reflects heat from a room back into it. It also reflects away heat from the sun without cutting out any light. Put simply, it helps to keep the house cool in summer and warm in winter. In addition, the gap between the twin panes of glass can be filled with an inert gas such as argon, which adds further insulation.

Adding an extra pane to an existing window, known as secondary glazing, cuts down on heat loss and does not have to meet Building Regulations. It is even possible to reduce heat loss by just adding a sheet of plastic. This should cover the window, without touching the pane, and be held in place with magnetic strips so that it can be removed.

When you sell your house, you may be asked by your purchaser's solicitors for proof that any windows that have been installed since April 2002 comply with Building Regulations. You will have to present either a certificate showing that the work has been carried out by an appropriate registered installer or a certificate from your local authority building control department, stating that the job was approved under the Building Regulations that were current at the time of installation.

● **Use safety glass** If you are undertaking improvements to your home that involve the installation of glazed doors and windows, including the construction of a conservatory or glass roof, you must use safety glass in areas that are prone to impact damage. For information about exactly where safety glass must be fitted, contact your local authority building control officer or ask a reputable glass merchant or installer.

You have a choice between two basic types of safety glass: toughened or laminated. Toughened glass is much harder to break than standard glass, but when it does, it shatters into tiny granules. It needs to be ordered to size because it cannot be cut or drilled once it has been made. Laminated glass is made up of two panes of glass with a plastic interlayer, sandwiched between them. It is extremely difficult to break and, although it can crack, it will not split into tiny fragments, because the interlayer holds any pieces together. Laminated glass makes excellent security glazing, so is a good choice for windows in garages or in workshops where you store valuable tools or other equipment. Another bonus of laminated glass is that the plastic interlayer acts as a filter, screening out most of the sun's damaging ultraviolet rays. This means that any soft furnishings, carpets and paintings in rooms that are fitted with it, should fade less.

● **Beware condensation**
Replacement double-glazed windows invariably have better draught proofing, so the downside of installing them is that you might introduce a condensation problem on the walls (now the coldest part of the structure) due to the reduced ventilation. One answer is to fit 'trickle' ventilators and also fit extractor fans in bathrooms and kitchens where most moisture is produced.

● **Shop around** Get at least three estimates before you choose a contractor to make or fit your windows. Write down a list of questions to ask each firm, then visit their showroom or invite a representative around to your home. Ask to see a portfolio of designs and discuss which would be suitable for you. If the company has fitted windows locally, ask if you could view them or talk to previous customers – a personal recommendation is worth a lot. Ask about security features – the types of locks fitted and how tough the glass is – and about the length and conditions of the guarantee for the work. Finally, don't be rushed into making a decision. Salesmen often push for a quick answer. Consider all the factors – ask further questions if necessary – and make your choice in your own time.

● **Keep the character** An important factor when choosing replacement windows is to match their design to that of your house, so that the character of the property is retained. Many brand new homes suit simple, rectangular, casement window frames, but these rarely look right in older properties that were built with a different, often more ornate, style of frame in mind. Box sash windows, for example, were commonly fitted in Victorian houses. Replacing these with metal or plastic-framed double glazing always ruins the look of the building. Another factor to bear in mind is that although using such glazing may be far cheaper than installing new, correctly styled wooden sashes, this is likely to push down the value of your Victorian house. Luckily, in recent years window manufacturers have broadened their range of designs, so maintaining the correct period style while increasing the energy efficiency of your home is becoming much easier.

In some areas, you should also check whether or not planning permission or conservation-area consent is required before fitting any replacement windows. You may find the type and size of windows you are allowed to fit has to conform to a strict set of rules.

● **Plan an escape** When choosing new windows, remember that any fixed double-glazed panels will be very difficult to break in an emergency. So make sure that there are sufficient windows that can be opened wide enough to allow someone to escape if a fire breaks out. This is especially important in upstairs rooms and is, in fact, a statutory requirement when fitting windows in a loft conversion. Keep the keys to any window locks to hand in a fixed place in each room and make sure everyone knows exactly where they are kept.

● **Block out prying eyes** To make sure that any valuables you keep in your garage or shed are not on view to passers-by, simply apply a sheet of coloured, self-adhesive plastic film to any glazed area. This can be purchased at car spares shops in silver or black, then cut to size and stuck on to the inside of the windows. Your shed or workshop will look just like an upmarket car or limousine.

ENERGY CONSERVATION MYTHS

PROGRAMMABLE THERMOSTATS SAVE YOU MONEY
Well, they do, but only if you programme them to do so. Many people mistakenly believe that these computer-chip, electronic devices will automatically set themselves to operate in the most energy efficient way. But they don't. You have to programme them so that they stop your central-heating boiler coming on when it isn't really needed – at night or when you're at work or on holiday. So read the manufacturer's instructions carefully and learn how to set your thermostat to suit your particular needs – you could save around 15 per cent on your monthly fuel costs.

FANS COOL A ROOM
Fans do not actually cool the air in a room, they cool the people in it by creating a wind-chill effect on their skin. So there is no point leaving a fan on when you are no longer in a room. Instead, treat it like a light and turn it off when you leave. Otherwise, you will just be wasting electricity and running up a large bill.

COMPUTER SCREENSAVERS SAVE ENERGY
All a screensaver does is prolong the life of your monitor by displaying a moving image while you are not using your computer, as any fixed image left on would eventually 'burn' itself into the screen, ruining it. Screensavers do nothing whatsoever to save electricity – in fact, they burn up quite a lot. If you want to save energy, without turning your computer off, check if it has a special energy-saving mode: go to your operating system's control panel and explore the power management options.

STAND-BY COSTS LESS THAN TURNING ON AND OFF
This is certainly not true. Leaving a machine constantly in stand-by mode consumes a surprisingly large amount of electricity. If you want to save energy – and money – you should always turn your computer off at night or when you will be away from it for a long period of time. Remember also to switch off other computer hardware, such as scanners, printers and external hard-drives and speakers at the mains. If they are powered via a plugged-in transformer, that will remain on even when the power button on the appliance has been switched off.

SELLING YOUR HOUSE

3 CLEVER WAYS to make your house seem more attractive to a potential buyer

● Create a good first impression

You've probably heard it before – that sprucing up the front of your house can help to lure in buyers. First impressions are so important that this advice bears mentioning yet again. This isn't something to consider only when you have someone coming to view the property. Keep the outside of your house looking good at all times, because a potential buyer might just be walking or driving past. Here's a step-by-step guide to making a good first impression:

Tidy up Stand outside your front door and take a good look around. Remove all the rubbish and clutter you see, including gardening tools, toys, broken plant pots and any left-over building materials. Store anything worth keeping – out of sight – in a shed or the loft.

Freshen up the entrance Your front door is the first feature a potential buyer will really notice. Clean it or, if necessary, scrape and repaint it.

Tend the garden Prune bushes and trees, especially if they're blocking your path or windows – remember that you can't sell a house if buyers can't see it properly. Remove all dead plants and either compost or clear these from your garden. Weed and mulch, and keep the lawn freshly cut and watered.

Clean and fix it Clear out the gutters. Remove any moss from the roof, fill in cracked windowsills and replace any rotting exterior timbers.

● Revamp the interior

This is not about making expensive changes, such as installing a new bathroom or kitchen. It's about tidying up and adding the odd item or two to make your home look more impressive. Known as 'home staging', this idea originated in the US, where it is now widely offered as a professional service, and it is starting to be used by some canny sellers in Britain, usually on a hard-to-sell property. But there's no need to wait until your home fails to sell. You can create interest – and possibly get a higher price – by making a few small changes to tempt would-be buyers (see page 126).

According to Steve Kerslake of Home Stagers UK, 'staging' your property means 'identifying what type of person is most likely to buy your home and then highlighting how your home might suit them. A good example is of an older couple, downsizing after 30 years in their home. They may now use an upstairs room as an office or hobby area. We'd say, put a bed back. A growing family is most likely to be looking around and needs to see that all upstairs rooms are roomy as bedrooms.'

● Employ a professional

Of course, you can do your own 'home staging', but you may feel more confident about its effect, or simply prefer it, if you engage someone to do it for you. A professional 'stager' might propose design ideas, recommend decorators or gardeners, rearrange furniture and even oversee the process. Often they buy accessories, such as vases and picture frames, on your behalf.

The cost of professional 'staging' can seem high, but you are almost certain to get the money back in an increased selling price – and you will probably want to keep some of the items you have purchased in the process.

5 things you should know about ESTATE AGENTS

ALTHOUGH YOU CAN SELL OR BUY A HOME on your own, it's tricky. Most of us opt to use the services of estate agents. But while these professionals can be very helpful in finding the right buyer or locating the perfect house, you have to remember that they are in the game to collect a hefty commission . . .

1 THEY WORK FOR THE SELLER
Yes of course, an estate agent is going to be helpful if you're the buyer – they only make money if you do buy. But you should always remember – especially if there are hitches during the buying process – that it's the seller – not you – who is paying them.

2 YOU CAN SET THE TERMS
If you don't agree with the valuation that an estate agent recommends for your home, you can ask them to market it at the price you think it should be. How much commission they charge is also up for discussion. If you have good reason to believe your home will be a fast, effortless sale, make this clear and insist on a lower commission rate.

3 VIEWING TIMES AREN'T SET JUST TO BE CONVENIENT FOR YOU
Estate agents often arrange a time for you to see a property that will hide the fact that, during rush hours, the traffic nearby is dire. Or at weekends, football fans park there before the match. If you really like a place, you should always go back for a second, or even third, look at a different time – one of your own choosing.

4 'OPEN HOUSES' RARELY SECURE A SALE
But they are a great way for agents to build up a list of potential clients. If you've been urged to set up an 'open house' and have been spending all week getting ready for it, be wary; it might not be worth the trouble – at least not for you. For the same reason, agents may try to include as few details as possible when advertising your house. They'll mention just enough to attract callers, so that if your home turns out to be unsuitable, the agent can now market other properties to them.

5 AGENTS DON'T ALWAYS PUSH FOR THE HIGHEST PRICE
Of course they're after the best possible commission, but sometimes a quick and easy sell for £200,000 is better than waiting for £205,000. That £5,000 difference is a lot of money to you but at 3 per cent commission, it's only £150 less to the agent.

HOME STAGING
MADE SIMPLE

12 SMART MOVES that will help to sell your house faster for the highest possible price

● **Think about the market** You need to regard your home as a product. It must be priced right and look better than similar properties in your area in order to be competitive.

● **Create a neutral look** Buyers decide to buy or not to buy a house in a matter of minutes. If they spend even a few moments admiring your personal possessions, such as photographs or a hobby collection, that's time wasted. A potential buyer needs to be able to picture their belongings in the space, so by removing your personal items, it is easier for someone to imagine their own things in it.

● **Thin out rooms** When you sell your home, you're going to have to pack up and move, so start now – and definitely before someone comes to view. Removing some of the furniture will make a space look larger, so take a few pieces out of every room in the house and rearrange what's left to give a more streamlined look. Clear all unnecessary objects from tabletops, desks and shelves. Keep decorative objects restricted to groups of one, three or five items – odd-numbered groups always look better. Simplify busy walls by taking down and rearranging pictures. If you need room to store everything you have removed, use the garage or rent a storage unit.

● **Free up kitchen counters** Store away gadgets and machines that you'd normally leave out, such as can openers or food processors. You want people to assume that you've enough space for all kitchen equipment. Remove notes and magnets from the front of the fridge.

● **Declutter the bathroom** Clear unnecessary items from the shelves. Keep only essential toiletries, preferably in a wall-mounted cabinet.

● **Organise wardrobes** If everything is crammed in and the doors won't shut, a buyer will think that there isn't enough storage space. So remove and pack away any clothes you never wear and hang up items left slung over chairs.

● **Clear under the stairs** Pull out all the coats and jackets that you have crammed in, sort out which you wear regularly and hang them up. Pack the rest away. You want visitors to think there's plenty of room there, as well.

● **Clean, patch and paint** Freshen up your walls, carpets and curtains, if they need it. Fill any holes and cracks in walls and apply a coat of fresh paint where necessary – remember that neutral wall colours, such as beige and cream, paired with a brilliant white trim give a classic and spacious look to rooms. If anything is beyond cleaning or revamping, replace it.

● **Furnish dead space** If you've got unused rooms, help buyers to see how they might fill them. Create a home office. Set up a desk and computer – even if you have to borrow one.

Clean windows. This will invite in plenty of natural light and help to enhance any views from the property

● **Let in the light** If you're selling your home, one thing that is guaranteed to impress buyers is how bright, airy and spacious your home is. Here are some secrets that will help to reinforce this impression:

Clean windows This will invite in plenty of natural light and help to enhance any views from the property.

Trim those shrubs If the branches are growing across your windows, they will stop sunlight from streaming in.

Illuminate the space Open curtains and blinds and fit high-wattage bulbs in all lamps, ready for evening viewings.

Brighten up surfaces If your walls are stained or cracked, fill them in, then repaint them in a light colour.

● **Check key points** Stand in the doorway of every room and survey the interior. Then walk into the centre of each room and stand and look around once more. This is what a potential buyer will do, so make sure all your rooms look good from these key points.

● **Forget fresh coffee** Tricks such as having coffee percolating on the stove or bread baking in the oven may fail to impress potential buyers. Beautiful, scented flowers can be a better bet. Fresh, clean paint in every room also gives the impression of a clean, well-maintained and desirable property.

BUYING A **HOUSE**

3 SIMPLE SECRETS that could save you time and money when you are looking for a new home

● **Be single-minded** Don't make any major purchases if you're also thinking of moving house. Taking out a loan for a new car, for instance, could radically change your financial status from the point of view of a bank or mortgage lender. That's because you will have to give details of regular outgoings on the application form before a lender can work out the level of debt you can comfortably take on. You could be turned down for a mortgage that you'd have got if you hadn't had other loans.

● **Don't mention your plans** Never mention any proposals you have in mind for refurbishing a property that you're hoping to buy. Doing so could cost you thousands. If you're an exceptionally

honest person, don't even meet the seller. Do it all through agents. Most people who sell a home have a lot of themselves invested in it and they like to feel that the next owner will appreciate what they're giving up. If you fall into a conversation about the panelling you want to rip out or the summerhouse you intend to knock down, the offended seller will be less likely to drop his price during negotiations. If you must meet the seller, keep it brief.

● **Note that no house is unique** If you fail to get a place that interests you, remember that there will always be another desirable property. It may be even better. Remember this and you will stop yourself from paying over the odds.

secrets for
YOUR GARDEN

Dozens of easy tricks from green-fingered professionals

THE GOOD EARTH

8 WAYS to create a rich, fertile growing environment for your lawn and plants

● **Don't waste money on soil testing** If you listened to the 'experts' in gardening magazines, you might think a soil-testing kit is essential. But many top professional gardeners would disagree. If you regularly add compost, manure and a good organic fertiliser, such as blood, fish and bone meal, to your soil, you should achieve the required pH balance and essential minerals. To learn more about the general nature of soils in your area, the best plan is to ask a neighbour with a flourishing plot or an expert at a local nursery, who will tell you what to expect and can make recommendations for additions to your soil. And always keep an eye open for the plants that do well in your locality, as this is a good indication of general soil conditions.

● **But know when testing is a must** If you are having difficulty growing a plant that should succeed in your area, especially if your neighbour's plants do well in a similar situation, it may indicate a problem with the soil and a test could help to identify a solution. It is also worth testing the soil if you plan to fertilise every year; you could save money and avoid pouring unnecessary chemicals into the garden when a dose of lime or manure is all it needs.

● **Save money on mulch** Mulch is essential for retaining soil moisture and inhibiting weeds, and the owners of your local garden centre or DIY store will be delighted if you buy it from them by the bag. But arboriculturists and tree trimmers usually sell or even give away their chippings, which make excellent mulch. Call a local tree contractor and ask if you can get a load of chippings dumped in your driveway at the end of their day's work. Many are happy to oblige. Also, ask if your local authority makes their chippings or composted waste available to the public. But always remember to check the source of the chippings to avoid making mulch from diseased or pest-infected trees.

To keep your car clean when collecting mulch, place a large piece of sturdy plastic, a dust sheet or an old duvet cover on the back seat or in the boot of the car to pile the chips onto.

● **Don't dump or burn your leaves** Make a container out of wire netting and empty all your autumn leaves into it. They will break down slowly to make leaf-mould, which is an excellent substitute for peat in compost and can also be used as a soil conditioner or a mulch. If you have a leaf collector with a built-in shredder, your leaves will make leaf-mould even more quickly.

● **Use compost, not fertiliser** A well-made compost will add nutrients to the soil just as efficiently as any concentrated fertiliser and it will also improve the texture of the soil. You'll need to add about 5kg of compost per square metre, so never throw away green or kitchen waste – it's a valuable commodity – and start building up your compost heap. Work the compost into the soil before planting and, every winter after harvesting, spread it over the garden to a depth of about 1.25–2.5cm. Your soil will be more fertile, easier to work and have better drainage.

● **Build a simple compost bin** To compost with lawn trimmings, leaves and other garden and kitchen waste, you'll need a good-sized composting bin, which can be expensive if it's bought at a garden centre or through a catalogue. But your local authority may supply them at a discount to local residents, so phone to find out if it does.

Or, try this tip from gardening expert and broadcaster Daphne Ledward. She suggests taking four 1 metre square pieces of polystyrene wall insulation and covering each with heavy-duty polythene on all sides. Use these to form the four walls of your compost bin, tying the pieces together at the corners with shoelaces. Place this in a corner of your garden and cover any compost that you put in it with a piece of old carpet to keep out most of the rain and to prevent heat from escaping. Don't turn or water the compost or you will cool off the rotting materials, which will soon reach a very high temperature. You can make usable compost in as little as two months in summer, using a bin like this. Most organically based materials, cut or shredded into small pieces, are suitable for composting, the exceptions being pet waste, diseased plant material and raw or cooked meat. Renew the polythene covering if it becomes damaged, or after two or three years, before it starts to biodegrade and cause a litter problem.

● **Make a kitchen composter** You will be far more likely to compost kitchen scraps if you have a composter that's closer to the kitchen than the compost bin at the bottom of your garden. And you don't need to spend a fortune on a suitable container. Instead, buy a cheap plastic dustbin from any DIY store, garden centre or hardware shop, fit it with a tap or bung near the bottom and stand it on bricks that are high enough to allow you to position a container underneath the tap. Place some straw or damp, shredded newspaper in the bottom, add a few red worms (you can usually find these in your garden compost bin, but there are plenty of advertisements for worms or worm eggs in the back of gardening magazines) and start adding your kitchen waste. The worms will quickly turn it into a material that looks very much like fine peat. Any liquid that starts to form at the bottom should be drained off regularly and can be used, diluted, as a liquid feed for pot plants.

● **Brew your own liquid fertiliser** Organic liquid fertilisers are the products of steeping compost or other plant remains in water until the resulting brew is rich in nutrients and beneficial bacteria. The liquid is more versatile than compost and can be used to feed

How they do it . . .
keeping tools handy

If you're constantly mislaying your tools when gardening, try these two expert tips to make it easier to keep them close to hand at all times:
• Paint the handles of all your garden tools with Day-Glo paint and they will show up easily even if dropped amid thick foliage.
• If you have a large garden, keep a series of waterproof, plastic dustbins in strategic places. Each should contain a set of your most frequently used tools: secateurs, trowel, hand fork, pruning saw, shears and loppers, for example. You'll save a great deal of time and effort by not having to walk backwards and forwards to the garden shed to collect tools you may have forgotten to take with you.

and other garden and kitchen waste

plants of all kinds, replacing expensive fertilisers. The simplest method is to suspend a muslin bag of rich organic compost in a bucket of water or a watering can for two to three days. Carefully remove the bag and its contents, then use the brew to feed your plants at once. You can also use sheep droppings if they are available. Comfrey and nettle liquid feeds are frequently used by organic gardeners. To make a comfrey feed, steep 3kg comfrey leaves in half a plastic dustbin of water. Cover with the lid and use, undiluted, after four weeks. For a nettle feed, soak 1kg nettles in approximately 10 litres of water and use after two weeks, diluted one part nettle liquid to ten parts water.

OUTDOOR PLANTS

9 WAYS to make the most of your plants – from the best price for new plants – to foolproof planting tricks

● **Try cheaper sources for plants**
Why pay top prices at a garden centre when you may be able to find plants every bit as good elsewhere? Arboretums and botanical gardens often hold plant sales, as do local gardening clubs and organisations. Charity events can be a great source of interesting plants at affordable prices, too.

● **Give the gift of perennials**
You could pay a lot of money for a gift of a potted plant. Or you could save a fortune and give beautiful plants from your own garden instead. Many perennial plants need to be divided every couple of years as they grow. Flowers that grow from bulbs, such as daffodils, snowdrops and bluebells, are the easiest to divide. When the foliage has died back, dig them up, separate the bulbs and dry them off. Once dry, they can be bagged up in a pretty wrapper and trimmed with ribbon. Snowdrops can even be transplanted while they are still in leaf. The recipient will be delighted as they will all come into flower the following spring.

● **Ask a neighbour** Although garden centres wouldn't recommend it, you may be able to get many of those pricey perennials that they stock free of charge – from the garden of a green-fingered neighbour. If any of your friends have perennial plants that you covet, ask them if they need to be divided – you could offer to help with the work in exchange for taking some home for your own garden.

se cret weapon

THE RING OR ONION HOE
The thick metal ring, sharpened at the base and attached to a long handle was designed in the USA to allow unskilled workers to hoe onions and other crops without damaging them. You can now buy ring or onion hoes in the UK from specialist gardening shops, some catalogues and on the internet. To use, you push and pull the ring over the soil. It is difficult to damage any of the plants being hoed as the side of the ring pushes them out of the way.

● **Buy a smaller pot** When buying flowering perennials, choose nothing larger than a 1 litre container of plants. Young perennials tend to grow quickly and within a single season will catch up in size with larger, more expensive plants. They will also adapt much better to their new conditions.

● **Beware of fast-growing plants**
Some plants can rapidly become overwhelming and may jump the garden fence or send roots beneath it and invade your neighbours' plots or nearby open spaces. Such invasive species can seriously alter the local plant environment. Most do have their place in a garden, but stop them spreading by pulling up shoots where they are not wanted, or by planting only in confined areas such as pots, containers and beds bounded by paving or raised beds. Plants to be avoid are Michaelmas daisies (*Aster*), golden rod (*Solidago*), knotweed (*Persicaria*), mint (*Mentha*), *Houttuynia* and gardener's garters (*Phalaris picta*).

● **Water 'drought-tolerant' plants**
To get a proper start in life, even drought-tolerant plants need regular watering for the first year after planting. After that, as long as you have planted suitable varieties, they should be able to live on the average rainfall in all but exceptional drought conditions.

● **Be selective with wild flowers**
Bags of premixed wild-flower seeds can seem like an easy recipe for instant blooms and colour: just scatter on the ground, add water and a beautiful meadow full of wild flowers will magically appear. But you do need to choose the wild flowers for the situation carefully. Those that thrive on chalky soil won't tolerate waterlogged peat; some that tolerate hedge-bottom conditions won't cope with full sun in a meadow. So how do you make sure your wild-flower garden is safe and appropriate for your area?

The best method is to select packets of seeds for individual wild flowers, rather than mixes, so you can choose your own blend and be sure what you are planting. If you opt for a seed mix, buy from a local company, because the more widely a mix is distributed, the more likely it is to contain inappropriate seeds. Make sure the packet lists all of the seeds it contains and look up any unfamiliar plants. Remember that if you intend to grow wild flowers in grass, you need native grass species, otherwise the precious flowers may be choked out by grasses that have been developed to make a smooth lawn that is suitable for regular, close mowing.

● **Pest-proof your roses** To keep pests on rose bushes to a minimum, leave plenty of space between them, or mix with other plants. Feed and water well, mulch in spring while the soil is damp and choose resistant varieties, like 'Silver Jubilee', 'Iced Ginger' and 'Arthur Bell'. If you have been unfortunate enough to see black spot and mildew over the flowering season, prune in the autumn, remove all remaining green leaves and dispose of the prunings at the local recycling centre, where green waste is composted in such a way that the resultant material is sterilised.

● **Go low-tech for drip-irrigation**
When watering flowerbeds and other planted areas, drip-irrigation is the best method – it is extremely efficient in its use of precious water and the slow, deep penetration of moisture is great for the roots. But you may not need the expense of a full, installed system – here is a simple way to give plants a deep soaking

at no cost at all. Save 2 litre, plastic, soft-drink bottles and large milk containers. Punch a small hole in the bottom of each, then fill it with water. Stand one water-filled container next to a plant – bury it a little, so it's stable and not too visible – and it will slowly release its water into the surrounding soil. To water trees, use 20 litre water carriers, designed for camping, with their taps adjusted to drip slowly. Even with a centralised drip-irrigation system, these portable waterers are useful for keeping isolated shrubs and trees damp.

CONTAINER PLANTS

6 SECRETS for making potted house and patio plants flourish for less

Biscuit tins, cans ... and old buckets make good outdoor flowerpots

● **Don't line pots with pebbles**
Although conventional wisdom used to be that pebbles or pieces of clay pots in a container improved drainage, plant experts now believe they take up space that plant roots need and may encourage fungal growth. What you need is soil that goes right down to the bottom of the container. If you're worried about soil washing out of the drainage hole, cover it with a small piece of clay pot or a couple of pieces of kitchen paper. The roots will soon bind the compost.

● **Make your own containers**
Ornamental pots can be expensive, but you probably throw away scores of household items that are perfect as garden containers. Biscuit tins, cans, plastic ice-cream boxes and old buckets make good outdoor flowerpots. Just drill holes in the bottom for drainage and paint in your chosen colour.

● **Keep plants happy while you're away** How do you care for plants while you're away from home? Asking a neighbour to come in and water them can be less than satisfactory if he or she doesn't give your plants priority. But you can reduce the need for watering by taking a few steps before you leave for your holiday.

✿ Use a potting mix that contains moisture-retaining granules (polymers) or add some to your mix. These retain water for later use by thirsty plants.

✿ Move your plants out of direct sunlight – behind windows shielded by net curtains is a great spot.

✿ Turn down the thermostat in winter to keep the interior of the house cool.

✿ Move pots and containers close together, so the plants will provide each other with shade and humidity.

✿ Place sensitive plants inside 'tents' – put a plastic bag upside down over each plant, using stakes as 'tent poles' to keep the plastic off the foliage. Cut holes in the bag so that air can reach the plant.

✿ To conserve water in outdoor containers, move to a location sheltered from the wind and group them together.

✿ In summer, bury potted plants to their rims in the garden temporarily and mulch around them.

● **Salvage dried-out plants** If your plants do dry out completely while you are away, you can revive them when you return by soaking the containers in a bucket, water butt or paddling pool. Use warm (but not hot) water, and submerge the pots until bubbles stop appearing from the soil. Remove the pot and drain any excess water.

● **Try the wet-carpet treatment**
Invest in a sheet of capillary matting, which is available from garden centres, dampen it and use it to cover a large tray. Stand a bucket of water close by, and place the plants on the matting-covered tray. Make a 'wick' out of another small piece of matting; put one end of it at the bottom of the bucket and the other on the tray. The wick will keep the matting damp, and the water will seep into the drainage holes of the pots and keep the compost moist.

● **Use a rope to water plants**
Another solution for holiday watering takes advantage of the capillary action of natural fibres. Place potted plants next to a bucket of water, then cut a thin natural-fibre rope into lengths that reach from the bucket to each pot. With a rock or brick, anchor one end of each cord in the bucket and coil the other ends around the surface soil of each pot. Water will flow through the rope to the plants.

VEGETABLE GARDENING

7 TRICKS for growing brilliant brassicas and other tasty crops in your vegetable patch

● **Don't sow too soon** Seed packet instructions often encourage you to start sowing too early. Most vegetables only start to germinate when the soil temperature reaches 10°C. Invest in a soil thermometer to save time and money. Speed up soil-warming by covering them with black polythene for a week or two before sowing . Early crops may need protecting from cold winds and frost with agricultural fleece. Crops that are sown later at warmer temperatures generally catch up with earlier sowings and the harvest date may end up less than a week behind.

● Start off with easy vegetables
Lettuce and other salad leaves, spring onions, carrots, beetroot and spinach beet are all easy crops for the first-time vegetable grower. You are almost guaranteed good results; once flushed with success, you will feel ready to graduate to more demanding crops.

● Jump-start spring crops
Once the weather has warmed up, you can sow half-hardy vegetables in a cold frame, to be planted out when the risk of frost has passed. Make your own frame from an old window, complete with glass, and enough bricks to make walls to stand it on – two bricks high is quite sufficient. A double glazed window is even better. You don't even need to mortar the bricks – they won't move far. This simple shelter will protect seedlings from cold winds, keeping the temperature inside several degrees warmer on frosty nights.

Always open up the window on sunny days or the plants inside will get too hot. When the danger of frost is past, you can use the cold frame for taking cuttings during summer or sow another, quick-maturing crop. It can be used to protect plants from frost in autumn or even to keep producing salad greens all winter.

● Protect seedlings with a homemade cloche
The French invented the glass cloche to protect seedlings from frost. You can buy beautiful cloches, but you can also make your own from a plastic 2 litre soft drink bottle. Using a sharp knife, carefully slice the entire bottom from the bottle. Place the bottle over the seedling,

leaving the cap off for ventilation. Bury the lower edge of the bottle in the soil to anchor it in place and deny slugs and snails access, or push a cane into the ground next to the seedling and place the bottle over the stick.

● Support your tomatoes the simple way
Many complicated devices are sold for supporting tomatoes and other plants in grow bags, but you can avoid the expense by placing your bag on soil rather than on a hard surface. If you then drive a stout cane right through the bottom of the bag into the soil, the tomatoes will be quite secure.

If you don't have a patch of bare earth, place the grow bag near a sunny wall or fence, attach an ornamental trellis to the upright surface and tie the tomatoes to this – they will look much more decorative grown this way.

● Extend your growing season
If you enjoy the fantastic flavours of home-grown produce, you can extend your growing season by planting the right vegetables and taking a few simple steps to protect them as autumn approaches. Broccoli, cauliflower, peas, spinach and many other greens can be planted in midsummer for an autumn harvest and root crops, such as beetroot, carrots, parsnips and turnips, will stay fresh in the ground through the autumn

Protect
seedlings
with a
homemade
cloche

How they do it . . .

thinning out seedlings

A well-known vegetable grower suggests this method for thinning out seedlings. Mix together carrot seeds and radish seeds. Then space the seeds evenly in the row, starting early in the growing season and continuing to plant every few weeks until midsummer. Radishes are among the quickest vegetables to sprout from seed and the fast-growing seedlings will mark-out the row within a week.

As the radishes are harvested, they break up the soil next to the maturing carrots, allowing them to grow more thickly and deeply; the carrots will then be easier to pull up when the time comes for harvesting them. This method has an additional benefit, as it saves handling the carrots to thin them out; when handled they give off a scent that attracts destructive carrot flies which may then lay their eggs in the soil around the seedlings.

goes to seed, don't forget about weeding as summer wanes, and cut back overgrown foliage near the garden so that your vegetables get enough sunlight.

Often the first frost of the season is only a warning sign and if you carefully protect your plants, you should get another two or three weeks of warm growing weather before regular frosts set in. Cover any tender plants with lightweight, old net curtains, a piece of horticultural fleece, sheets, newspapers, or even buckets or tubs. But remove these covers as soon as the temperature rises above freezing the next day. This way, you will impress your friends when you serve up home-grown vegetables for Sunday lunch or a special dinner.

● **Ripen tomatoes upside down**
If below-freezing weather is forecast and your tomato plants are laden with fruit that is still green, try this clever trick to make sure you don't lose your crop to frost. Pull the entire plant out of the ground and hang it upside down in a cool, dark place, such as a basement, a well-insulated shed or a garage. The fruit will ripen and you will be able to enjoy tasty home-grown tomatoes for another couple of weeks while the supermarkets are having to import theirs.

and into winter. Cover with agricultural fleece or straw to make them easier to dig up when the ground is frozen.

To keep plants producing for as long as possible, continue to water them regularly, keep picking fruit before it

YOUR **LAWN**

6 CRAFTY WAYS to help you to create a lush, low-care sea of green in your garden

● **Build up dips in the lawn** Low, yellow or dead spots in your lawn could be a sign of a pest or disease. Or they may simply be occurring in places where your lawn dips, especially if they appear

after heavy rain, as grass can suffocate or rot if it is left covered in standing water. Try spreading a layer of compost or fine soil, mixed with a little lawn seed, over the yellow spot to raise it up to the level of the surrounding ground. Within a week or two, new grass will sprout to fill the patch.

● Don't bag up grass cuttings

If you have a mower that shreds grass and returns it to the lawn, reduce the recommended amount of lawn fertiliser by at least a third and possibly even half. A mulching mower like this will save you the expense and effort of spreading a lot of chemical fertiliser every year.

● Keep your lawn well aerated

Most lawns only need aerating once a year – if that – to improve the drainage and break the soil up, but it is important to do it at the correct time for your area and grass type. Some lawns do better if they are aerated at the beginning of the growing season, while others will benefit more from being aerated at the end.

You don't have to pay through the nose to get your lawn treated and it's no more strenuous than mowing. You can hire a machine from a garden or DIY centre that will spike and slit your lawn – and perhaps your neighbours may be prepared to share the cost and do theirs at the same time. Then feed your sward with a proprietary lawn fertiliser, raise the blades slightly (most lawns are cut too short) and you'll have a piece of grass to be proud of.

● Treat your lawn to a tonic If you
cut your lawn to a reasonable length about once a week, use a mulching mower and aerate the surface periodically, you will probably find that you don't need to fertilise it regularly. But if you think it's looking a little lack-lustre, an application of seaweed extract or meal in early summer should soon bring back its verdant brilliance. And don't worry if it starts to turn brown after a spell of dry weather – one good shower of rain will restart the greening process.

EXPERT ADVICE
GREAT TIPS FROM THE PROFESSIONALS

Reseeding a lawn

Whether you have a small bare patch or half a lawn to reseed, do it in late summer or autumn, when cooler temperatures, higher humidity and warm soil will give the grass a good start:

1 Rake off any dead grass and debris. Loosen the soil in the bare patch to a depth of 2.5cm. If the grass was killed by dog urine or a chemical or petrol spill, it's best to dig out the area and replace it with fresh soil.

2 Spread 5–7.5cm of multi-purpose potting compost over the area, then smooth it with the back of a rake so that the compost is level with the surrounding soil.

3 Mix the seed with an equal amount of damp sand a day before you sow it. The moisture will jump-start germination. Scatter seeds evenly with the sand, so that they stay in place on the ground, even on a windy day.

4 Cover the seeds with a thin layer of compost, then water gently, being careful not to wash the seeds away.

5 Keep the area moist with a fine spray of water, two or three times a day, until the seeds germinate. Then water them regularly, until the grass becomes established.

Treat your lawn to a tonic

How they do it . . .
keeping a lawn lovely

Use these maintenance tips from the people who keep golf course greens looking pristine:

• Lawns mown in the same direction every time develop stripes that may grow back irregularly. Alternate mowing one way across the lawn the first time and then at right angles to this direction the next time. If you are really keen, follow the diagonals too.

• For the best cut, mow in mid to late morning, when it's cool but the morning dew has dried off.

• Don't rush mowing, because you may miss spots.

• Using a sit-on mower, keep the mower at a medium speed. Throttle down to lower speeds when turning corners and trimming borders for a closer cut.

• For a healthy lawn, never remove more than a third of the grass blade at one time.

• Grass no less than 2.5cm high usually looks better, encourages a deeper root system and helps to prevent weeds and moss from invading.

• Sharp lawn mower blades help to create a well-manicured lawn, and cleaner cuts promote healthier grass. Use a metal file or a grinding wheel to sharpen the blade, maintaining the blade-surface angle that came from the manufacturer.

• Water infrequently but deeply. A sprinkling of water may do more harm than good and a brown lawn will soon green up once the drought is over.

● Good ways to deter moles

Adorable to the animal lover, moles can be a real nightmare for someone who cherishes their well-manicured lawn. The number of devices available to deter them are almost as numerous as the molehills on the lawn, some more effectively than others. Areas that are in constant use are less likely to be affected, as moles dislike the vibrations, so in summer a twice weekly cut may be all that is necessary to give them a headache and encourage them to go elsewhere. Strong smelling substances, like mothballs, garlic powder and citrus-scented disinfectant, poured down the runs, may be a deterrent and a plastic children's windmill is as likely to cause them annoyance as an expensive specially designed ultrasound device.

● Don't be dogged by yellow patches on the grass

If you have a dog and your lawn is covered with yellow or brown circles, the dog's urine may be the culprit. In serious cases, the spots may require reseeding or returfing. The problem is caused by the nitrogen in the urine. Although nitrogen is a central ingredient in most fertilisers, the concentration in undiluted urine is too high for the grass and it dies from the stress. Some people believe that female canine urine contains a substance that causes the die-off. But female dogs probably cause more problems because they tend to urinate all at once on a flat surface and so concentrate their impact in one spot, rather than 'marking' as males do.

What is the most effective solution? It has been claimed that changing the pH in a dog's urine by altering its diet can reduce the damaging effect of the urine, but this is seldom effective and might affect the dog's health. The only sure-fire solution is to dilute the urine; this can be achieved in two ways. The most effective is to act quickly and pour water on the place where the dog has urinated within the first few minutes. Less effective, but also helpful, is adding more water to the dog's diet, by feeding it wet food or moistening dry food with water. The dog may urinate more often, but the concentration of nitrogen in the urine will be lower. Some breeds can cause more damage than others, but in general remember that it is difficult to keep a dog and also have a perfect lawn.

LANDSCAPING

8 GREAT STRATEGIES that will turn an ordinary plot
into your dream garden

● **Be a garden detective** Before
hiring a designer or spending a fortune
on new plants, take a walk around your
neighbourhood with a clipboard and a
digital camera. Make a checklist of the
types of plants you need in your
landscaping – flowers, ground cover,
shrubs and trees – then note the plants
you like or dislike in each category in
your area. Look at what grows well in
local gardens that are similar to your
own as the soil type and growing
conditions are likely to be much the
same as your own. If you see an
unfamiliar plant, take a photograph or
ask your neighbour for its name.

Armed with your checklist and the
photos of plants you like, go to a garden
centre and start shopping. The experts
there should help you for free and give
advice on when to plant each variety,
how big they will grow and how many
plants you need to fill a given space. You
will be well on your way to a beautiful
landscape – without the expense of a
landscape designer.

● **Use the local library** There are
plenty of excellent gardening books, but
most people don't want to buy a shelf-
full of new books in order to create a
dream garden. Gardening magazines are
an alternative way to pick up good, up-
to-date information, but for free advice,
try the gardening section of your local
library, where you may find everything
you're looking for, without having to
pay a monthly subscription. If you need
information on a particular topic, the
librarian should be able to help and will
also order in anything that is not already
on the shelves.

● **Use the World Wide Web** More
and more professional gardeners use the
internet to discover new plants and
techniques, so you can do the same
yourself rather than paying for advice. A
quick search should bring you more than
enough contacts for the information you
need, with links to even more fascinating
areas of the subject that will set you up
as your own expert in no time at all.

● **Investigate new garden centres**
Ask local people with striking gardens
where they shop for plants. Then visit
the garden centre they recommend, but
leave your cheque book or credit card at
home. Ask lots of questions about your
garden's problems and needs without
any intention of buying anything. If
staff give you ample attention and
answer questions coherently and
completely, you should feel happy
coming back to buy what you need.

● **Don't get rid of the grass** Garden
designers might prefer you not to think
about it, but decking, outdoor fountains
and even flowerbeds are generally more
work for the homeowner than simple
grass. Decks need resealing periodically
and become slippery when wet,
fountains need their filters cleaned and
flowerbeds require weeding, feeding,
deadheading and mulching. Maintaining
a decent lawn is less labour intensive
than any of these.

● **Store and save** If you have the
space to store items, such as fertiliser,
manure and potting compost, buy them
when your local DIY store, supermarket
or garden centre has them on special

Buy some brightly coloured clothes line ... lay this along the outline of the paths and beds you are planning

● Landscape the low-tech way

Many professional landscapers use specialised computer software to help their clients to visualise exactly how their new landscaping will look – and to tweak the design until it is just right. You can get the same results by buying your own program – or you can try this cheap, low-tech way to visualise the outlines of paths, beds and walls. Buy some brightly coloured clothes line or similar lightweight, highly visible rope. Lay this along the outline of the paths and beds you are planning. Now you can check the way your new layout will look from different vantage points – from the house, patio, street or any other suitable viewpoint. It helps to have a partner who can adjust the position of the lines as you make suggestions. When you are happy with the layout you have created, use some water-soluble marking spray (available at some DIY stores or garden centres) or emulsion paint, to mark the lines. Place dots every half-metre along the lines, a couple of centimetres inside the planned path or bed. Double-check the position from your different viewing points, then paint a solid line. This is where you will start to dig.

● Add a simple water feature

Although a small pond, a babbling stream or a splashing fountain is often a highly desirable addition to a garden landscape, building these features can be expensive and fraught with problems. But there is an easy way to add water and life to your garden that doesn't involve moving parts or hiring a pricey contractor. Buy a children's paddling pool and use it as the basis for creating a self-contained bog that will be the perfect place for growing some striking, water-loving plants, such as Japanese irises and marsh marigolds:

offer. If you're planning a large landscaping job, buy your fencing, stones and other materials when stockists are trying to move them, often at the end of summer, and store them over winter for big savings. Garden centres may be overstocked as winter approaches and need the space for Christmas items. Spring bulbs are often sold off at very low prices after Christmas and summer bulbs need clearing by the middle of spring, so look for bargains here. Bedding plants may be almost given away by the end of June. Landscaping contractors, too, may be eager to squeeze in a final job after most people have stopped thinking about their lawns and gardens; they may be more willing than usual to bargain with you.

✿ Choose a site where the new plants will look natural: the border of a wood or near a pond or ditch, for instance.

✿ Excavate a hole to the depth and diameter of the paddling pool. Test the pool's fit in the hole and remove or add soil until the pool sits flat on the bottom of the hole and its top rim is level with the ground or lawn.

✿ Using a screwdriver or sharp knife, punch holes around the sides of the pool 10cm below the rim, to allow some drainage during periods of heavy rain. Install the pool in the hole and pack soil firmly around the sides.

✿ Now fill the entire pool with a mixture of one half coarse sand and one half peat substitute. Level the surface, then use flat stones or pavers to cover the plastic lip. Add water until the sand and peat mix in the pool is saturated.

The best time to construct your paddling-pool bog is in the autumn, as this will allow it to settle over the winter. Make final adjustments or additions in the spring, before planting. Any plants that love getting their roots wet will thrive in your new bog, including water mint, brooklime (*Veronica beccabunga*), cardinal flower (*Lobelia cardinalis*) and monkey flower (*Mimulus*). To maintain it you simply need to ensure that the bog stays wet. By midsummer you should have a beautiful new addition to your garden without spending vast amounts of money on a water-garden specialist.

GARDEN CARE

6 MAINTENANCE TRICKS that every home gardener should be aware of

● **Beware of over-feeding** You may be tempted to fertilise your newly planted trees or shrubs immediately, but this can cause them severe stress. This is because the plants will then grow too much stem and foliage, without having the necessary root system to support them. Instead, you should wait for several months after planting before applying fertiliser – or stick to no more that the minimum application that is recommended by the manufacturer.

● **Avoid 'specialist' fertilisers**
There is no need to buy the costly feeds that are recommended exclusively for one purpose. For example, a liquid lawn tonic (without weedkiller) is really just a high-nitrogen fertiliser and can be used for any predominantly leafy plant, such as rhubarb, ornamental grasses and leeks, during the growing season. And soluble tomato fertiliser works just as well on all flowering and fruiting plants. Plants with low-nutrient requirements, such as orchids, may be fed on weak doses of any general purpose plant feed. And when you give your roses their annual dose of fertiliser in spring, remember that most other flowering shrubs and climbers, and particularly clematis, will also benefit from an application at the same time.

● **Use branches as levers to root out stumps** Digging out the stumps of large shrubs and trees is nasty work, but to avoid paying someone to do the job

GETTING HEALTHY PLANTS
AT A DISCOUNT CENTRE

GARDEN CENTRES AND NURSERIES would like you to believe that you are foolish to buy plants from garages, supermarkets and market stalls, but in many cases these outlets get their plants from the same growers and distributors as the top garden centres.

The difference is in what happens after the plants go on display at the store – generally, plants will receive more expert care and constant attention at a garden centre and will stay healthier. But you will pay for that privilege.

How do you avoid buying a fading rosebush from a garage forecourt or supermarket chain? Or, for that matter, even at your local garden centre? Fortunately, plants will usually show you how they are feeling, and if you know what to look for, you can buy healthy plants wherever you shop. So here are five things to look out for:

GENERAL SURROUNDINGS Take a quick look at all the plants on display. If they generally look good, they are probably getting decent care. If half of them are drooping or brown or the compost and display beds are covered in weeds, go somewhere else, even if the plants you want look healthy.

ROOTS If the roots are bunched up and growing profusely out of the drainage holes, the plant is pot-bound and most likely stressed. Conversely, if the plant lifts easily from the pot, it may have just been repotted, and its roots won't be ready for the garden. With trees or shrubs inside hessian covering, the rootball should feel solid.

OVERALL APPEARANCE The leaves should be green and shiny, not wilting or yellow and brown. The plant should be full and bushy, rather than tall and lean. Stems should be uncracked and scar-free.

BUDS Look for budding rather than fully flowering plants. Plants in bud will transplant easier and you will have the pleasure of the flowers for longer. Also, they prove they are capable of flowering well, even if it takes a couple of seasons for them to get established.

PESTS AND DISEASE Inspect the entire plant carefully, especially under the leaves, for any pests or signs of disease. If the plant passes this entire inspection with flying colours, it should thrive in your garden, no matter where it came from.

for you, you can make it easier. Leave a length of trunk or the main branches when you cut down the tree or shrub, rather than cutting it off at ground level. When you start digging, use these branches as levers to give you a major mechanical advantage for working the stump and roots out of the ground. If you have access to a winch, you can easily attach a chain to the trunk and winch the stump out when you have cut through some of the larger roots.

● **Steer clear of trees when using 'weed and feed'** All-in-one lawn treatments may save time, but can cause problems if applied carelessly. Many trees, shrubs and ornamental plants can be damaged or even killed by these products, applied to the lawn above their root areas. Certain plants are extremely sensitive to lawn herbicides, including apple, box elder, catalpa, dogwood, forsythia, honey locust, lilac and sycamore. Keep the spreader well away from them and treat specific weeds only as needed. Never add grass mowings from newly treated grass to the compost heap, though after a few weeks they may be added providing they are composted for at least six months.

● **Take care with weed-barriers** Landscaping fabric and other artificial weed barriers are effective options to herbicides, but can cause new problems and still fail to prevent weed growth in the long run. The best place to use barrier cloth is under gravel or rockeries, pathways, decking and other places where few or no plants are growing. In flowerbeds, especially in wet climates, weed barriers can hold too much moisture, causing some plants to rot. They can also promote the growth of moulds and fungi and may cause roots to grow less deep. When mulching with

---

EXPERT ADVICE
GREAT TIPS FROM THE PROFESSIONALS

How to apply herbicides safely

A drop of herbicide on the wrong leaf could kill a plant you love, so:
- Consider every alternative to chemical weed control.
- Keep animals and children away from the area for the length of time recommended by the manufacturer.
- Keep herbicides away from watercourses.
- Never buy and store more chemicals than you will need in a 12 month period.
- Spray first thing in the morning or in the evening, when it's cool and there is no wind.
- Spray at the manufacturer's recommended stage of weed development. Do not spray when rain is forecast.
- Follow the manufacturer's instructions when diluting.
- Never mix different herbicides unless recommended to do so on the label by the manufacturer.
- Adjust the nozzle to a medium to coarse spray. Keep the sprayer low to reduce drift of airborne chemicals.
- Use a 60cm square of cardboard as a shield.
- Wear eye protection and gloves. Wash hands and face after spraying.
- Do not make up more mixture than you will use.

---

bark or wood chippings over weed barriers, a new layer of topsoil is created as the mulch decomposes and the weeds that move into this fresh soil will be even harder to remove because their roots will intertwine with the barrier fabric. Even if you don't mulch over the fabric, organic material and seeds will blow in and weeds will take root.

Plastic barriers are the worst, blocking oxygen and preventing moisture from reaching the soil. They become brittle and disintegrate, making them a litter problem and very hard to remove. If you are using heavy-duty black polythene to eliminate weeds without chemical weedkillers, the

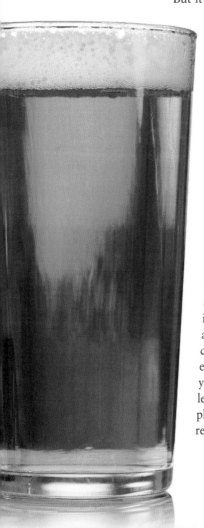

Kill slugs
with beer ...
Some pubs
may give
you the
dregs from
their bars
if asked

sheeting should be lifted for a day or two twice a year to let oxygen reach the soil. Fabric landscaping is better, because it will breathe. The best barriers are those that can be removed each season, so the soil can breathe or that decompose into the soil, such as ones made from recycled paper. The ideal way to keep weeds down is to work soil regularly and add plenty of organic matter, so they can be pulled out easily. Keep on top of them at the seedling stage by hand weeding or hoeing.

● **Try homemade hose guides**
Gardening catalogues are full of pricey hose guides to keep the hose from wrecking favourite plants or tipping over garden furniture as it is dragged around. But it's easy to make your own guides and install them anywhere that a hose might get caught up. Get your local DIY store or builders' merchant to cut you some 45cm lengths of timber,

no more than 18mm square. Treat these with preservative, then hammer them into the soil with a wooden mallet everywhere that you have a problem with the hose getting caught up. To keep your hose moving smoothly past the stakes, try covering them with one of the following:

✿ Paint a PVC pipe, 2.5cm in diameter, and cut it just long enough to cover the wooden stake. Place this over the stake. The pipe will spin as the hose rolls past.

✿ Cut pieces of bamboo or large-bore copper tubing to the appropriate lengths and use these as rollers.

✿ Find two ceramic pots that are about 10cm tall and have a large drainage hole in the bottom. Slide the two pots, the first facing down and the second facing up, over the wooden stake. The two stacked pots will create an hourglass-shaped roller. If the drainage hole is a little too small to fit over the wooden stake, widen it, using a pair of metal cutters, until it slides through easily.

PEST CONTROL

8 SPECIAL TRICKS for keeping your garden pest free

● **Learn more before you spray** More insects are beneficial or neutral to your plants than they are harmful. When beneficial insects, such as those that eat pests, are killed, a dependency on chemicals is created. Before you kill everything that moves, the minute you notice some holes in your plant leaves, take an affected leaf or photograph of the problem to a reputable garden centre or check in a

book on plant pests and diseases to find out what's wrong. Then, if necessary, you can choose the treatment that will attack that problem specifically. Remember that one or two holes, although not attractive, are not usually fatal and may not need any form of treatment. If you must resolve the problems with chemicals, remember that they are safer on indoor plants, because the environment is contained, and the chemicals are unlikely to affect creatures other than the target pests.

● **Control earwigs with newspaper** Trapping earwigs is much more effective and environmentally friendly than using an insecticide. In the evening, roll up sheets of wet newspaper and lay them around the garden. At sunrise, earwigs will crawl inside the wet pages to take shelter. Collect the papers, earwigs and all, before they dry out, but don't throw them into an open bin or refuse bag or the earwigs will soon escape and make their way back to the garden. You can burn the papers with the bugs or shake the earwigs into a toilet or sink and flush them down the drain or tie up the papers and bugs tightly inside a plastic bag, with absolutely no openings, and then put them in the dustbin. Another efficient trap is to fill plant pots with straw or hay and place them, upside down, on top of canes near plants that are likely to be seriously damaged by earwigs, such as dahlias. The earwigs will disappear into the pots overnight and can be disposed of every morning by burning the straw.

● **Kill slugs with beer or coffee**
You can buy expensive and toxic slug repellents, but natural methods are cheaper and just as effective. Slugs have a fatal vice – they like beer too much. Fill an empty baked bean or cat-food can with beer and bury it in your garden soil with its rim just proud of the earth to prevent beneficial creatures, such as ground beetles, from falling in and drowning as well. Overnight, the slugs will be attracted to the beer, fall into the trap and drown. You can throw out the entire can in the morning and replace it with a fresh batch. Some pubs may give you the dregs from their bars if asked. Alternatively, slugs hate coffee or at least caffeine, as much as they like beer. Research has found that a solution of 1 per cent to 2 per cent caffeine will kill

4 PERMITTED ORGANIC PEST CONTROLS

ORGANIC GARDENERS prefer not to use any kind of spray to control pests, relying instead on resistant plant varieties and good cultivation.

But there are certain times when this approach is just not enough. Organic gardeners then have to resort to something more drastic – and there are in fact several pesticides that they can use.
Here are four of the most effective:

1 DERRIS This is derived from the roots of a plant and is extremely effective against greenfly, blackfly and other aphids, as well as flea beetles, raspberry beetles and sawfly larvae. But it is harmful to some beneficial insects, such as ladybirds and lacewings, though not to bees.

2 PYRETHRUM An extract of the daisy-like pyrethrum flower, pyrethrum is harmful to all aphids – and many beneficial insects, although its effect is not long lasting. Use it in the evening, when most insects are not flying around.

3 RAPESEED OIL A quick spray of this oil will control aphids, greenhouse and brassica whitefly, thrips, scale insects and red spider mites by suffocating them. Seedlings and some plants, such as fuchsias and begonias, are damaged by rapeseed oil, so it should never be sprayed in areas where these are growing.

4 BT (BACILLUS THURINGIENSIS) These are bacterial spores that produce a protein which is toxic to some insects. BT, usually applied as a drench, kills caterpillars by paralysing their mouthparts and gut. It is often used as a last, organic resort to control cabbage-white caterpillars. But it should not be used near the host plants of non-harmful butterfly larvae, such as nettles.

slugs. That's much more than the average cup of coffee, but coffee may still act as a deterrent. Spray foliage with the brew or sprinkle the grounds around your plants. If nothing else, coffee grounds make a good addition to the soil, especially for plants that flourish in acid conditions.

● **Deter slugs and snails** Slugs and snails will avoid passing over certain substances, such as dry ash or soot. So sprinkle one of these in a ring around vulnerable plants such as hostas. The ash will need replacing once it gets wet. Dry cocoa shell, which is a by-product of the chocolate-making industry and sold at garden centres as a mulch, is also an effective deterrent, but only when it is fresh and dry.

● **Don't rely on marigolds** These cheerful yellow and orange flowers are often sold to gardeners with the promise that they will deter pests from attacking their vegetables, but their effectiveness is limited, although they'll work well as a defence against any nematodes that are lurking in your soil. But many organic gardeners claim to have had great success against aphids – greenfly and whitefly – especially in the greenhouse, by planting beds of tagetes, the French marigolds which produce clusters of small flowers.

● **Repel aphids with a citrus rind** Soap solutions are an effective method for dealing with aphids, but they can harm plants as much as the bugs with over-use. Instead, try this approach. Grate the rind of a lemon or orange and combine it with 500ml boiling water. Leave to steep overnight, then strain to remove the bits of rind. Pour the liquid into a spray bottle and spray it over any aphids that you spot on the leaves of your plants. Make sure you check underneath the leaves, where many aphids tend to gather. Reapply every four to seven days as long as the aphid problem persists. This citrus solution is an aphid repellent, not an insecticide, so it won't kill them but will deter them from coming near your plants.

● **Keep your crops chemical-free** If you prefer not to live on a diet of second-hand insecticides and pesticides, keep all pests and most diseases away from the vegetables and fruits you're growing by erecting a cage around them, made out of stout canes joined together with plastic cable ties, and covering it with a fleece. Keep the fleece on until the harvest, and only remove it for tending the plants when necessary. In this way, your crops will be free of most major pests, such as the caterpillars of cabbage-white butterflies, raspberry beetles, brassica whitefly, carrot and cabbage-root fly, pea and bean weevils and gooseberry sawfly.

Deter slugs and snails ...
[with] dry ash or soot

● **Banish leatherjackets** These are the larvae of the daddy-long-legs or cranefly. They usually appear in the soil in late summer and can decimate a lawn. The first signs of their presence are yellowing patches of grass and flocks of starlings probing the turf. To eliminate, water the lawn well where it is yellow and cover overnight with a tarpaulin or sacking. The larvae will come to the surface and in the morning they can be swept up and disposed of.

ANIMAL PESTS

5 STRATEGIES for making destructive four-legged visitors unwelcome in your garden

● **Stop cats using your garden as a lavatory** The better you cultivate your garden soil, the more attractive the neighbourhood moggies will find it. Some cats dislike the smell of cocoa shell, garlic and *Coleus canina* (the pee-off plant), so it is worth trying these, as well as proprietary cat deterrents, if the problem is particularly bad, although results tend to vary. Prickly branches, laid on the soil, will usually suggest to cats that they are not welcome there.

If you catch the culprit, a jet of cold water may be all that is needed to send him or her back home for good. Cats may also think twice about visiting a garden where there is a resident dog or feline. But the only real solution may be to cover the soil with landscape fabric and coarse chippings or to plant so closely that there is no bare soil that can be used as a cat toilet. In the vegetable garden, covering the crops with fleece should sort out the predicament.

● **Deter deer with eggs** Deer can wreak havoc in your garden. They breakfast on vegetables and munch away at your fruit trees at night. The most effective solution against them is a fence, but it must be 2.4m high and can be both ugly and expensive. A less pricey and easier alternative is eggs. Deer hate the taste and smell of raw eggs, so make a potion by beating half a dozen eggs into 2 litres water. Mix until all the yolks are well blended with the water. Sprinkle this mixture on the leaves of the plants you want to protect. It should remain effective until the next rainfall. Reapply after that.

● **Scent deer out** As well as the odour of eggs, several other scents have also been know to drive deer away. Try hanging up muslin bags of stinky socks, deodorant soap or human hair, ideally unwashed. These smells may make wary deer steer clear of your garden. If that doesn't appeal, there are also certain aromatic plants that deer don't like to brush against. So try planting artemisia, lavender and Russian sage as a natural fence line. If, after all this, you still can't get the deer to steer clear of your garden, consider replanting with plants that they hate. These include begonias, cosmos, daffodils, foxgloves, irises, marigolds, peonies, snapdragons and zinnias, along with shrubs and trees, such as boxwood, holly, juniper, lilac, pine and spruce.

To protect your vegetable garden, a rabbit-proof fence is the best solution

❀ Clean up spilled birdseed.

❀ Post realistic rubber models of snakes or owls. Or slice up an old hose into snake-like lengths and coil these among the plants.

❀ Hang dog hair in muslin bags or distribute it among the plants to frighten away rabbits. Strong-smelling soaps are also said to deter rabbits.

❀ Surround plants with spiky clippings, like those from holly and berberis.

Remember that rabbits will get used to these deterrents, so you will have to mix up the methods to keep them on their toes. Also, older tress and shrubs are less likely to be targetted by rabbits and some shrubs, like buddleja, bamboo, box, daphne, euphorbia, hypericum, philadelphus and yew are reasonably rabbit-proof, even when they are young.

● **Fence off your veg** To protect your vegetable garden, a rabbit-proof fence is the best solution. Use chicken wire and make sure the fence's bottom is buried by at least 15cm, or the rabbits may tunnel under it. It also needs to extend to a height of at least 80cm above the ground.

● **Rabbit-proof the garden** Here are several low-impact deterrents to try against voracious bunnies:

❀ Remove piles of wood and branches and other hiding places for rabbits.

GARDENING **TOOLS**

7 EASY WAYS to get a handle on the tools and other equipment that you use to care for your garden

● **Make your tools dirt-repellent** There's a secret weapon you can use to guard against messy tools – it's the cooking-oil mister you buy to keep fat to a minimum when frying. Spray a coating of oil on a shovel or trowel before using it and you will find that even sticky clay soil will slide straight off. Spray the blades and underside of your lawn mower and wet grass won't stick to them. Another trick is to keep a bucket of sand in the garage or shed and plunge a spade or hoe into the sand before putting it away. The sand will scrape off any dirt or other mess.

● **Don't buy gardening kneepads**
If you find that your knees ache after kneeling for hours to plant out new seedlings, make your own pads to protect them. Cut a couple of pieces from an old, foam, camping or yoga mat. This will protect your knees just as well as the special versions you can find in gardening catalogues or garden centres. The covered foam is tough, shock absorbent and easy to clean with soap and water. Alternatively, if you have any to spare, tie a computer mouse mat to each knee. As the modern computer mouse usually doesn't need a special mat, most of us have a couple that we don't need any more.

● **Make tools easy to spot** Why do garden tool manufacturers paint their products in colours that blend in so well with the garden? Perhaps they think they will sell more replacements that way. Beat them at their own game. To keep your hand tools from disappearing, wrap brightly coloured electrical tape round the handles. It only takes a moment, costs next to nothing and will save you a great deal of money because you won't mislay your tools so often. But even if they are easier to find, don't leave expensive tools lying among your flowerbeds, shrubs and long grass. Exposure to the weather will damage them and stray tools in the garden also pose a danger to pets and children.

● **Make a simple tool rack** There is nothing more irritating and dangerous than a heap of carelessly piled garden tools in one corner of the shed or garage; if you try to take one out, they may all fall over and hit you. But you don't need to be a professional builder to make a rack to hold them safely.

Screw a wooden roof batten to the wall, using rawlplugs if the wall is made of brick or concrete. Buy enough tool hooks – readily obtainable from a local hardware store – to accommodate all your tools, with a few spares in case you acquire some more. Screw these to the batten, leaving enough space to accommodate each tool comfortably. Write the name of the tool over the top of its designated hook, then you will never have a problem finding what you want to use – and where to hang it when you have finished with it.

● **Move rubbish more easily**
Instead of trying to get all your prunings and trimmings into your wheelbarrow – usually with minimal success – make a sledge from a cheap tarpaulin with eyeholes around the edges. Attach ropes to one end of the tarpaulin so you can

THE LEAF BLOWER VERSUS THE GOOD, OLD-FASHIONED RAKE

A leaf blower is a useful gadget if you have a lot of trees and shrubs but, before you buy one, there are one or two points to bear in mind. Most blowers will suck up leaves as well as blowing them into a convenient heap – these are the ones to consider. And many shred the leaves so you can get more into the collecting bag before it needs emptying, although this can make the piece of equipment very heavy and unwieldy before it is emptied on to the leaf-mould heap. Electric leaf blowers are a little less noisy than petrol ones, but if noise bothers you, you probably won't want to buy either. For a small to medium-sized garden, you would do well to forget about leaf blowers altogether and buy a wide-tined, large headed, plastic leaf rake instead. This is lighter, quieter, and almost as quick to use as a leaf blower in confined spaces. But in a larger garden that is full of deciduous trees, a leaf blower could save you quite a bit of time and effort.

GIVE YOUR MOWER A TUNE-UP

WHEN THE LAWNMOWER STARTS to sound a bit rough, you may not need expensive repairs or a costly replacement. In some cases, a single, new spark plug could fix it. Even the least handy homeowner can keep a lawnmower in tip-top condition with a simple annual tune-up.

You should consult your owner's manual for the specifics of your machine. But these basics apply to most models:

✿ Before you work on a lawnmower, always remove the wire leading to the spark plug so that it is impossible to accidentally start the mower.

✿ Clean the underside of the mower thoroughly, scraping off dried-up grass clippings with a putty knife. Clean out any air vents and channels.

✿ Unscrew the spark plug with a deep-socket wrench that fits the hexagonal nut. Install a new plug of the same type, having set the spark plug gap to the manufacturer's recommendation. Fit the hexagonal nut back in place, taking care not to cross-thread it (that is, setting it in askew, so that the threads get damaged as you turn it). Then gently tighten the nut, again using the deep-socket wrench.

✿ Unscrew the engine cover and vacuum up any dirt and grass clippings that have become lodged in there.

✿ If you have a petrol mower, unscrew the oil dipstick and carefully tip the mower onto its side, allowing the dirty oil to drain into a pan, such as an old baking tin. (Some mowers have an oil drain plug that can be removed with a wrench, so

the oil can be drained without tilting the mower.) Check the owner's manual for the correct oil type, and pour in new oil until the dipstick reads 'full'. Clean up spilled oil with a rag.

✿ Unscrew the air-filter cover, remove the filter and discard it. Clean the filter area thoroughly with a rag and an old toothbrush. Insert a new paper air-filter with the pleated side facing out. If you're inserting a new foam filter, it should be soaked first in clean, new engine oil; squeeze out surplus oil on to a rag, then insert the foam filter into the correct position. Replace the cover.

BEFORE STORING A PETROL MOWER FOR THE WINTER
Run it until the petrol tank is empty. Disconnect the petrol line and, if possible, lift off or unscrew the petrol tank and clean it by putting half a cup of fresh petrol inside and swilling it round vigorously. Do not store petrol in any container over the winter; always use fresh in the spring.

Parts for many popular mowers are available from agricultural and horticultural engineers. And you won't pay a repair shop's mark-up to get them.

pull it along the ground. Pile all your rubbish onto this and you will save endless time and effort taking it to the compost heap. This method of carting rubbish is particularly useful when you are trimming a hedge – the tarpaulin can be laid out so the clippings fall onto it; when full they can be dragged away and the ground underneath will be more or less clean.

● Put old golf equipment to work

Your gardening catalogue probably features an array of fancy carts and racks for carrying your rakes and trowels around the garden. But you can ignore them all if you have an old golf bag on wheels. Long tools will fit neatly into the main compartment and hand tools can be clipped to the outside. The pockets can hold seeds, shears and other smaller items. And if you discover any tees inside one of those pockets, they can be put to use too. Wooden or plastic tees make terrific colour-coded markers for newly seeded gardens. If you're not a golfer, visit a local car-boot sale; you will often find what you are looking for there. Or try a golfing friend who has moved on to new equipment.

● Make a handy tool caddy You

may not be able to move the holes off the golf course, but you can borrow the idea. Take a 25cm length of PVC piping that's around 38mm in diameter and bury it so that it stands vertically in the ground near the edge of your vegetable plot or flowerbed. In an instant, you have made yourself a caddy that can be used to hold your rake, hoe or shovel at the ready. Just turn the tool upside down and slide its handle into the pipe. Make more of these tool caddies and then strategically locate them around your garden or allotment, so you always have the right tools in the right place, whenever you need them.

● Coil a hose without assistance

You can buy all sorts of hose reels and carts – some of which are so elaborate that they look like machines the fire brigade ought to be in charge of. But if you know how to handle your hose correctly, you can coil it easily without any of these complicated devices. If you use a hose with longitudinal stripes, it will be easy to coil without twisting it – just keep the stripes running straight as you coil and uncoil.

Unkink a hose by pulling one end across the lawn; the weight of the hose will help to pull out the twists and you can judge by the stripes when it is straight. Leaving a stiff hose in the sun for an hour or so will make it much more pliable and easy to coil.

● Create your own hose storage

Wall-hung racks for coiling and storing a hose are usually quite inexpensive, but if you prefer to recycle something from your home, try one of these alternatives:
❀ Cut down an old plastic dustbin until you have a tub about 50cm deep. Punch drainage holes in the base, then coil and store the hose inside it.
❀ Transform an old car wheel with a coat or two of special green or white metal paint and, with the wheel lying flat on the ground, spin the hose around it. Hang or lean in a corner to store.
❀ Turn a large old terracotta pot upside down and wrap the hose around it.
❀ To store a hose for a long period of time, such as over the winter, drive a stout nail into the wall of your garage or shed, hang an old bicycle inner tube over the nail, loop the lower part through the coiled hose, then pull that up to hang it over the nail. Before storing a hose for any length of time, screw the two ends of the hose together so that snails, spiders and insects won't be tempted to nest inside it.

12 who'd have thought it
GARDENING AIDS

WHO SAYS YOU CAN ONLY USE PROPER TOOLS IN THE GARDEN?
These common household and workshop objects, including a couple of items normally considered candidates for the rubbish bin, can be put to work as gardening aids in surprising ways.

Cushion the sole of your foot as you dig

1 PAPER CUPS If new seedlings are vanishing from a flowerbed overnight, you need a shield to protect them from pests, such as cutworms and slugs. Cut the bottom off a paper cup and place the cup over your seedling to keep the hungry creatures at bay.

2 CARPENTER'S BELT If you have an old carpenter's belt, use it to carry all of your little gardening implements around with you – twine, hand tools, measuring tape and other similar items. During a day's gardening, you'll save yourself a lot of trips to the shed.

3 OLD HOSE A length of old garden hose will help to keep tool edges sharp and prevent them from cutting accidentally. Use heavy shears or a utility knife to cut the hose to the length of the tool edge. Then slit the hose lengthways down one side to make an opening for your tool edge. Slide the edge of the tool into the hose, and secure it with twine or bungee cord. To provide a protective layer for your feet when you're digging, slit a piece of hose to the width of your spade or fork, make a hole in it and slip it over the handle.

Sow a few grass seeds on a tea bag ... to patch small bare spots in the lawn

4 TEA BAGS Sow a few grass seeds onto a wet tea bag. The grass will quickly germinate and the 'plugs' can then be used to patch small bare spots in the lawn.

5 CLOTHES LINE To make a more comfortable grip on your trowel or another garden tool, wrap the handle tightly with a length of cotton cord, then cover the cord with several layers of gaffer tape. In the long term, the bulkier, softer grip will be much easier on your hands.

6 BAR OF SOAP Before you dig your hands into the soil, scrape your fingernails across a bar of hand soap. The soap that collects under your nails will create a barrier, preventing an embedded, impossible-to-clean rim of dirt from settling underneath. When you wash your hands, the soap barrier will dissolve.

7 ALUMINIUM FOIL To keep slugs away from your vegetables, try mixing some strips of aluminium foil in with a mulch. Or help plant cuttings to grow straight by starting them in a container covered with foil. Make a few holes in the foil and insert the cuttings through the holes.

8 SOLDERING IRON If a garden hose that's still in use has sprung pinpoint leaks, go to your toolbox and get out your soldering iron. Heat it up for a few minutes until it's nice and hot, then touch it carefully to the leaky spot on your hose, letting the surface melt and seal.

9 PLASTIC CABLE TIES These are available in various thicknesses, lengths and colours from DIY stores and are invaluable in the garden for everything from plant ties to making a temporary fruit cage.

10 KITCHEN TONGS Take a pair of kitchen tongs outside with you when it's time to trim back any prickly vines or rosebushes. The tongs will allow you to hold or bend the branches painlessly while you snip with the other hand.

11 SANDPAPER Keep a sheet of fine sandpaper or emery cloth handy in your tool shed. When rust appears on a pruning-saw blade or another metal tool, rub it away with a light sanding. Follow up with a light coating of oil – from a rag carrying a touch of motor or olive oil.

12 COFFEE GROUNDS Once your coffee grounds have 'done their job' inside the house, put them to work outside too. Sprinkle them in your garden, where they will decompose and add nutrients to the soil.

secrets for **YOUR WARDROBE**

How fashionistas and
garment gurus dress to impress

BUYING **CLOTHES**

12 SMART STRATEGIES for finding flattering garments at reasonable prices

● **Work the seasons** If you know when clothes are likely to first hit the shops, you'll be primed to take advantage, either by getting in first for must-have pieces or by anticipating sales. In the high street, summer is considered the longest retail season – first deliveries of garments into stores are, incredibly, around the first week of November and the last intake is around mid July. The high street is also becoming increasingly geared to mini trends, with changes of stock every five to eight weeks. The main designer seasons are spring/summer (from March to the end of August) and autumn/winter (August to the end of February), but there may also be 'transitional' seasons, influenced by the weather, as well as collections of party wear for the Christmas market and 'taster' offerings that highlight key new looks before the main collections reach the rails.

● **Invest in the best** The key to controlling clothing costs and looking fabulous is to buy one key piece of classic, luxury-label clothing – that really suits you – each season. If you look good in it, you'll definitely wear it and if you look after it, it should last for years. Go for items that are comfortable and effortlessly stylish, rather than being fashion led. Mix and match such pieces with inexpensive finds from the high street. They will lend class and style to anything else you wear. And, if they help you to sever the all too common habit of buying too many cheap, throwaway items that won't wear well or last long, you won't need to increase your total spending on clothes by much – if at all.

● **Buy classic jeans** Manufacturers love it when you pay inflated prices for trendy versions of staple garments, such as jeans. They'll go out of fashion within months and you'll be buying the next look. So invest, instead, in classic five-pocket, dark blue demins. Buy the best you can afford: heavy, tightly woven cloth, dyed with natural indigo. Look for the red and cream edging that comes when the cross threads of the fabric are woven in to stop fraying. They will last for years, looking better as they fade.

EXPERT ADVICE
GREAT TIPS FROM THE PROFESSIONALS

Learn all about dress sizing

Are you unsure which size fits you? It's a common dilemma for British women, because the sizing of UK womenswear is determined by a base size that is aimed at a store's target market, with sizes graded up or down to suit that market. So, for instance, you can be size 10 in one store and as much as size 14 in another. In France and Italy, where many top fashion labels make their clothes, sizes are related to body measurements – 38 (S), 40 (M), 42 (L), 44 (XL). So there's more chance you'll be able to predict what will fit you if you buy from designer ranges. But it's not just numbers. Where a garment is made will affect its proportions and therefore how it hangs. In Malaysia and Sri Lanka, the cut is based on UK sizing; in Turkey, on German sizing, which can be larger than French or Italian sizing; and in Egypt, on American sizing. The smart shopper takes several sizes of one garment into the changing room. You need to think about shrinkage, too – up to 3 per cent is considered acceptable by most manufacturers, particularly for jeans and T-shirts.

● **Check the quality** The British high street is the envy of the world for its ability to replicate designer looks at great speed and affordable prices. But how do you judge the quality? The first thing to take note of is the fabric. Stylist Mary Mathieson, who worked on the costumes for the Harry Potter films, has some tips for doing this. To test whether cotton jersey or knitwear will keep its shape, she suggests giving the fabric a little tug. If the garment doesn't recover its original appearance, take that as an indication of how badly it will wear. When buying cotton-jersey items, keep an eye out for double-knit quality – it is heavier and has a closer texture that will hang well, feel good against the skin and survive repeated washing.

Look out for loose threads and ruched-up stitching; they indicate that a garment has been run-off quickly, using the wrong stitch length. Both may also mean that the manufacturer hasn't bothered to check the finish – a sign of sweat-shop labour. Examine the inside of knitwear, too. If spare yarn loops across the back, rather than being knitted in, the garment has been produced cheaply and is likely to pull. And check that buttons are firmly sewn on, with the thread knotted at the back, or they may come off in the washing machine.

... check that buttons are firmly sewn on

● **Buy at factory outlets** At the end of each selling season, manufacturers and designer boutiques are swamped with garments they can no longer sell and need to off-load. Many end up in factory shops, specialist designer outlets and discount stores, where you can pick them up for up to 70 per cent less than the standard retail price. Shop for classic shapes and hand-worked fabrics and steer clear of last year's must-haves and fashion-led colours and prints. Keep an eye out for garments that have low 'hanger appeal', but will look stunning on, such as strappy items and tops and dresses with complicated draping.

● **Learn price-slashing strategies** Boutiques and department stores may be so desperate to shift merchandise that you can gain substantial discounts if you know how to ask for them:

◎ **Ask for a multi-buy price** If you're buying more than one item, corner the manager and ask for a discount. This works best on quiet days, just before closing time, and in unseasonal weather.

◎ **Grab a pre-sale special** If you know that the sale starts in a few days, ask to pay the lower price now. Again, negotiate with a senior member of staff.

◎ **Get fitted for free** If a full-priced garment doesn't quite fit you, in a shop that offers an alteration service, barter to have it altered without charge. Though this is usually a paid-for service, they may oblige to complete the sale.

◎ **Look for fresh talent** To get a more expensive look at minimal cost, shop at small, independent boutiques that champion up-and-coming designers. They offer quality and an individual look without the premium prices commanded by the major names.

◎ **Make friends with salespeople** If they get to know your personal look, they may call you when something suitable comes in. Many retailers of designerwear even buy collections with specific customers in mind.

◎ **Join the mailing list** High-end shops often hold preview sales at discounted prices for regular customers.

◎ **Use a store card** When making a big purchase at a department store, get a discount by accepting a store credit card. It will qualify you for future discounts, too. But pay off the balance immediately – store credit cards tend to charge exorbitant interest rates.

● **Feel the nap** Does your suit catch the light strangely, but you can't think why? Not all manufacturers pay attention to the direction of the nap – the way the raised fibres of fabrics such as corduroy or velvet lie. When buying clothes made from these materials, you need to check that the nap runs the same way over the entire garment. Stroke the sleeve of a jacket, for example, from top to bottom, then run your hand over the back and front from top to bottom, too. It doesn't matter how the fabric feels, as long as it feels the same everywhere.

● **Buy satin-weave cotton** Nobody wants to arrive at work in a shirt that looks as if they've slept in it. Textile expert Sally-Ann Gill says that there is a special weave of cotton that resists wrinkles and drapes beautifully, but most shop assistants will have no idea how to identify it for you. It's called satin-weave cotton and because it's woven to achieve a ribbon-like surface, it feels exceptionally smooth. It's also heavier than plain-weave cotton. To be sure you're getting satin-weave, grab a handful, squeeze, then let go. If the garment holds the wrinkles, it's basic plain-weave cotton. If the fabric springs back relatively wrinkle-free, you've found satin-weave. Double-check by looking at the inside of the fabric – it will look different from the outside. Plain cotton is the same on both sides.

● **Colour-test before buying** Next time you buy clothing, conduct two quick tests to make sure the colouring is of high quality. First, slip on a pair of sunglasses – the brown-tinted type work best – and check that the colours in the various parts of a garment – collar, cuffs, waistband – match. Then remove the glasses and carry the garment over to a window to check that the colours match in daylight, too. By doing this, you're looking out for an important quality issue known as 'metamerism' – where the colouring of a fabric can vary from one piece to another, depending on lighting conditions. It's something shoppers are rarely told anything about, but reputable clothing manufacturers carry out rigorous tests to make sure that the colour of their clothes is consistent in all light sources. So if you find a garment that fails your tests, don't buy it. And be especially careful in discount stores. That bargain could be marked down for a good reason.

HIDDEN TRUTHS What clothing retailers don't want you to know about **PRICING**

It's impossible to know precisely what a particular retailer paid for the clothes on display, but having an insight into the pricing process may help you to decide when to buy. A manufacturer creates a garment and offers it to a retailer for roughly double what it cost to make. If a shirt cost £10 to make, for example, it will be offered for £20 – this is the wholesale price. Retailers then double, or more often treble, that to cover their overheads. So, the shirt may appear on a shop's rail with a price tag of £60. But in many stores, only 10 to 20 per cent of customers buy at the original price. Slow sales may mean that by the end of a selling season, a garment gets marked down to the price the retailer paid for it. But don't feel bad if you get it at this bargain price. The retailer will be happy as long as the average selling price across a range of garments is about twice what they all cost wholesale. So if you lust after an expensive item, think about whether it's worth waiting until the end of the season to get it at a substantial discount.

5 quick fixes for your WARDROBE

YOU DON'T HAVE THE TIME or know-how to keep your clothes in perfect order. But here are some rapid solutions that will guarantee that you always look immaculate.

1 TAPE IT
Keep a few strips of double-sided tape in your bag for use in emergencies, says costume designer Pam Verran. It will take care of a drooping hem, or secure a gaping neckline or unruly collar, or hold a dangling belt or buttonless sleeve neatly in position – until you have the time to mend them properly. One of the best double-sided tapes is that used for securing wigs. Ask for it in large chemists, in the lingerie section of department stores and at specialist theatrical costumiers and wig shops, or search for it on beauty-supply websites.

2 AVOID IRONING MARKS
Make sure you turn your clothes inside-out to iron them, especially when pressing jacket sleeves and trouser legs. This will avoid any unsightly shiny patches ruining that perfect finish. And press shirts in the following order for maximum efficiency: collar, sleeves, yoke, back and finally the front.

3 STEAM AWAY THAT SHINE
If after ironing dark trousers, there are shiny spots on the fabric, don't fret. Here's a rapid cure: mix 2 tablespoons distilled white vinegar with 10 tablespoons cold water. Dip a clean cloth into the mixture and use it to gently blot the offending spots. Then switch on your steam iron and, holding it an inch or two above the fabric, pass it over the affected area several times. The steam will help the vinegar to break up the shine. Hang the garment up to dry for 5-10 minutes and it will be ready to wear.

4 RACE TO THAT SPOT
The quicker you treat a stain, the better your chances of removing it. If possible, take the garment off immediately and blot the stain with a paper towel or clean cloth to remove as much of it as you can. Then either squirt some pre-wash stain remover onto the spot and wash the garment, or take it to a dry cleaner as soon as you can. Remember that heat, like time, works against you. Never put a stained garment in the tumble dryer or leave in a warm place.

5 BLOT, DON'T RUB
If you notice a stain on your clothes, don't try to rub it off. All you'll do is damage the fabric and probably force the stain deeper into the weave. Instead, moisten some kitchen paper or a napkin with water and blot the stain gently to draw it off. Many people swear by using soda water – yes, the stuff you mix with drinks – rather than plain water.

● **Slip into something old** It pays to prowl boutiques that regularly sell vintage clothing, since they receive new stock at any time, regardless of the season. They can offer you a unique look, with a sure-fire guarantee that no one else at a party will be wearing the same outfit. You can keep to the classic styles that these shops sell for years; even modern designers are continually returning to them for inspiration. Many of the fabrics that were used from the 1950s and 1960s are of especially good quality, but you should be wary of fabrics from the 1940s, as they were often made from low-grade, waste cotton. Vintage clothing is also a good buy for someone of less than average stature, since the garments were sized smaller than they are today. To follow vintage sizing, you may need to know your bust measurement in inches. A UK size 34, for example, was made to fit someone with a 34 inch bust. The current way of indicating size, using numbers – 10, 12, 14, 18 – was introduced in the 1960s, but a size 12 from that period is unlikely to match the proportions of a modern size 12 garment, manufactured in the UK.

● **Restyle your clothes** Seamstress Mari Maurice is one of a burgeoning breed of designers who are urging us to revamp what we already have. She suggests that you don't buy any new clothes for at least two months. Instead, you should pull everything you love – but which is looking a little dated or no longer fits – out of your wardrobe and make it into something new. Or you could employ someone with her skills to do it for you.

● **Individualise high street buys** Give those inexpensive clothes a touch of class and make them more distinctive at the same time. Buy cards of unusual buttons from antique fairs or wherever you see them and use them to replace the cheap original fastenings. Add a good-quality belt, pin on an interesting brooch and your bargain garment suddenly becomes bespoke.

CLEANING CLOTHES

6 WAYS to keep your garments looking their best for longer

● **Launder less often** Do you clean a garment every time you wear it? Well, it's a waste of effort and detergent – and it shortens the garment's life. Don't throw clothes into the laundry basket when you take them off at night. Check first if they need any of the following:
◎ **Repairs** If there are buttons missing, falling hems or broken zips, put them in a special 'to mend' pile, or fix them now.

◎ **Stains removed** Are there any tough or oily stains? They should be taken to the dry cleaner within a day to maximise the chances of them being removed successfully.
◎ **Washing** Only do this if a garment has noticeable smudges and dirt on it.
◎ **Airing or pressing** Some items don't require a full launder. An hour on the

washing line and a reviving iron will freshen them up, removing all traces of body odour and other smells. Then you can return them to your wardrobe, ready to wear again.

● **Cut down on detergent** Most of us use far too much washing powder or liquid. Malgosia Dzik Holden, a designer for Britain's oldest knitwear manufacturer, John Smedley, urges us to ditch biological cleansers as they weaken fibres. A regular wash can be done perfectly well using half the amount of non-bio detergent recommended on the packet – and you should set the machine at no more than 30°C. You only need to use a higher temperature and a full dose of detergent for really dirty white cotton or linen.

● **Only use extras when necessary** Household product manufacturers try to sell us all kinds of washing aids, but clothes don't really need fabric softener and anti-static agents. If garments do cling to each other because of static electricity, simply dampen your hands and brush them across the material to kill the electrical charge. Towelling items absorb water better when they are not doused in fabric softener. But softener can be useful for garments containing mohair, cashmere and angora. Their longer fibres will eventually 'pill' (entwine into little balls where subjected to friction, such as under the arms) and the only way to avoid this is to keep these garments for special occasions and use fabric softener to 'relax' the fibres.

● **Update your washing machine** Some companies, including Miele and Bosch, have developed drums for their machines that are kinder to fabric. The holes in regular drums draw fabric in during the spinning part of a washing cycle, breaking the fibres. But the textured surface of the newer fabric-friendly drums contains smaller holes set in the corners of a honeycomb-like structure to lessen the destruction. Also, avoid tumble drying whenever possible. To see the wrecking effect it has on the fibres of a fabric, look at the alarmingly high number of threads in your filter.

● **Preserve precious pieces** Before you put a special evening dress or interview suit into storage, always launder or dry-clean it. Even if it appears to be spotless, you risk ruining the garment if you store it as it is. It may be covered in 'invisible' stains, such as lemonade, white wine and even sweat, that will turn yellow or brown over time and then be almost impossible to remove. Take note also that moths are not only drawn by natural fibres, such as wool and cotton; they love clothing that is soiled, stained or sweaty too.

Pay particular attention to your wedding dress, possibly the most expensive and fragile item of clothing you'll ever own. Ask about how to care for it when you buy it; or track down a dry-cleaner that offers special protective treatment. It you use a dry-cleaner, make sure that the company really does have the expertise to do a good job. If you can, get recommendations from other people who have used them. Ask if they send your gown out for servicing. If they do, this probably indicates that it is going to a specialist.

Also ask how your gown will be packed for storage. Check if it is going to be vacuum sealed. This preserves the fabric and stops it from oxidising and turning a yellow brown. If it isn't vacuum sealed, it should be wrapped in acid-free tissue paper – again to prevent yellowing – and packed in a breathable and pH-neutral cardboard box.

> A regular wash can be done perfectly well using half the amount ... recommended on the packet

● **Ration the dry-cleaning**

Obviously, your dry-cleaner is unlikely to tell you this – but most people bring in items far too often. The chemicals used to dry-clean will gradually weaken the fabric in your clothing, shortening its lifespan. Suits, in particular, can look dreadful after only a few months' wear, if you have them dry-cleaned every two to three weeks. Aim to dry-clean a suit approximately once every three to four months. If your suit is just a little creased, use a steam iron to relax the fabric – or ask your dry cleaner to give it a light steam for you. If you get a spot or two on your suit, try removing them by using a disposable fabric-cleaning wipe. Most people in the fashion trade confide that many garments marked 'dry-clean only' can be laundered by hand or even washed on the wool setting of a modern washing machine.

How they do it . . .
removing stains

You don't get to be a top costume designer for stage and screen like Birgit Mueller, without learning to think quickly on your feet. Here are some of her tips for making sure stains make a rapid exit:

• Sprinkle oily stains with baby powder. Leave for a minute or so, then brush oil and powder clean away.
• Keep a square of velvet in your bag and use it to wipe off smears of food, make-up or lipstick.
• To remove blood spots, ball up a thread of cotton in your mouth, then use it to blot them off. For large areas of blood, pour on salt, then blot.
• Douse ink stains in hair spray, then wash them out.
• Dab gin or white wine onto red-wine stains and they'll float out in the wash.
• If a shirt smells sweaty, mix 2 tablespoons vodka with 4 tablespoons water in a sqeezy bottle and spray it onto the underarm area of the garment.

STORING GARMENTS

5 GUIDELINES for creating an orderly wardrobe and ensuring wrinkle-free clothes

● **Strip off the plastic bags** Never store your clothing in dry-cleaners' plastic bags. Clothing needs to breathe, and the moisture that gets trapped inside these bags can cause mildew, which damages garments permanently. If you want to protect an item in storage, put it in a breathable, cotton garment bag.

● **Store out-of-season clothes**

Now that we all snatch up so many high street 'bargains', our wardrobe rails are groaning with crammed-in garments. This is a problem, because clothes need room to hang freely if they are to emerge from the wardrobe fresh and wrinkle-free. But one key manoeuvre will free-up space – removing all the clothes that are not currently in season from your wardrobe. You could store your out-of-season clothes in an empty guest room or in a hall cupboard, or on a hanging rail in the laundry or utility room. Every spring and autumn, rotate the rails, bringing clothing for the new season back into your wardrobe.

If you rotate your clothes in this way every six months and your wardrobe is still jam packed, try changing them around four times a year instead of two,

HOW GOOD IS YOUR
DRY-CLEANER?

QUALITY OF WORK VARIES GREATLY FROM ONE DRY-CLEANER TO ANOTHER. So how can you be confident that they won't ruin your clothes? Here are a few insider tips that might help.

SET UP AN 'AUDITION' If you're considering taking clothing somewhere unfamiliar, take a tip from the professionals by testing the new cleaner's skills first on three basic items: a cotton shirt, a light-coloured linen shirt or blouse and a light-coloured silk garment. These three offer enough variety for you to evaluate a dry-cleaner's work.

When you collect your clothes, here's what to look for:

COLOUR Is it the same as it was before cleaning? If it looks duller, then the dry-cleaner is not changing filters often enough. Dry-cleaning fluid can be used again and again but, after tackling one set of clothes, it must be passed through a carbon filter to purify it before it's ready to tackle the next load. If a dry-cleaner tries to get too much mileage out of a filter, it will eventually become less efficient, leaving impurities in the cleaning fluid that will make your clothes look duller.

TEXTURE Does the garment look and feel the way it did when it was new? It should if it's been cleaned correctly; if not, it will be limp, like an old rag. Have a sniff, too. If the fabric has a stale odour, it indicates either a lack of care or dirty cleaning fluid. As an antidote, remove the plastic cover and hang the garment outdoors for 2 hours to freshen it up.

STAINS Assess how well the dry-cleaner talks to you about any stains before and after cleaning, advises Garry Woo, who runs a highly respected dry-cleaning business in London's theatreland. You should be asked what type a stain is – wine, blood, food, pollen – and how long it has been there. Then you should be given an estimate of how successful its removal is likely to be, based on the nature of the mark and the fabric.

PRESSING Is it neatly done? Each garment should look perfect and be ready to wear. The cotton shirt is a good test of pressing quality, because it's difficult to iron well. If you want to throw in an extra challenge, hand in a pleated skirt. To get right, pleats require time and close attention to detail.

BUTTONS Hand in a garment with broken, loose or missing buttons. A good dry cleaner will bend over backwards to replace lost or damaged buttons for free – even when the problem is not their fault. They will retrieve any loose buttons that come off during cleaning from their machinery, find a replacement from their in-house supply, or even trek to a shop or button supplier to find the right match. If all those measures fail, the best dry cleaners might even offer to replace an entire set of buttons on a garment with a new set for free.

so that you have only three months' worth of clothes within easy access. It might also be a good idea to review your everyday clothing needs. If you wear casual clothes five days a week, you might not need to store smart suits and dresses in your main wardrobe. Perhaps keeping them with your out-of-season garments would be a better idea.

● Buy less and get rid of more

Take your time reorganising your wardrobe – make sure you're making the best use of that precious space. And while you are doing it, don't buy anything new. That should give you enough of a gap to break your fashion-buying habit and help you to review the way you shop. As you rotate your clothing, examine every item. If a piece no longer fits – no matter how cute it is or what fond memories it might evoke – get rid of it. Do the same with any garment that makes you feel fat, frumpy or old. You can't afford to allow it to keep cluttering up your mind, your self-confidence and your home. Then think hard about your age and lifestyle. How many garments do you have that aren't really suitable any longer? Ask a friend for an honest opinion. Pull out everything that you haven't worn in the last year and off-load it – give it away, take it to a charity shop or simply throw it out. You could invite some of your friends round for a clothes swapping evening. Consider storing classic pieces that might come back into fashion or are good enough to pass on as heirlooms. Take any items that you can't bear to lose to a creative seamstress, who may be able to remake them into something that you can wear again. Think of this 'editing' out of your wardrobe as an ongoing review that you will repeat season after season.

● Section your wardrobe

'Visualise your hanging space as a costume department on a film set,' advises designer Pam Verran. Pre-iron every garment, hang them singly on good wooden hangers – no plastic or wire – and store in groups: trousers, skirts, strappy tops, dresses, jackets and so on. You might also find it helpful to arrange items by their colour. 'It's like being an artist with all your pots of paint on view,' says Verran, 'ready to be thrown at the canvas.' But the most important thing is to make sure you can see what you have clearly and that there is room to move the hangers along the rail to inspect a garment. This makes it easier to pick out matching outfits.

● Learn what keeps moths at bay

Do you suspect that your precious knitwear has been infiltrated by moths? If you do, hand-wash it in a gentle wool shampoo, allow it to dry, then stick it in the freezer for a couple of days. This will kill any moths – and their eggs – that are present in your clothes. Also, be aware that the bug-repellent powers of cedar wardrobes and chests are grossly overrated. A moth will run when it gets a strong whiff of cedar, but the pungent smell peters out after a year or two. Reviving the scent requires sanding the surface layer of wood. By the same token, if a dry-cleaner asks if you want to pay to moth-proof garments that are going into storage, say, 'No'. This type of moth-proofing only lasts a month or two. A better way to store vulnerable wool and silk garments is to slide them into sealable moth-proof garment bags, available from some department stores and dry-cleaners. Or you can put them in an airtight container (look out for Mottlock moth boxes) with a handful of cedar wood cubes that should be replaced when they lose their scent.

10 space-saving CLOTHING storage tricks

IS YOUR BEDROOM FLOOR OVER-RUN WITH SHOES? Are you strapped for belt storage? Are you up to your neck in accessories? You are not alone – most of us have amassed so many clothes that we don't have enough space in which to keep them.

The ultimate solution, of course, is to take an honest look at your wardrobe and to get rid of all those items that you never wear – and to learn to resist the temptation to buy a new-look T-shirt when you already have six that are similar. But if you can't bear to part with anything or tame your addiction to fashion, there are a number of clever and inexpensive aids to help you to squeeze every conceivable inch of clothing storage out of your home.

1 CLOSET IT IN CANVAS
Pick up a free-standing canvas wardrobe – from IKEA or a department store or a specialist storage shop. Set it up in a spare room and you'll have an extra metre or so of hanging space, plus room for folded jumpers or shoes, too. Canvas is perfect for keeping clothes dust-free, while allowing air to cirulate around them. If you are storing in an unused room or basement, do check for damp; if necessary, invest in a dehumidifier and leave it on overnight, once or twice a week, when the weather is particularly wet or really cold.

2 BUY HARD-WORKING FURNITURE
When selecting items to furnish your home, choose those that perform more than one function. A day bed with a hinged top, for example, allows items to be stored underneath it, as does a sofa that has hidden drawers, set beneath the seat cushions.

3 SLEEP ON IT
To find an extra cubic metre or so of storage space, look under your bed. Container manufacturers have devised a variety of clever devices for making maximum use of this space, including wide storage boxes on wheels, with either snap-on lids or side-drawer access, and ranges of clear vinyl cases that make shoes and other accessories stored in them easy to peruse.

4 GET HOOKED
In the bathroom, install several hooks on the back of the door for hanging up robes.

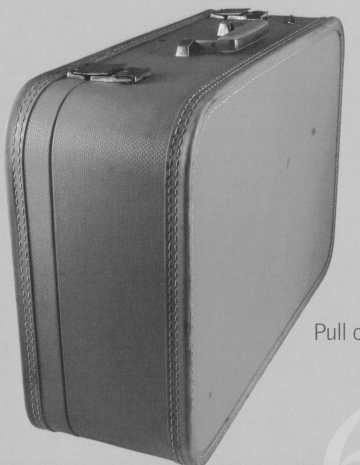

5 **SEND THEM PACKING** Pull out any empty suitcases that aren't in current use and fill them with all your out-of-season garments and clothing that you don't need access to day-in, day-out. You'll gain elbow room in your wardrobe – and your luggage will take up no more space than it did before you filled it.

Pull out any empty suitcases ... and fill them

6 **STAND IN A CORNER** Compact, free-standing coat stands can pack a lot of clothes storage into a very small area of floor space. To free up a crowded cloakroom, park a coat stand by the front door – and plant one in your children's bedrooms, too. Draped with an array of coats, jackets, hats, scarves and umbrellas, a coat stand can look surprisingly decorative.

7 **SHOW THEM THE DOOR** Hang one of those canvas shoe-organisers on the back of your cupboard, wardrobe and bedroom doors. A typical one will have hooks that fit over the top of the door, allowing a dozen or so canvas pockets to drape over the surface of the door. As well as being a splendid way to keep your shoes organised and off the floor, they also provide imaginative storage place for rolled-up scarves, lingerie and other small items of clothing.

8 **HANG TOGETHER** To save hanging space, invest in a selection of the speciality hangers that are designed to accommodate several skirts or a dozen scarves, belts or ties. But don't be tempted into loading regular one-garment hangers with several layers of clothing.

9 **GO VERTICAL** See-through, stacking bins are ideal for storing sweaters, other foldable clothing and accessories such as handbags and shoes. When stacked, they take up little floor space, and the transparent sides help you to identify items quickly. Those with drawer-type fronts make access easier.

10 **LOOK UP** Install some high shelves around your bedroom to accommodate hats, bags, small storage boxes or special shoes that you only wear occasionally. A wide shelf, mounted about 30-46 cm below the ceiling, will be in no one's way and will provide a neat 'relief' for an overstuffed wardrobe. A high storage shelf is a very good way to make use of that 'dead' space above the door frame.

In the bathroom ... hooks for hanging up robes

secrets for
YOUR
GIZMOS

Insider tips from £50-an-hour
repairers and electronics whiz kids

RESEARCHING PURCHASES

6 SMART STRATEGIES to minimise hassle and help you to make big cash savings

● Keep on top of changing prices

Many retailers boast about their 30 day price guarantees, claiming that if the price of a product, such as a television or DVD player, drops within 30 days of your purchase, the shop will refund the difference. But this is a calculated marketing decision. What they don't mention is that they know that few shoppers check the price after they've made their purchase. Not long ago, watching a price meant returning to the shop. But thanks to the internet, you can beat them at their own game by watching the price online. It should only take a couple of minutes a day. And if the price goes down because of a sale, you'll get some of your money back.

● Ask if they work on commission

Salespeople are legally obliged to tell you the truth about this. So, if they depend on commission and you're looking for an honest opinion about a computer or television, you'll know to try another store, where you can be sure you're not simply listening to sales patter aimed at getting you to buy the product with the biggest cash reward for the person selling it to you. But remember that such patter can mean that a deal may be there for the asking, as people who work on commission usually have the flexibility to slash prices. In stores that pay their employees on a commission-only basis, always ask for a discount – but do your product research somewhere else.

● Beware of incentive-led advice

Retailers often offer their salespeople special incentives to sell products that are not selling quickly enough. While commission might already make salespeople biased towards the more expensive products, incentives encourage them to sell an unpopular or brand-new product, as yet untested on the market. If you've done your homework online or by talking to others, you can quickly figure out which ones are being pushed in this way.

● Check out warranties

Salespeople have been known to play down a manufacturer's warranty if they think they can sell you their own version. You're usually much better off with a warranty that comes from the company that made a product, rather than from the store. Ask to see a copy of the manufacturer's warranty and read it over carefully. You may find that it covers problems for much longer than the salesperson would have you believe. Refrigerator compressors, the most expensive replacement part on any fridge or freezer, often come with a warranty that lasts up to five years.

● Skip most extended warranties

Salespeople are good at making two to five year warranties sound worth the extra money, but some of these plans can cost you hundreds of pounds – and can be difficult to claim on once the item is over a certain age. Here's what they don't tell you: profit margins on electronics are only about 10 per cent. Extended warranties are one way that retailers and manufacturers can make up the difference. The repair rate for the first three years of ownership for camcorders, digital cameras and most televisions is less than 10 per cent. That

continued on page 170 ➜

Consider the potential benefits of buying from a small, local dealer ...

BUYING
APPLIANCES
at large retail outlets & superstores

WHEN YOU DECIDE TO BUY a new washing machine, fridge or power tool, it may seem only natural to make a local home superstore your first stop. But purchasing a complex piece of machinery is not the same as picking up some paint or wallpaper and you may not be getting the same good deal. **Here are some things that you should consider before buying at a large retail outlet or superstore.**

THEY DON'T ALWAYS HAVE THE LOWEST PRICES

Because they entered the appliance-selling game relatively late, retailers such as B&Q and Focus don't command the same volume discounts that they do on commodities such as timber and plasterboard. Nor do appliance manufacturers want to alienate the thousands of independent, specialist shops across the country that stock their products – stores that may still offer very competitive prices.

Consider the potential benefits of buying from a small, local dealer – you'll get dependable service and accountability, and you'll be supporting the local economy. But if you do decide to buy an appliance from a large retail outlet or superstore – perhaps because you want to purchase everything for your new kitchen in one place – bring the top competitor's lowest price quote with you. Most will match, or beat, it. But remember that quality of service may not be their main objective and, when it comes to large appliances, good service is important. This is what the large retail outlets and superstores don't want you to know about how their businesses operate:

● They are typically too short-staffed to be able to handle service well – remember that to make a profit, they have to keep overheads low.

● They will give you a number for a customer service department rather than the name of a person in charge, so it will take longer to deal with any problem that you may have.

● Their organisational structure means that it is very difficult to communicate with either your original salesperson or an individual customer-service representative.

25 per cent. Sometimes these installation companies are new businesses that aren't able to generate enough business on their own and need the extra work for cashflow. The whole setup creates a gap in accountability that can make it hard to solve any problems that crop up.

BUYING TOOLS THAT ARE EXCLUSIVE TO ONE RETAILER IS RISKY
Some brands of power tools are sold at just one retail chain and large retail outlets and superstores often have their own brand-name tools. This can spell trouble for contractors working long distances from home and for people who move to an area

If you are going to use a tool more than once or twice … it makes sense to buy, rather than rent

where there is no branch of that particular store. Without easy access to the outlet that sells your brand, you might not be able to buy suitable replacement parts or accessories for your tools. Before you choose a brand, find out where accessories and parts for that brand are available, where repairs are made and then consider if it's convenient for you. Ideally choose one that is widely available everywhere.

POWER TOOLS THAT USE ONE KIND OF BATTERY ARE A GREAT IDEA
The battery is typically the most expensive part of a new cordless drill, saw or other power tool. And it's always a good idea to have a back-up battery. Buying several power tools that use the same battery will allow you to keep one that is already charged up and ready to use at a moment's notice, without having to buy a spare. It also cuts down on the number of battery chargers you have around the house, which reduces clutter and saves you money.

RENTING TOOLS CAN COST AS MUCH AS BUYING THEM
Renting a power or garden tool can cost nearly as much as buying the same tool new. If you are going to use a tool more than once or twice and have space to store it, it makes sense to buy, rather than rent. Even if it only takes you an hour to aerate your lawn, you may have to rent the tool for a minimum time period, for instance 24 hours. Instead, if you need expensive lawn tools such as a ride-on lawnmower or rotavator, ask your neighbours if they'd like to pitch in so you can buy one and share it.

Besides, employees in many superstores are far too busy trying to deal with all the other customers to really be able to give you their full attention. It's best to think of large retail outlets and superstores simply as retailers.

MOST LARGE RETAIL OUTLETS AND SUPERSTORES DO NOT HAVE THEIR OWN INSTALLERS
When you purchase a large appliance that needs professional installation, it is not employees from the store who will come into your home; they are probably employed by an installation company that the shop has hired on contract. The large retail outlets and superstores simply act as the middleman, charging you the installation fee, plus a mark-up that can be in the region of

means 90 per cent of the time, all of the extended warranty money goes to the store or manufacturer.

One extended warranty that you might want to consider is for a laptop computer. Laptops have a three year repair rate of 33 per cent, so consider a one to three year extension of the standard one year manufacturers' warranty. Buying the extended warranty from the manufacturer usually means you will get technical support as well.

Warranties from retailers tend to cover only problems with the hardware and not the technical support.

● **Get the dealer to install it** There can be a lot of finger-pointing if a new appliance doesn't work. The dealer may say it's the installer's fault, while the installer may claim the retailer is responsible. Prevent this by asking the retailer to install it. When the same business sells and installs your appliances, they will usually take responsibility for problems that occur.

APPLIANCE CARE

5 PROFESSIONAL SECRETS for
keeping your gizmos in tip-top shape

● **Unclog your dishwasher** Repair people can often make easy money from customers who complain that their dishwasher isn't cleaning as well as it used to. Before calling a repairman, have a go at fixing the problem yourself with this easy, 3 minute procedure. Look at the top of the spray arms inside your dishwasher (there are usually two, one at the bottom and one under the upper rack) – all the holes should be clear. If mineral deposits or other debris are closing off the holes along the top of the spray arms, they won't clean correctly. Unfasten the clips or screws holding the spray arms in place and put the spray arms in the sink. Unbend a paper clip, insert the end into each spray hole and move it around to dislodge the blockage. Rinse the arms out under the tap to flush out the debris and return them to the dishwasher – which should now work properly again.

● **Source parts on the internet** It's now much easier to get hold of spare parts, so if you can get access to a broken dryer belt or worn dishwasher spring, you can replace it yourself and save on repair bills. Instead of driving to the nearest appliance-parts dealer, leafing through old catalogues or annoying a behind-the-counter type who's used to selling to trained technicians, you can now turn to the internet for parts – and advice about installing them.

● **Know your limits** Modern manufacturers have made many machines harder for do-it-yourselfers to get into. 'I was servicing appliances in the 1970s and 80s', says Graham Dixon, former field-technician and appliance repair instructor. 'Access has become a little trickier, but appliances are essentially easier to work on once you get in there. Replacing parts is usually a matter of removing a few screws or brackets. Manufacturers build them so that highly paid technicians can fix parts and get out quickly.'

Some repairs will also be too complicated, or potentially dangerous, for homeowners to attempt on their own and the DIYer will have to make a decision whether to attempt them or not. But you can usually use the internet to diagnose your problem, track down repair manuals (sometimes manuals for similar models give you all you need to know about accessing a machine) and buy parts through mail order. Good places for appliance DIYers to start online are www.ukwhitegoods.co.uk and www.amazon.co.uk – which you can use to search for various appliance repair books.

● **Clear the drain tube** Inside the main compartment of a typical fridge, there is a V-shaped trough, moulded into the plastic on the back, beneath the cooling plate. At the base of the 'V' is a small hole leading to the outside of the appliance. At the exit point on the rear of the appliance, a tube is attached which leads to a plastic evaporation tray that is mounted on the compressor. The purpose of this system is to drain the run-off that develops when your unit periodically allows any build-up of ice to melt, so that your fridge remains – as advertised – 'frost-free'.

The problem with this kind of drainage system is that algal spores often develop in the hole and tube, blocking them. This causes water to back up on the floor of the cooling compartment, which can then turn into ice. The solution is simple – use a turkey baster to force a small amount of fresh water through to flush it out. You may have to turn off the fridge to let the ice melt first. The water will run into the tray at

How they do it . . .
checking reliability

'Choosing a brand can be bewildering,' says Graham Dixon, an appliance consultant. He suggests getting the lowdown from the repairman. 'Go to an independent dealer and talk to the salespeople. Then talk to one of the repair people. Once, when I was shopping for a heating system for one of my clients, I checked with a plumbing supplier, who recommended a certain brand. Then I talked to a local plumber, who installs these types of systems. He also liked the brand, but he didn't like a competing one because a number of his customers had experienced problems with it. The installer or service engineer knows the performance of a product in real-life, local situations. Salespeople, even from a local independent dealer, may be pushing a particular product for incentive or commission.'

the rear of the appliance, so empty it. Then pour a teaspoon of chlorine bleach into the tube to prevent any recurrence of the algae spores. It's a simple job that could save you a hefty repair bill.

● **Lubricate your ice-maker** They were once a luxury, but today many freezers have ice-makers installed as a standard feature. If the ice-maker in your freezer has ground to a halt, try this simple cure before you spend money on a repair call. Take out the ice-cube tray and remove any remaining ice. Buff the tray with a kitchen towel until it's perfectly dry. Then give the inside of the tray a light spray of vegetable oil. One of the most common reasons that ice-makers stop giving out ice is that the tray clings to the new ice cubes and can't eject them. The thin film of oil will prevent this bond forming and will leave no taste at all on your ice.

how to ruin **YOUR** APPLIANCES

APPLIANCES EVENTUALLY WEAR OUT. Certain parts simply fail with time. It's inevitable. But abuse and neglect can speed up the breakdown rate of cookers, dishwashers, fridges, tumble driers and washing machines, helping to keep repairmen busy. **Here are some of the most common ways that homeowners contribute to the demise of their appliances, along with advice for avoiding these errors.**

WASHING MACHINES Some parts are easy to replace, but damage to the inner drum or outer tub, caused by coins or metal objects left in pockets can sound the death knell for your machine. Inner-drum damage can result in torn or pulled clothing, while outer-tub damage can lead to leaks. The high price of such a major appliance, plus the cost of installation, makes any repairs or replacement prohibitively expensive.

REPAIRMAN'S TIP:
● Never wash anything with heavy metal fasteners.
● Always check the pockets of clothing before placing them in the drum of your machine.

BONUS TIP:
● Overloading your machine may not ruin it, but it will create additional wear and tear on certain parts such as bearings and suspension, making them prone to premature failure and forcing you to call the repairman or fix it yourself. Be sure to always follow the manufacturer's suggestions for load size.

TUMBLE DRIERS When the typical 5kg load of laundry comes out of the washing machine, it can contain up to 2 litres of water. The drier's job is to remove this water. It heats the clothes, converting the water in them into water vapour and forcing it out of the drier through the exhaust vent, along with any fluff and lint. Tumble driers are designed to push this moisture-laden air only so far. Every bend in the vent hose or ducting – around a corner or up a wall – dramatically reduces the airflow, so that your drier has to work harder to dry your clothes, leading to increased running costs and possible premature failure. Moisture problems may arise and lint can build up in the vent pipe and the machine. The latter is the most serious, because lint is inflammable. In the UK, tumble driers account for several hundred fires a year, with lint and fluff build-up being a key factor. No matter what the reason for the call-out, all manufacturers recommend that service personnel de-lint the inside of the driers they attend. Removing lint and fluff from inside a drier cabinet can be too complicated, or potentially dangerous, for a homeowner to attempt.

REPAIRMAN'S TIP:
● Follow your drier-manual's instructions for proper venting. Whenever possible replace plastic or vinyl exhaust hoses with rigid or flexible metal venting, making the pathway from the drier to the outside vent as straight as possible.
● Make sure that you remove any lint and fluff from all the accessible places in the drier where they tend to collect – the

Never force too many pans

back, air vents, around the mouth of the lint filter and around the door. Once a year, it may be worth getting a professional to clean the interior of your machine.

BONUS TIP:
● Ensure that all accessible lint filters are cleaned after each use, as this ensures that the drier works to peak performance.
● Clean and check the vent hose or duct regularly.
● Get the inside of the drier inspected for lint and fluff build-up and cleaned on a regular basis.

GLASS-TOP ELECTRIC HOBS

Because electric hobs don't have many moving parts, they can last a long time. But damage to the glass top can cost £300 or more to replace, often making the repair uneconomic. The most obvious way to break the glass is to bang it – an impact break. But improper heating can also crack the glass. Using concave-bottomed or over-sized pans can trap heat and cause the glass to crack. Cosmetic damage can be caused by using unsuitable cleaning products or utensils. Always use hob-safe cleaning products and utensils and remove food spillages quickly before they burn on.

REPAIRMAN'S TIP:
● Use flat-bottomed pots and pans and make sure that they are not larger than each burner.

FRIDGES AND FREEZERS

The most expensive part of a fridge or freezer is the compressor, a part of the sealed cooling system which is often protected under a special five-year warranty and should last at least twice as long. But you must clean the dust that builds up on the condenser coils, usually located behind a grille at the back or the bottom of the appliance. If not, the compressor will be forced to work harder and may overheat. If it fails prematurely, but after the warranty is void, a repair may be too costly and you will have to replace the appliance.

REPAIRMAN'S TIP:
Once a year – twice if you have furry pets – carefully clean the dust from the condenser coils and air vents using a vacuum cleaner and a condenser-coil cleaning brush (a tapered bottle-type brush on a short handle). Gently brush the surface and in between the coils, then vacuum. Repeat until the coils are dust-free. Do not poke at the coils with a vacuum cleaner's hard-plastic crevice tool or use any metal items at all as this will result in damage to the coils.

BONUS TIP:
● A full freezer is more efficient than an empty one, which has nothing to hold the cold. An efficient freezer not only

prolongs the life of the compressor and the fridge itself – but also saves energy. Fill empty freezer shelves with bags of ice, frozen veggies or even plastic milk jugs filled with water.

DISHWASHER

One small nick in the vinyl-coated rack can start off rusting that may ruin a dishwasher. Once the metal inside begins to rust, you can't stop it. The rust will stain the dishes until you replace either the rack or the machine. Replacing a dish rack can cost 25 per cent of the price of a brand-new machine. Incorrect loading and failure to keep the appliance topped up with salt and rinse aid are major factors in poor wash results.

REPAIRMAN'S TIP:
● Hand-wash pans, colanders and other kitchenware that has sharp edges. Never force too many pans or glass items into a small space.

BONUS TIP:
● To keep the dishwasher at peak performance, ensure you have the water hardness selector correctly set for your area – refer to your instruction manual for details.
● To get a 'squeaky' clean finish on all your items, ensure that the rinse-aid dosage selector is set correctly. Small circular ring marks indicate that the setting needs to be increased (or the rinse-aid reservoir needs filling – see below). A sticky film on items means the setting needs to be reduced.
● Keep salt and rinse-aid containers topped up. A container full of rinse-aid can last for three months, but in hard-water areas, a container of 4kg salt may be used in just two weeks.

or glass items into a small space ...

COMPUTER CARE
5 SLICK TIPS to save money and do your own fixes

Leaving your laptop plugged into the wall all the time will actually make the battery weaker

● **Cut down on repair time** Here's a little-known secret among techies: the first thing a computer repairperson does when he or she arrives is to make sure your operating system is updated. If you're like most people, you probably use Microsoft Windows. You can – and should – update Windows yourself, before the £40 an hour IT expert arrives. And if you're lucky, updating Windows might even solve the problem you called about. If a plug-in, such as a digital camera, MP3 player or printer isn't working, it could be because your drivers are out of date. A Windows update will take care of this. Think how good you'll feel if you can call up and cancel the appointment.

To update Windows, here's what to do if Internet Explorer is your browser (advice differs for other browsers). Log onto Explorer, go to the 'Tools' menu at the top of the page, then click on 'Windows Update'. You will be taken to the Microsoft website, which will check to see if your computer needs any upgrades. If it does, follow the prompts to download the upgrades. If you have Windows Vista or XP, you can get your computer to download the upgrades automatically. To do so, click on the 'Start' menu in the lower left corner of your screen, click on 'Control Panel', click on 'Security Centre', then turn on 'Automatic Updates'.

Apple computers can be a little more expensive than most PCs. But since only about 2 per cent of the population uses Apple's Macintosh computers, very few spyware and virus programs are written to affect them. Virus writers would rather get at 98 per cent of computer users than Apple's small user base. So, if you are having a lot of problems with spyware and viruses, consider buying a Mac next. The peace of mind might be worth the slightly higher cost.

● **Kick-start a failed connection**
If your high-speed internet service fails to work after a power loss or computer crash, it could be that some of your devices have powered-up in the wrong order. Save yourself some time and hassle by trying the following procedure. First, shut down your computer. Then turn off or unplug your modem – the device that connects you to your cable or phone line. If you have one, turn off or unplug your router – the device that links the modem to your home network. Wait at least 30 seconds. Now turn everything back on in the following order:
1 Modem – it will send a message to your internet service provider (ISP) saying you need a new connection.
2 Router – it tells your modem to connect.
3 Computer
Nine out of ten times, doing this will fix your connection problem. If it doesn't, the problem probably has something to do with your internet service provider, not your computer. At that point, it's time to call a specialist.

● **Boost your computer's speed**
The many software programs that come bundled on your computer take up valuable space. They also fight for your computer's resources by constantly searching for updates of themselves, even when you don't have the program open. What computer companies don't

tell you is that when you buy one of their machines, it will already be running slower than it should because of all the extra programs. You can free up space and resources by removing all the programs you don't use.

Simply deleting the icon on your desktop will not remove the programs – you have to uninstall them. If you use a Windows Vista or XP-based PC, do this by clicking on the 'Start' menu in the bottom left corner of your computer screen. Next, click 'Control Panel', then 'Uninstall a Program' (Vista users) or 'Add or Remove Programs' (XP users). Scroll down the list of programs and remove the ones you are certain you don't need. The rule-of-thumb that computer technicians use with clients who want faster machines is: if you haven't used a program for a year, you can remove it without worry.

● **Drain, then recharge** You probably don't need a spare laptop battery, unless you travel frequently. A second battery is bulky and is almost never worth the money. Since batteries drain more quickly as they get older – after only a few years, a battery may only reach 95 per cent of its original charge – it is best to stick with one battery and keep it healthy. The best way to do this is to charge it only after it has been fully drained. Leaving your laptop plugged into the wall all the time will actually make the battery weaker. Before a big trip, when you'll need as much battery power as possible, drain your laptop battery completely – running a CD or DVD is a good way to quickly sap all the power – and then recharge it completely.

● **Upgrade your PC** Computer companies thrive on a marketing strategy known as planned obsolescence

HIDDEN TRUTHS What software manufacturers don't want you to know about **FREE SPYWARE**

Makers of spyware, the insidious software that secretly gathers information about your Web surfing habits while also slowing down your surfing speed, have become very clever at fooling consumers into downloading their software onto your computer. They have even been known to advertise spyware as 'free spyware blockers'. You should only download free spyware blockers from www.download.com – one of the most trustworthy sites for downloads on the internet, according to computer technicians. Two of the best free spyware blockers are Spybot Search and Destroy and Ad-Aware from Lavasoft.

– the idea that today's brand-new machine will be out of date in just a few years, thanks to ever-faster processors, bigger hard drives and more memory. They reckon that most of their customers would never dream of tinkering with electronics in the same way that they might replace a belt in a vacuum cleaner. But despite the short-term nature of computer software, many desktop computer hardware parts fit together like high-tech Lego.

Instead of spending upwards of £300 on a brand-new computer, just upgrade a few parts. If you need more memory, plug in a random-access memory (RAM) upgrade, which usually costs less than £50. If you want to burn DVDs, buy a DVD burner – another £50 purchase – and add it to one of the empty slots on the computer. This way, you can keep your old keyboard, monitor and speakers, all of which work perfectly.

COMPUTER SECURITY

11 WAYS to keep your personal information
out of the hands of strangers

... spending £30 to £40 on a router can slam the door on all potential hackers

● Remember that nothing is free

When you see a pop-up ad for free screensavers, you might think they look cool. They may seem innocent enough. But you pay a price, as they contaminate your system with spyware. When spyware builds up on your computer, every time you start it up, you have a line of people at your internet 'door' waiting to collect information about you. It also slows down your computer a great deal.

● Read your licence agreement

If you download 'free' software, you must first click a button that says 'I accept'. Most people click without reading the end-user licence agreement (EULA) accompanying it, which is like signing a contract without reading it. Read the EULA and it will explain that in exchange for the free screensavers, the company will plant spyware on your computer.

● Install security programs If your

computer is hooked up to the internet, it is absolutely essential that you have reputable security programs installed on it. Spend the extra to get a good-quality security package. Norton and McAfee are two of the biggest names in computer security software. They each sell bundles that include an antivirus program, a firewall to stop hackers, a spyware

blocker and an email checker (it will scan incoming mail for contaminants). You need all of these.

● Get a router for broadband

When you use DSL or cable to link directly to the internet, you are entering what some experts call the demilitarised zone (DMZ). This leaves you wide open to hackers who use scanning software to locate your open internet protocol (IP) ports and remotely access your computer, allowing them to read any personal data, as well as download viruses and spam.

To avoid letting hackers into your system, buy yourself a router, a small box that looks like a modem and routes data between the cable or phone and a small network of computers. Even if you only have one computer at home and no plans for creating a network, spending £30 to £40 on a router can slam the door on all potential hackers. If you add a broadband router and link it to your modem, you should be invisible. Now when the hacker scans, all he can see is your router. He or she can hack that all day long and not get through it, because there are no ports open.

● Secure your wireless network

Many people who have more than one computer at home are discovering the benefits of wireless networks – which use a router to link up those computers. But there is a big potential problem. Like anything computer-related, routers for wireless networks are all designed to work straight out of the box. So once you plug it in, you are immediately online and surfing. The downside is that if you can surf at once, so can anybody else. Any passer-by can get onto your network and spread viruses or even traffic in criminal activities, such as child pornography. Some lawyers have even suggested that homeowners are legally liable for lack of security on their networks.

Securing your wireless network is simple. You will find instructions inside the router box. Typically, you'll be asked to open your internet browser and type in a series of numbers (your IP address, which in most cases is 192.168.1.1). This takes you to your router settings. Click on the 'Wireless' tab and then click on 'Security'. Follow the instructions for creating a password, sometimes called a wired equivalent privacy (WEP) key. Choose a password and your network is safe.

● Never download from a site that advertises on another site
You'll often see a pop-up saying something like, 'Viruses detected on your PC – click here for a free scan and clean of your system'. Or, 'Want to stop Junk emails – Click Here'. Avoid them. Only download directly from a known and trusted site like Norton or McAfee.

● Don't be tempted by the prize
If you see a message similar to, 'You are the 999,999th visitor – Congratulations You've WON!!! Click here to claim your prize'. Don't, whatever you do, be tempted to click. Nothing is for free and only heartache can come from this. There are two possible outcomes: they

can get into your system and get your email address which is a form of phishing (see below), or you may be downloading a dormant virus that is set to activate and attack your system at some time in the future.

● Avoid the phishers
If you receive an email that says it's from your bank and it has been sent to other accounts as well as yours, it's 99.9 per cent likely to be bogus. Sometimes it will ask you to confirm your username and password, but never give this type of information. In fact, don't even open the email; just delete it. No genuine banking organisation would contact you for sensitive information in this manner.

THE MAGIC MEMORY STICK
Always back up your data at the end of each session. It's so easy with a USB flash drive, also known as a 'pen driver' or 'memory stick'.

A tiny 1Gb flash drive is capable of holding a large number of documents at a very low cost. It is a small, lightweight, removable and rewritable drive, that contains a printed circuit board that is powered when plugged into a USB port on a PC or Apple Mac.

Memory sticks can be used to store documents, photographs and music files, and offer significant advantages over other portable storage devices, particularly floppy disks. They are extremely compact (barely 5-7cm long) and very light. They are also generally faster, hold more data (at present up to 64Gb) and are more reliable – due to both their lack of moving parts and more durable design – than floppy disks, Zip or Jaz drives.

And they are so simple to use. All you have to do is plug one into any available USB port and drag and drop your files from the folders on your PC to the flash drive.

● **Check your message links** If you use an instant messenger service such as MSN or Yahoo) and are sent a link to a web site, always ask the sender if they actually sent it, even if you know them. If you click, you may unwittingly accept a virus. Be especially aware of attached 'executable' files with the suffix .exe as these may be programmed to launch and attack the system when clicked.

● **Cut down on Spam** If you are getting annoying emails advertising 'Welcome to the VIP casino', you can put in a simple filter to redirect them so they don't reach your inbox. You can set up a rule that catches any incoming mail with the word 'casino', say, in the subject line and either re-direct it to another folder or immediately delete it.

● **Declutter regularly** Always make sure that you delete any cookies and temporary internet files, especially after using an online banking service or other site where you have been asked to give personal details.

MOBILE PHONES

3 TIPS for outsmarting mobile phone companies' clever tactics

● **Buy at the end of the month**
An employee of a major mobile-phone retailer gave us some inside information. The best time to buy is at the end of the month. Most sales teams have a specific 'discount budget' or allocation of money they are allowed to discount in order to close deals. At the end of the month, when sales quotas must be met, they will dip more deeply into their discount budgets. So bargain hard for your phone at the end of the month – and don't let them tell you they 'can't do any better on the price'. You could offer to sign on for two years if they give a good price.

● **Skip the accessories** People who sell mobile phones typically only make commission from the accessories they sell you, not the phone itself. That's why they can seem so insistent that you buy extra chargers and cases. So only buy accessories that you will really use. If, for example, you seldom travel by car, an in-car charger won't be much use.

● **Skimp on 'replacement' insurance and save your old phone**
Mobile-phone salespeople will leap at the opportunity to sign you up for a phone replacement policy, costing from £5 to £10 per month. It may not sound like much, especially when compared with the quote for a full-price replacement – but at the end of the year, you could have spent over £100 and have nothing to show for it.

Save money by creating your own insurance against breakage: keep the old phone. You can then simply insert your SIM card back into your old phone. And check if your home insurance covers the phone. If not, it may not cost much to add it to the policy.

5 ways to get cheaper
DIGITAL SERVICES

DIGITAL COMPANIES COMPETE FIERCELY for your money. Here are some insider tips for gaining your own competitive edge when it comes to getting the best TV, telephone and internet services.

1 USE YOUR LOYALTY AS A BARGAINING TOOL Because of marketing costs, it can cost digital companies – who often provide TV, telephone and internet services – ten times more to recruit a new customer than to retain an old one. You can use this to your advantage the next time you find yourself dissatisfied with their service. Simply say that you'll take your business elsewhere. Chances are they will address your problem and they may even give you a better deal.

2 SHOP AROUND If there are several service providers in your area, call around for the lowest price. If your current provider's price is relatively high, quote the lowest competitor's price (including incentives). Chances are that they will match or beat that price to keep your business.

3 ASK FOR CREDIT Every now and again, you may have trouble with your TV, telephone or broadband service. The next time things go wrong, don't just settle for restored service. Ask for credit. If you don't have any luck with the first customer-service representative, insisting on speaking to a supervisor.

4 DON'T BUY SERVICES YOU DON'T NEED Most companies offer a range of TV packages with names like basic, standard and premium, each step up adding more channels and more cost. Take a very close look at the channels offered at each level and compare them with the channels you actually watch. You may well find that you are paying for a lot of channels that you never watch. Most people have, at most, ten channels that they watch regularly.

5 GET NEW-CUSTOMER BENEFITS Often digital companies may not require you to sign a contract, which gives you the opportunity to cancel your service, possibly without penalty, and then sign up again the next day to take advantage of incentives such as reduced fees or six months of free premium channels. Better still, just call the provider and say you're going elsewhere unless they offer you the new-customer rates.

Don't buy services you don't need ... most people have, at most, ten channels that they watch regularly

EVERYDAY

DO YOU KNOW the best time to get **seasonal bargains** and how junk mail could save you pounds on your utilities?

THAT YOU CAN often get the **best deal on a car** at the end of the month? How few rights you have at car-boot sales and two essential tools you'll need to check out the goods?

DISCOVER WHY YOU should be wary if your broker is constantly offering you 'hot tips'. Why 'googling' your name could

LIVING

save embarrassment at a job interview and how mixing business with pleasure could **help your career.**

AND IF YOU WANT to firmly deter burglars, which six key precautions should you take? Our experts reveal dozens of ways to **safeguard your property** and yourself.

JUST TURN THE PAGE to start discovering many, many more **rarely disclosed tricks and secrets.**

secrets for
YOUR CAR

The inside track for keeping your
wheels turning smoothly

CAR MAINTENANCE

10 ESSENTIAL FACTS about car-care that will help you to keep running costs under control

● **Know when to change the oil**
In America, cars are festooned with stickers urging drivers to change the oil every 3,000 miles. In Europe, some manufacturers insist their cars will run for 20,000 miles between refills. But they can't both be correct. The fact is that oil begins to contaminate after a certain time. Changes every 6,000 miles are recommended – and don't leave it for more than 7,500 miles. Money spent on oil is a wise safeguard against costly long-term repairs.

● **Check out the best fuel for you**
Don't simply follow the advice of forecourt posters that urge you to buy the highest-grade fuel. Do comparative runs on similar journeys, one with ordinary unleaded and one with premium. Some cars run better on the pricier stuff, some don't. And also note that fuel with a high detergent content benefits all types of engines.

● **Keep your warranty on track**
Servicing a car is just like any other professional activity: some companies are good at it, some aren't. You won't invalidate your warranty by getting your car serviced independently as long as the work is carried out to manufacturer standards using the correct parts. But you will miss out on any Technical Service Bulletin (TSB) modifications – work that manufacturers get their official franchises to carry out free of charge during a service. Once a car is more than three years old, when the manufacturer's warranty has expired and it has passed the point at which TSB modifications are likely to be made, it

may be time to find a good independent garage, whose labour rates will be cheaper. This will reduce future resale value, but it makes less and less difference as the car gets older.

● **Ignore 'dented' tyre warnings**
If a tyre salesman points out dents in your tyres' sidewalls, don't worry – he's just trying to make a quick buck. An unscrupulous dealer will tell you these dents are a problem and that you need new tyres, but these little concave depressions are perfectly normal. And they are not really dents; they form where the tyre's poly-cords join together. On the other hand, if you have a tyre *bulge* – a convex lump – it is a sign of an impending blow-out and you will need to buy a replacement.

● **Keep tabs on tyre pressure**
Checking your tyre pressure regularly – at least once a month – is the easiest way to reduce expenditure on car-related repairs. Why? First, it's not safe to have under or over-inflated tyres, because it increases the risk of a blow-out. Also, incorrect tyre pressure will have an adverse effect on fuel economy and increase wear and tear on your brakes and suspension. The maximum permissible pressure should be marked on a tyre's sidewall and the manufacturer's driving manual will advise optimum running pressures. These may also be indicated by a sticker on the rear edge of the driver's door.

● **Polish it yourself** Many car dealers offer to give a new car a wax and polish treatment before you take delivery. This will add lustre, but it might also cost from £150 to £300. The alternative is to buy the same protective wax – for about £40 – and apply it yourself. All you then need is a dry day and a little elbow grease. And you'll get protection that is much longer-lasting than a hot-wax spray at a drive-through car wash.

● **Hot wax for free** You will almost certainly get some of the protective benefits of hot-wax treatment every time you use a car wash – even if you don't pay for it. The need for environmental sensitivity obliges garages to recycle their car-wash water. So a garage's water supply will contain residues of the spray-on wax that gets applied during other motorists' washes and some of it will be transferred to your car.

● **Put a mechanic at the wheel**
You may book your car in for a check-up, because something at the front is squeaking. If it's placed on a ramp and 20 minutes later you're told that you need new brake discs and pads, be cautious. How does the garage know that if they haven't taken your car for a test drive? Seek an alternative opinion. A mechanic needs to take a car for a spin to diagnose problems: those that don't might just be trying to sell you the most expensive fix.

● **Avoid shock-absorber betrayal**
It has been known for unscrupulous mechanics to spray oil on a car's shock absorbers, to create the impression that a leak has occurred. If you're given this grim news, always go to another garage and ask for a second opinion.

● **Find a garage you can trust**
Several schemes have been set up in a bid to ensure a fairer deal for motorists. The Retail Motor Industry Federation (www.rmif.co.uk) covers England, Wales, Northern Ireland and the Isle of Man and it also has links with the Scottish Motor Trade Association (www.smta.co.uk). It provides a consumer advice service, a helpline to guide you to the nearest RMIF-approved garage and an arbitration service to help with any complaints that may arise.

The voluntary Good Garage Scheme (www.goodgaragescheme.co.uk) seeks to ensure a decent standard of service. Motoring adviser to *The Daily Telegraph*, 'Honest John' has a directory of good garages – based solely on positive customer feedback – on his website (www.honestjohn.co.uk).

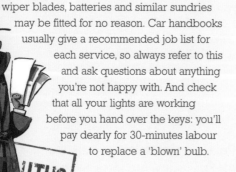

HIDDEN TRUTHS What your garage is happy for you not to know about **CAR MAINTENANCE**

Some garages have a habit of charging for 'extras' that you don't need, when you take you car in for a service. Their mechanics may routinely empty the window-cleaning solution from the washer bottle and then charge for a refill. Or you may be billed for unnecessary lubricants. It's also common for garages to clean rather than replace oil filters and then charge for a full replacement – and new wiper blades, batteries and similar sundries may be fitted for no reason. Car handbooks usually give a recommended job list for each service, so always refer to this and ask questions about anything you're not happy with. And check that all your lights are working before you hand over the keys: you'll pay dearly for 30-minutes labour to replace a 'blown' bulb.

It's always wise to take blankets, energy bars and water on any car journey in poor weather

ROAD SAFETY

6 TOP TIPS for coping with dangerous driving conditions

● **Stop aquaplaning** This occurs when the tyres are on water, rather than directly on asphalt, usually when you're driving quickly and suddenly hit a deep puddle. If it's raining hard enough, you don't even need to drive through a puddle to aquaplane. This is potentially dangerous and creates a risk that you will lose control. Don't brake, but let the car coast until the aquaplaning subsides. If your car has manual transmission, engage the clutch to cut off the supply of power to the driven wheels.

● **Deal with skids on ice and snow** Take your foot off the throttle and steer in the direction that you are skidding. If you must use the brakes, apply steady, gentle pressure but do not pump them or allow them to lock. The brakes will probably make some noise, but you should soon regain control. Note that anti-lock (ABS) brakes increase stopping distances on snow or ice, but some manufacturers enable such systems to be deactivated via a dashboard switch.

● **Don't get hurt by an airbag** Airbags have enhanced occupant safety in the event of a significant impact, but they can inflict injury on those who sit too close to the wheel. Leave at least 25cm between yourself and the steering wheel and always wear a seatbelt (now compulsory in many countries). Frontal airbags can injure young children, who risk being struck in the face or neck. Keep offspring in the back and use an approved car seat to ensure they are effectively belted in.

● **Minimise the impact** What action should you take if another vehicle is coming towards you? The other driver may be distracted or, worse, asleep at the wheel. So flash your headlights and/or sound your horn in a bid to get the other person's attention (flashed headlights are only ever meant to be used as a warning). Drive as close to the left side of your lane as you can, so that you're as far away from oncoming traffic as possible (this applies to Britain and other countries that drive on the left; if you're elsewhere, stick

CAR EMERGENCY KIT

HERE ARE 15 EXTRA ITEMS that will help if you break down or get stuck

Keep them in your boot or glove compartment so that they are always handy. Note that in some countries it is a legal requirement to carry spare bulbs, warning triangles, protective fluorescent jackets and other such safety aids. Check local legislation before you travel. And if you are a member of a roadside breakdown recovery service, always carry your membership card.

These are the extra items:
- MAPS   (or a portable satellite-navigation unit, but make sure you keep it charged)
- FIRST-AID KIT
- JUMP LEADS
- PAPER TOWELS
- A TORCH   (plus spare batteries)
- A PORTABLE FLASHING LIGHT   (plus spare batteries)
- ENERGY BARS   (or similar non-perishable food)
- DRINKING WATER
- A BRIGHTLY COLOURED 'HELP' SIGN

In winter, add these, if appropriate for the weather:
- CAT LITTER, SAND OR SALT   (provides good traction in the snow)
- A SHOVEL
- ICE SCRAPER
- EXTRA CLOTHING AND SHOES, PARTICULARLY WARM JACKETS, HATS AND GLOVES
- WINDSCREEN AND/OR DE-ICING FLUID
- ANTIFREEZE

Check your torch batteries regularly

as far to the right as you can). If the car is in your lane and not moving, slow down to minimise the force of any impact. As long as there are no pedestrians around, try to veer off the road to the left, away from approaching traffic. If it looks as though you might hit a street sign, at least it's not another vehicle travelling at speed. And if you run out of options and a collision is inevitable, try to hit the other obstacle at an angle rather than head on.

● **Don't swerve for animals** In physical terms, some animals are, clearly, potentially more damaging than others. On dark country lanes, use of full beams – when there is no oncoming traffic – will illuminate an animal's eyes and make it easier to spot. It's always better to keep a straight course. Swerving increases the risk of loss of control and might lead you to collide with something more damaging than a deer or a badger – a wall or a telegraph pole, perhaps.

● **Stay calm if you get stranded** Extreme weather is rare in the UK. But if you do get stuck somewhere in difficult conditions, limit your exposure to the elements and conserve your energy. If you can't shovel your vehicle out of a snowdrift – or there's a blizzard – stay in the car. Don't venture out unless help is clearly visible within about 90m. Turn on your hazard warning lights or, in daylight, tie a brightly coloured cloth to the aerial to make your car more visible. Run the engine for about 10 minutes every hour to provide heat, making sure that the exhaust pipe isn't clogged with snow, and open a window slightly on the side away from the wind. Wrap up in a blanket, if you have one, but don't fall asleep – or, if there's more than one person in the car, take turns at sleeping. It's always wise to take blankets, energy bars and water on any car journey in poor weather.

DRIVING OFFENCES
5 INSIDER STRATEGIES for dealing with them

● **Make a good impression** Many officers decide whether you're going to get a ticket before they approach your vehicle. So it's advisable to keep your car clean, tidy and forgo spoilers and tinted windows. You want to look responsible and law abiding rather than anarchic.

● **Wave at lurking police cars** If you're driving a little faster than you should be and spot a police vehicle, it might help if you wave politely, says a former police officer. The policeman may either think that you know each other and wave back, or else that you're acknowledging your error and are letting him know that you're slowing down.

● **Don't admit you were speeding** If you do get pulled over, says a former police officer, never acknowledge that you were speeding. You don't want to give the police any ammunition against you. Admitting guilt at the roadside will condemn you to defeat in court. When an officer claims you were speeding, give a brief, non-committal response such as, 'I see,' or 'I was not aware of my speed'. Deal with the police as quickly and politely as possible. You don't want them to remember anything about you, except that you did as you were told.

● **Know how to plead your case** If you know you're guilty, it's probably best to accept the situation, pay your fixed penalty fine (plus points) and move on. Fighting a lost cause through the legal system can be both expensive and fruitless. Or you could ask if you can take road-safety tuition as an alternative to penalty points. When the ticket carries the risk of a ban, it's best to seek legal advice if you want to stay on the road, although logging onto the website www.speed-trap.co.uk may help. If you plan to contest charges, make notes at the scene to keep your evidence as accurate as that of the prosecution.

● **Get the charges dropped?** Most motorists don't contest speeding tickets, but there are circumstances in which they possibly could:

🚍 If, due to local authority negligence, speed limits are not clearly posted or signs are obscured, you could appeal.

🚍 When a speed limit has recently been changed and no clear notice has been given, a court might accept an appeal if you didn't exceed the previous limit.

🚍 If you are caught by a speed camera, the police must send you a Notice of Intended Prosecution within 14 days for a subsequent charge to be valid. If they don't meet this deadline, it's not.

SATELLITE NAVIGATION

Many satellite navigation systems contain the locations of fixed safety camera sites, and you can subscribe to monthly updates that can be uploaded via your computer. The use of GPS-based camera locators is perfectly acceptable in most countries (including France, although local police might try to convince you otherwise), but laser detectors, which actively seek out speed traps, are often illegal. Check before you travel. And though a sat-nav might inform you about camera locations and speed limits, only your eyes and judgment can determine a safe speed.

BUYING A CAR

6 PROFESSIONAL TIPS to help you to cut through the sales hype and save some cash into the bargain

● **Check how you're protected**
It's common practice, especially among independent traders, to adorn cars with banners bearing terms such as 'certified' or 'approved', but they mean relatively little. A car might have had certain checks, but that doesn't guarantee brakes, tyres and everything else will be in perfect working order. But consumers are protected against unscrupulous practice, in certain situations, at least. Most major dealers offer reasonably comprehensive 12 month warranties on used cars and independent traders are obliged, under the terms of the Sale and Supply of Goods Act 2002, to provide an implied six months of cover on all cars sold. Buyers have no such legal protection if a car purchased from a private seller turns out to be faulty. If you find a car you like, a number of firms offer an independent checking service – for a fee. It is also worth paying to verify a car's history, to make sure that no finance is still owing, or that it isn't stolen.

● **Know your warranty options**
Extortionate finance rates are a way for car sellers to increase profits and so are extended warranties. There are cheaper alternatives. Online companies (such as www.warrantydirect.co.uk) offer policies that could beat those offered by the dealer. You might not want to buy your warranty over the internet, but understanding the market gives you a better platform from which to negotiate.

● **Go for comfort, not looks** When ordering a new car, do you stick with the plain but functional wheels that come as standard or go for a set of racy alloys with low-profile tyres? The latter will look good, but your back might not appreciate the investment. Deeper-profile tyres aren't just cheaper: they also provide extra cushioning on roads with speed humps and potential potholes.

● **Time it right** Major dealers receive bonuses for sales performance and towards the end of a month you'll find sales staff might be prepared to offer extra customer incentives as they strive to hit targets. If you are not fashion-conscious, it's worth remembering that you can get a good deal on cars approaching the end of their life cycle.

How they do it . . .
getting a car-hire bargain

At many popular destinations, there aren't enough compact and economy cars to fill the needs of everyone who wants to save a few pounds and you can use this to your advantage.

If you are heading to a tourist mecca, such as Las Vegas, your best bet is to book the smallest car possible, says Peter Wu, a frequent traveller and former chief purser of a major airline. Chances are you're not the only one trying to be prudent, so the smallest cars are invariably the first ones to go. And if they've all gone by the time you arrive at the hire company's office, you'll be given a free upgrade. If the rental agency hasn't run out of small cars and you really want something larger, you can then say you've changed your mind and pay the higher rate. Upgrading is easier than switching from big to small.

Dealers need to make space for new stock and you'll get a good bargain on a late example of a proven model. Finally, if you want a convertible, buy it in winter as prices rise in spring, when the sun begins to break through.

● **Go online and save** Don't be nervous about buying a vehicle online – just check out the reputation of the seller, if possible, first. The internet has been around long enough for some justifiably strong reputations to have been established. Good brokers buy in bulk from major dealers, so full warranties still apply and they get

discounts not available to individuals. Part of the saving is passed on to you.

● **Don't pay for rust-proofing** It's unlikely that today's sales personnel will try to sell you rust protection for a new car, but there are a few who prey on the unsuspecting. Cars are now made so well that rust protection is unnecessary. Some manufacturers have long-term anti-rust warranties – up to 30 years, in the case of Mercedes-Benz.

GETTING A **FAIR DEAL**

8 SMART MOVES to make sure that you buy or sell at the best price, with the least hassle

When ordering a new car ... go for comfort, not looks

● **Know your market** Every car showroom – from gleaming, main-dealer franchises to dusty sites on street corners – will have a shelf full of well-thumbed books, such as the *CAP Black Book* (www.cap.co.uk) or *Glass's Guide* (www.glass.co.uk). Updated every month, these are trade 'bibles' that provide a rough guide to the used value of all makes and models, based on criteria such as age, condition and mileage. If you are looking for a part-exchange deal, a trader will almost always offer you less than the figure quoted in any of the above, but you can check out the ballpark figure to aim for, before you ask for a deal, by using similar guides that are available to the general public: try the *What Car? Price Guide* or *Parker's* (www.parkers.co.uk). As always, the internet is a ripe source

of useful information for car buyers and sellers. Check manufacturers' official sites to get a feel for new and used prices. Most have sections that enable you to create a virtual new car to your own specifications and you can also search nationwide to see what's available on the used market, and how much it is likely to cost.

● **Don't be fooled by the badge** Britain tends to be a nation of car snobs – and manufacturers know it. There is nothing wrong with premium-brand cars, but in some cases the badge's perceived aura accounts for a significant percentage of the elevated purchase price. Today, many manufacturers share componentry (an industry-wide cost-saving measure) and you will find cars with radically different prices but very similar running gear. The Volkswagen Group, for instance, has a stable of brands including VW, Audi, Skoda and Seat. All are different on the outside, but beneath the skin you'll find that they have the same chassis and engine. If engineering integrity means more to you than impressing the neighbours, and you can live with slightly lower-grade interior trim, try a little lateral thinking.

● **Fine-tune your sales pitch** If you are trying to sell your car privately and the telephone isn't ringing at all, try consulting a general car-sales website such as www.autotrader.co.uk for guidance. Do a nationwide search for cars of similar age, condition and mileage to find out what others are asking. If you have set your price much

higher than that, the absence of potential buyers will be answered at a stroke. The wisest approach is to do this research before you put your car on the market – and offer it for slightly less than the going rate if you want to attract a quick sale. Equally, if you are in the market to buy and see a potentially attractive car advertised, conduct the same search to see if the seller's asking price reflects market trends. If it is too high – and they won't budge – walk away.

● **Take a short-cut to a discount** Car dealers always prefer to sell you a car from stock rather than making a special order on your behalf. You can use this fact to your benefit. Inform the dealer that you would like to purchase a low-specification model without the expensive options that are habitually fitted to showroom vehicles. Chances are that they will offer to cut the price of a well-equipped car, if you agree to take current stock off their hands.

● **Be wise to the pitfalls** Trading in your old car can put you at a disadvantage, because it gives sales staff more variables to factor into the deal they might offer you – a chance for the unscrupulous to baffle the unwary. Be aware that no dealer is going to give you more than the trade value for your part-exchange car, so it will almost certainly be more lucrative to sell it privately. But that opens the door to a host of other potential problems. Private advertisers have been exposed to various new scams in recent years. One of the most common is the cold-calling agency that tells you it has a number of people looking for a car like yours. In return for a nominal fee (usually about £80), they guarantee to find a buyer who will pay your asking rate: once they have taken your money, they do absolutely nothing

HIDDEN TRUTHS What dealers don't want you to know about **CAR FINANCE ...**

Ask these questions to see if the car finance package you're offered is really a good deal:
● Does the loan require an enormous down payment or a 'balloon payment' at the end?
● Is the price of the car higher for people who accept low-interest financing?
● How long are you given to repay the loan? If it's only 12 months, be wary.
● Must you buy extras you don't want, such as an extended warranty?
● Will you have to give up any of the manufacturer's cashback offers?
You might want to establish your credit rating so you know exactly what you're entitled to. Companies like Equifax (www.equifax.co.uk) will do this for you.

in return. Part-exchanging your car with a dealer might cost a little more, but for many people it's a convenient, stress-free option. Major dealers will generally pay more for a part-exchange vehicle than some of the car-sales supersites that have sprung up in recent years, but that extra cash is likely to be swallowed up by their higher selling prices.

● Pick part-exchange deals apart

Sometimes a car dealer will promise you a generous part-exchange allowance on your old car and neglect to mention that he is putting up the cost of the new one. The cost of your new car should be the same whether or not you intend to part exchange. You should also ask the dealer whether any generous offers apply to all incoming part-exchange cars, no matter how much wear and tear they have. And establish whether special offers apply exclusively to in-stock vehicles, or to those with the most expensive options packages.

● Learn about car auctions

Auctions can be fantastic places to source a genuine bargain – in theory, cars will sell for whatever is seen to be a fair trade price on a given day. At the same time, they can be a trap for the unwary. Most modern auction houses are highly professional, but it is still a good idea to pay several visits to get a feel for the style and mood of the place before you attempt to buy. There are many specialist auction houses that deal in niche markets, such as classic cars, ex-fleet vehicles or 4 x 4s, but it's always best to know exactly what you're looking for before you visit any auction. Before you bid, have a good look at potentially suitable cars in the viewing area. Check for signs of repaired accident damage (a respray, evidence of misaligned panels or patches of filler),

unevenly worn tyres or a creamy residue beneath the oil filler cap, which could imply a blown head gasket. Also, make sure the car has a full service history. Remember that the purpose of auctions is to shift lots quickly and, unlike buying from a dealer, you have no legal comeback against the seller in the event of technical problems. Auctions are probably the cheapest way of buying a car, but there are risks attached.

● Get it checked independently

There are various independent bodies that provide professional car-checking services that can save time and money when buying a car. To verify that the car you want is not stolen, has no finance owing and is not an insurance write-off that has been restored illicitly, you can contact companies such as HPI (www.hpicheck.com) or the AA (www.aacardatacheck.co.uk). The charge for their services is likely to be about £30, but it's a lot cheaper than having a car repossessed, for reasons beyond your control, and being unable to claim compensation.

Several motoring organisations also offer independent technical inspections to advise private buyers of a car's potential roadworthiness. These include the AA (www.theaa.com/motoring-advice/index.jsp) and the RAC (www.rac.co.uk/web/vehiclechecks). You may pay up to £150 for this service, but think how much more you could lose if you buy a car with problems.

If you want to buy something out of the ordinary, such as a Jaguar E-type, it is worth consulting a marque specialist or an owners' club for advice before you commit to a purchase.

Professional car-checking services ... can save time and money when buying a car

CAR **INSURANCE**

4 GREAT TIPS for getting a good deal on insurance

● **Keep a healthy credit rating**
According to experts, drivers with long, stable credit histories are less likely to be involved in accidents. People who are lax with their financial affairs are statistically more likely to file a claim, so insurance companies consider them to be a higher risk. It might sound odd, but this is a method insurance companies employ when determining your car insurance premium.

● **Train for a discount** Insurance is not optional; it is mandatory for all car drivers in the United Kingdom. And, at the younger end of the spectrum, for drivers aged 17-24, annual premiums can be as expensive as the car they drive. But there are ways to soften the financial blow. Pass Plus (www.passplus.org.uk) is a course that teaches newly qualified drivers things they won't have had to learn to pass their test. It's not free, but is designed to enhance confidence and improve road awareness. Many insurers offer discounts to those who pass.

● **Keep your insurer up to date**
If you alter your car in any way, always let your insurance company know. The modifications might be cosmetic – a set of alloy wheels with low-profile tyres, for example – and unlikely to make any difference to your car's performance – but it's still best to inform the insurer of the changes.

If you don't divulge such information and the insurance company finds out, it could try to use it as an excuse to invalidate any future claims. But if it tries to charge you extra for an inconsequential adjustment to your car's specification, take your business to another company.

● **Cut premiums on a 'banger'**
Your insurance broker will be delighted every time you renew a comprehensive policy for a car that's worth relatively little – perhaps less than £1,000. It might make more sense to take out cheaper cover and put the cash you save into a high-interest account. Then if you have an accident or your car is vandalised, you can dip into your savings to cover the repairs.

Check before you do this though. Ask your broker how much your premiums will drop if you raise your excess or take out a third party, fire and theft policy.

EXPERT ADVICE
GREAT TIPS FROM THE PROFESSIONALS

Things to remember about insurance

It's a fact of life that you need to do a lot of comparison shopping in order to find the most competitive car insurance rates. You might be eligible for some discounts that a broker won't divulge while giving you a quote. Here are some of the things that can qualify you for cheaper car insurance:

• Insuring more than one car on the same policy (not many UK companies do this, but Primo does – www.primoplc.com)
• A clean track record in terms of accidents and/or traffic violations
• Being aged 55-70
• Passing an advanced driver training course
• Using a reputable anti-theft device
• A relatively low annual mileage
• Being a long-term customer

MOTORHOMES

4 POINTS to ponder when buying a home on wheels

● **Check American prices** It might be worth sourcing your vehicle in the US, where the motorhome is an institution. Even with import costs and paying for a single vehicle approval (SVA) test, which is mandatory for any import not approved to British or European standards, you may pay less.

● **Think about left-hand drive** This notion may fill you with trepidation. But if your motorhome is likely to be used mainly for holidays in mainland Europe, left-hand drive could be a much better option, particularly if you're likely to have to travel alone on toll motorways.

● **Consider dual-fuel** Liquefied petroleum gas (LPG) is cheaper than petrol or diesel. So it might be worth having a large, fuel-guzzling vehicle, such as a motorhome, converted to dual-fuel specification. Ideally, this should be carried out by a company that has LPG Association approval.

● **Watch your weight** Some large motorhomes are close to their chassis's recommended maximum weight – and that's before you've added a family of four, filled the cupboards and topped up the water tank. Overloaded vehicles are prone to instability, so be vigilant.

> On the road, be wary of manhole covers ... in wet weather they can cause your tyres to lose their grip

MOTORCYCLES

4 TRICKS to help make motorcycling safer and cheaper

● **Beware of slippery surfaces** Watch out for diesel spills in fuel stations, taking extra care as you turn in and pull away. On the road, be wary of manhole covers and the shiny strips of tar that seal the edges of road repairs; in wet weather they can cause your tyres to lose their grip.

● **Keep your visor clear** To stop it fogging up, shake a drop of washing-up liquid onto the inside of the visor. Then rub it around until it's no longer visible.

● **Clean it for less** Wash your bike with warm soapy water, then rub plastic bodywork with silicon-based furniture polish and a soft duster; clean and

protect metal parts with WD40 and then wipe the excess off with a clean rag; polish out scratches on your screen with toothpaste and clean your visor with a baby wipe.

● **Cut insurance costs** Fit an approved alarm and immobiliser and keep the bike off-road or in a locked garage overnight. Take a course of training and a test with the Institute of Advanced Motorcyclists. And if if your bill is still crippling, you could consider getting married. Married riders with family responsibilities pay less for insurance than single people.

chapter **9**

secrets for
BUYING STUFF

favourite tricks of experienced
bargain-hunters and champion shoppers

GENERAL SAVINGS

8 SMART STRATEGIES for staying at the top of your game when it comes to finding bargains

● Watch the financial news

Towards the end of the year, pay special attention to the financial section of the newspapers and stories on the news about the economy. Even in a recession, the retail industry will never broadcast the fact that business is slow, but the media will let you know. If news forecasts are saying that Christmas sales figures will be sluggish, you can bet that stores will start discounting their goods during the autumn shopping season. Head to the high street and start scouting for early bargains. And if you learn on the news the day after Christmas that the festive shopping season was very disappointing for retailers, plan another shopping expedition and stock up on New Year bargains, as prices will be lower still.

● Check your junk mail

Day in and day out, all sorts of offers for cheaper versions of services you purchase every month, such as mobile phones, gas, electricity and insurance, come through the post. Don't just drop them into the recycling bin – use them to your advantage. When a great offer turns up on your doormat, call up your current provider and explain that you are considering switching to one of its competitors. Read the competitor's offer to your current supplier over the phone and ask whether it can match this deal. Your existing provider may match the deal – saving you money without having to switch. But if your provider will not cooperate, switch with the help of a comparison website: www.uswitch.com, www.moneysupermarket.com or www.gocompare.com for example.

● Become a pro at shopping

An old trick will put thousands of pounds into your pocket every year. Here's what to do: establish a specific price in your mind – let's say £20. Whenever you are planning to buy an item that costs more than this amount, first find out all you can about the product, urges Alan Zell, a retail expert who calls himself 'the ambassador of selling'. Long ago, shoppers used to research the difference between quality brands and those of a lower quality. They learned to recognise high prices and bargains. They thought long and hard over their purchases before they put their money on the counter. Shopping carefully like this has become a lost art nowadays and that's how businesses like it. Retailers are more than happy for you to simply grab whichever item is convenient, since you often give them more of your money than you would if you took a little time to make a well-informed purchase. Remember: shops are professionals at selling you things. Level the playing field by becoming a pro at shopping. Once the price passes £20, give all purchases your full attention.

● Use credit to your advantage

If you pay off your credit-card balance in full each month and your card doesn't offer cashbacks or other worthwhile incentives, sign up for a credit card that does and take out a pair of scissors and cut up the old one. Credit-card companies have blanketed the country with their cards so thoroughly – and pleas in the mail for even more people to get them – that they are desperate for your business. Use this information to

... buy a
bargain fan
in winter

your advantage. Many credit-card companies are offering incentives for you to use their cards nowadays. The best incentives are cashback (typically 0.5 or 1.5 per cent of the amount you spend) and points schemes – which are good provided the goods you can exchange the points for are things you wanted anyway.

Another good deal is free travel insurance, but don't confuse this with free travel accident insurance (which pays a lump sum if you die or are injured while on holiday or travelling on public transport). The likelihood of claiming on the latter is so small that it's a perk that is definitely not worth having. Also, don't be conned by offers of internet-fraud protection (the law protects you anyway), purchase protection cover (which has a lot of exclusions and your home contents insurance probably covers you already) and extended warranties on electrical goods (very few these days break down in the first couple of years).

Do remember that incentives are bait – the credit-card companies are trying to lure you into giving them more money than you will save. Avoid these sneaky traps by paying off your balance every month by direct debit so that you aren't hit with interest charges and late fees. And never have a card with an annual fee, because they eat into your benefits.

● **Pay bills by direct debit** Some phone and fuel suppliers charge extra if you opt to pay bills quarterly by cheque. Most offer a discount – say 5 or 10 per cent – if you agree to pay monthly by

direct debit. You still get a quarterly bill, but the supplier estimates your likely charges for the whole year and sets your monthly direct debit at one-twelfth of the total. Your balance builds up as the monthly payments go in and falls again when the quarterly charge is taken.

Just beware of the supplier setting the monthly charge too high. The company – not you – is earning interest on the balance. If too much credit does build up, ask for a repayment and for the monthly charge to be reduced. Suppliers also offer discounts if you agree to manage your account online instead of having paper bills.

● **Plan ahead and buy off-season**
When it's hot, people want to buy fans, garden furniture and barbecues. When it's cold, they want sweaters and winter coats. And businesses charge a lot of money for these items when demand is high. Instead of shopping with the herd, make your purchases at times when demand is low, so you hold the upper hand. The shopkeepers will be happy to offer you a bargain just to get the stock off their shelves. This will require you to look a little farther down the road when planning your purchases and also to know when shops are likely to be eager to reduce their stock levels. So if your barbecue is on its last legs, buy a replacement during the early autumn and buy a bargain fan in winter. Watch out too for the launch of new models of cookers, TVs and the like. Shops will often give you a great deal on last year's model, because they simply want it out of the showroom.

● **Learn the skill of negotiation**
In plenty of countries around the world, the price tag on an item is merely the starting point – you then discuss a more

reasonable price with the shopkeeper. Make haggling a regular part of your shopping experience. You'll be amazed how often retailers will give a discount in order to make a sale. Look for a small imperfection in the item – perhaps a bouquet of flowers looks less than fresh or a small blemish on an item of clothing – and ask for a discount. But never name the discount you'd like. Ask 'What is your best price?' and let the salesperson give a figure. When you name the price, you may be offering a figure that's higher than the salesperson would suggest.

● **Stock up on gifts** A steady stream of work colleagues, neighbours and distant relatives will always be having birthdays. It's a fact of life. And when you suddenly remember that a birthday is coming up in a few days, you'll probably buy a knick-knack that's too expensive just because it's convenient. That's often a fact of life too – but it doesn't have to be. Instead, always be on the lookout for bargain prices on items that you think would make good gifts. You're not picking out the perfect present for a specific person. Try a candle in a nice candleholder or a funny book or a smart, newfangled kitchen implement. Tuck your finds into the back of a drawer, then when a birthday comes along, take an item from your stash, wrap it carefully in attractive paper and enjoy the lack of stress and money saved.

SPECIAL
SAVINGS TRICKS

8 SECRET WAYS that a little ingenuity can help you to cut your cash outflow

● **Form a 'hand-me-down' club**
Children's clothes are great business: as kids grow so fast, their clothes quickly become unwearable, even though they still look good. So parents have to buy a constant stream of new garments, just to keep up with their growing offspring. But instead of enriching the coffers of expensive children's shops, organise a club of parents from your child's school or nursery to exchange hand-me-down clothing. Twice a year, in autumn and spring, everyone can bring in the clothing that's still in good condition but no longer fits. You'll be able to quickly assemble a new wardrobe for your child, while getting rid of items that you no longer need. Just make sure a wide range of ages is represented at the gathering, rather than children in only one year group. This way you'll always have larger clothes working their way into your trading system.

● **Buy socks in one colour** Always buy the same colour and style of socks for your child, preferably white, since you can bleach them when they're stained. Socks invariably vanish, so when you lose one of a pair, you can simply pair it up with another, because they're all identical. You'll never be stuck with an 'orphaned' sock that has no match. Just imagine how clothing retailers will grit their teeth as you stroll straight past a display stand of socks in every imaginable colour and texture.

● Pay less at the petrol pump

When petrol prices soar, every extra mile you drive to find bargains puts more money into the pockets of supermarkets and big oil companies. But you can do a bit of damage limitation and keep the price down by shopping around before you get behind the wheel, using the website www.petrolprices.com Just type in your postcode and the site tells you which outlet within a 2 to 20-mile radius is selling the cheapest fuel. The site is free to use but you have to register and the consumer database that you join may be used by the website owner (a firm called Fubra) to market other websites. Local prices can easily differ by 5p a litre or more. On that basis, if you drive 10,000 miles a year, using the site could save you around £50 a year.

● Take a job ... and a discount

If you're looking for a part-time job, fill out applications at shops where you frequently make purchases, such as clothing stores or sports outlets, which give their employees a discount. And if you have teenagers at home who need extra cash, encourage them to get jobs at your family's favourite retailers and receive employee discounts too. Not only will you benefit from any discounts, you'll also gain access to a new world of insider information on upcoming sales.

● Cancel that premium channel

If you're paying for a premium TV channel just to watch a particular series, call the satellite or cable company today and cancel your subscription to that channel. Many series only contain 12 episodes per season and you then have to wait for months before the next season begins – and all that time, you're paying bloated fees. Instead, switch to Freeview, which gives you 40 digital channels for only the cost of the set top box – as little as £20. If you have digital, you may find that for the cost of the box, Freesat has the channel you want. You may even be able to see the show on your computer through Iplayer and ITV Player. Otherwise, watch the series with a friend who already has that channel or rent the whole season when it comes out on DVD. Even better, go to your local library and borrow it for free.

● Cut costly snacks and drinks

Would you like a £450 pay rise next year? Stop buying snacks and drinks at work from coffee bars and vending

HIDDEN TRUTHS What the card companies prefer not to mention about **CREDIT-CARD PURCHASES**

When you pay for goods or services costing more than £100 but less than £30,000 using a credit card, the card company is equally liable with the retailer to compensate you if goods are faulty or don't turn up. And following a Court of Appeal judgment in March 2006, this applies whether you are using your card in the UK or buying abroad, such as over the internet or on holiday. Companies may say that they need a court judgment before they will step in. But the Financial Ombudsman Service says this is wrong. 'Customers can choose whether to claim against the supplier, the card issuer or both'. Similar protection applies to Visa debit cards, but there is no protection for charge card or credit-card cheques.

machines. Your £2 skinny latte five days a week, 46 weeks a year works out at £460 a year. A bottle a day of mineral water costs £345 a year. Add in a bag of crisps from the vending machine and you are wasting hundreds of pounds a year. Use the water cooler. Stock up on snacks at the supermarket. Organise a kettle so that you and your colleagues can make your own coffees and teas.

● **Help a friend move** Always help friends pack their belongings and load the van when they're moving – this simple favour could save you big money. When people load their home contents into boxes, they usually find items that they no longer need or don't want to bother packing and unpacking. As a result, you may be able to bring home hundreds of pounds' worth of spices, frozen food, videos and DVDs, books, toys, furniture and other handy household items. Best of all, your friends will think you've done them a favour.

● **Get a reporter's help** Companies live in dread of looking like 'the bad guys' in newspaper or TV news stories. If you have been through every possible way to air a consumer complaint via the offending company, contact the consumer desk at your local newspaper or television station – or threaten to. Reporters love 'little guy vs. hard-nosed company' stories. Once they make an inquiry, your consumer problem will probably be solved very quickly.

GROCERY SAVINGS

9 CLEVER TRICKS for getting the best quality and quantity when you go shopping for food

● **Buy food once a week** If you're hooked on impromptu food shopping, break the habit right now – it's expensive. Attach a magnet-backed notepad and pen to the fridge and the moment you run out of something, add it to the list. This simple discipline will have a major impact on your family budget. If you don't keep a list, you're likely to drop into shops for one item here and two items there. Instead, establish a time each week when you can go food shopping and have time to focus on what you're buying, and aren't in a rush. Be sure that you have your list with you, as you go out of the door. Supermarket managers love it when you don't keep a shopping list, for several reasons. First, the more times you go into the shop, the more chances you'll have of picking up unnecessary items on impulse. Also, when you buy goods on the spur of the moment, you are more likely to pay the full price for them, as you haven't had time to check for a sale or wait for one to arrive. In addition, the more shopping trips you make by car, the more fuel you use, which adds an invisible cost to your groceries.

● **Get the smallest carrier** If you only need one item, don't get a basket. If you're only buying three items, get a basket, not a trolley. Only get a trolley – and even then choose a small one – if you're shopping for a lot of items. When

How they do it . . .
get a supermarket bargain

You don't have to monitor the constant pricing activities at every local supermarket to save on food shopping, according to Stephanie Nelson, a bargain-hunting expert. 'All the sales will ultimately come to each store,' she says. 'Running back and forth between supermarkets eats up both your precious time and expensive petrol.' But she does think that it's a good idea to develop a fundamental understanding of each supermarket's sales strategy. If a store offers a loyalty card, apply for it and use it. Watch out for periods when the shop is offering double or triple points on items that you would buy anyway. Check the supermarket's advertising flyers for forthcoming bargains. When you see a great sale on an item, buy a six-week supply so that you'll have enough to last you until the item goes on sale again.

you venture into the shop knowing you are going to have to carry your purchases in your hand or a small basket up to the counter, you probably won't make impulse buys. As you've already checked out the bargains and made a list of the items you need, you shouldn't be buying more than you need anyway.

● **Look out for limited buys** When you see a sign in a supermarket or a clothes shop that advertises a low price – but only lets you buy a few items at this price – take advantage of the deal. You may never see this product at a price this low again. When a shop sets these limits, it's a sign that it's selling the products at, or even below, the price that it paid for them, says Eugene Fram, a professor of marketing. Shops don't set limits because they're worried that customers will pile their trolleys high with the discounted

items – they are afraid that owners of small businesses will buy all the stock and resell it at a higher price in their own shops. So your high street shops may be out of luck when these limited offers come around – but you can take advantage of them.

● **Track the price of your dozen key purchases** Buy a small notebook and look through your fridge, freezer and food cupboards for the 12 products you buy most often. For many people, this list will include items such as milk, cheese, fruit juice and bread. Give each item its own page and write the name at the top of the page. Take the notebook with you whenever you go shopping and each time you buy the item, jot down the price. And each time you see the item listed in a supermarket flyer, note the price in your notebook too. It won't take long for you to become aware of when you should stock up on bargains and when you should wait for a sale. As clever shoppers have learned through their adventures in bargain-finding, you have to know the difference between great prices and expensive markups in order to save money. Although a large supermarket may contain 30,000 items, just being able to find your top 12 items at a discount will save you big money. A frugal expert told us that simply by stocking up on chicken breasts only when they're on sale – rather than paying the going price every week – she saves £162 every year.

● **Watch the cash register** The checkout operator may want to make small-talk with you as he or she rings up your purchases. They may or may not have been trained to do that to help the store make more money from you, but either way, this distraction can certainly do it. Politely respond that you need to pay attention to something else instead – and keep your eyes trained like a hawk on the cash register readout. Cash registers aren't always updated with the latest sales prices on items. Since you know exactly how much the items should cost, alert the operator if any incorrect prices come up to ensure that you are getting the low price that you found. It's always a good idea to check your till receipt and query any mistakes.

● **Use your loyalty card** Many supermarkets offer loyalty cards that earn you points to save money on future shopping trips. Some checkout operators ask for them when they take your money; others don't. Before you go into the shop, put the loyalty card with the card that you intend to pay with – or with your cash – so that you don't forget to hand it over. Be sure not to overspend just for the sake of a few points and remember to reclaim your points when there's a good deal on an item you want.

● **Go to the farmers' market late** Farmers' markets are wonderful places to buy fruit and vegetables, cheeses, meat and a whole host of goodies – the produce is often fresher because it's grown close to your home or has been very recently picked or packed. And when you visit at the right time, you

may be able to take home your favourite foods at a steep discount. Late in the day, sellers are faced with the prospect of having to cart home or throw away unsold stock. They hate having to do that. So they're likely to sell you their remaining items at a reduced price, in order not to have to bother working out what to do with them.

To find your nearest farmers' market, visit the National Farmers' Retail & Markets Association (FARMA) website at www.farmersmarkets.net. Although FARMA membership is UK-wide, you'll find a more comprehensive list of Scottish farmers' markets at www.scottishfarmersmarkets.co.uk.

● **Do it yourself and save** Food companies like you to think that they're doing you a favour by offering bags of prewashed salad and individual servings of soup or pasta in sauce. Actually, they're just looking for a way to charge you more money. Buy individual salad components, instead of bagged salads and soups; and pasta, pasta sauce, cereals and other foods in normal-sized tins and packets, instead of in tiny ones. It only takes a few seconds to wash your own salad and divide food into multiple bowls – and you won't pay extra for conveniences that you don't really need.

... wash your own salad – and you won't pay extra for conveniences you don't really need

● Keep your beer in the dark

If you – or members of the family – enjoy drinking beer, you can save money by taking a tip from wine connoisseurs. Create your own 'beer cellar'. Find a cool, dark spot where you can leave cases of beer without moving them – under these conditions, beer will stay fresh for at least six months. Then wait for the summer sales to begin. You should then be able to buy in bulk and get the best discounts on all your favourite brands. And if you live near any of the Channel ports, you can easily nip over to France and stock up even more cheaply. For tips on shopping on the French side of the Channel, see www.day-tripper.net

USING **COUPONS**

3 CANNY WAYS to get the most from coupons when you shop for groceries

● **Get more coupons** Coupons are a great way to gradually save big money. So why stop with one set of coupons from magazines and mail flyers when you can get more? Find out if friends and family get coupons but don't use them. If so, ask for them. If your main source of coupons is flyers in the supermarket or the website of the supermarket chain, you can pick up or print out as many coupons as you want.

● **Use coupons immediately** Look out when you're shopping for items with a coupon that gives money off your next purchase. These are often used to promote new products and are great if it is an item you want to try anyway. If you are shopping with someone else, get money off immediately: go through the checkout first, detach the coupon and pass it to your friend to use at once.

● **Use the internet** Many companies have a website where you can register for special offers, like www.heinz.co.uk and www.twiningsandyou.co.uk You must agree to receive regular news about products but in return you get a stream of coupons and other offers. Before you shop online, visit websites such as www.zfreebies.co.uk for a big range of coupons and discounts, some for online supermarkets, such as Tesco and Asda.

HIDDEN TRUTHS What the supermarkets don't want you to know about **PRODUCT PLACEMENT**

While you're wheeling your trolley down the aisles, do plenty of stooping down low and reaching up high. Food makers may pay extra to shops to have their products stocked at eye-level, so that consumers see them more easily. And guess who pays the extra cost so these foods have a prime position on the shelves? That's right – you. Supermarket managers cross their fingers and hope you will drift through the store with your gaze firmly at eye-level. So always look up and down. The items on the highest and lowest shelves will probably be a better bargain.

Use every trick to be a smart shopper ...

RETAIL SHOPPING

11 SECRETS that the canniest shoppers use when buying clothing, electronics and other merchandise

● **Speak your mind** If you needed to find out if the pair of jeans you admired on your friend were available in your size – but the 20-something assistant was too engrossed on her mobile to help you – don't handle the situation by getting angry and vowing never to go near the shop again. If you're annoyed over any issue with a store – from an encounter with a rude or unhelpful salesperson to shoddy goods – use the situation to your advantage. Shop managers want customers to return and they have a lot of leeway to give you a special offer when you're disgruntled to ensure that you do. So when you complain about poor goods or service, make sure you ask for a discount, store credit or some other incentive on your next purchase.

● **Ask for a discount** Forget about being embarrassed or uncomfortable when you call a company and threaten to take your business elsewhere if it won't offer you a discount. This call might be the best conversation the customer-service representative has had all day. 'Many customer-service staff get bonuses for keeping customers who are thinking about leaving,' says Jeffrey Strain, an expert on living frugally

(www.frugal.org.uk). That's because it costs companies a lot of money to bring in new customers and many are happy to offer a discount to stop you cancelling their service. So make the call – the company should be happy to work with you and offer you a deal – and those few minutes on the phone may put hundreds of pounds back into your pocket.

● **Follow the returns policy** Before you hand over £100 at an electronics store for a portable DVD player for your kids to watch in the car, visit the customer-service desk and read the small print about the store's returns policy. If you don't, you could get stuck with a bad buy. The small print often requires you to follow complicated directions in order to return a product. You'll need to provide the receipt and usually all of the item's original packaging to get a refund or replacement item. So be sure to review the returns policy before you leave the shop to cut down on any confusion later.

When you get home from shopping, take your receipt out of the bag and keep it in a special folder in your desk drawer. Then put the item's box and other packaging in the original carrier bag at the back of a cupboard until the period of time in which you can return it has passed. If you become dissatisfied with the item, you can then quickly reassemble all the elements you need to return it to the shop.

● **Write a fan letter** Wouldn't it be nice if manufacturers filled your post with free cosmetics and other products? They're happy to do so; all you have to do is say something nice to them. Manufacturers get lots of letters from customers complaining about items and it makes their day when they get a letter complimenting their products. 'If you use a product often and really enjoy it, write a letter to the manufacturer,' recommends Donna Montaldo, a coupon and bargain expert. She has written letters to show her support for her favourite cosmetics and by doing so, she says, 'you can

usually get a ton of coupons in the mail.' Find the postal address of the company on the product's package or on the company's website. Make sure you mention the exact name of the product you enjoy and how long you've been using it, when you write the letter. Apply a stamp, cross your fingers and wait for the coupons – and possibly samples – as a thank-you for your letter.

● **Act promptly on cashbacks** On some items, especially mobile phones and some electronic goods, you may be offered a rebate or cashback offer. You pay the full price initially, but can then claim back part of the cost – typically £10 to £70. But companies don't always make the cashback process easy and, when you don't follow their rules, you probably won't get your money. After all, they count on a certain percentage of their customers failing to apply for it. Since you often need to post in a receipt to claim your rebate, ask for a duplicate of the receipt when you pay. This way you will have a back-up copy, in case the company loses the one you send in or you need to return the item if it's faulty. There's usually a time limit for claiming the rebate, so you need to be quick off the mark. With mobile-phone deals, you may have to send in your first few bills and there often isn't long between receiving the last one and the closing date for the cashback. Check the instructions for claiming the cashback carefully and follow them to the letter. If you don't put all the correct bits of paper into an envelope and post it off on time, the odds are your cashback will slip away.

● **Befriend the shop's staff** You have your eye on a particular backpack that you're planning to buy before a hiking trip later in the summer, but it's not on sale yet. Engage the salesperson –

HIDDEN TRUTHS What the discount stores don't want you to know about **PRICES**

Managers of discount supermarkets, such as Lidl and Aldi, want you to think that they have the best bargains. That's not necessarily true. They usually give better deals than you'd get if you simply filled your trolley at a mainstream supermarket without comparison shopping. But you can pay less for many items than the prices that these discounters offer. When you use coupons and wait to buy products that are on sale, you'll usually get household goods more cheaply at a mainstream supermarket. You can save 50 per cent or more on cereals, bread, meat, toilet paper and other staples, when they're discounted at a main supermarket versus a discount store.

sale

or even better, the manager – in a little chat to establish a friendly atmosphere, then ask if the item will be on sale at any time soon. You're not just a run-of-the-mill customer anymore – you're someone about to reel in an inside scoop. Since you have a casual banter going, the staff may share some inside information on upcoming sales that the other shoppers don't know about. Next weekend or even a few months from now, you may be able to stroll back in and get the backpack at a 20 per cent – or even bigger – discount.

● **Take advantage of loss leaders**
Shops often advertise products at an extra-low price just to bring you inside. They may lose money on these 'loss leaders', but they will make even more money because they are using the bargains to lure customers towards other items in the store that are marked up in price. So when you go into a shop to buy one of these great bargains, just buy the loss leader, turn right around, pay for it and leave. When you buy other things, you're almost guaranteed to blow any money you've saved on the bargain.

● **Check new clothes thoroughly**
Clothing retailers are not going to worry if you take home damaged goods and decide later that complaining is not worth the bother. So check *before* buying – there's a good chance that another

customer has tried on the garment that you want to buy. A shopper in a hurry may have broken the zip or got a foot caught in a hem and ripped it. Some unscrupulous shoppers take buttons or belts from garments while they're in the fitting room. Before you head for the cash register, check that hems, extra buttons, fasteners and other details are intact and operating correctly. If there's a problem, ask if there's another garment in your size that's perfect – or if not, and you really want the item – see if the manager will offer you a discount. This may affect your right to return the garment, but at least you'll know what the faults are before you take it home.

● **Be cautious of 'sales' bins** In a department store, most of the display racks will be in impeccable order – until you come across a bin of items dumped in a dishevelled heap in the corner. Your immediate reaction may be that you've unearthed some major discounts. But that's just what the store manager wants you to think. So check the prices carefully on everything that you fish out of that bargain bin. An unkempt display does not necessarily mean a good deal.

● **Benefit from a storecard** In some shops, staff will always encourage you to sign you up for a storecard. Most storecards are a rip off if you borrow on

HIDDEN TRUTHS What product makers don't want you to know about **RECOMMENDED AMOUNTS**

Even though labels tell you to put a specific dose of detergent into your washing machine or add a level scoop of coffee to your coffee-maker, you don't have to use this much. Manufacturers are in business to make money and the more times you return to the shop to replace their products, the more money they make. Experiment by using a little less. Reduce your washing powder by a quarter. Keep your toothbrush a week beyond the recommended time. Squirt only half as much cleaner into the toilet bowl. You'll find that you can cut back on many household products, without seeing a difference in results – and all those bottles, jars and tubes will last longer.

them, because they charge sky-high rates of interest. But if you have the willpower either never to buy with a storecard or always to pay off the bill in full each month, it can be worth signing up for one. You will probably be invited to special evenings where you'll get first pick of the bargains, you may be offered extra discounts when you buy with your card and the bumph that comes with your bill may include a coupon or two to lure you back to the store.

● **Look for price-match promises**
Some retailers aim to beat competitors on price and will pay you for shopping around. If you find a cheaper deal, they will match it. Some retailers, especially for electrical goods, even make this promise for website sales. Price comparison sites like www.kelkoo.co.uk and dooyoo.co.uk make shopping around easy. Any cheaper product must be the identical make and model and available for immediate purchase.

SHOPPING ALTERNATIVES

6 TRICKS for finding the best bargains at car-boot sales, jumble sales, factory outlets and charity shops

● **Plan your attack on car-boot and jumble sales** One of the most penny-pinching people on the planet revealed to us her personal game plan for scooping up scores of car-boot and jumble bargains in a single weekend. This is it: get yourself a street map that covers all the residential areas near you. Next, get a local weekly newspaper which will have a classified section brimming with ads for car-boot sales, jumble sales and garage sales. Now you

are equipped to plan your attack. Circle the sales that fall within more upmarket areas and use your map to list the order in which you will visit each one. Jumble and car-boot sales in more expensive parts of town, or more exclusive villages, tend to offer more upmarket goods. The same is true for smaller car-boot sales, but large sales attract dealers and dedicated car-booters from a wide area, so home in on the non-professional stalls for the real bargains. By carefully planning your route to all these sales, you should cut down on wasted miles driving backwards and forwards. And when you spend £5 or £10 less on petrol, the bargains you find will become even better deals.

● **Go equipped** Finding great deals at car-boot and jumble sales depends on speed – so you can find the good items before other shoppers get to them – and a discerning eye that lets you pick out the quality merchandise from the junk. Equip yourself with the following weapons so that you can move quickly from sale to sale and pounce when you find a great deal:

☑ **Small notes and coins** Debit and credit cards are no use in the casual sale world and sellers usually won't take cheques. You don't want to lose a special item because you run out of cash.

☑ **A tape measure** From curtains to chairs and mirrors to mantlepieces, you need to know if certain items will fit in your home before you buy them. Know what sizes you are looking for before you take off to the sales and measure these sorts of objects at the sale before you buy. If you forget your tape measure, you can use a £20 pound note to estimate sizes – it's 15cm long.

☑ **A magnifying glass** Check for dents, loose threads and other imperfections before you hand over any cash.

☑ **A map** When you finish at one sale, it's time to make a quick beeline for the next one.

● **Haggle with the best of them**
Haggling at car-boot sales and garage sales is *de rigueur*. To get the best price, follow these tips:

☑ **Dress down** Look as if you really need a bargain or two.

☑ **Cram your purse with coins** You can ostentatiously check through these to make it look as if you are on a tight budget. Keep your notes well hidden.

☑ **Begin with a low offer** If sellers won't budge, start to walk away. They might accept it, rather than lose your custom.

● **Take a piece home** If you find a particularly special chest of drawers at a sale late in the day, after you've spent most of your money on other bargains and you're short on cash, you could give the owner a few pounds as a deposit. But it won't guarantee that he or she won't sell it to someone else, so use this crafty trick gleaned from one of the world's best bargain-hunters. Hand over as much cash as you can to the owner as a deposit, then, before leaving to get the

---

EXPERT ADVICE
GREAT TIPS FROM THE PROFESSIONALS

Know your rights at car-boot sales

If you're buying at a car-boot sale, you really have very few rights, so you should always check items that you're thinking of purchasing very carefully. Trading Standards officers recommend that you steer clear of the following: electrical equipment, such as heaters, irons and electric blankets; nightwear, which might be made of inflammable material; food; cosmetics (unless the manufacturer's seal is unbroken); and pushchairs or children's car seats. If you buy any toys, make sure that they don't have sharp edges or loose parts. And be wary of DVDs and software, which may be blank or poor-quality, illegal copies. If you unwittingly buy goods that you later discover are stolen – common items include bikes and gardening equipment – you're entitled to a full refund from the seller.

Regular car-booters, who often buy in goods for resale, are in reality traders. So, if you buy anything from them, you have, in theory, the same protection as you would if you were buying from a shop – though in practice, you may find it hard to enforce your rights.

rest of the money, take a drawer with you. No other shopper is going to be willing to buy the incomplete chest, so you're assured that it will be waiting for you when you return.

● **Go for seconds** A salesperson in an ordinary shop would never steer you away from a full-priced pair of jeans and suggest you buy a slightly damaged version for a 30 per cent discount. But that's exactly the sort of offer you'll find at factory outlets and seconds shops. Many clothing chains and kitchenware suppliers operate factory shops, where goods are offered for a lower price than you'll find in the high street. Some of the best bargains are items with minor, imperfections. These are often so small that you'll fail to find them. Ask the sales assistant to show you the seconds. Once you pick the item you want, ask the assistant for his or her opinion on whether the defect will significantly decrease the usefulness or life span of the product. The odds are high that it won't. But note that you do have to be careful of brand-name merchandise that is made specifically for factory outlets and is of a lower quality than the brand's department-store goods. So inspect items carefully for workmanship and quality of materials.

● **Take a post-Christmas trip to local charity shops** Charity shops are a great place to find second-hand clothes and household goods, with the added satisfaction that you are helping a good cause, such as Oxfam or your local hospice. These shops would like your business all year round – and dropping in from time to time is a good idea, since you may get items for a fraction of what you would pay to buy them brand new. But there's a special time of year when you'll find an extra-large range of bargain goods – late December and January, when crowds of people flock to these shops to drop off unwanted Christmas gifts and take the opportunity to offload other surplus items at the same time. If you only go to a charity shop once a year, this is the time to visit.

BUYING ON-LINE
5 LITTLE-KNOWN WAYS to safely get great savings in cyberspace

● **Bid on bank-holiday weekends** When you bid on items on eBay and other auction websites, it shows when the bidding will end. So look out for items for which the bidding will close at a time when most people are likely to be away from their computers. If bidding stops at 9pm on Easter Monday or 8am on Christmas morning, few people will be adding bids and so running up the price at the last minute. You can sneak in during the closing seconds, place your bid and claim the item for yourself.

● **Be creative with spelling** If you're looking for a particular item on an online auction site – an Armani suit, for example – try searching for it under a few misspellings of the brand name as well. Sellers who aren't good spellers may be offering what you want as an 'Aramani' or 'Armane'. Since most people searching through the site would only look for a listing of the suit under the brand's correct spelling, you could be competing with fewer shoppers when you cast your search a little wider.

● Look for a reputable rating

When considering whether to buy an item on eBay, check the seller's rating. Unscrupulous sellers hiding behind a pseudonym, may take your money and never send you the product. But people who buy from the site can rate sellers based on criteria such as whether the item was described accurately, whether it arrived on time and if it showed up undamaged. Steer clear of sellers with less than a 98 per cent positive rating. Your risk of having an unhappy transaction goes up as the seller's approval rating drops. If you're tempted to buy an item but the seller's reputation seems questionable, send the person an email asking about the product. If you receive a thoughtful response in a timely manner, this is a good sign that you're dealing with an honest individual.

● Let the Web shop for you
Use the internet's price comparison sites to help you to track down the cheapest online prices, without having to visit every individual retailer's site. You could try Kelkoo (www.kelkoo.co.uk), Ciao (www.ciao.co.uk), PriceRunner (www.pricerunner.co.uk) or Shopzilla (www.shopzilla.co.uk). The Web can also help you to shop around if you want to buy in a real shop. Following a trend already established in the USA, the UK now has its first bricks-and-mortar comparison website: AskTheLocal (www.askthelocal.com). This lets you compare prices on clothing, electronic appliances and other household goods.

Type in what you are looking for and your postcode for a rundown of local retailers and their prices.

● 'Google' online vendors
Always check the reputation of any company you buy from over the internet. There

---

EXPERT ADVICE
GREAT TIPS FROM THE PROFESSIONALS

Finding a safe online payment service

Online auction sites are a great place to find bargains, but they're also used by crooks who offer merchandise at tantalising prices, take your money and run. From 30 September 2008 there has been greater protection given to buyers on eBay. Whereas previously buyers had a maximum of £500 of protection, now if you buy something on eBay using PayPal you are protected if the goods don't turn up or are significantly different to how they were described up to the full value of the purchase including postage. If you have a problem you must raise the dispute with the seller within 45 days of payment and this needs to be escalated to a claim within 20 days of the dispute being raised. The new protection also applies to people selling items on eBay.

If you buy something from a retailer online that costs more than £100 using a credit card, you are covered under Section 75 of the Consumer Credit Act 1974 if something goes wrong –for example, the goods aren't delivered or aren't as they were described.

Using an escrow account is a way of making large purchases on the internet more safely. The service holds on to your payment until you've verified that the goods have been received and are as described, then the money is passed on to the seller. There is a fee attached to this service. Be wary of escrow services recommended by the seller and check that it is a legitimate service. In the UK escrow agents are normally solicitors or accountants, bound by the rules of their professional body. If you use an escrow agent based abroad, make sure they are regulated by the relevant professional organisation or regulatory body.

EXPERT ADVICE
GREAT TIPS FROM THE PROFESSIONALS

How to pay the minimum for what you want

Whenever you need to buy anything, always work your way up the 'shopping hierarchy' from the cheapest to most expensive to find the best deal:

• First, try to borrow the item. If you only need to trim a few branches, borrow a chainsaw, don't buy one.

• If you can't borrow it? Try to get it free. Websites such as www.free2collect.co.uk, www.eFreeko.co.uk and www.gumtree.com will identify all sorts of items that locals are giving away free. Many local authorities are also starting exchange schemes which let residents swap items to reduce the amount of rubbish going into landfill sites. If your passion is books, check out the free book exchange at www.readitswapit.co.uk.

• If you can't get things free, buy a slightly damaged version – a new washing machine with a scratch will work fine. Electrical retailer, Comet, does online clearance auctions of slightly damaged stock and ex-display models at www.clearance-comet.co.uk.

• If a second isn't available, then shop around for a store offering the unblemished item at a discount.

• Finally, if you can't get the item free or cheap, only then should you pay full price. But you'll probably find what you're looking for long before reaching this stage.

are lots of reputable name-brands, but also too many fly-by-night rogues. Such companies would be embarrassed to have you do this, but go to your favourite internet search engine and enter the company's name. You will probably be able to click your way to a forum where other customers air their opinions of the service they received. Also click your way onto Dooyoo (www.dooyoo.co.uk), a dedicated consumer and business website which includes reviews from people who have bought before you. Another check is to go onto the company's own website and make sure that there's a phone number and an address – these are signs of the company's stability. Then make sure that the address and phone number are accurate by checking them in the business listings of the phonebook or on an online directory enquiries site, such as www.bt.com or www.192.com You might also want to call the phone number. Be wary of doing business with websites that have offices that are based abroad, since they are harder to check and you'll have fewer alternatives if your deal goes awry.

AUCTION STRATEGIES

6 GOOD BETS for getting the best bargains when you buy by bidding

● **Check out police auctions** What happens to lost and stolen items that the police recover but can't trace back to the owners? They're sold at auctions up and down the country and also online. The police online auction site, Bumblebee (www.bumblebeeauctions.co.uk), generally reflects the taste of your average crook, so you'll find loads of bikes, electrical equipment and clothes, but other items too. Bidding starts at £1, so you can pick up some real bargains – a bike for a fiver is not uncommon. Many police forces also use real-world auctions – for details, check out www.policeinformation.co.uk

● **Buy a jet online ... or some thermal socks** Some government departments use auctions and sales. The Ministry of Defence sells surplus equipment through the Disposal Services Authority at www.edisposals.com You can buy anything from a Lynx helicopter to generators, quad bikes, quartz watches and thermal socks. The DVLA regularly auctions personalised number plates. You can bid in person, by phone and you can even place a bid on the internet (www.dvlaregistrations.co.uk).

● **Know your auctioneer** At an auction, the auctioneer's obligation is to make money for the seller. But he or she wants you to leave satisfied with your purchases too. Strike up a conversation with the auctioneer before the sale. Mention the items you're interested in and ask if he knows any information about them, such as their age, condition and value. Once you get to know an auctioneer, he can help you out in a number of ways. He may choose to 'ignore' your bid if he thinks you're trying to pay too much for the item. Or if he notices that you're not paying attention to an item that you'd probably be interested in, he may mention during his high-speed patter that you should consider bidding. By having a good rapport with the auctioneer, you'll notice these helpful little signals.

● **Bid reasonably** If you're going to put out the first bid at an auction, start with a low price, but not a price that would be a 'steal' for the item. For example, if you think the item is worth £1,000, don't start your bidding at £5. Offer £100 or £200 instead. The auctioneer needs to make money for the seller hosting the auction and if certain items aren't going to fetch a reasonable price, the auctioneer can halt the bidding. If few people were going to bid against you anyway, your excessive bargaining may lose you the prize.

● **Set your limit ahead of time** Before bidding begins on an item, whether it's an in-person or online auction, write down how much you're willing to spend, then add an extra 10 per cent. During a heated exchange of bids, most people lose their ability to stick to a reasonable price. Once you reach your limit and then the added wiggle room you've allowed yourself, stop. Don't go any higher. Let the winning bidder realise that he or she has just paid too much and save your money to win on an auction bid on another day.

● **Ignore faxes offering bargains** One of the biggest scams is faxback services that promise to tell you where to get amazing deals at auction. You'll pay through the nose on a premium-rate phone line for a list of police and government auctions that you could have got yourself for free online.

Buy a jet online ...

secrets for
YOUR MONEY

Bankers, brokers and financial advisers
reveal their cash-keeping tactics

BUDGET & SAVINGS

6 EASY WAYS to keep more cash in your pocket

● **Keep a contingency fund handy**
Something – a car repair, emergency
dental work or even a redundancy –
always comes up to throw you off your
monthly budget. To keep these incidents
from putting you into debt, you need to
have an emergency stash of cash that is
easily accessible, preferably in an instant
access account or even an individual
savings account (ISA) where the interest
is tax-free and often at a higher rate. It
is worth noting though that once you
have taken money out of an ISA it
cannot be replaced in the same tax year.

Just how much money gets you out
of a bind? That's easy to calculate.
Track all of your spending for a month,
from your mortgage payment to lunch,
and multiply that total by three. That
three-month operating budget is a scary
amount, isn't it? But this is the minimum
you should have on hand in case the
roof caves in – literally or figuratively –
and you need ready cash to get you
through the rough spots.

● **Hide the credit card** We're always
making impulse purchases, from the
latest kitchen gadget at the supermarket
to a new CD. Doing this can lead you
into debt, so how do you stop this debt
from rocketing out of control? Simple.
Leave your credit card at home when
you go out. It's too easy to flash the
plastic, when all you went out for was
some milk. Instead, figure out how much
cash you'll need each week for your
regular purchases – things like your
supermarket shop, daily cup of coffee
and chocolate bar. Then head to the cash
machine and get your weekly money
ration. With a finite amount of cash,
you'll think twice before embarking on
spur-of-the-moment spending sprees.

● **Check out credit unions** If you
need to borrow money, there may be a
better source than your bank or credit
card. It's called a credit union. Credit
unions are cooperative ventures that don't
have to make profits for shareholders
and therefore usually charge less interest
than banks. The people who do business
with a credit union – you, with your
savings accounts and loans – more or less
'own' it. Some credit unions now offer
the same services as banks, including
debit cards and bill-payment services, and
even full current accounts. The members
of a particular credit union must have a
common bond; for example, they may
live in the same area, belong to the same

BUDGET FORMULA

So you diligently track your income and every expense
that you have. But how do you know if you're spending
reasonable amounts of money on things such as housing,
debt and groceries? Here, as a guide, is what government
figures say the average UK household spends:

32 per cent: Living expenses – food, clothing, transport,
childcare, education and healthcare

25 per cent: Housing and household bills – mortgage or
rent, council tax and utilities

18 per cent: Leisure and entertainment – eating out,
alcohol and tobacco, cinema, concert and theatre tickets
hotels and days out

17 per cent: Taxes – income tax and national insurance

4 per cent: Pension contributions, savings and loan
repayments (The average UK savings rate is notoriously
low. If you want a secure retirement, you'll normally need
to save a lot more than this.)

4 per cent: Insurance – life, health, home and car

EXPERT ADVICE
GREAT TIPS FROM THE PROFESSIONALS

Three ways to ensure financial health

1 When buying a home, the price should ideally not be more than three times your annual gross household income – or 2.5 times your joint income, if you're a couple – plus however much you can manage to put down as a deposit.

2 Your total monthly debt payments – including mortgage, student loans, car and credit-card payments – should not be more than 35 per cent of your monthly gross income. Some experts will stretch this ratio up to 40 per cent, but that leaves you very little wiggle room.

3 To retire comfortably, your nest egg at age 65 should be about 20 times what you want your annual income to be. If you anticipate needing about £20,000 a year to live on when you retire, you'll need to save a nest egg of about £400,000. Of course, this will vary if you retire early or continue to work longer than usual.

get tax relief on yearly pension savings of up to £3,600 or 100 per cent of your UK earnings, whichever is the greater. That gives most people plenty of scope to save. The big question is, how much do you need to save for a comfortable retirement? One big bank suggests you halve your age to find the percentage of your gross earnings you should save. So if you start saving at age 30, save 15 per cent; if you start at 50, save 25 per cent.

● Make, and stick to, a budget
A budget is the first step to gaining some financial order in your home. The Consumer Credit Counselling Service (CCCS) suggests three steps to taking control of your budget:

Step 1: Start with the reality of your current situation. Keep a record of your spending and be conservative in estimating your income.

Step 2: Complete a monthly budget. For example, using the headings CCCS suggests on its website (see below).

Step 3: Evaluate and reduce your spending. Decide which items are essential and which you can do without.

For lots of ideas on budgeting and free templates you can use, see the websites of the CCCS (www.cccs.co.uk), National Debtline (www.nationaldebtline.co.uk) or Credit Action (www.creditaction.org.uk).

church or work for the same employer. To find out if there is a credit union you could join, go the website of the Association of British Credit Unions Limited (ABCUL), www.abcul.org It has a list of credit unions, broken down by geographical area and common bond.

● Put yourself on your 'payroll'
Every month, the bills pile in regular as clockwork. You may be so busy paying everyone else, that you forget about yourself. Put your retirement savings in high gear by setting up a standing order to a pension plan. Since April 2006, you

● Divvy up unexpected income
When you have a windfall – a bonus, gift or cash for extra work – watch debts shrink and savings grow, without feeling deprived, by using the rule of thirds:

○ **One third for the past** Use a third of your windfall to pay off any debts.

○ **One third for the future** Put a second third, immediately, into some sort of savings or investment account.

○ **One third for the present** Use the final third to make a purchase that you want or a home or personal improvement.

A budget is the first step to gaining some financial order ...

CREDIT CARDS

8 LITTLE-KNOWN TIPS that will help to get you out of debt fast

● **Settle the expensive debt first**
Let's say you have a £2,000 balance on a high-interest credit card (perhaps 18 per cent or more), £100,000 mortgage and £10,000 student loan. You only have so much money to devote to paying off loans each month, so which of these debts should get priority? First pay off the high-interest-rate debt – in this case, the credit card – even if it's the least amount of money you owe, say financial advisers. If your earnings are high enough, you'll have to pay off some of the student loan, but don't pay off any more than you have to, as it's cheaper than the mortgage or the credit card. Tackling the expensive loans first and paying off the cheapest loans at a slower pace will save you a lot of interest in the long run.

● **Make them an offer** Here's something that you'll seldom hear from a Visa or Mastercard customer service centre: if you owe so much money on your credit cards that you're considering an individual voluntary arrangement (IVA) or bankruptcy, chances are the credit-card companies will strike a deal with you. They know that if you go down the route of an IVA or bankruptcy, they're unlikely to get all their money back. They also know that if they apply for a County Court Judgment (CCJ) in order to recover their money, a court will simply order you to pay off the debt in small instalments – maybe just £1 or £2 a month – according to what you can afford. So you can pre-empt a court order and save the card company legal fees by making an offer to pay off the debt, bit by bit, in small, regular sums.

Ask the card company to freeze the interest while you do this – they don't have to, but probably will. For free help negotiating with the card company, contact the Citizens' Advice Bureau (CAB, www.citizensadvice.org.uk), the Consumer Credit Counselling Service (0800 138 1111) or the National Debtline (0808 808 4000).

● **Pay twice a month** If you owe a lot on high-interest-rate credit cards, it might be worth making a payment every two weeks instead of once a month,

HIDDEN TRUTHS What credit reference agencies don't want you to know about **CHECKING YOUR CREDIT FILES**

There are three main credit reference agencies (CRAs): Equifax (www.equifax.co.uk), Experian (www.experian.co.uk) and Callcredit (www.callcredit.co.uk). All sensibly advise that you check your credit files regularly for errors and signs of identity theft. But they give the impression that you can only do this by signing up for their expensive online services. In fact, you have a statutory right to have a copy of your credit file sent to you at a cost of just £2 per file. Aim to check your CRA files once every 18 months. Just write to each CRA, requesting a copy of your file in accordance with your statutory right (under section 7 of the Data Protection Act 1998), enclosing a cheque or postal order for £2. If anything on your file is wrong, you have the right to correct it.

HIDDEN TRUTHS

ZOPA

Zopa is a market for social lending that allows you to borrow money from and lend to ordinary people, cutting out the banks and other middlemen. So its interest rates are typically much lower than a bank's or card company's. Simply go to www.zopa.com, key in the loan amount you need and for what period and then check out the rates being offered by lenders today. If you like what's on offer, sign up. Zopa will review your financial status and match you to the lenders in the market – but if your credit rating is very poor, you won't be eligible to borrow through Zopa. Zopa acts as the mediator and charges a small transaction fee – set at £118.50 for borrowers while lenders are charged 1 per cent of the money they lend each year.

even if you're just paying the minimum amount due. Check with your card provider if they will use payments made mid month to reduce the balance because, if they do, it will cut into the interest as it accrues. Over time, you'll save a considerable sum of money.

● **Pay in full – immediately** If at all possible, pay off your credit-card bills in full every month. If you can't clear the whole balance, it can be worthwhile paying off what you can as soon as the bill arrives. Different cards work in different ways, but interest typically starts from the purchase date or when the transaction reaches your account. Check with your card company but, in many cases, from the date your payment arrives interest continues to be charged only on the remaining balance, so the longer you wait to make a payment the more interest builds up. Don't file that bill away for later – pay straight away.

● **Never miss a deadline** The Office of Fair Trading (OFT) reckons that card companies have been ripping off their customers to the extent of £300 million a year, through excessive charges for missing the monthly payment deadline and other defaults. Penalties are now effectively capped, but you'll still typically be charged £12 if you pay late. Remove the risk by setting up a direct debit to pay your credit-card bill automatically each month. You can choose to pay the bill in full, pay a fixed sum or pay the minimum amount – but be wary of the last option.

● **Pay more than minimum** Paying the minimum each month spins out your debt and will cost you dear in interest. For example, suppose you borrowed £1,000 at 10 per cent. If you only pay the minimum required every month – typically the greater of 2 per cent of the outstanding balance or £5 – your monthly repayments would start at £20 but fall with your outstanding balance. It would take nearly 15 years to pay off the debt and you would have handed over a total of £568 in interest. If, instead, you pay off a fixed sum of £20 every month, it would take less than five-and-a-half years to pay off the debt and cost just £281 in interest.

● **Resist pre-approved offers** Credit-card companies know how to ensnare new customers – keep up that barrage of offers. Once you take the bait and have a card, chances are that you're going to run up some debt. One way to resist temptation is to stop receiving the offers. You can opt out of receiving credit-card offers and most other UK-sourced junk mail by signing up with the Mailing Preference Service (MPS); call 0845 703 4599 or visit the website at www.mpsonline.org.uk. Once registered, about 95 per cent of junk mail addressed to you personally should dry up – it won't stop mail shots from abroad or small local firms, or letters addressed to 'The Occupier'. To stop unaddressed mail, register with the Royal Mail Door-to-Door Opt-Out service (08457 950 950 or email optout@royalmail.com). To only stop credit-card mail, but still receive other unsolicited offers, you have to write to each card company separately, asking to be removed from their mailing list.

● **Bin credit-card cheques** Don't be fooled if your card company sends you blank cheques to spend. They look like ordinary cheques, but carry the same massive charges as a cash withdrawal on your credit card. This can mean a handling charge – say 2.5 per cent of the transaction value – and interest from the date of the transaction, and your purchases aren't protected in the same way that credit card purchases are. Resist temptation. Shred and bin these cheques as soon as they arrive.

REDUCE **YOUR BILLS**

19 SHARP MOVES to make sure you pay less

● **Make weekly menus** If you plan your meals for the week, then write out a shopping list to fit your menus, you'll be less susceptible to impulse buys when you enter the supermarket. Stores are deliberately laid out to take you past lots of tempting extras while you shop for staples. So decide in advance what you'll buy and stick to the list. And if you do need to drop into your supermarket for the odd item you've forgotten during the week, always use a basket. It's far too easy to start adding extras to a trolley.

● **Get the best deal** Before you set out, you could check which supermarket in your area offers the best overall deal for your weekly shopping list. Click on to www.mysupermarket.co.uk and enter your postcode; you'll be able to compare current prices for individual products that you're planning to buy. Remember also to go for own-brand goods whenever suitable products are available; they're usually cheaper than branded items of the same quality.

● **Go online or to a discount store** Another way to cut the cost might be to shop online. Prices are often cheaper and it's easier to stick to your list. But remember to factor in delivery charges. Discount stores, such as the local Lidl or Aldi, may also be good places to get your basics – milk, eggs, pasta, rice and flour – for less.

● **Buy in bulk** Buying in quantity is usually cheaper. It's particularly great for things that store well like pasta and rice, but you do need the space to keep them. If you don't or you're attracted by the savings on a bulk-buy of a perishable item, such as meat or cheese, why not shop with your parents or a friend and divide your purchases up between you.

● **Study sales patterns** They might not admit to this, but many supermarket chains discount foods at regular intervals – for example, a certain ice-cream might be half price once every four weeks.

Buying in quantity is usually cheaper ... great for things like pasta and rice

Other foods that are discounted on a regular basis include breads, orange juice, pasta sauce, apples, lettuce, chicken breasts, yoghurt and cereals. Once you're aware of the pattern, you need never buy these products at the full price. You could also make a habit of doing your supermarket shopping in the last hour or two before the store closes – that's when you'll find big discounts on perishable products, such as bread, meat, fish and many chilled items on the deli counter.

● **Collect coupons and vouchers** You'll find these in magazines, on websites (see www.ukfrenzy.co.uk) and some may even be delivered directly to your mobile phone. Or go straight to the source: pretty much every national brand has a website, and many of them provide printable coupons, so you can print out as many as you need, plus rebates and other special offers – sometimes including free samples.

● **Seek out double offers** While most retailers limit you to one discount at a time on a product, supermarkets often allow you to apply multiple discounts at the same time. For example, a store may be promoting a food product that you love and for which you have coupons. At moments like these, stock up if you can – you'll be getting a favourite food almost free of charge. If others have beaten you to it and the item you have vouchers for is out-of-stock, tell the supermarket manager. You'll probably be offered new vouchers that you can use later, when new stock is in.

● **Be discerning** Never buy anything, no matter how tempting the offer on it, unless you're really going to use it. BOGOFs (buy-one, get-one-free deals) are great, but only for goods that you use a lot and store well. They may be less of a bargain for perishable goods.

● **Use loyalty cards** The deals on these are not usually good enough to sway your choice of supermarket, but if you are shopping in a particular store anyway, you might as well make use of what that shop's card has to offer.

● **Keep your eye on the till** You may think that modern scanner systems don't make mistakes. But studies reveal that discrepancies between the price label and the scanned price occur in about 5 per cent of all cash-register transactions. So look closely at your bill and speak up if you spot an error.

HIDDEN TRUTHS What your bank or lender doesn't want you to know about **CHARGES**

• **Credit-card late-payment fees** Any charge over £12 is now generally deemed unfair, unless the card company can justify the extra. If you are charged more, you may be able to demand a refund.

• **Overdraft charges** The Office of Fair Trading is investigating this topic, but thus far the majority of people who have challenged high bank charges for unauthorised overdrafts have got a partial or full refund. Download a template claim letter from www.moneysavingexpert.com or www.which.co.uk

• **Mortgage exit fees** The Financial Services Authority (FSA) has said it is unfair for lenders to change the terms of the mortgage exit fee. Challenge your lender if this happens to you and also claim a refund if it has happened within the past six years.

• **Complaints** Contact the Financial Ombudsman Service on 0845 080 1800 or via their website (www.financial-ombudsman.org.uk).

HIDDEN TRUTHS

● **Try local markets** Low overheads mean these are often much cheaper than the supermarket. And try haggling – especially if it's late in the day, the fruit and veg are not of the best quality or you need an unusually large amount.

● **Plant herbs – not vegetables** Fresh herbs sold in supermarkets are incredibly expensive, no matter what time of the year you buy them. You can save a small fortune if you can harvest basil, oregano, thyme, mint and rosemary from your own garden. But you won't see the same cost benefit with vegetables. The week your courgette harvest comes in is usually the same week that it comes in at local farms – meaning the market stall or supermarket will be selling them at a heavy discount.

● **Learn to cook – with the seasons** Ditch the ready-meals and other convenience foods. Cooking from scratch is cheaper and it doesn't have to be time-consuming. Bookshops and charity shops are crammed with meals-in-minutes cookery books, so getting the know-how isn't costly either. And try to use ingredients that are in season – they'll cost less then and will probably be fresher and taste better too.

● **Be creative with leftovers** You'll be amazed by the delicious meals you can rustle up from the assortment of leftovers lingering in your fridge. Go to www.cookingbynumbers.com for some inspiration.

● **Forget loyalty** If you stick with the same gas, electricity, water, phone, broadband or digital TV provider year after year, chances are that you're paying over the odds. Be prepared to switch regularly to get the best deals. Checking what's on offer and making the switch is easy at www.uswitch.com Once you've found the best deal, it's always worth phoning your current supplier to say you are switching: they may offer you an improved deal to keep your custom.

● **Use online directory enquiries for F-R-E-E** 118 calls often have a fixed charge of around 20 to 70 pence plus additional per minute charges, but the same services are free if you access them online. There are around 200 providers, including www.192.com, www.118.com and www.bt.com Source one with Google if you don't already have a favourite. If you prefer the phone, you can call Freedirectoryenquiries on 0800 100 100 or The Number on 0800 118 3733. There is no charge, but you will hear advertisements during the calls.

● **Get free calls over the internet** If you have broadband internet service, then you can use your computer as a telephone at no charge. All you need is a headset with a microphone or a telephone that connects to a USB port on your computer, and some free software that you can download. Skype (www.skype.com) is the best-known internet phone service; it allows you to call any other similarly equipped computer around the world for free. If you both have webcams, you can make video calls. You can also use Skype to call landline phones and mobiles in the UK and overseas; there is a charge for this service, but it is less than making the call from a BT phone, for example.

● **Do your homework on mobiles** You could be throwing money away if you sign up for the wrong mobile package. If you're an infrequent user, a pay-as-you-go service might suit you better than a

Do your homework on mobiles ... you could be throwing money away

monthly pre-pay deal. But if you use your mobile a lot, then paying monthly is probably right for you. Think about when you make your calls – day, evening or weekend – and whether you text or talk and what networks your friends are on. Be wary of signing up to text-alert services and photo and video messages; these typically cost extra. Check out how you will be charged for internet downloads to your phone; paying by amount of content can be expensive.

● **Cut energy use** You'll pay less and help to fight global warming, too. See www.energysavingtrust.org.uk for ideas on how to conserve energy. These range from turning down your central heating by 1°C – saving about £40 a year – and fitting energy-saving lightbulbs – just one can save £100 over the lifetime of the bulb – to generating your own solar or wind power. There's information, too, about grants to help with the cost of energy-efficient home improvements.

SHARES & **INVESTMENTS**

3 **SMART STRATEGIES** to help you to determine if you have the right stockbroker

HIDDEN TRUTHS What financial advisers don't want you to know about COMMISSIONS

Using a financial adviser who is paid by commission from product providers makes the advice look free. But ultimately you pay the commission through the charges for the product you take out. It also means your adviser stands to gain by selling you one product that pays a higher commission instead of a better product that pays less, by selling you more than you want or by encouraging you to switch unnecessarily from your existing product to a new one. Truly independent advisers must either charge you a fee or offer you the choice of paying by fee or commission. If you choose the latter, ask for a commission rebate – you get back a share of the commission either as a cashback offer or through enhanced terms for the product you're buying.

● **Research the firm** To make sure that your stockbroker is legit, always check that the firm is registered with the Financial Services Authority (FSA) – www.fsa.gov.uk/register/home.do or 0845 606 1234. If the firm is on the register and listed as 'authorised', you get a range of protection when you use it, including checks on its solvency and probity, proper complaints procedure and access to a compensation scheme if things go wrong. If the firm is not on the FSA register, avoid it like the plague and notify the FSA. Such a firm is trading illegally and you will have no protection if you use it.

● **Steer clear of pushy brokers** Start worrying if your broker is pushing a particular stock, especially one that has been in the doldrums recently. Unscrupulous firms sometimes engage in what's known as a pump-and-dump scheme: they highly recommend a stock to their customers, the price rises as those customers buy it up and the brokers quickly sell their own shares of the stock behind the scenes, pocketing bucketloads of cash. It's an ugly practice – and it's illegal – but it does happen. This is also a favourite scam of offshore firms – often called 'boiler rooms' – that cold-call you out of the blue. Don't fall for it.

● **Be wary of 'hot tips'?** Does your broker constantly go on about his 'hot tips'. The odds of one broker knowing something the rest of them don't know are almost nil. By the time the 'secret' reaches you, chances are that the City high-fliers have already made their move on the stock, leaving latecomers little chance of making a profit.

secret weapon

PRICE-TO-CASH-FLOW RATIO

To pick successful stock, try the price-to-cash-flow ratio measure that many City analysts use. Get a company's report and accounts from its website, find its cash-flow from the operations statement and stop at the total before any deductions for dividend payments and acquisitions. That's the 'free cash-flow', the cash available to buy new assets, fund takeovers, pay dividends or buy back shares. Next, take the company's market capitalisation (published on the share pages of newpapers and websites) and divide it by the free cash-flow figure. This gives you the price-to-cash-flow ratio. You can feel pretty good about buying stock in a company with a price-to-cash ratio of ten or less. Don't like doing the maths? Your stockbroker should be able to get you the price-to-cash-flow ratio very easily.

INVESTMENT CAUTIONS

2 TRAPS to avoid in the pursuit of quick wealth

● **Sniff out investment scams** The moment you get a few extra pounds in your pocket, investment advice starts leaping at you from every area of your life – from a favourite uncle, from colleagues at work, from drinking buddies, from strangers on the telephone, from unsolicited emails, and from magazine ads. Greet all unsolicited investment suggestions with an enormous amount of scepticism. Here are seven signs of a possible investment scam trying to pluck the cash out of your wallet:
○ A promise that there's no risk
○ A promise that you'll get rich quick
○ A promise of tax sheltering in an 'offshore' investment
○ An offer of an offbeat investment in, for example, artwork, coins or jewels

○ A woeful story from a stranger who wants your help in accessing a large bank account or other funds
○ An investment based on information that, supposedly, no one else can access
○ An investment plan that asks you to recruit other investors

● **Wise-up on 'day-trading'** It sounds like the ideal life. Rather than toiling in an office or waiting at tables every day, you're going to sit at a computer at home in your pyjamas, making quick, buy-and-sell stock decisions and racking in masses of cash. Well, here's a reality check:
○ **Don't gamble away your livelihood** The truth is that most day-traders lose a lot of money. So never, ever day-trade with money you need for day-to-day living,

continued on page 224 ➡

6 secrets for BOOSTING your credit score

IN OUR MODERN SOCIETY, MOST PEOPLE PAY for all their major purchases – from houses to appliances and cars – with mortgages, personal loans or credit cards, so your credit rating is extremely important. The better it is, the more likely you are to get a good interest rate, and a few points difference in the rate can add up to a substantial amount of money over the life of a car loan or a house mortgage. **Here are some insider tips on keeping your credit rating in tip-top shape.**

1 ASK FOR LENIENCY The quickest path to a low credit score is making late payments on obligations such as your credit card, mortgage, or car payment. But if you're running short this month and have been a model borrower up to this point, there's an easy solution – call the lender and ask for an extension. Or ask if you can make a smaller payment this month. If you have a good track record, the chances are you'll get the OK and be able to keep your credit rating high. But keep in mind that this is a one-off strategy designed to give you a little breathing room. You can't call up month after month and expect to receive an extension from your lender.

2 SHRED YOUR FINANCIAL STATEMENTS The one surefire way to see your credit rating plummet is to get your identity stolen. Not only will it ruin your credit rating, but it's also going to take a lot of time, effort and patience to restore it to its previous high level. So how do you avoid this mess in the first place? Don't simply bin personal papers – shred them first. This includes bank statements, credit card bills and anything with financial information on it. Shredders range in price from £10 for an electric cross-cut shredder which cuts documents in two directions, to around £1,000 for one that turns your important financial documents into dust. In truth, a simple shredder is all you need. That's because crooks always take the easiest route. It's a lot easier to read a bank statement that was ripped in half than the one that was shredded into 50 pieces.

3 LIMIT THE NUMBER of credit applications you make. Never apply for more than, say, two credit cards or other loan deals at any one time. If a lender sees that you have applied for three or more cards or loans in a short period of time, it will probably assume you're in desperate need of cash – and desperate people do not make good credit risks. Even worse, it might think your identity has been stolen, which would also send your credit rating down the tubes.

Don't simply bin personal papers – shred them ...

4 PROJECT A STABLE IMAGE

The more settled and stable you seem, the higher your credit rating will be. For example, homeowners score more highly than renters, employees more highly than the self-employed. The longer you have been at your current address, in a job and with the same current bank account, the better your rating will be. Give your landline telephone number rather than just a mobile. If your circumstances are about to change – for instance, if you are about to move house or get divorced – try to make any loan applications before the change happens. Although all lenders use their own credit scoring system, you can get a good idea of how you are likely to score, using the free credit-score tool at www.checkmyfile.com

5 DON'T BE RUINED BY LATE PAYMENTS

Did you know that if you miss a payment deadline on one type of credit – say, your pre-pay mobile, car loan or a credit card – many credit-card companies reserve the right to raise your rate on their card because you are now deemed to be a higher credit risk? If you read the small print on your credit-card agreement, you may see wording such as 'we may make changes that are personal to you based on changes in your credit risk' – effectively what this means is that the interest rate you are charged by the credit-card company can be affected by how you run your accounts. Your low 0 per cent deal could skyrocket to 20 per cent. Remember, your credit reference agency information will be seen by anyone who's providing you with credit, and if you're making late payments to one lender, you can be sure all your credit-card companies are going to find out. Be sure to make your payments like clockwork, for example, by setting up standing orders and direct debits to make the payments automatically and ensuring you have enough money in your account to cover them.

6 CHECK YOUR CREDIT STATEMENTS

Identity theft is a multi-billion pound business now, and hordes of thieves are hoping you won't check your card statements. But if you check them as soon as you receive them – or, better still, manage your credit account online so you can check it between statement dates – you'll spot any criminal spending quickly and be able to take action. Check your hard-copy statement or go to your credit card company's website for information on how to get online access to your account.

... manage your credit account online so you can check it between statement dates

such as cash for covering household bills, pension and retirement plans and your children's university funding.

● **Understand the expenses** Day-traders often have to pay the company to which they're affiliated enormous commissions in exchange for training and equipment. They work with borrowed ('on margin') money and can quickly ring up large debts. Given these hefty expenses, have a clear idea of what it takes to turn a profit in this scenario.

● **There's no such thing as 'easy'** Day-trading requires you to be glued to a computer all day long, monitoring prices and trends. This is hard and nerve-wracking work. Anyone who tells you otherwise is fooling you.

● **Consider the source** Once you become known as a day-trader, you will be barraged with hot 'insider' advice, primarily from people who are trying to drive up their own investments. Don't act on this advice if you aren't sure of the source.

● **Check out that seminar** You may have been invited to find out about day-trading at a special seminar or workshop. Find out whether the instructor will benefit if you decide to become a day-trader. If so, the information provided may be seriously biased.

INSURANCE

6 INSIDER SECRETS to help you buy the right policies for yourself and your family

● **Be wary of income protection** Some income protection insurance pays out only if it's impossible for you to work at any job. For example, if an IT consultant could still earn a crust selling burgers, no insurance payout. Don't buy this kind of cover. Instead, ask your insurance company or broker for an 'own occupation' policy, as this will pay out if you're prevented from doing the job you have; for instance, if you're a writer and lose your ability to type, the insurance will pay the claim. You'll continue to get paid even if you change careers and go back to work, although the payout will reduce to take account of the earnings. This kind of insurance makes a lot of sense, considering that government figures show that 1 in 16 people of working age has been off work sick for more than six months.

● **Don't pay by instalments** Here's another reason for building up some savings: to pay your car or home insurance in a single lump sum when the annual renewal falls due. You'll pay over the odds if you spread the payments over 12 months. Insurers and brokers treat the outstanding premium as a loan and charge you interest on it, usually at a hefty 15 to 20 per cent.

● **Choose the right life cover** Don't be seduced by costly investment-type life policies, such as endowment insurance and whole-life policies, if all you need is protection. The cheapest way to get lots of cover is to choose term insurance; this pays out if you die during your chosen term, but pays out nothing if you survive. You can cut the cost even further if you opt for the type of term insurance called 'family income benefit'. If you die, it pays out a yearly income for the remaining term rather than paying out a fixed lump sum.

● **Factor in inflation** You've got your life cover and income protection insurance – great. But don't let the insurance companies catch you out later. Today's £5,000-a-month cover might be just pocket money in 50 years, so make sure inflation, and your own advancing age, don't get you in the end. When you buy your policy, you'll be faced with two choices for combating inflation: you can choose either to buy more cover at a later date, or to have the insurance company automatically increase your cover each year in line with inflation. Go for the latter, because if you have to buy added insurance down the road to keep up with inflation, you're going to be charged a price in relation to your then current age.

● **Know what's covered** Here's something that you need to know when it comes to your insurance, especially homeowners' policies: unless the policy specifically excludes something, the insurance company has to cover it. Let's use a wildly hypothetical example to explore this. Say aliens from the planet Xenon land in your living room and demand your self-cleaning oven. They claim they need it to get back to their homeland. Because they have their laser guns pointed at your dog, you allow them to take the oven. Now you need a new one, so you call your insurance company to file a claim. If you tell your insurers that aliens stole your oven, they'll probably say. 'Sorry, you're not covered for alien robbery.' Well, in fact, it's likely that your are, because if it isn't excluded on your policy, then it's included.

● **Forget about loyalty** Car, home and annual travel insurers often trumpet great deals for new customers, but a year later your renewal premium doesn't look so great. Firms rely on customer inertia – your tendency to renew automatically to make life easier. But you can usually save a lot of money if you shop around. It's easy; just go to a price comparison website, such as www.confused.com, www.uswitch.com, www.comparethe-market.com or www.moneysuper-market.com You can compare the quotes with a broker; contact the British Insurance Brokers Association (BIBA) on 0870 950 1790, or www.biba.org.uk

HIDDEN TRUTHS What shops, lenders and insurers don't want you to know about **PAYMENT PROTECTION INSURANCE (PPI)**

When you take out shop credit or a personal loan, you may be offered PPI, which covers your loan repayment for up to two years if you become unemployed or can't work due to illness. But think carefully, as this insurance is expensive, so will greatly increase your repayments, and is riddled with exclusions. Typically, there is no cover for claims arising from existing health conditions, for people working on short-term contracts, or for part-timers and the self-employed, and no unemployment cover at all for the first six months. Salespeople are keen to push PPI because of the fat commission they make. Recently the FSA has declared an end to the sale of single premium PPI alongside loans.

If you have been sold an unsuitable policy or were misled into believing that it was a compulsory part of the loan deal, check with www.which.co.uk/ppi, and then contact the insurer for a refund. If you are unhappy with its response, contact the Financial Ombudsman Service (0845 080 1800, www.financial-ombudsman.org.uk).

TAXES AND
ESTATE PLANNING

8 TOP TIPS for surviving tax returns, revenue enquiries, wills and probate

● **Check your tax code** The vast majority of the UK's 32 million income-taxpayers pay tax through PAYE (Pay As You Earn). You might think this means you can rely on your employer or pension provider to get your tax bill right. But according to the National Audit Office, 5.7 million PAYE taxpayers could be paying the wrong amount of tax. It reckons some £500 million is overpaid each year. And although the estimated £1 billion underpaid sounds like good news, it's not so sweet when the problem comes to light and back-payments are collected through hefty extra deductions from your salary or pension. So make sure your tax office sends you a coding notice every year and whenever your circumstances change. Check the code is right and also check each payslip as soon as it arrives. If you spot a problem, raise it with your employer, pension provider or tax office. Bear in mind, you can go back nearly six years to reclaim tax overpaid in the past.

Think twice before opting to work out your own tax bill ...

● **Don't work out your own taxes** If you are one of the 9 million people who has to fill in a self-assessment tax return each year, think twice before opting to work out your own tax bill: the UK tax system is notoriously complicated and it's easy to make mistakes. There is no need to struggle through the figures yourself: in most cases, you can get someone else to do it for free. From the 2009 returns, if you file a paper return, it has to be in by 31 October, but the Revenue will then work out your tax bill for you. If you file your return online, the HM Revenue & Custom's free tax software calculates the tax you owe. Another advantage of filing online is that the deadline for submitting your form is extended to 31 January. The Revenue's free tax software does not cover the most complex tax situations – for example, if you have income from trusts or capital gains, in which case your options are to let the Revenue crunch the numbers (so file by end of October), buy commercial software (see www.hmrc.gov.uk/efiling/sa_efiling/soft_dev.htm for a list), or pay for the help of an accountant or other tax adviser.

● **Use your allowances** The UK tax system doesn't offer many tax breaks these days, so it makes sense to make full use of the few that are available:

○ **Invest your full cash ISA allowance each year.** The interest is tax-free.

○ **Stocks and shares ISAs are tax-efficient** if you pay tax at the higher rate and, because income and gains from ISAs do not have to be declared on your tax return, they save you loads of tedious admin.

○ **Don't waste your capital gains** Consider investments that, instead of taxable income, produce a capital gain. You are allowed to make several thousand pounds a year of capital gains completely tax free.

● **Save yourself £100** If you pay tax through self-assessment, at the latest, your tax return must be in by 31 January following the end of the relevant tax year. If you're late, there's normally an automatic £100 penalty. Each year, the Revenue rakes in around £90 million in late filing penalties. Get organised and keep your money.

● **Get help for an enquiry** The Revenue generally has a year from the date you file your return within which to open an enquiry if it thinks you have declared too little income. Enquiries are

---

EXPERT ADVICE
GREAT TIPS FROM THE PROFESSIONALS

Big Brother's watching – here are some of the ways the Revenue can find out what you're up to:

● **Offshore alert** If your permanent home is in the UK, you are liable for tax on all your income from anywhere in the world. Banks have been forced to release records of customers who have – or have had – offshore accounts or credit cards linked to such accounts. As a result, the Revenue is poised to claw in huge amounts of tax from people who have not declared the interest they receive.

● **eBay blues** Usually there's no tax on money you make selling stuff you've cleared out of the attic. But if you buy in goods to resell, sell things you make, buy or sell on behalf of other people or sell services, the Revenue will say you are running a business and should pay income tax and maybe VAT too. The Revenue keeps a good watch on eBay and other online platforms.

● **Small ads** The Revenue also regularly scans classified ads to spot people who are working in the black economy without paying tax.

---

most likely if you are self-employed or you have complicated personal tax affairs, but some returns are chosen at random. Mainly, the Revenue uses a risk-based approach to selecting cases for enquiry. For example, if you are in business, it will compare your profits with other people in a similar line of work. If your profit margin looks out of step, it could look as if you're not declaring all your income or you're claiming excessive expenses. Expect the Revenue to be tough. You'll be made to feel guilty even if you haven't done anything wrong and the Revenue will demand all sorts of documents, some of which it has a right to see and maybe some which it does not. This is the time

... get someone else to do it for free

to get a professional on your side. If you do not already have an accountant or tax adviser, check out members of the Chartered Institute of Taxation (www.tax.org.uk). If you are on a low income (£15,000 a year before tax or less, £17,000 for those over 60), you might qualify for free help from Tax Aid (0845 120 3779, www.taxaid.org.uk) or Tax Help for Older People (0845 601 3321, www.litrg.org.uk).

● **Make a will** If you don't, the law decides who will inherit all your wordly goods. The law favours husbands, wives, civil partners and children, but cuts off unmarried partners and stepchildren without a bean. If you have no close relatives, your wealth could end up going to the Crown. Even if you are a classic married-with-two-kids type, the law can leave a mess with, say, your spouse having to sell the family home so that others can take the share the law says they should get.

● **Put your trust in trusts** Often your spouse or partner will need the use of your assets – especially your share of the family home – during their lifetime and after that you might want the assets to pass to your children. You can make sure this happens by setting up a suitable trust in your will. This is not a DIY job.

Enlist the help of a solicitor with experience in this area, for example, a member of the Society of Trust and Estate Practitioners (www.step.org).

● **Review your will to save tax** There may be inheritance tax on what you leave when you die, though everyone has a tax-free allowance (£325,000 in 2009–10 increasing to £350,000 by 2010–11). But anything you leave your husband, wife or civil partner is tax-free anyway. In the past, this meant if you left everything to your other half, you wasted your tax-free allowance and increased the size of their estate, often triggering a big tax bill when they died. But, from 9 October 2007 onwards, when a surviving spouse or civil partner dies, in addition to their own tax allowance, they get any unused allowance from their late partner (whenever they died). This extra allowance is given at the rate current at the time of the second death. For example, a widow dying in May 2010 could have a tax-free allowance of £750,000 if her late husband had used none of his allowance. Couples using will trusts miss out on the increase in the allowance between the two deaths. So, if you have a will trust, get your solicitor to check whether you would now be better off changing your will.

RETIREMENT
3 CLEVER MOVES for your career endgame

● **Play catch-up** Maybe during your first few decades of work, you failed to see the wisdom of squirrelling away cash for retirement when there were so many 'better' things to do with it. If you're now

age 50-plus, retirement is just around the corner and it is time to pause and take stock. Traditionally, two pieces of investing advice applied to those getting close to retirement, first, that it's never

... it's never too late to save ...

too late to save and, secondly, that it is worth making extra contributions to an existing occupational or personal pension plan. Now, the most sage advice is to work out exactly which investments will give you the best return on your money with the least risk and do this as soon as possible. The essential first step is to get independent financial advice and review the investments and pension plans that you already have in place.

● **Play smart with your offspring**
Children and grandchildren don't have to follow in your wanton footsteps. Anyone of any age can have a personal pension and anyone can pay into the plan for them. For a planholder without earnings, the maximum contributions on which tax relief is available are £3,600 a year. So you could start paying into a pension plan for each of your grandchildren. They'll really thank you for this head start later.

● **Work longer** If you want to carry on working and can afford to delay the point at which you start your retirement,

you can earn extra pension funds from both the state scheme and from any occupational and personal plans that you have. With the latter, for every year that you delay retirement, that's an extra year of earnings from which you can make contributions, plus an extra year's investment growth and one year less that your pension has to be paid out. All these factors boost your pension. On top of that, once you've reached state pension age, you can earn extra pension or, if you prefer, a lump sum, by putting off the start of your state pension. If you delay taking your pension for one extra year, you can earn either a 10.4 per cent increase in your pension for each year of deferral or a lump sum. For example, if you were entitled to £105 a week at 65 and delayed receiving your pension until you were 70 you would get £159.60 a week. That means that you would be getting an extra £2,839 a year of pension. Both the pension and the lump sum are taxable, but tax on the lump sum will be charged only at the top rate that you were paying before taking the lump sum into account.

secrets of
YOUR WORK

Everything that human resources left
out of the office manual

GETTING HIRED

9 INSIDER TIPS on what to do and what not to do when you are looking for a job

● **'Google' your own name** It may never have crossed your mind, but it is now quite possible that prospective employers will punch your name into an internet search engine to find out every little detail of your life that's posted online. 'Googling' job applicants is becoming standard practice, although it's not a practice that human resources directors are always happy to admit to.

Actually, getting 'googled' is a positive sign, because it means that a company is interested in you. But it also means that just about everything you've ever 'shared' in cyberspace is available for them to see and judge you by. You probably don't consider that this is fair – but it's a job-hunting reality these days.

Your first countermove is to do an internet search on yourself to see exactly what information on you is lurking out there. Then run through all the sites you have ever posted to – chat groups, discussion forums, friends' blogs or home pages, your own blog or home page and networking sites like MySpace or Facebook. If you find something you'd rather not have come up at a job interview – drunken beach-party photos, say, or an angry tirade you once wrote about the very industry you're trying to land a job in – see what you can do to make it disappear. Ask friends to take any potentially damaging photographs off their sites and check if more formal sites offer a 'private access only' option for their archived material.

You might be stuck with some of that embarrassing material that's been posted online. But at least you'll be aware of what a prospective employer might have seen and you'll have time to consider how to deal with it. And from now on, remember – never post anything on the internet that you wouldn't want to discuss at a job interview.

● **Give your letter character** Here's a secret straight out of the human resources office – you're being judged even before your CV is opened. Did you use stationery from your current employer when applying for your next job? Did you run your letter through the company franking machine? If so, the HR person receiving it is going to make some instant judgments about your character – and will probably drop your CV straight onto the reject pile.

Make sure that any correspondence you send to your future employer has a look that says 'this one is special'. Choose a good-quality, businesslike envelope and always address it to a specific person, such as the head of human resources or the person in charge of the department you're applying to. Use that person's name on the envelope, not just a title. Make sure you spell both their name and job title correctly – do some research if you have to. Stick a personal name and address sticker on the back, crisply printed in lettering that says, 'I am somebody'. You want to make an good impression. The best CV in the world won't do you any good if it doesn't get opened.

● **Use email like a professional** Are you applying for a job by email? If you are, then bear in mind that the person who reads your application might notice things that you don't. Rule number one is to always demonstrate your professionalism. Will an email address such as gogirl@yahoo.com be the first thing your prospective employer sees? That's hardly professional. Nor is using a jokey screen name or signing-off without giving sufficient contact information, because you're assuming the recipient will just hit 'Reply' to get back to you. It might also be a good idea to set up an email account that you use only for job applications.

Other things prospective employers will be looking at are your spelling and grammar. Forget about the sloppy typing that's connected with casual email culture. Proofread your covering letter and CV. If a recruitment officer see typos and poor grammar, you're unlikely to be considered for a job, even if your CV is managing-director material. If the staff in HR think that you don't care enough

to check for errors, they're unlikely to think you'll make a good employee. Also, remember that directing correspondence to a specific person, by name, is even more important when you're applying by email than by post. You can usually find out the names of HR personnel, as well as their email addresses, by checking a company's website. If you can't find the information online, ring and ask, or consult your local library for reference books that may provide this type of company data.

● Be prepared for a phone call
There's a new trend in HR departments that you should be aware of – they're likely to hit any job applicants that look promising with an unexpected phone call – as the first step in the interview procedure. It's nothing to worry or panic about. It's just that they've read your covering letter and CV and may have even checked your references and looked you up on the internet; now they want to learn a little more about you before committing to a face-to-face interview. So be prepared for that phone call and put some thought into how you might answer it, if it comes.

You may now be wondering what you should do if an HR manager phones at a bad time. Well, it's okay to say so. It's far better to arrange for them to call you back in an hour's time than to try to make a good impression while your children are screaming, the dog is

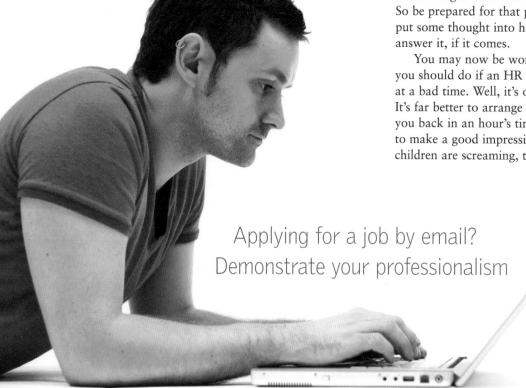

Applying for a job by email?
Demonstrate your professionalism

barking or dinner is boiling over on the stove. And giving yourself a little extra time to collect your thoughts is probably no bad thing either.

● Tout your skills, not your hopes

One of the most common CV formats calls for placing an 'objective' at the top of the first page. You may consider writing something like 'Experienced product designer seeks new challenges within an innovative company …'. But potential employers who read this are unlikely to be impressed – they really don't care what your hopes and ambitions are. What they want to know is what skills, talents and strengths you have that will benefit their company. Instead you should craft a concise, one or two-sentence 'positioning statement' at the top of your CV. And remember that this feature, in particular, should be individually tailored for every prospective employer you write to.

● Leap on job prospects

Have every element of your personal presentation ready, so that you can spring into action at a moment's notice – particularly a polished CV, samples of your work, if appropriate, and a list of references. If you see a classified ad for the ideal job in the weekend newspaper, you want your application on the recruitment manager's desk by Monday morning. Why? Because companies typically select candidates that are worth considering from the first batch of applicants. This approach may not be very scientific or wise on their part, but it's human nature. If you respond immediately, you could be getting called in for a job interview while other applicants are still dusting off their out-of-date CVs.

● Respect the HR interviewer

Many a job opportunity is lost because an applicant doesn't realise that the

---

EXPERT ADVICE
GREAT TIPS FROM THE PROFESSIONALS

How to crack that job interview

You'd probably make a fool of yourself if you tried to follow all the advice floating around on how to handle job interviews. Just stick to these simple tips:

• **Rehearse the interview** Have a friend play the role of interviewer and practise answering questions. Some career coaches even suggest interviewing for jobs you don't really want just to get used to the procedure.

• **Do a dry run** Make sure you get to your interview on time by doing the same journey the day before. Check on the best route and how long it takes to get there – door-to-door – allowing for any reasonable delays.

• **Dress to show you care** For most office jobs, that means a suit and tie for men, and a suit or something as smart for women. You're not making a fashion statement; you're showing the job is important to you.

• **Enter confidently** Never walk in while chatting on your mobile or finishing a drink. Walk in purposefully, smile and shake hands firmly.

• **Only bring what you need** Samples of work might help your cause. Shuffling through bulky folders won't.

---

person from human resources on the interview panel has as much say about whether you get hired as the head of the department with the vacancy. Often your first interview will be with a member of the HR team. Treat it as the real thing, not a preliminary formality, or you may never get beyond it. True, HR personnel usually don't have the expertise to assess your technical ability, but they're there to assess how well you are likely to fit into the company culture and make a useful team player. Also, good HR professionals usually make sure they know enough about the day-to-day workings of jobs in their company to ask intelligent questions about them.

'Lunch' is where you need to show ... that you can represent the company well to outsiders

● **Leave your personal life behind** In a job interview, avoid mentioning personal matters; focus solely on professional issues. If you blather on about your children or your marriage, the interviewer may assume that you will allow personal issues to intrude upon your work life as well.

● **Take the 'lunch' seriously** So, your potential boss and two other top company executives have invited you to lunch. It may seem like a nice, friendly gesture, but remember that it's really just a further step on in the interview procedure. Their motive is to evaluate you in a social setting. For some jobs – especially high-level ones – 'lunch' is where you need to show that you have good communication skills and that you can represent the company well to outsiders. Are you up to it? Of course you are. You wouldn't have made it this far if you weren't. But get the details right. Arrive on time. If the others order a pre-meal drink, feel relaxed by doing the same, but don't worry about not having one if you don't want it. They invited you, so let them pay. Turn off your mobile phone, your BlackBerry and any other gadget you have that might intrude. You're not impressing anybody about how busy you are by taking calls or messages during lunch. You need to show that you've come prepared to be totally focused on the matter at hand, as you would be if you were doing business for the company. Don't order the most expensive thing on the menu, but don't be a killjoy by saying something like, 'I think I'll just have a small salad today'. Order something you know and like. Show them that you can enjoy yourself and be professional at the same time.

Finally, feel free to cheat by checking out the restaurant in advance. If possible, familiarise yourself with the menu and wine list and even find out what the general dress code is and where the toilets are – anything that will help you to feel more at ease.

MAXIMISING YOUR REMUNERATION

5 IMPORTANT POINTS to keep in mind when you are negotiating your salary and benefits

● **Pin down the benefits** Don't accept a job offer without being clear about the benefits package you'll be getting, even if you're happy with the actual salary on offer. Sometimes a company can meet your requirements regarding pay, only because they are seriously skimping on any benefits you'll receive. As much as 40 per cent of a remuneration package may be made up of employee benefits. If the company is not prepared to make a decent contribution to your pension or there's no private medical cover being offered, that 'acceptable' salary is, in effect, considerably reduced.

● **Never undersell yourself** When you appear keen to take on a job, despite the low salary and inadequate benefits, you're probably assuming that the recruitment manager thinks you're eager to work for the company and are a good team player. And you hope that you'll be rewarded sometime in the future. Forget it. What the manager is actually thinking is that the company can get your skills at a cut-price rate. And the chances are that this won't change for years to come, no matter how good a job you do. A prospective employer expects you to ask for the salary – and benefits package – you think you deserve. Then you negotiate from there. You are not scoring any points by selling yourself off cheaply; you're only undermining your position.

● **Sympathy is not a factor** The person on the other side of the desk will probably nod with sympathy when you say you need better private medical cover or more money because your child or partner is ill. But that doesn't mean you're going to get it. The only thing on the HR manager's mind is negotiating in the best interests of the company. Push for what you think your skills and qualifications deserve, not for what you feel you need, based on personal circumstances.

● **Be patient about a pay increase** You have to build up to it. You not only have to do your own basic job well, but you need to take on extra responsibilities and acquire a reputation as someone who can get things done. When you do ask for an increase, have a list of your

---

EXPERT ADVICE
GREAT TIPS FROM THE PROFESSIONALS

Understanding a company's benefits package

Benefits packages can be confusing. But many companies like it that way, because it leaves you at their mercy. Here's a checklist that may help:
● **Start date** Do you get your benefits right away or only after a trial period?
● **Holidays** What is your annual entitlement? How does this increase with length of service? Do you lose any holiday allowance you don't take each year? How long can you take at once? Must any be taken at a set time, say over the Christmas or Easter break?
● **Pension scheme** How much does the company contribute? What are you likely to get on retirement?
● **Private medical insurance** Will you have to pay some of the premium? Is your family or partner covered? Are pre-existing conditions covered?
● **Disability and life insurance** What cover, if any, is provided? Do you have to pay anything towards it?
● **Childcare** Is it offered? Is it on-site? Is it free?
● **Training** Are work-related courses usually paid for?
● **Parking** Does it exist? Is it free?

---

achievements – and documentary evidence to back them up. If you can show where you've saved the company money or increased profits – even better.

● **Money isn't everything** If your request for a rise in salary is turned down, you may be able to get the equivalent of what you were asking for in better benefits. That could be a mix of an increase in pension contributions, longer paid holidays, better medical insurance or more flexible hours. But even though your boss may be in a position to boost your benefits and even think you deserve more, it will be your job to raise the issue.

GETTING AHEAD

9 SECRETS for honing that competitive edge and advancing your career

● **Find a mentor** The basic skills you use to do your job were almost certainly acquired by studying with a suitably qualified teacher. So why not learn the skills needed to advance your career from someone who has the relevant experience. Look out for someone who can offer you advice, act as a sounding board and give objective feedback and professional support.

Once you've done some people-watching in the workplace and found somebody you might want to enlist as your mentor, simply ingratiate yourself with that person. There doesn't have to be anything formal about a mentor-mentored relationship. First offer help. For example, you might show interest in a project he or she is working on. Ask if it is possible to help in order to gain experience. If you're graceful in your approach and not too pushy, and the person turns out to be a good choice, things may work out far better than you could imagine. Someone who's sharp enough to have become a success in the company, is likely to guess what you're up to, but will usually appreciate being picked out as your mentor.

● **Respect support staff** One of the main pipelines to useful information in a typical workplace runs through the administrative and support staff. Personal assistants and receptionists know this, but some of your colleagues may be too busy feeling superior to give them the time of day. So get ahead of the competition by making sure you're friendly, helpful and respectful to everyone in your organisation, both up and down the ladder. To succeed, you need informal as well as formal sources of information. And you can be sure that a good administrative or personal assistant will often be one of the first to know what's going on in the company. In fact, the best ones almost appear to know what's happening before it happens. So make it a habit of saying 'good morning' to everyone in your office and from time to time ask the receptionist 'what's new?'. You might occasionally get some very interesting and useful answers.

HIDDEN TRUTHS What your WORKPLACE COMPETITORS won't tell you about getting promotion

Simply being good at your job is never going to be enough to get you the promotion you think you deserve. If you don't fit in with the company culture, communicate well and stay informed, someone with less talent than you is going to pass you by on the way up the ladder. And you need to make sure that you expand your horizons beyond your own department, too. Don't be surprised to discover that your more successful colleagues have been busy building up contacts and making allies across the entire company. They've probably also joined professional associations and forged links with prime movers in other companies – because they know that useful information can come from outside their own workplace. While you stick firmly to the rules, they're willing to bend them a little and take a more creative approach in order to solve problems and get the job done efficiently.

● **Stop clock-watching** Good managers don't expect you to be a slave to the company. In fact, many bosses respect people who value and guard their private time. But if you consistently put in the minimum number of hours required, or insist on getting every available half-day off, or always take every single minute of your lunch break, no matter what deadlines are looming, you are sending out a clear message that what comes first for you, is definitely not your work. A better approach is to show you're willing to adjust your schedule, where necessary, to get things done and that you're passionate about your job. More than anything, managers love a worker they can depend on, especially in a crisis or when time is tight. Show you can be trusted and are flexible – and the free time you need will probably take care of itself.

● **Demonstrate your involvement**
If you're really focused on your work, you may be able to spot areas where problems could arise in the future and pehaps suggest innovative solutions that will nip them in the bud. Never ever criticise the current set-up; instead offer constructive, practical solutions and, if appropriate, time to help to implement them. Your interest in the company and your commitment to its success are likely to be noticed – and rewarded at some time in the near future.

● **Keep up with new technology**
An estimated 80 per cent of jobs in the modern workplace involve the daily use of a computer. So go out of your way to learn all the computer skills you need to thrive at work. Then go to the next step and monitor what's hot in terms of electronic gear, software and websites. No work manual will tell you this, but people who are savvy about technology often move ahead faster than people who don't care about it or who shy away from learning the software packages that will make their work more productive and give it an edge.

● **Write power-packed emails**
Emails are key to communication in the office. Yet, as a rule, they are badly written. So by consistently sending sharp, well-composed electronic messages, you will make yourself stand out from the crowd. Take careful note of the following:

✎ **Hone your subject line** Try to be more specific. Instead of giving your email the name 'Byrne project', call it 'Byrne project: new deadline for phase 2'. Your email is already more interesting than most.

✎ **Don't bury the lead** If you want to annoy people, make them read three paragraphs before you get to the point. If you want to rise in the company, state your purpose in the first sentence or two and then get to the why and how of the matter.

✎ **Request further action** End emails with a suggestion or a request for action. An example would be: 'I will call you on Monday at 10am to discuss this' or 'When can we get this done?'. Otherwise, nothing is likely to happen.

✎ **Be human** People who would never dream of being cold and abrupt in person, often come across that way in their emails. Being businesslike doesn't mean being impersonal. Try to remember that the recipient, like you, is a human being.

✎ **Proof your email** Just one misspelling, grammatical error or typo can make a sender look careless and disrespectful. Sending 'clean' emails lifts you above the sloppy crowd.

Stop clock-watching ... show you're willing to adjust your schedule

How they do it . . .

self-promotion

Before careers' adviser Dale Kurow starting helping others to get ahead, she was doing the hiring and promoting herself, as part of the human resources team at a major company. It was there she learned a key trick: 'I once had a boss who was trying to get me fired, but it had more to do with his problems … than my performance. I knew I was doing a good job, so I asked colleagues to let him know that. They did and everything turned out fine.'

The moral of the story is not to wait until there's trouble. Enlist others to sing your praises, when the need arises. Dale suggests that if your colleagues or another manager tells you how good a job you're doing, make sure that that message is passed on to your boss. Ask the person who said it to do this. It's more effective than doing it yourself, because the praise comes from a third party.

✏ **Check the address** Always make sure that you are sending your emails to the right person. It's so easy to press the 'send' button, only to discover that your message is heading straight to the desk of the very person you don't want to see it. Be especially careful about the content. You never know who may unwittingly forward your email on.

✏ **Behave yourself** Avoid sensitive subjects, such as sex, race, age, religion and disabilities. Apart from being inappropriate email topics, especially in the workplace, you could find yourself in a lot of trouble over them. You may not think you are causing any harm, but others may think differently. You could end with a discrimination claim being made against you.

✏ **Stop copying in everybody** All you're doing is irritating people who are not directly involved in the project.

✏ **Pick up the phone** If you have to spend more than 5 minutes on an email, call instead. It's easier to explain things on the phone, and you can always follow up with a shorter email to confirm the details of your conversation. In some cases, it might be even better to make face-to-face contact.

● **Read the trade journals** Every industry has newsletters, magazines and websites devoted to it. Subscribe to the ones that are relevant to your work. You'll learn about current trends, the competition and maybe even a thing or two about your own company. You'll be more knowledgeable about your job and may benefit by impressing managers and colleagues with your expertise.

● **Manage 'sideways' and 'up' too** If you're a manager, don't just focus on the people you oversee. You need to manage your peers – those on the same level as you – and your bosses as well. These two groups are often harder to win over than those working under you. But when your peers respect you and your bosses appreciate the way you communicate with and assist them, you increase your value to the company.

● **Never let your boss be surprised** This is one of the unstated rules of workplace survival – don't let your boss learn about bad news, angry customers or even positive developments from anyone but you. There is nothing worse for a senior manager than not being up on the latest news – and to then hear all about it from an angry superior or a cut-throat peer. So make it a policy to keep tuned into what's happening around you and to let your boss know quickly about anything of note that is going on – good or bad. You may be well rewarded for your efforts.

OFFICE POLITICS

4 CLEVER TACTICS for dealing with the variety of human interactions you encounter in the workplace

● Learn to love office politics

Hard workers may not want to hear this, but 'keeping your nose to the grindstone' – that is, concentrating solely on the job at hand – is a strategy for failure. You may think it's admirable to stay away from office politics, but all it really means is that you're limiting your potential. 'Office politics' is just a term for the range of human interactions that go on in any workplace. Being involved in office politics doesn't have to be something cold and calculating. It is simply about forging links with those around you, which means you're more likely to be involved in your job, helping you to do it better and have a more successful career.

So the most important tip concerning office politics is to get good at it. Do what real politicians do – form strategic alliances. Establish relationships with some peers, some superiors and some below you in the hierarchy. Go out of your way to help a person you like or respect. Then ask that person to help you. That may lead to a link with somebody else as well. If not, create a second link yourself, then a third.

Cultivate these work relationships. No matter how well you do your job, you're going to need allies to help you up the ladder. That's why you need to be involved in office politics.

● Mix business with pleasure The

advice you usually get is to keep your social life separate from your work life. But not only are office friendships natural, they're also essential if you want to shine. Friends make for loyal allies, honest advisers, information sources and links to other allies, advisers and sources. So by all means, cultivate friendships at work.

But don't limit your socialising to individual relationships. Try not to miss the company boat trip, quiz night or Christmas party. Even if you'd rather stay at home, make an effort to go to at least a few of these events. They offer priceless opportunities for making connections with others in a more relaxed setting.

● Keep an eye on fellow workers

You'll never find this in the employees' manual, but the most useful habit you can develop at work is to carefully

HIDDEN TRUTHS What your **SAVVY COLLEAGUES** don't want you to know about office politics

You're involved in office politics whether you like it or not. Staying aloof can mean you're perceived as lacking in social skills and not a 'people person', deserving of promotion. Managers like the creativity that can arise from employee interaction and the stability that can result from in-house relationships, since studies show that those who socialise at work are less likely to leave. In fact, managers often like to watch office interactions closely to see who swims best in the office-politics pool.

But there's no shortage of people who mistakenly think that bad-mouthing is what office politics is all about. A good office politician makes alliances, not enemies.

Hear it through the grapevine ... it can be priceless

observe your colleagues' actions and behaviour. And the best time to do it is when they don't know you're watching. Start looking from the first day on the job and don't stop until you get your gold watch. Watch everybody – your peers, subordinates and superiors. Watch them at meetings, at parties, at lunch and during the workday routine. Eavesdrop when you can – without being sneaky, of course. Observe body language. Use small-talk to probe.

Here are some of the things you're looking for when you're new: who takes lunch together; who does what at lunch (staff restaurant, packed lunch, the gym or a run); who commutes together; who laughs at whose jokes; who supports whom at meetings; who comes in early; who stays late. Learn your fellow employees' individual interests, their status in the office, their family situations and their hobbies. Notice how they talk and the tone of voice they use. Discern their values and their tastes. You need to care about all this information, because it constitutes the workplace culture in which you're operating. It's the raw material of your success. It will help you to make better decisions, make it more likely that you'll spot opportunities and, when you do, enable you to act on them more efficiently. For example, your surveillance reveals to you that Mary in IT is an avid collector of dolls. A month later you run across an article on a famous person who is also a doll collector, so you can pass it along to her, saying you thought she might be interested. Then in a few months time, when you need urgent help from IT on a project, you'll have a casual contact in that department.

Are you spying on people by doing this. Not really, because you're not seeking information to use against them. You're seeking information in order to work with them – albeit for your own benefit. Besides, a lot of your colleagues will be watching you too.

● Hear it through the grapevine

As a source of factual information, the company grapevine is by definition unreliable, since rumours aren't facts. But as a barometer of workplace mood and attitude, the grapevine a very good thing to be tuned into. And as an indicator of what the future may hold, it can be priceless. But there's another reason for the grapevine's value that you're not supposed to know about – that is that the management uses it to float ideas, to test employee reactions to possible new policies and to slowly break the news of likely redundancies. You can't afford to ignore the grapevine.

Find out who the grapevine's main perpetrators are. Then, instead of shunning them as hopeless gossips, cultivate them as sources of vital information. But never take their word at face value. Register it and then follow it up to find out how accurate it is. Remember that, in the world of office politics, information passed on in this informal manner can be just as valuable as information that is conveyed by more formal means. And, in many cases, if you know that the top brass is monitoring your reaction to all the rumours that are being put about, you can make sure that you respond in ways that will make you look good.

LEGAL PROBLEMS

3 WISE WAYS to handle difficulties arising from
harassment and discrimination on the job

● **After complaining, stick it out**
Once you lodge an official complaint
that you've been a victim of harassment
at work, the company management may
try to make your life difficult by giving
you dead-end projects that are almost
impossible to complete or overburdening
you with unnecessary paperwork. Their
secret goal is to get you to resign – but
don't. Once the company can claim you
'abandoned' your job, your harassment
case will become so weak that no lawyer
is likely to take it on.

But if you can prove you're being
treated unfairly – simply because you've
already registered a complaint – you
may be able to sue your employer for
victimisation as well. If fact, you're far
more likely to win an award on those
grounds than on the original harassment
issue. So make sure you keep a detailed
record of all post-complaint actions that
smack of victimisation – even if they're
so subtle that you feel they will be hard
to pin down. Leave it to your lawyer to
select the evidence that's most relevant
to your case.

● **Don't be put off** Employers often
try to spread the word that taking out
a harassment or discrimination case
against them is a losing proposition.
And, in general, they've been successful
at making employees think that there's
little chance of winning and even less
chance of collecting a worthwhile sum
of money. They wouldn't want you to
know that punitive damages are not as
rare as you've been led to believe. They
don't want the truth to get out – that
you really can't lose in most cases. If you
win, your employer will have to pay

EXPERT ADVICE
GREAT TIPS FROM THE PROFESSIONALS

How to document discrimination on the job

At the first sign of any discriminatory behaviour or
harassment, start making a record of what took place.
Keep a diary in which you write down the date and
time when anything you consider might relate to your
case occurred, along with where it happened, who did
what and who witnessed it. Make sure you also keep
any documentary evidence, even if it doesn't amount to
much on its own. A note or email with, for example, an
ethnic slur that possibly refers to you, should go
straight into your discrimination case file. If the
offence is a public one, such as a racist or sexist
cartoon being posted on the toilet door, you have the
legal right to take it down and copy it, or even keep
the original in your file.

But note that, tempting as it may be, there's no
point in taping any conversations you may have with
the person who you feel is discriminating against you
or harassing you. These recordings will not be
admissible as evidence at a tribunal.

---

your legal fees, but if you lose there is
only a slight chance you'll have to pay
theirs. And these days, many legal
practices offer a 'no win, no fee'
arrangement for such cases.

If your case is solid, judgment in
your favour is likely and could involve a
considerable amount of money as
recompense. After all, discrimination
and harassment are odious practices.

● **Get counselling** It's not uncommon for victims of discrimination, bullying or harassment at work to suffer from depression or other debilitating mental conditions, such as post-traumatic stress disorder. But it's also not uncommon for such victims to refuse counselling, or at least to put it off until their cases are resolved. That's a big mistake. By seeking out professional care for any health problems relating to your case, you're not only making sure that you're getting the support you need to deal with your situation, you're helping yourself from a legal point of view, too. The mere fact that the conditions surrounding your poor treatment at work – and the resultant legal action – have led to you seeking treatment from a mental health expert is highly likely to increase any award that might be offered to you by a tribunal.

GETTING FIRED

8 KEY ACTIONS you should consider taking if you are about to lose your job

● **Ask for a reference** How crazy is it to ask somebody who has just fired you to provide a reference for your next job? Under the circumstances, what are your chances of getting a positive one? Well, it's certainly not crazy and the chances of walking out with a decent reference are better than you might think. In fact, it's always worth trying to negotiate some sort of reference before you empty out your desk or locker and leave. Securing some sort of reference will help to diffuse any worries you may have about explaining your exit to prospective future employers.

And here's the good news. These days, employers are so worried about possible legal issues that can result from giving a poor reference, that you'll find that they're generally very limited on detail. They will often just confirm your job title and dates of employment – and only occasionally give details of reasons for leaving. So unless you've been fired for gross misconduct – in other words, you've done something really bad, such as punching a colleague – your employers will be loth to say anything negative about you in a reference.

In some cases, particularly if you've entered into a compromise agreement with your employers (see page 244), a reference may be included as part of the package. But don't always bank on this. Many companies are happy to say they will provide a good reference in order to get you to sign on the dotted line of a severance package that suits them. Then the reference is soon forgotten about.

● **Approach a friendly manager** If the company itself won't provide a reference, seek out another high-ranking colleague – a supervisor, a manager in another department with whom you worked regularly and well, or a respected veteran. Even if that person cannot go on record with a formal letter on your behalf, he or she may agree to be listed as a reference and will be happy to speak well of you if telephoned by a prospective employer.

● Quit before you're fired You may remember the old cliché: 'You can't fire me, because I quit!' This line is usually heard in films, when a character says it to save their pride. But in real life, resigning before it gets to an unpleasant dismissal does make more sense if you're truly dissatisfied with your job. Your boss may have noticed something you haven't – that your performance has been suffering recently. The real forbidden knowledge in this case may be something you're keeping from yourself – that deep down inside, you know you're slacking because, frankly, you hate your job. You may even subconsciously want to be fired. If that's the case, the solution is to start looking for another job right away.

Don't just resign; the best time to look for a new job is when you already have one. You will then retain the security of a regular salary coming in, and still be out there in the working world with all its energy and useful connections, instead of making phone calls from the isolation of your kitchen table. Don't feel guilty about looking while you're working; in fact, it's likely that you'll be doing your current job far better, fueled with new energy because you have finally made a constructive decision about your future.

Be honest with prospective employers about your current situation. And do tell your current boss about your plans too – but not straight away. First decide what you're really looking for. Then send out a batch of CVs and wait until you've had favourable responses and the prospect of a job offer before breaking the news. Your boss may be hurt or even angry, but if your poor performance and attitude have been noticed, he or she may also be relieved that the situation is moving towards a solution that won't include a messy dismissal.

Quit before you're fired ...

● Ask for a promotion Here's a variation on your pre-emptive dodge-the-axe strategy. After you've done some soul-searching, you decide that you're so dissatisfied with your job that resigning is the best solution. Your next move is to march straight into the boss's office – not to say you're leaving, but to air your grievances. Say how you feel, state clearly what you want and ask what plans, if any, the company really has for your future in the company. What have you got to lose?

You may wonder why you should bother to take this approach, if you're thinking of leaving anyway? Well, it's because that's the best time to do it.

Voicing your desires provides a context when you do give notice and may even help to make what you're seeking much clearer in your own mind, as you look for a new job. But be aware that your employer may be sympathetic to your problems and offer to help to improve your conditions of employment. You may end up not resigning after all. Sometimes an employer has no idea that you have any difficulties with your job and, if your work is satisfactory and valued, may make an effort to accommodate your concerns. And if you're not valued enough for them to do that, then you'll know that your decision to leave was certainly the right one.

HIDDEN TRUTHS What HUMAN RESOURCES may avoid telling you about holiday entitlement

By law, all full-time workers in the UK should receive at least 28 days paid holiday a year, including bank holidays. It is also a legal requirement that an employee has a written contract of employment, stating exactly what their holiday entitlement is. Even if you've signed a contract giving you less paid holiday than the statutory minimum, you're still entitled to receive it. Part-time workers are covered, too. For example, if you work two days a week, you are legally entitled to two-fifths of the statutory 28 days. Never be afraid about raising the issue with your boss, if you think you're missing out – remember, the law is on your side.
Also, check if you're due any money in lieu of unused holiday entitlement when you leave a job. Your contract should make this issue clear but, if it doesn't and HR are less than helpful when asked, consult your local Citizens Advice Bureau.

● **Learn to compromise** If, when you express your dissatisfaction with your job, your boss decides that the current situation is untenable, you may be offered what is known as a compromise agreement. This means that your employer agrees to terminate your contract of employment by offering a package of, say, a one-off severance payment and a good reference. In exchange, you must agree not to air any of your grievances in public or to sue the company for unfair dismissal. A compromise agreement may not be appropriate for your situation, so don't be surprised if you're not offered one. But if you are, consider it carefully. It could be you're best option. And make sure you check all the details of the agreement very thoroughly before you sign on the dotted line. The wisest way to deal with it is to hire a lawyer to represent you and make sure you get the best possible deal. And, if you're considering doing this, the good news, is that your employer will have to pay your legal fees.

● **Turn getting fired into an asset** The moment of truth has arrived – when an interviewer asks you why you left your previous job. Don't panic. You can handle it if you know what the people interviewing you are really thinking. Prospective employers are not interested in being your judge and jury, nor are they interested in rescuing your career. All they're trying to ascertain is if there's a problem or not with your attitude and approach to your work.

Don't plead your case. Don't try to defend yourself with detailed complaints about what 'they' did to you. Don't be morose or express anger or bitterness over the situation. And, most important of all, don't bad-mouth anybody. All that you will accomplish with such defensive behaviour is to convince your would-be employer that the business of your dismissal is still festering. They may be worried that this may affect the way you handle all future business dealings.

Instead, compose a carefully considered response, well in advance of your interview. Spend some time putting together three or four sentences that sum up how you have dealt with, understood and moved on from your dismissal. Rehearse this little speech over and over again, until it begins to sound believable and will leave the interviewer wondering how you could have possibly stayed on in your job under the circumstances you describe. Close with something like this: 'It was one of those unfortunate situations that was bound to end in a parting of company, and they took action before I did. I realise now that I should have expressed my own concerns about the job, instead of letting things fester, but I've learned from the experience.' If you put this type of positive spin on the situation, a prospective employer will usually accept it and may even be impressed by your ability to handle problems and to learn something from them.

● **Call the Benefits Agency** Even if you've managed to walk away from your old job with several weeks' or months' worth of severance pay, you should still contact your local Benefits Agency to inform them of your situation and to find out what, if any, benefits may be available to you and when you can claim them. There are many different options on offer, depending on the circumstances under which you left your job. So make sure that you're not missing out on something that you may be entitled to. Get on the phone immediately – some benefits take longer to sort out than you might think.

Get on the phone immediately – some benefits take longer to sort than you might think

● **Ashamed? Get over it**
You might never have imagined that someone as skilled and talented as you could possibly be without paid employment for an extended period of time. What's more, the idea of filing for unemployment benefits makes you feel uneasy. It's as if you're asking for a handout, when you're not actually destitute. Get past that mental block. If your car or your home got damaged, you would happily accept money from your insurance company to cover any necessary repairs and other problems that arise. Unemployment benefits are just another form of insurance, that happens to be run by the government. Anyway, you've been contributing your hard-earned cash – year after year, while you were gainfully employed – to the funds from which any benefits you receive are drawn. So don't feel embarrassed about accepting what's on offer. Take it with a clean conscience – after all, you've worked hard for it.

secrets for
YOUR SAFETY

Tips to protect you and your property
from thieves and rogues

HOME SECURITY

6 BASIC PRECAUTIONS that will deter burglars from targeting your home

● **Safety-check your front door**
You'll feel safe and secure knowing that you have good-quality security locks fitted to your front door, and it may save you money on your house insurance as well. Most new plastic doors will have good security built in, but if you live in a house with timber doors, start by checking the door and frame. The harder, thicker and stronger the timber, the better. If the door frame is a thin section and could break if the door were pushed really hard, reinforce the internal side with a long strip of flat steel, known as a London bar. This is screwed to the frame and has a D-shaped section to secure the lock staple. To add strength to the hinge side of the door and frame, fit two hinge bolts.

● **Update your locks** The simple surface-mounted night latch found on many front doors is easily opened by a burglar. It is worth replacing it with a surface-mounted rim lock, which can be deadlocked. This type of lock cannot be opened without a key after it has been locked from the outside and the inside handle cannot be forced if a burglar breaks a glass door panel or window. Most insurance companies also require you to have a five-lever mortise lock.

● **Check the lock's Kitemark**
When choosing locks for external doors, check for the British Standards Institution Kitemark and the number BS 3621:2004, which ensures that the lock is made to a reasonable standard. If in doubt, check with a locksmith or consult your local crime prevention officer.

● **Fit a door viewer** If your door has no glazing, fit a door viewer so that you can see who is on the other side before opening the door. To avoid callers forcing their way in after you've opened the door, fit a strong door chain on the inside of the door, just below the lock. Having an outside light fitted above your front door will also help you to see night visitors. And when your front door security is up to scratch, move on to upgrading your back door and any other external doors.

HIDDEN TRUTHS What **BURGLARS** don't want you to know about break-ins

• **Burglars don't just work at night**, they're equally likely to strike during the day if a house appears to be empty. A favourite tactic is to knock on your front door. If nobody's home, they can look for a hidden key or an open window (Home Office statistics reveal that in nearly half of all burglaries there is no forced entry), or try to kick the door in.
• **They hate barking dogs** Even a small dog will help to protect a home, as long as it barks loudly when strangers approach. Put up a 'Beware of the Dog' sign. If you can't have a dog, or don't want one, you could get a recording of a dog barking to play every now and again (and have it running on your answering machine's message).
• **They don't care if your income is modest** The average burglar wants small, easy-to grab and easy-to-sell items – like laptops, DVD players, watches, jewellery, CDs and mobile phones.

HIDDEN TRUTHS

WOOF WOOF!

Burglars ... hate barking dogs

Simple window catches or stays that do not have a key to lock them are a potential weak point. Burglars' most common method of breaking in is to smash the glass on a small window, lean in and release the catch. To upgrade your window security, replace simple catches with locking ones, fit a type of lock to the existing catch or stay that locks it in position, or fit separate window locks.

● **Do these seven things too**
Thieves usually go for easy pickings. So they won't normally target homes that don't offer easy access:

● **Secure your windows** According to Home Office statistics, a third of burglars get in through the window. Security-system installers want you to believe that barred windows are the solution but, unless you live in a high risk area, the truth is that burglars are usually looking for open windows. (Drive around any residential area and you'll be amazed at how many windows are left open.) Just closing and locking your windows makes your home much safer. In fact, houses with simple security measures such as window locks are ten times less likely to be burgled than those with no security measures in place.

★ Keep ladders locked away.
★ Padlock sheds that house equipment.
★ Install security lights that operate when movement is detected outside.
★ Never attach a name tag to your keys and don't leave spare keys in obvious places.
★ Cancel milk and paper deliveries when you go on holiday.
★ Buy a timer to switch on lights at different times when you're away.
★ Find out how secure your home is at www.homeoffice.gov.uk/secureyourhome and see how you can improve things.

PERSONAL SECURITY

6 EXPERT SAFETY TIPS that can save your life

● **Don't be an easy target** You know the cliché: 'It can happen to anybody.' But criminologists know something else – that muggers pick on people who walk along looking lost, distracted or vulnerable. Don't be like them. Stay aware of your surroundings and adopt purposeful, assertive body language that projects confidence. The government's Crime Prevention Team advices the following:

★ If you think someone's following you, check by crossing the street, several times if necessary and make for a crowded place if you're still worried.

★ Avoid short-cuts through dark alleys, parks or over waste ground.

★ Walk facing traffic so a car can't pull up behind you unnoticed.

★ Hold a handbag firmly with the clasp facing inwards and carry house keys separately in a pocket.

★ Hide an expensive watch or jewellery. But, if you are unlucky enough to be mugged, give up your property; your safety is more important.

● **Get an alarm** If you often walk home alone in the dark, you should get a personal attack alarm, says the Crime Prevention Team. Ask at a DIY store or take advice from the crime prevention officer at your local police station. Carry it in your hand so you can immediately scare off an attacker, and choose a model that continues to sound if it falls to the ground.

● **Stay safe in taxis** When taking a taxi or private hire vehicle, make sure it is licensed by checking its signage or plate or the driver's badge. If travelling alone always sit in the back seat and, if you're at all concerned or feel uneasy, simply ask to be let out in a well-lit public area where there are plenty of people. At night, when you reach your destination, ask the driver to wait until you have gone inside.

● **Safety on public transport** Being alone at night makes you vulnerable. Stay away from isolated bus stops after dark. If you get onto a near-empty bus or it empties during the journey, sit near the driver. On an overground or underground train, choose a compartment where there are other people and make a mental note of where the emergency chain is.

● **Don't bring your stalker home** If someone is following you, your natural instinct may be to get home as quickly as you can and lock the doors. In truth, though, heading for home is a bad idea – you don't want your stalker to know where you live. If you're being followed, never lead the person back to your home. Do not stop or get out of the car. Drive to the nearest public place where you'll be able to call the police. 'If you think you're being stalked while on foot, don't wait to be sure. Use your mobile phone to call the police immediately while heading for a busy place with lots of people,' says Daniel Riley of the Suzy Lamplugh Trust, the national charity for personal safety. If you don't have a personal alarm, make as much noise as possible to attract attention. 'Scream, run, yell if you are able,' says Riley.

● **Repel a potential rapist** Stay calm. That's the key message from personal safety expert, Sarah Haddon. 'If you panic, it will be difficult to think of your available options. Focus on your breathing. Then, assess your situation – what are the available escape routes? Can you activate a personal alarm? Can you shout or scream? Does the attacker have a weapon?' Sarah adds, 'These considerations can help you to evaluate the best course of action. If you call for help, be specific – "Call the police! I'm being attacked!" Or you might pretend to be sick or claim to have an STD (sexually transmitted disease). These options are not risk free but in a situation where your safety is at risk, you may want to try whatever you can.'

TELEPHONE
TRICKS & TIPS

6 CLEVER WAYS to stop eavesdroppers, unwanted calls, premium rate charges and text scams

● **Find out if someone is tapping your phone** More than 200,000 electronic bugging devices and covert cameras are sold in Britain every year and possibly used by stalkers, snoopers, jealous spouses and a range of other unsavoury characters, according to a BBC website. Buying and selling bugging equipment is not illegal in the UK, although phone tapping is and punishable with a £1,000 fine.

Although bugs are generally hard to find without highly sophisticated equipment, Peter Heims, past president of the Association of British Investigators, has revealed one simple way to track them down. All bugs go out on the FM wavelength, so they can be detected with a small portable FM set, which will emit feedback – a high pitched noise – if you go through the wavelengths and find the one that the bug is operating on. The bug will be hidden where the feedback is noisiest. 'It is an amateur way and it actually works', Heims told a BBC forum.

● **Banish unsolicited phone calls** You're sitting down to Sunday lunch when the phone rings. You rush to pick it up and someone – irritatingly – presses you to buy their company's double glazing. The easiest way to stop such unsolicited sales and marketing calls to

---

EXPERT ADVICE
GREAT TIPS FROM THE PROFESSIONALS

How to find out a caller's location

Ever had a mystery caller? Or perhaps a worrying, malicious call from an unknown source? On landlines throughout the United Kingdom, you can now usually trace the caller thanks to visual display units or 'caller return' services that most phone service providers supply. Although a malicious caller can withhold their number, the police or a phone service provider can still trace the caller's number if it is reported as a nuisance call. If you are receiving malicious calls or text messages on your mobile phone, do not delete them if you wish to make a formal complaint. Keep a log and keep all caller numbers or IDs. The police can then investigate and you may be asked to make a statement.

Find out if someone's tapping your phone

your home landline or mobile phone is to register with the Telephone Preference Service (TPS) www.tpsonline.org.uk/tps/

If you're registered, it is then illegal for any organisation, including charities, voluntary organisations and political parties, to call you without your consent. While the TPS protects mobile phone users from unwanted calls, you may still receive unwanted SMS marketing messages (texts) and will have to send an 'opt-out' request to the company concerned to stop these.

● **Stop the silent treatment** It is also intimidating to receive calls when the phone rings and there is no one there. The explanation may be innocuous: some silent calls are generated by automatic dialling equipment which dials more numbers than there are operators available to handle the calls. But if you have worries ring the Telephone Preference Service on 0870 443969 and protect yourself against this intrusion by registering with

the Silent Callgard Service on 0844 372 2325. This and all the TPS services are free of charge.

● **Ban recorded messages** Equally irritating are the sales and marketing calls you try to field and then discover that you're listening to a recording. The company responsible must stop if you ask them to. But if you can't track them down, complain directly to the Information Commissioner's Office (ICO), the government body responsible for enforcing the regulations. Phone their helpline on 01625 545745 or see their website at www.ico.gov.uk

● **Beware of premium rate services** They can be useful and even entertaining but premium rate numbers will also send your phone bill rocketing sky high. Such services, which provide weather information, offer competitions and message exchange services usually start with '090' while services of an adult nature start with '0909'. If you don't want anyone to dial these numbers from your family phone or computer, you can contact your phone service provider and have them barred. If you have any other problem with a premium rate telephone service or have been wrongly charged for using a premium rate number, you can again complain to PhonepayPlus (previously known as ICSTIS) – tel. 0800 500212 or see their website: www.phonepayplus.org.uk/

● **Stop the text scams** An increasingly common scam is the reverse billed text message where you get charged for receiving premium rate texts on your mobile phone. The Citizens Advice Bureau suggests replying to the short code number with 'STOP' or 'STOP ALL'; sending texts to those who specify they don't want them is illegal. Complain to your network provider and then to PhonepayPlus if it continues.

IDENTITY THEFT

11 SURE-FIRE WAYS to protect yourself from prying thieves

● **Guard your National Insurance number like the Crown Jewels** Be selective about giving out this number because a National Insurance number (or a Personal Public Service Number in the Republic of Ireland) is a boon to identity thieves. Don't hand it over lightly. Only work and tax-related dealings usually require your NI or PPS number. Even then, hold out until you're convinced it's necessary. For example, when filling out a job application, ask if, for security reasons, you can withhold your number until you're offered the job. 'And don't forget to look after your passport and driving licence,' warns Kate Beddington-Brown from CIFAS, the UK's fraud prevention service. 'If thieves take them, they can commit crimes in your name and get rich at your expense.'

● **Keep your credit cards safe** Most internet, phone and mail-order fraud results from stolen cards. If your cards are lost or stolen, cancel them immediately. Keep a note of your cards' emergency numbers and see the Card Watch website (www.cardwatch.org.uk) for more information.

● **Don't reveal PINs or details** When giving card details or personal information over the phone, internet or in a shop, make sure that others cannot see or hear the transaction. Shield the keypad when punching in your PIN at a cashpoint or till, and beware of 'shoulder surfers' who may be watching from behind you. If you think that someone may have seen your PIN or copied your card when it was out of your sight, change your PIN immediately at a cash machine. Choose a number that is not easy to guess, and never use the same one for different cards. Vary your passwords for different accounts.

● **Check bank and card statements** Take a look as soon as they arrive. If you spot anything you don't recognise, contact the bank or card company immediately; they will then be responsible for undertaking further verification and investigation, and, as appropriate, reporting cases of criminal activity to the police.

● **Update your computer protection frequently** Software companies may not like you to use 'borrowed' or otherwise illicitly installed computer privacy protection programs, but hackers love it when you do. That's because unlicensed spyware, personal firewall protection and anti-viral programs aren't eligible for free software updates. There's a reason why all those updates are offered: identity thieves are constantly finding ways around existing software to get into hard drives to steal your passwords and financial data.

Using protective software that has not been updated is like taking last year's flu vaccine. It won't work. For extra protection, put password protection on files that contain sensitive personal information, like your credit card or bank account numbers. Just click the help button on your computer and follow the instructions. Also use the latest browser and enable your PC to install any new updates automatically. Monitor the volume of pop-up ads, and avoid clicking on them as you may inadvertently download spyware onto your machine. Enable encryption on wireless immediately after setting up a home network. If you download free software, check licence agreements carefully; be wary of disclosures saying that information collected about you will be sent to a company's website.

● **Check your personal credit file regularly** To ensure that no identity thief can run up bills in your name and affect your personal financial standing,

How they do it . . .
destroy personal information

Jemma Smith from APACS, the UK trade body associated with payment transactions, recommends shredding bank statements, credit card offers or any other financial documents that reveal personal information. She suggests using a crosscut shreadder – the kind that turns paper into confetti – so identity thieves can't fit the pieces together. If a shredder is too expensive, you might consider tearing up papers and putting them in a home composter, along with any left-over food.

Or, as one radio listener once suggested, she adds, you could use waste paper to provide bedding for a hamster or rabbit. Another idea, suggested by an elderly lady, is to tear up papers and put them in a large mixing bowl. Then pour boiling water over and leave them overnight. In the morning the papers will be reduced to an unrecognisable mass of pulp.

the Home Office suggests that you regularly obtain a copy of your personal credit file to see which financial organisations have accessed your details. It is particularly helpful to do this a few months after you have moved house, just in case any personal financial details have gone astray.

There are three credit reference agencies, Callcredit, Equifax and Experian, who collect and store information on everyone's financial situation. This can include details of county court judgments, bankruptcy, property repossessed, your credit accounts and a record of everyone who has requested a credit check on your file. Credit information is usually held for six years.

For a small fee (usually £2), you can review the information held by the credit reference companies. Write to

any one of them asking for a copy, or apply online via their websites:
★ Callcredit, www.callcredit.co.uk, tel. 0870 060 1414
★ Equifax, www.equifax.co.uk, tel. 0870 010 0583
★ Experian, www.experian.co.uk, tel. 0870 241 6212 or 0800 656 9000

You can ask them to correct any inaccuracies, but you can't ask them to amend or remove correct information. As well as the basic version of the report, some credit reference agencies offer a superior standard of report. This might give additional information or a faster response time, but will cost more.

In Ireland, contact the Irish Credit Bureau, www.icb.ie, tel. (01) 260 0388; the report costs 6€.

● **Shred unwanted mail – and, if necessary, stop it coming** One of the most common ways crooks can obtain personal details is by 'bin raiding'. Certain simple precautions can reduce the risk: before you throw away anything containing personal information, make sure you rip it up, or even better, pass it through a paper shredder so that prying eyes cannot read it or decipher the information. The same applies to any financial statements you are throwing away.

Unwanted, unread junk mail may contain personal details – even your birthday – and could be of use to an identity thief. Do put a stop to it, if it serves no purpose – to you, or to the advertisers who send it.

The last thing advertisers want is to waste their valuable resources by mailing people who are simply not interested. Most of your junk mail problem will disappear if you 'opt' yourself out of marketing offers by registering with the Mailing Preference Service at: www.mpsonline.org.uk (UK only).

● **Get your identity back ... without paying for it** The good news is that the authorities are getting better at catching high-tech thieves who impersonate others for monetary gain. In 2006 Britain's banks and financial institutions detected two out of three frauds before applications could be approved. But, if you've been the victim of identity theft, report it to the police immediately. 'Don't panic,' says CIFAS's Beddington-Brown, 'but act quickly.' Go to the Home Office website www.identity-theft.org.uk where you'll find a list of organisations that can help you with the process of recovering your identity with simple, clear instructions.

Yes, you'll have some paperwork to fill out, but you'll have to do that even if you pay a restoration service to help you. According to a 2006 report by CIFAS, in more than half of all identity-theft cases, victims spent less than 24 hours putting matters right. Usually, the only costs you have to pay are postage, telephone calls and any other expenses incurred as you contact credit card agencies or banks about your case to replace cards and documentation.

● **Choose a hack-resistant online password** Just as you wouldn't give your ATM code to a stranger, it's as important to protect your online passwords; otherwise, computer hackers could have access to your financial records, email account, credit card and online banking information. Here are a few guidelines:
★ Don't use birthdays, children's names, anniversaries or other such personal information. These are the first bits of data that thieves and hackers will use when trying to break into your accounts.
★ Don't think that spelling your spouse's name (or any other easy password) backwards will work either.

Internet shop only on secure sites.
Thieves can ... even forge the padlock or key

Hackers have programs that will detect words spelled out backwards.

★ Don't use one password for all of your different accounts. If online thieves work it out, you're in big trouble.

★ Choose passwords that have both letters and numbers. Pick a password that's not even a real word – just jumble up some letters and numbers. And change your password frequently.

● **Beat the 'phishing' scams**
Identity thieves would like you to be lazy, but beware. If you ever receive an email that appears to come from your bank, broker or some other financial business, double-check that it's genuine. Thieves often send bogus emails (known as 'phishing') from addresses that contain some element of a reputable institution's name – just to fool you – and sometimes include upsetting or exciting (but false) statements in their emails to try to persuade you to react immediately.

They may ask you for personal information such as your username, password, credit card or bank account details. Or it may be a trap designed by an identity thief to get you to click on a link. Instead of taking you to the business, that link will take you to a phony website, cleverly designed to look like the real thing. There the thief will try to extract as much personal information from you as possible, such as your password, National Insurance number or mother's maiden name.

If you're suspicious, print out the email, call the financial institution named and speak to a representative. If you bank online, go directly to the website by typing the name into your browser.

● **Internet shop only on secure websites** When you make a purchase through a secure connection, the retailer's web address should change from 'http' to 'https' and you will often see a padlock or key symbol at the bottom of the page. But, warns the Anti-Phishing Working Group, an industry association that fights the scams, thieves can now spoof both the 'https' and even forge the padlock or key in order to steal your credit or debit card details.

To avoid this, first make sure that you have personally entered the web address (rather than clicking on a link from another website) and when you see the padlock, double-click on it. If the address displayed doesn't match the security certificate, don't continue the transaction. Modern internet browsers can also be set to alert you if you are sending details to an insecure site.

VEHICLE & BIKE THEFT
4 WAYS to deter potential car and bike thieves

● **Use a steering-wheel locking device** Any car-alarm vendor will want to sell you the latest high-tech device, like hidden 'kill switches' that cut off the ignition, engine and fuel supply, automatically so that even the most skilled hot-wire pro can't start your car, let alone steal it. But think about it: for the gizmo to work, the bad guy has to already be in your car. Do you really want that? Instead of the kill switch, use an easily installable mechanical device that locks to the steering wheel or steering column. Until you unlock it, nobody can turn the steering wheel, which means nobody can drive the car away. But best of all, these devices are highly visible, so they act as a deterrent. If car thieves spot a good anti-theft device in your car, they're likely to look for another car to steal.

● **Reduce the risks when your car is parked** Here's how to park so that it's harder for thieves to make off with your vehicle. When parking on the street, park between two other cars (practise that parallel parking) and turn your wheels towards the kerb. Thieves are looking for fast getaways, and won't want to waste time manoeuvring out of a tight spot. And if possible, choose a busy street to park on – the more light and traffic around, the safer the parking place. Car thieves hate audiences.

When leaving your car in a car park, choose one with an attendant or an electronic barrier, and never leave the ticket clearly visible on your dashboard – in fact, always take the ticket with you. Car thieves look for the tickets so they can take cars out of the car park without having to stop and explain to the attendant how they 'lost the ticket'.

If your home has a garage, always use it. A car sitting out on a residential street is an inviting target, even if it's locked. If you have a driveway and have more than one car, always park the most expensive or attractive one at the top of the drive and block it in with the less valuable one. If your driveway is open, consider having lockable gates fitted to the drive. If you have lockable gates, always lock them.

And finally, when you return home don't leave the car keys (or any other keys) near the front door on a table or other open place; it makes it easy for thieves to pass a stick equipped with a hook or magnet through the letter box to 'fish' the keys out.

● **Pay attention to prevent carjacking** Carjacking – when thieves physically overpower you and steal your car – is a rare crime in the UK but it does occasionally occur and high performance vehicles are usually the target. Carjackers, like street robbers, depend on the element of surprise. You can avoid being a victim by following Home Office crime prevention advice:
★ Keep your doors locked in built-up areas, and try to keep the windows wound up, especially when stopped at traffic lights or junctions.
★ Be aware of the people around you.
★ Use the middle lane, if there is one, when waiting at junctions or traffic lights, so that your car is harder to get to from the pavement.
★ Do not stop to help someone who has broken down. If you want to help, drive to the next garage or police station and get assistance from there.
★ Be very wary if someone tries to pull you over for no reason, or if you are

Practise that parallel parking ...
thieves won't want to
waste time manoeuvring out of a tight spot

involved in a minor accident – sometimes carjackers will 'accidentally' bump into your car, aiming to get you out of the car so they can steal it.

'If you are unhappy with the circumstances, or suspicious about the motives of the other party, keep driving to the nearest police station, garage or other public space,' says West Yorkshire Police's Crime Reduction Officer Detective Inspector John Minary. 'Call the police on a mobile phone if it is safe to do so, or get a passenger to make a call for you. Make a note of the car registration number and description, and a description of the occupants.'

If confronted by an armed carjacker, don't resist. Give up your keys and hand over money if it's demanded. Don't argue, fight or give chase. These people have no qualms about hurting you. Try to remember as many details as possible about the thieves and their vehicles.

● Mind your bike Cycle thieves are trying to ruin your fun and your fitness. Throughout the UK, around 440,000 bikes are stolen every year. To beat the thieves, always secure your cycle with a hardened steel U-type lock, as cable locks are easily cut, and lock it up in a garage or outhouse overnight. While even the strongest lock may not deter some thieves, using it will help your insurance claim as most companies won't cover unsecured bicycles. Check to ensure your home insurance policy covers your bike; if not, ask if it can be included; this usually adds little to your premium. You might also consider joining the CTC, the UK's national cyclists' organisation; if you buy CTC's CycleCover, free personal accident cover is also included. For the £36 annual CTC membership fee, you also receive free third-party insurance plus access to specialist legal advice, if required.

secrets of
THE LAW

Fight back and win: how
legal eagles work the system

GETTING **LEGAL ADVICE**

7 SECRETS for obtaining help with legal problems without paying a fortune

● **Check your insurance policies**
People don't realise that legal protection cover is often included with regular house or motor insurance. Your policy documents will usually tell you what is covered, and give a helpline number to call for initial advice. For example, house policies may cover any problems with defective purchases or tradespeople working on your home, while car insurance policies may enable you to claim compensation from another road user if an accident was not your fault.

● **Consult your local Citizens Advice Bureau** They will provide free advice on most issues and can direct you to further help if needed. See their website www.citizensadvice.org.uk or look in your telephone directory for your nearest branch.

● **Call your council** The Trading Standards Department can often help you with consumer concerns, such as problems with tradespeople or with goods you have bought. They cannot help you to bring a case individually but may take direct action if a trader is breaking the law. Look in the telephone directory under your local council or go to www.tradingstandards.gov.uk

● **Speak to your trade union representative** If it's a work-related matter your trade union or professional body may help, and in some cases even take action on your behalf.

● **Check out relevant organisations**
Some organisations offer their members free legal advice in relevant areas, for example the AA and RAC on motoring issues. Many professional or trade organisations will assist consumers who have problems with one of their members, and even if they can't help directly, knowing that you have contacted them may encourage the tradesperson to be helpful. If you think you have been discriminated against on grounds of race or sex, you could talk to the Commission for Racial Equality or the Equal Opportunities Commission; for problems with financial services, talk to the Financial Ombudsman Service. The Citizens Advice Bureau can often tell you which organisations to approach for specific problems.

● **Find out if you are eligible for free legal services** Free legal representation – what used to be called 'legal aid' – is available in some cases if people meet fairly strict financial criteria for both income and savings. In England and Wales it is run by the Community Legal Service (CLS) Fund (for information see www.clsdirect.org.uk, helpline 0845 345 4345). In Scotland contact the Scottish Legal Aid Board (www.slab.org.uk, helpline 0845 122 8686), in Northern Ireland the Northern Ireland Legal Services Commission (www.nilsc.org.uk, 028 9040 8888). The Republic of Ireland operates a similar system through a network of local law centres (www.legalaidboard.ie or tel. 066 947 1000).

If you are not eligible for legal aid, you may be able to get 'pro bono' help – which means that the solicitor does not charge, or provides services at reduced cost. You cannot get help with crime, family or immigration issues. If you are eligible, you need to fill in a form – available from legal advice centres such as the Citizens Advice Bureau – to see whether a solicitor is prepared to take on your case pro bono. Talk to your local CAB or see www.lawworks.org.uk for more information.

● **Find a solicitor who offers a 'no win, no fee' arrangement** Known as 'conditional fee agreements' in the trade, this means that your solicitor will only charge if you win your case, and even then the person you are suing will usually have to pay most or all of the solicitor's fees and expenses.

The solicitor may take a 'success fee' from your compensation if you win, but often the losing side pays this as well.

If you lose there may still be fees to pay, such as the other side's costs and expenses, but you can take out an insurance policy to cover such costs – and if you win, the premium will often be included in your award. Usually the initial interview to discuss your case is free. Practitioners are now regulated but, to be sure of getting someone reputable, choose a solicitor from Accident Line, the only personal injury referral scheme endorsed by the Law Society (www.accidentlinedirect.co.uk or tel. 0800 192939).

MAKE THE
LAW WORK FOR YOU
5 HELPFUL HINTS from the experts

Faulty goods? Make full use of your rights

● **Know your rights** These days you don't need a degree or access to a specialist law library to find out your legal position on most issues. A little searching on the internet can often answer basic questions with a few clicks. Do your research first and you could find an easy answer to your problem, or at least know where to go next for help. If you don't have internet access at home, you can use the computers available in most libraries, where staff will be happy to help. Try these sources:

The Community Legal Service (CLS) (www.clsdirect.org.uk) – offers free information leaflets on most areas of the law and detailed factsheets about problems with benefits, tax credits, housing, employment, education and debt.

AdviceNow (www.advicenow.org.uk) – an independent, not-for-profit website providing accurate, up-to-date information on rights and legal issues.
BBC Consumer (www.bbc.co.uk/consumer) – look at their 'guides to …' section for information on issues ranging from buying a house to eating out, and much more. There is also a guide to complaining and even downloadable letters of complaint.
Consumer Direct (www.consumerdirect.gov.uk, 0845 404 0506) – the government's advice site explains your rights in most consumer areas and gives tips on what to do if you have a problem.

● **Demand customer service** If the problem is with a large company or public utility, contact the customer service (or complaints) department. They often have a set procedure to deal with common issues, and usually don't want legal hassles any more than you do. You might be able to work something out in a simple telephone call. Decide what outcome you want (for example, a refund, compensation or faulty work put right) and do your research first so you know where you stand in law (see the previous section). Sometimes just using the right jargon is enough to convince those you're dealing with that they'll save themselves a lot of unnecessary trouble by giving you what you want without further prevarication.

For a fast and simple approach to complaining to large organisations, check out the 'How to Complain' website (www.howtocomplain.com). This offers detailed advice on consumer rights and specific complaints procedures for a wide variety of organisations, including major retailers and public bodies. You can even fill in an online form and submit your complaint there and then.

● **Faulty goods? Make full use of your rights** By law, all goods sold in British shops must be of satisfactory quality, fit for purpose and must match any description given – if not, you are entitled to a full refund. This has to be claimed within a reasonable time (what is reasonable is not defined, though a seller can be liable for up to six years, depending on the type of goods).

Until recently, it was up to the buyer to prove that goods were faulty when sold, or that it was not reasonable to expect that kind of item to develop such a fault in the time concerned. Now, under European consumer regulations, within the first six months the onus is on the seller to show that the goods were not faulty when purchased. This

---

> ## EXPERT ADVICE
> ### GREAT TIPS FROM THE PROFESSIONALS
>
> #### How to size up a lawyer
>
> It's not easy to judge the skills of a potential legal advocate. Intuition and good character judgement help, but productive questions planned in advance will give you much more to go on. Try these:
> ● Do I need a lawyer, or is mediation or arbitration an option? What are the possible outcomes of my case, and what are the chances of a settlement out of court?
> ● In what area of law do you have the most experience? Have you handled matters like mine before? What have been the results of similar cases you've been involved in?
> ● How long will the case take and how will you keep me informed of progress?
> ● Will you be working on my case personally? Can I meet any other people who will be involved in my case?
> ● What are your exact rates and how are they determined? How do you charge for expenses? How often will I be billed? And what's a rough figure for the likely total cost?
> ● Are there things I can do myself to help things along, or to save me money? And if I am dissatisfied with how things are going, can I 'fire' you?

effectively means that if an item proves faulty within six months of buying it, you can usually claim a refund or free repair. Not all sellers are aware of this – but now you can tell them, if need be.

● **Protect yourself with plastic – pay by credit card when you can** Another handy little piece of legislation that gives British buyers stellar consumer rights is the Consumer Credit Act 1974. The boring title conceals a great bonus for buyers. The law says that for all purchases of over £100 (and up to £30,000) made with a credit card, the card company is jointly liable with the seller for anything that goes wrong.

So if a trader is difficult about sorting out a problem, you can complain to the credit-card company, who will often deal with it for you. Plus, if the trader goes out of business, you can claim against the card company. Note though, this only applies to credit cards (and some other forms of credit agreement), not debit cards, store cards or credit-card cheques.

● **Get your legal advice 'à la carte'** The legal profession may have you convinced that seeking its help involves a major permanent commitment. You must 'retain' a lawyer, they may say, so that he or she can 'represent' you in all matters. Well, we'll let you in on a secret: you don't have to do anything of the kind. Instead, think of lawyers as the legal version of electricians and plumbers.

Just because you need to consult a lawyer from time to time does not mean that you need to retain a lawyer – you can just pay for the specific service you need. So you can hire one solicitor to do the conveyancing when you buy your house, a different one to handle your divorce, and yet another to make or update your will. That way, you can take advantage of cheaper deals from lawyers who specialise in one area rather than paying standard rates from a single high-street solicitor.

DIVORCE CASES

4 WAYS to keep the pain to a minimum when a breakup is inevitable

● **Have a kinder, gentler split-up** Many people view divorce as a battle where the spouses fight out every issue from child custody and financial arrangements to who keeps the wedding presents and who gets the goldfish. But in fact, most people end their marriages with dignity and fairly quickly move on with their lives. A cooperative, uncontested divorce will not only save you immense stress but also a lot of money, and is the way most people do it.

So once you decide to split up, the first person you should talk to is not your lawyer but your soon-to-be ex-spouse. The conference agenda: can we do this together? Can we agree now on the big issues and work out the details as we go along? Can we talk about who needs to end up with what, where the children are going to live, and who's going to pay how much for their support?

If your spouse is reluctant to try the cooperative approach, trot out the facts about contested divorces: they take much longer, they are infinitely more expensive, they create more problems than they solve, and they can leave the two of you permanent adversaries. That can make for a lifetime of tension-packed encounters at events such as your children's school performances, graduations and weddings, and grandchildren's birthdays.

You don't have to like each other. Just be sensible and avoid

A cooperative, uncontested divorce will not only save you immense stress but also a lot of money

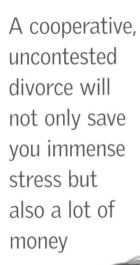

EXPERT ADVICE
GREAT TIPS FROM THE PROFESSIONALS

A top divorce lawyer's counsel:

• **Speak to Relate before you speak to a lawyer** That's the advice of Tony Roe, leading divorce specialist with the law firm Boyes Turner in Reading, Berkshire. While it may seem an odd thing for a divorce lawyer to say, as he points out, there are very few perfect relationships. 'Don't assume all is lost.' Relate (www.relate.org.uk) offers counselling to couples or individuals, and says that if the couple do decide to split, they still benefit from counselling in order to build better post-separation relationships for themselves and their children.

• **Focus on the children** Avoid them seeing any tensions between you and your partner.

• **Make best use of your time with your solicitor** Speak to your chosen solicitor on the phone before arranging a meeting – personal chemistry matters. Ask about likely fees. Before the meeting, jot down a list of the questions you want to ask. Think about taking a friend or relative with you to the first meeting: it helps to bounce the issues around afterwards. Remember that getting confidential advice does not mean that you are giving up on the relationship.

• **Keep channels of communication open** If you can still discuss things with your partner, or former partner, it can help in the long run.

• **Write down the financial history of the marriage** All the circumstances are important, according to the law, so it helps to know the chronology – when one side received an inheritance, or the other got a redundancy payment, for example. 'This helps the lawyer to advise and also helps the person to focus,' says Roe. 'Divorce is a difficult time emotionally even for the strongest of people – getting things down on paper helps to create some objectivity.'

• **Don't neglect your health** If the stress gets too much, consult your GP.

se cret weapon

RESOLUTION, MEDIATION

• **Choose a solicitor who is a member of Resolution**, the Solicitors' Family Law Association (www.resolution.org.uk). This organisation of around 5,000 lawyers and other family justice professionals was specifically set up to avoid the legal process increasing acrimony between separating couples. All members follow a standard, constructive, non-confrontational approach to family law. Couples are encouraged to settle disputes by negotiation wherever possible, with referral to counsellors and mediators where this may be helpful. Court action is seen as a last resort. Separating parents are urged to focus on their continuing role in relation to their children and disputes over financial matters and childcare arrangements are kept separate.

• **Go for mediation.** This process enables you to discuss issues with the help of an experienced and impartial mediator. It aims to find practical and fair solutions in areas of disagreement, which saves time and reduces legal costs. You can still take independent advice from your own lawyer on the issues discussed. Any Resolution solicitor can refer you to a trained mediator, who will also be an expert in family law. Once you reach an agreement, your lawyers can deal with the legal side to make it binding.

getting involved in bitter hostilities if you possibly can. In the end, being able to share your children's triumphs is more important than who gets the stereo.

● Keep relatives on the sidelines

Why do people who never gave a moment's thought to your marriage suddenly present themselves as indispensable guides as soon as you start down the road to divorce? Because, they tell you, they 'have your best interests at heart'; because they 'know how you feel'; because they 'know a good lawyer/counsellor/detective/psychic' you simply must see. Because, some will say, they've 'been there'. And because, all will say, they knew all along what a rat that no-good spouse of yours is.

The only thing they don't seem to know is that this is your divorce and yours alone. You and only you must control it. No matter how well intentioned or well informed your family members are, it is almost always best to accept their emotional support but keep them away from the action.

So yes, go ahead and listen – to your wise uncle, to your parents, to your sisters, and cousins and aunts. Listen to your friend, to your hairdresser, to your child's football coach … but then make your own decisions.

● Check your financial situation

As soon as you contemplate divorce, the most important thing to do is review your financial circumstances, advises family law solicitor Tony Roe. Make sure you understand your present financial position. Do a budget. If your spouse is responsible for the family finances, check the status of any joint accounts and that any joint mortgage payments are up to date. The more legwork you can do yourself the better. As the nature of the divorce process depends on mutual financial disclosure, don't throw away anything relevant – keep bank statements and details of pension arrangements, for example. It's important that your solicitor understands the full picture.

● Be honest about finances.

Dividing up assets and sorting out future financial arrangements is often the most complicated part of a divorce, and can create considerable tension. Assets include savings and investments, the family home and personal property. The law now allows pension funds to be split in a divorce settlement, though this will not always apply. The two of you can agree on a 'clean break' settlement rather than ongoing maintenance payments, but there will still have to be a maintenance agreement for any dependant children. It's important to remember that if you can't agree, the court will decide – so you will pay more in legal fees to end up with greater uncertainty. In England and Wales, in Northern Ireland and in the Republic of Ireland, the courts have wide discretion when dividing up property and setting up financial arrangements. In Scotland the aim is usually to make a clean break, and to divide the matrimonial property equally, although an unequal division may be made to take account of children and other circumstances. Your solicitor can advise on what is a fair division, suggest ways of achieving this, and produce an order that will be recognised and enforceable by the courts.

Either the solicitor or the court needs to know what each of you earns and who owns what, so that the assets can be divided fairly and future financial needs assessed – especially if you have children. If you don't both share your details freely, your lawyers could spend months in the attempt to extract information, racking up billable hours in the process. Better for you and your spouse to sit down together like adults and get it done in a day or two. Both of you will gain, financially and emotionally, from sharing this information, which eventually is going to come out anyway.

CHILDREN & DIVORCE

3 UNEXPECTED SUGGESTIONS for making clear-headed arrangements that benefit your children

● **Don't listen to what your kids say they want** Yes, you read that right. It may seem counterintuitive to play down the children's expressed desires at a time when you're fighting for their best interests, but it's the big picture that matters. Many a child-custody arrangement turns unnecessarily complicated because one or both of the separating parents goes out of their way to accommodate little Brittany's Friday-night sleepovers or Jimmy's absolutely non-negotiable need to take his tae kwon do lessons from the same teacher that he started with. But a year from now, Brittany may completely lose interest in those sleepovers, and the tae kwon do teacher may take a position with an accounting firm in Australia. As in any family situation, your kids are going to change, their schedules are going to change, and your own situations are going to change.

So don't spend time, money and emotional energy bickering over scheduling details. Your concern should be with nurturing the best family relationships possible under the new circumstances, so focus on the broad outlines of a custody arrangement that works for both parents and places the children where it's best for them to be.

● **Think twice about keeping the house** You may view your home as the most important thing to hang onto after

EXPERT ADVICE
GREAT TIPS FROM THE PROFESSIONALS

Helping your children through your divorce

Parentline Plus (www.parentlineplus.org.uk, 24-hour Parentline 0808 800 2222) is a national charity that works for, and with, parents. Recognising how difficult and painful the process can be, here's what they have to say about divorce and separation arrangements:
• The earlier you ask for help (from families and friends, schools, GPs and so on), the better you and your children will manage the difficult task of family change.
• However angry you may be with each other, don't take it out on the children, or ask them to take sides.
• Children may blame themselves (or someone else) for a family breakup, or 'act up' because they feel angry or frustrated. Reassure them that the breakup was none of their doing; they may need help to talk through feelings.
• Children often show distress during meetings with a non-resident parent but unless there is evidence of harm, this is likely to be because the child wants and needs more, not less, contact – face to face or by phone, post or email. The National Association of Child Contact Centres (0845 450 0280) run neutral venues where non-resident parents can spend time with their children.

your divorce. But think carefully; after a time that dear, memory-filled house may be more of a burden than an asset.

From the outset, consider what your situation might be like. This is typical: you're going to be a single parent. You have managed to keep the house, but even with contributions from your ex, your income is going to be less than when both of you were earning. And the mortgage payments, maintenance costs and council tax won't go down. Yes, the children will live in the house they're familiar with. But will their – and your – quality of life suffer as you struggle to pay for it?

Living below the standards of your own neighbourhood is a tough position for a single parent to be in. And it's tough on the kids too. They know their friends and neighbours have better toys, better clothes and better cars. They know that if they're invited on a ski trip, they probably can't go. They're aware that other children's birthday parties are more elaborate than their own.

If it's realistic to keep the house, go for it. But if it's not, bite the bullet, downsize, and start your new life in a more financially comfortable situation. Your children will adjust, and they'll feel a lot better about it once you and they take that nice holiday you wouldn't otherwise have been able to afford.

● Forget the win-at-all-costs approach
Most parents agree about arrangements for the children, but family law professionals will tell you: if a dispute occurs, it can get very nasty –

Children may blame themselves ... they may need help to talk through their feelings

especially if it's also tied in with financial arrangements. When you file for divorce, you have to make a Statement of Arrangements that sets out what you propose for the children. If you both agree, the court will usually let these arrangements stand. If not, the judge may suggest a meeting to see if you can come to an agreement with the court's help, or may point you towards

mediation, and may ask for court welfare reports or meetings with you and the children. The key legal principle is to act in the best interests of the child, and in most cases, that will be helped by parents working out a mutually acceptable solution. An arrangement made when parents agree is much more likely to work in the long term than one imposed by the court.

WILLS & **LIVING WILLS**

7 important thoughts on end-of-life documents

● **Wills are not just for rich people**
Whoever you are, however much (or little) you own, you should make a will. Why? Well, most importantly, if you have children under 18, so that you can leave instructions on who should be their guardian. And if you don't make a will, your property will be subject to intestacy rules (that just means, rules for people who haven't made a will), and that may have consequences you haven't foreseen.

Your house may not always go to your spouse, for example. If you've been living with someone you're not married to, they may get nothing. Your children may get less than you wished. If you have no dependants, everything may pass to your nearest relative – even if it's someone you haven't seen for decades. And if you have no traceable relatives it all goes to the Crown – the government.

If you die without a will, it may increase your liability to inheritance tax. You can't specify your wishes for your funeral arrangements. You can't leave money to charity. You can't nominate an executor to handle your affairs. Not having a will makes dealing with your estate immensely complicated, and it

could take months or even years to sort out. It could mean great stress and heartache for your nearest and dearest, at the worst possible time, and possibly bickering among your next of kin.

Have we convinced you? Every adult should make a will (in Scotland you can make one from the age of 12), and review it regularly and after any major life changes, like getting married or having a baby. Yet, according to the Law Society, even among people over 65, more than a third have no will – and this proportion rises to half of those aged 45 to 65, and nearly 90 per cent of under-45s. However old you are, don't be one of them!

● **Read a will carefully before signing it** You might have paid a solicitor so that you don't have to deal with all the legal language, but it's crucial to read through your will carefully before signing it. Although it's not the image law firms like to project, wills are usually put together from form documents. With all that cutting and pasting going on, incorrect information can and does sneak into (or correct information fall out of) the final printout.

● Explore what a will won't cover

A common estate-planning blunder is assuming that the will 'trumps' previous arrangements. But a will only arranges for the transfer of assets that aren't already spoken for in some other way; some assets might automatically go to somebody upon your death regardless of what the will says.

For example, when you began your pension plan, you might have named your first born – and, at the time, only child – as the beneficiary. That money still goes to your first child if you die before retirement age, even if your will says that all your assets are to be divided among the three children you now have. Similarly, your life insurance beneficiary gets the life insurance money no matter what. Or, if you own your house with your wife under a 'joint tenancy' agreement (rather than as 'tenants in common'), she will gain full ownership of the house when you die, even if you wanted to leave your share to children from a former relationship. The same thing applies to your share of money in joint accounts. ('Joint tenancy' arrangements do not apply in Scotland, so joint assets are treated differently.)

So you should check the beneficiaries on all your pension plans and insurance policies, and change them if necessary.

Also look carefully at jointly owned assets; you may wish to restructure your house ownership or joint bank accounts to change who gets what on your death.

● ... and note legal differences in other parts of the UK

The laws about making a will are broadly similar in England and Wales and in Northern Ireland. Scotland has a different legal system, and there are some important differences. In Scotland your spouse, children and other dependants may have a right to claim against your 'movable' property (everything other than land and buildings) even if your will stipulates otherwise. In England your will takes precedence, though its provisions can be altered by the Court to provide for dependants; also, a will is invalidated by marriage, unless you include a specific clause saying that it remains valid after marriage to a named person – if you divorce, your ex cannot inherit under your old will. In Scotland, your will remains valid irrespective – if you marry or divorce, you need to make a new one.

In the Republic of Ireland the law stipulates that proper provision must be made in your will for your spouse and any children, who have an automatic legal claim against your estate if you do not do so. A will is revoked by marriage unless it was made expressly with that marriage in mind.

● Make sure those who need it can find your will

If no one knows where your will is and it can't be found, your estate may be subject to intestacy rules (see above), so make sure your executor and your nearest relatives know where it is kept. Usually when a solicitor drafts your will, he or she will send you a copy and keep the original. Tell them where your copy is and make sure those who need to know have the

name and address of your solicitor. If you register your details with a company such as Willdata (www.willdata.info, 0845 009 7000), even if others forget, the location of the latest copy of your will can be found relatively easily.

● Most wills are made public

Your will normally becomes a public document after the formalities are dealt with. So if any of the provisions made in your will reveal secrets that you would rather keep private, even after your death, discuss this with your solicitor first.

● End-of-life decisions

No one wants to think about it but, sooner or later we are all going to die. Sadly, for many people, that's preceded by a period when we're unable to take decisions for ourselves; and if you're in an accident or suddenly fall seriously ill, you can be in this position at any age. Very few people plan for this – but doing so will not only ensure that your wishes are respected, but will also save your loved ones a great deal of trouble and soul-searching.

Lasting Power of Attorney (LPA) Like its predecessor, the Enduring Power of Attorney (EPA), the new LPA enables you to appoint someone else – a proxy – to take decisions on your behalf and to manage your affairs, if you cannot do so yourself. But the LPA offers more safeguards to protect against abuse and enables your proxy to take both financial and health care or personal welfare decisions. An LPA is a complex document and you will need a solicitor to help prepare one. More information is available from the Public Guardianship Office (www.guardianship.gov.uk, 0845 330 2900 or 020 7664 7000).

Advance directive You can make an advance directive (or 'living will') to express your wishes on medical treatment; standard forms are widely available online and elsewhere. Any refusal of treatment you make in advance is legally binding, provided it covers the situation that has arisen. As it can be difficult to specify exactly what should happen in any potential situation, you are encouraged to add a statement of your values, to help to guide medical staff caring for you. Appointing a health care proxy in this way does not have the same legal standing as appointing one using an LPA, though it can be valuable to have someone who will express your wishes to those caring for you.

WHAT YOU MAY NOT KNOW ABOUT INHERITANCE TAX

Not many people realise – until faced with the problem – that if your estate is liable to inheritance tax (IHT), the tax has to be paid before your beneficiaries receive the money from your estate. What's more, IHT must usually be paid within six months from the end of the month in which the death occurs; otherwise interest is charged on the amount owing. Tax on some assets, including the deceased person's house, can be deferred and paid in equal instalments over ten years, but usually interest will still be charged.

There is one saving grace: the Inheritance Tax Direct Payment Scheme allows the personal representative to pay IHT direct from the deceased's bank account (and certain other financial instruments). But not all banks belong to the scheme, and it isn't much help if there isn't enough money in the account to pay the tax – for example, if most of the value of the estate is tied up in property.

Another possible solution is to have a life insurance policy in favour of your beneficiaries. As it doesn't form part of your estate for tax purposes, the money is paid out fairly rapidly and can be used to pay your IHT bill, so that they can have access to the rest of your estate.

Or you could keep sufficient cash to pay the tax in a joint account. Sole bank accounts are instantly frozen when someone dies, but money in a joint account automatically passes to the survivor. Your share still counts as part of your estate for tax purposes, but at least the money is available.

FAMILY

MARRIAGE COUNSELLORS will **seldom reveal** that marital spats are healthy and mutual respect is more important than love for a happy marriage. And **discover wise ways** to deal with family flashpoints and keep everyone happy.

BE READY TO REVERSE other long-held beliefs. The best parenting policy for sibling scuffles is **often hands off.** Teens *need* pocket money to learn how to handle it – and a bank account

AND FUN

secrets for
**LEISURE
TIME**

296

PRIVATE

is no bad idea, either. And learn from top educational experts how to steer a child to success at school and beyond.

ALSO, DISCOVER how to win at cards and on the racetrack. Why it's cheaper to host a sit-down dinner than a buffet or why 'Sold out' live events rarely are. Travel the world in style at budget prices and **profit from a wealth of other secrets** that those who make money out of our ignorance are normally loth to reveal.

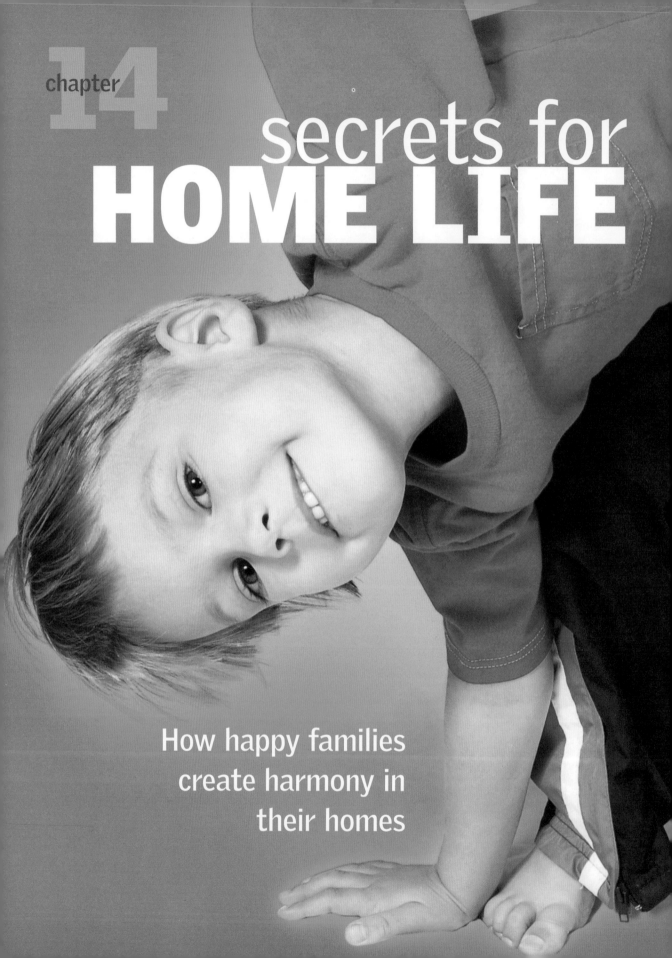

secrets for
HOME LIFE

How happy families
create harmony in
their homes

LOVE & MARRIAGE

4 STRATEGIES for making romance and attachment last

● **Look beyond love** Try not to lose your head as well as your heart, when you're romantically involved. You can actually predict to some extent whether someone is likely to make a suitable spouse. Here's a list of pointers that may help to guide you towards a successful partnership:

☺ **Listen carefully** Identify how your potential partner communicates. Also pay attention to how he or she handles sticky situations and painful emotions. Do you feel comfortable or threatened?

☺ **Look for true intimacy** We're not talking about sex here, but about the closeness that comes from being able to share life's experiences – both good and bad. Are you happy to spend time with your partner when he or she is ill or not feeling good? Can you discuss problems and work through them together?

☺ **Observe the parents** If you want an indication of how your beloved is likely to behave in a marriage, watch how his or her own family members relate to each other, especially the parents. What we learn about relationships as children, we often play out as adults.

☺ **Go for compromise** If you're forever giving in, then you've got a problem. Compromise is one of the key elements of a healthy relationship.

☺ **Be wary** Addictive behaviour, such as alcoholism, doesn't necessarily run in families, but it often does. Also watch out for a family history of depression or excessive anxiety.

● **Keep romance alive** Here are a few ways to show your mate how much you really care:

☺ **Plan a surprise treat** Don't fall into the trap of taking your partner for granted. From time to time, arrange to get home early and cook a special dinner, or reserve a table at a favourite restaurant, or even book a short break.

☺ **Send something special** For birthdays and anniversaries, send flowers, wine or chocolate to your spouse's office. You could also do this as a surprise, whether you have something to celebrate or not.

☺ **Give a massage** Learn how to give your partner a soothing foot or back massage at the end of a tiring day.

☺ **Leave a message** Make technology work for you. Send a text or leave a voicemail on your partner's phone, saying, 'I'm thinking about you'.

● **Enjoy common rituals** Studies show that couples with similar backgrounds and shared beliefs tend to

---

HIDDEN TRUTHS What your marriage counsellor may not always tell you about **COMPATIBILITY**

Good marriages don't have to be perfect, say psychologists Karen Sherman and Wendy Allen:

• A couple that doesn't fight is in trouble.

• Around 70 per cent of arguments between you and your partner will never be resolved. So relax, accept your differences and don't try so hard. Letting go is sometimes better than discussing everything to death.

• A 'good enough' marriage is the most couples can realistically expect and is actually quite an achievement.

• Genuine respect – not sex or money – is the most important factor in a happy marriage.

Few – if any – couples are happy or compatible all the time.

A PARENTS' GUIDE TO
ONLINE SOCIAL NETWORKING

WHEN TEENAGERS TALK ABOUT BEBO OR MYSPACE – known as social networking sites – parents tend to nod vaguely and go back to the ironing. But the impact of such websites has been huge.

MySpace, for example, was founded in 2003, and became so popular and influential that it launched the careers of the Arctic Monkeys and Lily Allen – and was then bought by Rupert Murdoch's News Corporation. Sites such as MySpace, Bebo, Friendster and Facebook loom large in the world of most adolescents – who often home in on them in order to keep in touch with friends or find romance. New sites are launched all the time – each one promising to be the next 'big thing'.

BEBO.COM This site, founded in 2005, tends to attract more younger users than other social networking sites. Its 'whiteboard' feature seems to be one of its main attractions, allowing users to draw online pictures of their friends' antics. The site is currently developing the facility for its members to share and download music.

FACEBOOK.COM Launched in 2004, Facebook's focus was originally communication between undergraduate students in North America. It's now widely used by many age groups as a way of keeping in touch. You don't say 'hello' to people on Facebook – you 'poke' them. Details of Facebook members are available on search engines, though you can opt out by changing your settings on the 'search privacy' page.

FRIENDSTER.COM Created in California in 2002, Friendster works like the other major sites. Users create an online identity by uploading a user portrait and answering a questionnaire profile. They then add 'galleries' of their friends. Most Friendster members are aged 21 to 30.

MYSPACE.COM Essentially a music lovers' site, MySpace is full of individual profiles and bands' pages. Your homepage lists your likes and dislikes, favourite bands and 'relationship status'. Unfortunately, this site is regularly targeted by paedophiles and stalkers, so has had some bad press.

Teach your children that people are not always what they seem ...

SAFETY GUIDELINES

There has been a lot of publicity about the dangers of social networking sites such as Bebo and MySpace. The risk that attracts most press coverage is that of paedophiles using these sites to meet children. But cyber-bullying can also be a problem. This is what you need to know in order to help your teenagers to stay safe:

1 Most social networking sites have a minimum age for users – 13 for Bebo, 14 for MySpace. If your younger child is logged in, report this to the site, which will remove the child's profile.

2 Some photos of individuals on their site profiles are very provocative. Warn youngsters about the dangers – risqué photos can be downloaded easily or even edited by unscrupulous people.

3 Teach your children that people are not always what they seem to be. If the person making contact is not a friend in real life, they must not accept them as a friend on their contact list or give out personal information.

4 Warn your children never to give their full name, age, address, usual email address or phone number. For safety's sake, get them to open a brand new email address, solely for their Bebo or other networking account. Then, if they encounter any unpleasantness, they can abandon that email address, but continue to use their main one.

5 Alert your children to the very real dangers of meeting someone in person whom they've only previously met online. If they're determined to do so, insist that you go along as well – or that a trusted adult friend accompanies them.

6 Report strange behaviour or bullying to the site itself or to the Child Exploitation and Online Protection Centre (CEOP) – www.ceop.gov.uk – and reassure your child that the bullying or unpleasant behaviour is not their fault.

7 Advise your teenager never to use his or her real name on any networking sites, but to choose a nickname instead. Apart from helping to maintain privacy, this advice could enhance job prospects, too. Prospective employers often conduct a Google search on people they interview, so they can pick up someone's profile when it's written under their real name – which might include something that could jeopardise their chances of a job offer in the future.

have better marriages. Taking part in certain events and rituals, especially religious rituals, together helps people to forge strong bonds.

● **Take 'alone time'** One of the toughest times in a marriage is when you have young children. Be creative about grabbing some time for just the two of you:

☺ **Take advantage of nap-time** Who says that you always have to do the laundry or catch up on household chores while your two year old takes an afternoon nap?

☺ **Invest in hardware** That means buying a lock or a even a simple gate hook and fitting it to your bedroom door.

☺ **Set the alarm** Wake up at 3am, make love and then go back to sleep.

TODDLERS TO TEENAGERS

10 KEY TACTICS
for bringing up healthy, responsible children

● **Take the TV out of the bedroom**
There are good reasons for removing TVs from bedrooms and keeping them only in rooms used by the whole family. For a start, research has shown that children with TVs in their rooms are more likely to be overweight, because they watch more and tend to snack as they view. Secondly, you have little or no control over what a child is watching. And finally, you lose opportunities for 'family time' – when you all curl up together on the sofa to watch *Doctor Who*.

● **Steer clear of sibling scuffles** Stay out of fights between siblings, unless you think that they might seriously injure each other. Fighting teaches valuable skills such as

EATING TOGETHER

Research shows that children who enjoy traditional family mealtimes have fewer mental health problems and do better at school. Parenting organisation Raisingkids (www.raisingkids.co.uk) has found that British children often have meals alone in their bedrooms, while watching television or playing computer games. The Government and parenting experts all agree that the disappearance of family mealtimes is one factor that can turn youngsters into yobs. Growing numbers of children are unable to use a knife and fork properly; solitary teenagers take food from freezer to microwave and up to their rooms without speaking to anyone. So listen to the experts and eat round the table, as a family, whenever you can.

☺ **Two to four years old** Ask them to put toys away, help to lay the table and put dirty clothes in the laundry basket.

☺ **Five to seven years old** They can begin to help with emptying the dishwasher, clearing the table and in the garden – weeding or raking leaves.

☺ **Eight to ten years old** By now, they are capable of making their own beds, dusting and bringing bags of shopping from the car into the house.

☺ **Eleven and up** Your children are now capable of almost any household task. They can vacuum, sweep up and clean the bathroom. It's a good idea to teach them some basic cooking skills, too. Most kids love being able to put together a simple family meal, unaided.

● **Get them a bank account** Stop handing out pocket money to your teenagers. Instead, get them to open their own bank accounts, give them a budget and tell them what it needs to cover – clothes, going out, mobile-phone bills – and let them learn to manage the cash themselves. Pay in a set amount each month and when they start to earn, cut back the amount you pay in by the amount they're being paid.

● **Talk about sex** Let your teenagers know that they can talk to you about sex without fear of judgment or lectures. Bookmark www.thesite.org and www.ruthinking.co.uk on the family computer and leave your teens to read what's on these websites in private, without breathing down their necks.

● **Don't let them drive too fast** Teenagers who break the speed limit are more likely to flout the law in other ways too, such as gambling, using drugs and drinking too much alcohol. Take speeding as an early warning sign and stamp on it.

assertion, managing anger and compromise. If ignoring a fight doesn't work, send your warring offspring to separate rooms until they cool off.

● **Limit choices** An inexperienced parent will ask a four year old, 'What do you want to wear today?' Offering such an open-ended choice will guarantee that your little girl will choose mauve tights, a pink tutu, a yellow fleece and sandals. A better strategy would be to lay two outfits on the bed and ask which she wants to wear. The same goes for food. Replace 'What would you like for lunch?' with 'spaghetti bolognese or cheese and tomato sandwiches?'

● **Let them help** A child as young as two is old enough to start helping around the house. Here are some chores that will teach your children to take some responsibility for the everyday comforts they enjoy, rather than taking them for granted:

8 ways to teach your CHILDREN about money

WE'VE ALL HEARD HORROR STORIES about children who go off to university – armed with only a student loan, an overdraft facility and perhaps a credit card – and run up mountains of debt in the first few months. Make sure that doesn't happen to your offspring by teaching them the true value of money before they leave home.

1 SHOW THEM THAT YOU PAY MONEY IN AS WELL AS TAKING IT OUT OF THE BANK If all your children ever see is you withdrawing £20 notes from the cashpoint, they'll grow up thinking that machines dole out money. Make sure they also see you depositing funds.

2 DIFFERENTIATE BETWEEN 'WANT' AND 'NEED' She needs trainers, but she wants the coolest brand. You need food, but you want to eat out. Apply this rule to anything you buy and to any of their requests for 'stuff'.

3 TEACH THEM TO SET GOALS AND SAVE FOR THEM Label a jar with a set amount of money to be used for something specific. Start small – for example, £5 to buy some Lego or paints. Collect £5 worth of change in the jar and count it out before buying the treat. Keep the money separate when you go to the shop, so your child can pay for the item, using the cash.

4 SHOW THEM YOU'RE PLANNING FOR THE FUTURE As well as using a moneybox to save for treats, make sure your children hear you talking about paying bills on time, saving for a new fence, paying off the car loan or investing for their university education.

5 GIVE TO OTHERS Next to the treat jar, keep another, labelled 'for charity'. Get younger children to put in a few pennies a week from their pocket money and teenagers to donate some of their allowance or earnings. They need to see you giving to others, too – whether it's a standing order to a local hospice or volunteering your time for a charitable cause.

6 MAKE CHOICES, NOT SACRIFICES Instead of saying, 'we can't afford that', 'that's too expensive', or just 'no', use a phrase that expresses a deliberate choice. Try, 'I'd rather stay at home this year and have some fun days out so we can save for a special holiday next year'; or 'I prefer to bring your juice and my Thermos of coffee with me rather than buying them at the café, so we can keep that money for more important things.' That way, instead of feeling that 'no' means sacrifice, scarcity or embarrassment, children learn that life is about making choices.

7 HELP THEM TO UNDERSTAND ADVERTISING Explain that 'only £99.99' is a marketing trick. Analyse ads on the TV and radio and see if your children can work out for themselves how advertisers push their products.

8 BOOKMARK WWW.DOUGHUK.COM This excellent website, aimed at 14 to 24 year olds, gives information on various aspects of personal finance – from banking to bills. There are role-play activities and quizzes to test knowledge of money matters, case studies and lots of useful links.

● **Avoid drifting apart** If you're starting to feel redundant, think again. The closer mothers and fathers are to their teenage offspring, the less likely those children are to start going off the rails. One or other parent could take a teenager out for a meal once a week or go shopping together or watch a live sporting event. Just make it something you both enjoy, so you'll both want to repeat the experience.

● **Make rules – and stick to them** You may have given in to the double ear piercing or the dreadlocks, but when it comes to tattoos or other permanent body markings, that are going to be difficult, painful and costly to remove, say 'no'. And make it clear that you don't expect them to get drunk or to take drugs, either.

● **Visualise their future** It's never too early to begin talking to your child about his or her future. By the age of ten, children are old enough to start looking ahead and understanding the value of education. Studies show that children who can visualise their future are less likely to do things that can destroy it – such as getting pregnant too young or ending up in prison.

PARENTS & SIBLINGS
5 SECRETS for boosting family harmony

Involve your dad ... ask his advice

● **Involve your dad** As we get older, our fathers often seem to blend into the background, while we may gossip, laugh and go shopping with our mothers. Instead of leaving him pottering in the greenhouse or reading the papers while you and your mum put the world to rights, find ways to involve him. Ask his advice about that door lock that's always sticking, get him to come and test drive a new car with you, persuade him to read to your daughter or see if your son can teach him how to play one of his computer games – but most of all, talk to each other. You'll really wish you had when it's too late.

● **Record your family digitally, then share the memories** As well as building up family photo albums, embrace modern technology. Buy and learn to use a camcorder and start filming, particularly those older relatives who may not be with you much longer. Then you can make DVDs on your home computer and send copies of them to other members of the family.

● **Start sharing it out** In the UK, no inheritance tax (IHT) is charged on anything you leave to your spouse. And, following a legislative change in October 2007, a spouse or partner gets any unused tax allowance you have, as well. But there's nothing to stop you from making financial gifts to your children or grandchildren now – many lifetime gifts are tax-free and most others suffer IHT only if you die within seven years of making them. If you're in robust health and want to help out your family, don't worry about giving it away.

● **Practise saying 'no' to relatives** Do you always find yourself saying 'yes' – albeit reluctantly – when your sister asks for money? Then practise ten ways to say 'no' in front of the mirror before you next plan to meet. Try 'No, I can't. All my money is tied up in a pension fund/life insurance policy/school fees plan and I can't take it out without being penalised'; or 'No, I'm sorry, but I'm going back to university to do an MA and I'm going to need every penny'; or 'I wish I could, but the boiler has just broken and we've got to replace it'.

● **Ask about family illnesses** It's a good idea to find out as much as you can about the health of all your extended family members – including any chronic conditions that affected grandparents, aunts and uncles. This

DOS AND DON'TS FOR FITTING IN WITH THE IN-LAWS

You've just got married and as well as a spouse, you've acquired a whole new family. Here are some ways to survive the transition and thrive in the long term:

DO try to understand how your spouse relates to his or her parents and any siblings.

DON'T assume that relationships in your partner's family will mirror those in yours.

DO make the time and effort to get to know your in-laws. If you live a long distance apart, keep in regular contact.

DON'T take offence easily. You may just not understand the way your new family works.

DO check with your spouse about family traditions. Do you take a gift when you go for lunch? Should you write a thank-you letter or simply pick up the phone? What do they like to eat and drink? What's their sense of humour like? Is it safe to discuss politics or religion with them?

DON'T criticise your partner's family. It's much better to ask for explanations of things you don't understand.

DO be polite and friendly. Charm them, but don't smarm.

DON'T assume they understand how you feel. And don't take their comments and reactions personally – you may have got the wrong end of the stick.

DO think about what will work best for you and your partner before you try to please your partner's family.

DON'T ignore your partner while you're with your own family. By all means talk to your sister and catch up with your father, but make sure you reassure one another frequently by including your partner in conversations.

DO ask your spouse how it went after a meeting with in-laws. A 'debriefing' may be useful to both of you.

information can be important in diagnosing any medical problems that you may develop. Ask about incidences of heart disease, high blood pressure, stroke, depression, diabetes, Alzheimer's, obesity, blindness, deafness and cancer. Find out what age the relative was when the condition was diagnosed and if he or she was treated successfully. Other conditions that families may share include allergies, asthma, migraines, fertility problems or learning disabilities.

FAMILY CONFLICT

6 WISE WAYS to deal with family flashpoints

● **Put it in perspective** Whenever you're in the middle of a heated family argument, ask yourself if the issue that's upsetting everyone is going to be that important to you in an hour or in 2 hours' time? Or tomorrow? By and large, the answer will be 'no'.

● **Rise above it** The next time you feel exasperated with your spouse or children, remind yourself of all the difficult times they may have experienced – perhaps dealing with *your* problems or irrational behaviour.

● **Take some 'time out'** You can't exactly banish warring family members who won't listen to your pleas for calm and reason from the house – but you can make an excuse and go out yourself. Leave them to it and go for a walk or do some shopping. They'll probably have

forgotten what they were arguing about and be chatting amicably by the time you return home.

● **Remember, it's them, not you** If members of your family are being obnoxious, that's their problem, not yours. Try not to snap or say something that you'll regret later.

● **Maintain a dignified silence** Not getting involved is sometimes the best way to deal with a difficult situation. Silence is a powerful tool, so use it.

● **Be kind to yourself** If your mother upsets you by mentioning your failed first marriage – yet again – don't criticise yourself for feeling angry. Your reaction is normal. But do avoid conflict over it. Instead, take a few deep breaths, count to ten, smile and change the subject.

YOUR PETS

7 HINTS for keeping the four-legged family members happy and healthy

● **Teach a cat the house rules** Cats can be trained to use a litter tray, to come when called, not to jump on to the kitchen worktops and not to destroy furniture and carpets with their claws. But remember that a cat's attention span is limited, so keep those training sessions short and sweet. And cats respond to bribery, so have a delicious selection of favourite treats to hand to reward them when they've successfully mastered a new pattern of behaviour.

Teach a cat the house rules

Here are some ideas for keeping your cat in order and happy:

☺ **Buy a scratching post** Or make one by covering a stump of wood with sisal rope, corrugated cardboard or carpet turned the wrong side out – but be careful not to have the same stuff on the scratching post and the floor – your cat may not be able to tell the difference.

☺ **Treat your wiring** Stop a kitten from chewing any accessible electric cables by painting them with a chilli powder-and-water paste.

☺ **Make the sofa less appealing** Teach a kitten not to jump up or curl up on your armchairs or sofa by temporarily sticking some double-sided tape on the seats. They'll hate the feeling of their fur being tugged by the tape.

● **Think of the neighbours** If your dog is always barking, you're not going to be very popular with the people next door. You could even be taken to court and face a fixed penalty if you do nothing to stop the problem. Here are some ways to tackle it:

☺ **Do some home-alone training** Your dog may not like you going out, but needs to get used to the idea. Leave your pet alone in another room – at first for a few minutes, building up to longer periods – at different times of day. Don't return until your dog has been quiet for a while, then go in and offer praise and a treat as a reward.

☺ **Provide company** If you have to leave a dog alone for a long time, arrange for a neighbour to pop in and perhaps take your pet for a walk. Even the sound of a human voice can be reassuring to an animal, so leave the radio on at low volume, tuned into a talk channel.

☺ **Change rooms** Some dogs bark because they can see what's happening out in the street. Keep your pet somewhere with a garden view instead.

How they do it ...
brushing a cat's teeth

Cats with bad teeth are susceptible to infection and are likely to have bad breath. Vets also charge high prices for animal dentistry, as a costly general anaesthetic is often required. So although the idea may seem odd, tooth brushing is no joke and can even save you money. The UK animal charity, The Blue Cross, recommends getting your cat used to teeth-cleaning as early as possible, but you can train an older cat to accept it. It's best to wait until your pet is relaxed and keep the first attempts short. Start by gently placing your fingers on the teeth while stroking your cat. Progress to rubbing the teeth with a soft cloth – soak it in the liquid from a tin of tuna to make it taste appealing. Finally try a toothbrush. Buy a special one from the vet or pet shop and hold it so that the bristles are at a 45° angle to the teeth. Brush daily, if you can, and always offer a treat afterwards.

☺ **Buy an anti-barking collar** You can now buy or hire these ingenious collars which work by releasing a spray of citronella oil when the dog barks, which surprises but causes no pain or harm.

● **Take them on holiday** It won't make your local kennel or cattery happy, but with a bit of planning, you and your pets can holiday together. You'll find pet-friendly hotels, camping sites and holiday cottages all over the UK. Type 'holidays with pets' into your favourite search engine and explore the numerous options, such as www.dogsinvited.co.uk

Since the introduction of 'pet passports' in July 2004, you can take your pets abroad, too. Britanny Ferries reported that almost 30,000 dogs and cats travelled with the company in 2006 and the trend is growing. Under the pet travel scheme you can take dogs, cats – and even ferrets – on holiday to Europe

Don't forget
to pack
your pet's
toys ...

and bring them home without the need for quarantine. Visit the Defra website (www.defra.gov.uk) for detailed information on taking your pet abroad.

● **Pack for your pet** If you're taking Flossie or Rufus on holiday, or even to your in-laws for Christmas, be sure to pack the following:
☺ **Health certificate** Get your vet to issue one, along with information about any vaccines and medications. It's also a good idea to have your vet's phone number to hand.
☺ **Medication** If your pet is currently taking any medicines, make sure you bring enough for the entire trip.
☺ **Food** Unless you're sure you'll find it at your destination, bring sufficient quantities of your pet's usual food. An abrupt change of diet could give your pet a nasty bout of diarrhoea – not ideal in a hotel or someone else's house.
☺ **Comfort and amusement** Don't forget to pack your pet's toys, bedding and, if appropriate, some cat litter.

● **Clean up that poo** There is nothing nastier than stepping in a pile of dog poo. Dog faeces are also a potential health risk, particularly to children. Since the Dogs (Fouling of Land) Act was passed in 1996, it's actually an offence not to clean up after your dog, and a successful prosecution can lead to a £1,000 fine. So whenever you walk your dog, take some old plastic carrier bags or scented nappy sacks in your pocket. Some areas give away free poop-scoop bags – ask your vet whether such a scheme operates where you live.

● **Safe walks for city cats** Walking your cat may make being outdoors safer for city animals. Whatever your cat's age, it can be taught to walk on a lead, if you follow some simple rules:

☺ **Get the right kit** Buy a comfortable harness – not a collar – and a lead. Leave the new harness near your cat's toys for a few days, so that your pet can sniff it, play with it and get used to it.
☺ **Take it slowly** Try putting the harness on, without the lead, for a minute or two. Give the cat a treat and take the harness off. Gradually increase the harness-wearing period, then follow the same pattern with the lead. Fix it to the harness and let the cat walk around the house trailing the lead. Keep rewarding with treats and cuddles, so the harness and lead have pleasurable associations.
☺ **Step out with caution** A cat that has never been outside before, may be frightened to begin with. So put on the harness and lead and carry your pet into the street. Hold your cat while it looks around and only put your pet down when you are sure it's happy with its surroundings. Let your pet's natural curiosity lead the way.

● **Tackle the allergy, keep the pet** Most allergy sufferers are sensitive to more than one allergen. If you react to pet dander (minute flakes of shed skin), the chances are you're sensitive to other common allergens such as dust, cigarette smoke or pollen. So before you dispatch kitty to the animal rescue centre, talk to your doctor about allergy jabs and antihistamines and try lowering the allergen levels in your house. Vacuum frequently using a cleaner designed for allergy sufferers, such as the Medivac Microfilter. Use HEPA air cleaners throughout the house and cut back on dander-collecting soft furnishings. Launder pillowcases, loose covers and pet bedding regularly. Make your bedroom an allergy-free retreat, from which the animal is banned. And lastly, give your pet a weekly bath – even cats can be trained to tolerate bathing.

OWNING A **PET HAMSTER**

HAMSTERS MAKE ENGAGING FAMILY PETS. They are inexpensive to buy, cheap to feed, need very little space and are easy to look after – so even the youngest members of the family can be involved. Hamsters are nocturnal and sleep during the day, but they are happy to play when the children come home from school.

Remember, though, that a hamster's lifespan is brief – usually eighteen months to two years – so you'll inevitably have to help your children through the experience of bereavement.

WHAT TO BUY Choose a Syrian, or 'golden', hamster. These little animals should be kept alone – one Syrian hamster to one cage – as they fight if kept together.

WHAT TO LOOK FOR Your new hamster should be four to eight weeks old, with bright eyes and ears that are held erect. It should not bite when you pick it up and there shouldn't be any signs of injury. Make sure you hold the hamster just above a solid surface, in case it takes fright and jumps.

WHERE THEY LIVE Hamsters need lots of exercise, so choose a big cage. The best type is a wire cage or a modular stacking system such as Rotostak. These provide a stimulating environment for your pet – but make sure you join the tubes and 'rooms' together securely to prevent escapes. Spread a thick layer of sawdust on the base of the cage and provide a handful of bedding – shredded tissue paper seems to be the safest. Don't use paper from your document shredder as the inks on it may be poisonous to a hamster.

WHAT TO FEED THEM Hamsters are omnivores, so they need seeds, fresh fruit and vegetables and animal protein. Make sure that you choose a hamster mix that includes peanuts and seeds as well as rodent pellets, which contain animal protein.

WHAT THEY DRINK Hamsters need water, but a water bowl is easily fouled. The best solution is a water bottle fixed to the cage so that the spout is within reach of your hamster.

KEEP IT CLEAN Hamsters don't smell if you keep their cages clean. They usually wet in the same area, so you can scoop out and replace any soggy sawdust every couple of days. Once a week, clean the whole cage. Throw away all the sawdust and old food and wash and dry the cage base. Put in fresh sawdust and new bedding if necessary. Then rinse the water bottle and refill it.

... choose a hamster mix that includes peanuts and seeds

secrets of
SOCIAL LIFE

How to succeed in love, master
etiquette and much more ...

DATING & RELATIONSHIPS

8 WAYS to find and nurture true love

● **Use a winning formula** After analysing the success of lonely hearts advertisements, Professor Richard Wiseman of Hertfordshire University concludes that the key is to make 70 per cent of the information about yourself and 30 per cent a description of the type of person you're looking for. 'There's a huge amount of psychology in personal ads', he concludes. 'You've got 25 words to impress someone, and that's your lot. So you need to choose those words carefully.' For speed dating he recommends asking open-ended questions and adding a touch of humour to lighten things up. His favourite is: 'If you were a pizza topping, which one would you be?'

● **Embrace chivalry on a first date** No matter who asked who to go out on that first date, etiquette experts say that a man should always pay (for same-sex couples, the asker buys). Here's a trick: if you are a female on a first date and the man doesn't reach for the bill, take a trip to the ladies' room. If he doesn't pay while you're away, offer to split the bill. If he lets you, then find yourself another man.

● **Do an instant brain test** To find out what kind of a person you're dating ask your companion to interlock their hands and place one thumb on top of the other. The result: left thumb on top indicates someone who excels at right-brain activities – those that are visual, spatial and intuitive. Right thumb on top reveals someone who is more logical, verbal and analytical, skills associated with the left hemisphere of the brain.

● **Tread carefully with office romance** A fifth of us meet our partners at work. The news of an office romance spreads like wildfire and the relationship could quickly be construed as inappropriate. To handle an office romance professionally, keep the following rules in mind:

❋ Make sure you like your colleague enough to take a risk. Chat at leaving parties and other social occasions. If it's just a fling and the person has no potential as the love of your life, end it.

❋ Never let a relationship compromise your work.

❋ Be certain the person likes you back: people are quick to cry sexual harassment these days.

❋ Do not speak to anyone in Human Resources. They may appear to be friendly and understanding but there could be unexpected repercussions.

❋ If it is serious, one of you may have to be prepared to leave, especially if you both work in the same department.

secret weapon

A BRIGHT TIE

At social gatherings where you are likely to meet potential dating partners, wear some distinctive article of clothing or jewellery. It not only makes you stand out from the crowd, but also offers anyone interested in you an excuse to start a conversation. For a man it might be a bright red or unusually patterned tie or a designer watch (it can be a fake), while a woman might try distinctive earrings, a striking necklace or an embroidered jacket.

● **Let your date do the talking** If you're painfully shy and on a first date, try asking a few easy questions, such as 'where was your last holiday?' If you become a good listener, you'll soon forget your nerves.

● **Freedom to flirt** When dining out with a date, it's quite acceptable to flirt and play footsie under the table, but overt kissing and groping will soon spoil the atmosphere and other diners will find it offensive.

● **A friend's ex? Tread carefully** Dating a friend's former partner is dangerous territory. If you truly feel he or she is your soulmate, try waiting (the rule of thumb is three months for every year the couple was together – up to a year or so). Or ask the friend for permission; if he or she did the breaking up, that also makes it easier.

And if your friend is now happily re-coupled, there should be nothing stopping you.

Champagne – for romance, it's an obvious choice

● **Set the mood with food** If you are preparing a romantic meal, certain foods can make the evening more pleasurable for both of you ... without your date suspecting a thing.

❋ **A game animal** According to historical theory, if you eat a wild animal, you take on some of its wildness. Given that your beloved is not a vegetarian, serve something like venison or roasted duck.

❋ **Oysters** Eaten since ancient times as aphrodisiacs, oysters contain zinc, which is stored in the prostate and is thought to prolong sexual pleasure in men. Enough said.

❋ **Champagne** For romance, it's an obvious choice, but be careful not to overdo it, remembering the words of Shakespeare, 'Liquor provoketh the desire but taketh away the performance.'

❋ **Chocolate** This popular food contains a chemical called phenylethylamine, a compound that the body naturally produces when a person is in love. Your date may instantly feel more amorous.

PARTIES &
ENTERTAINING

7 WAYS to be a good host (and guest)

● **Be a perfect mixer** Most people think that wine is cheaper than spirits, but, in fact, serving spirit-based cocktails or a wine-based punch instead of wine will actually save you money, since a bottle of wine yields only five glasses, which will serve, at best, three to five guests. Try the following options:

❋ Combine cranberry or pomegranate juice or sparkling elderflower pressé with a litre of vodka, or make a Pimms substitute with gin, lemonade and a dash

of Campari. Top with orange slices and mint. As a rule, using one part spirits to three of mixer juice gives you about 30 cocktails from a litre of spirits, which costs about the same as a bottle of wine. ❄ Make Buck's fizz with sparkling wine and orange juice, or mix a bottle of sparkling wine or champagne with 500ml orange juice and two 355ml cans of ginger ale or lemonade in a punch bowl, adding a few glasses of brandy for an extra kick, if you like. Stir and let guests serve themselves.

● **Don't drink if you don't want to**
If you're teetotal or driving home, you may find yourself being encouraged or even pressured to have an alcoholic drink. Ask your host or the bartender for a virgin drink such as tomato juice, a cola or plain tonic water with ice and lemon. If anyone asks and you don't want to admit it, you can tell them it's a Bloody Mary, rum and Coke, or a gin and tonic. Or, it may be easier to come up with a plausible excuse such as 'I'm on antibiotics' or 'I'm under doctor's orders'. Sometimes it's easier to put up a façade when you're being bullied. But it's also perfectly fine to refuse alcohol and, as you could point out, illegal and dangerous if you do drink and drive.

● **Ditch the dishes** If you're hosting a party using outside caterers, ask the company to itemise all charges in advance. If they plan to charge you extra for accessories such as dishes, cutlery and tablecloths, use the figure they quote as a starting point for making price comparisons. Ring around a few party suppliers to compare hiring charges, or ask your local village or church hall if they have crockery and cutlery they could hire out for a reasonable fee. If you're on a very tight budget, friends and neighbours may lend you all you need. The caterer may complain, but you're in charge. If you do a lot of entertaining it may pay you to invest in the major items. Surf the net or look for dishwasher-safe bargains at sale times.

● **Check out the toilets** Avoid embarrassment for you and your guests by making sure that all your toilets are

---

HOW TO HOST AN EVENING TO REMEMBER

An inventive host will go the extra mile to inject fun into a party, and get guests to mingle and enjoy themselves.
• Give people secret tasks they have to accomplish throughout the evening such as discovering how many guests have the same occupation, whether two people in the room share the same birthday or the same middle name. Give prizes – adult 'goody bags' can be fun – to those who have completed their tasks.
• Play charades, pass the parcel, musical chairs or pin the tail on the donkey. At a party, people often love to let their hair down and it will make older guests feel young again.
• Hire a karaoke and discover all those would-be Elvises and Madonnas. (But check out the noise rules in your area. Loud noise that disturbs the neighbourhood after 10.30pm or 11pm is a no-no.)
• Get out your digital camera and ask guests to strike silly poses – and, perhaps, send them photos later as an amusing memento.
• For a small party, take everyone out to your local ice-cream parlour (if you have one) for dessert, then back to your place for a night cap.

spotlessly clean and supplied with plenty of toilet paper. If you are hosting a sizeable summer event you may want to think about hiring portable toilets. Spending £250 for a superior set of four, complete with an area for wash basins and mirrors, will save domestic overload. If you have any doubts about the state of your home's plumbing be sure to have it checked out professionally before a big event.

● **Celebrate age and diversity** For a group of mixed ages, break the ice by getting everyone to come dressed in the fashion of the decade in which they were born. To celebrate a mix of people from different backgrounds, and to save yourself from having to make all the food yourself, ask each person or couple to bring a favourite dish which, if they wish, can be typical of their childhood or their cultural origins. Find out in advance what each is bringing so you can match up drinks and add additional items as necessary. Then sit back and enjoy everything from Cornish pasties to Madras curry.

● **Make a single outstanding dish** When you try to be the quintessential host or hostess, there is a natural tendency to overdo it. Because you want every course or dish to be perfect, you're likely to break your budget and drive yourself mad. The solution is simple. Make one main course dish the star of the meal and spend all your extra effort and money on that. If the other parts of the meal are simple – but made with fresh, tasty ingredients – they will set off your extra-special dish rather than compete with it. As a result you'll gain all the more compliments.

● **There's always one ...** Be prepared to cope with a guest who has had too much to drink. If you can't get rid of him or her before the shouting, arguing or throwing up begins, and if a polite warning and a drink of water doesn't work, try to get the person to lie down (have a bed made up, in case) or call a taxi. Give the taxi driver the address he's to go to and whatever you do, don't let the person drive home. Having a few sensible, sober friends on hand to help will pay dividends on occasions like this.

TYING THE **KNOT**

8 **TIPS** for the big day from seasoned wedding planners

● **Don't mention the 'W' word** Whether you're hiring a disco, hairdresser, marquee or a hat for the big day, just say that you're having a party. Companies and individuals hear the cash tills ringing when the word 'wedding' is mentioned. Fix the price, and get it confirmed in writing before you spill the beans. You may be planning a once-in-a-lifetime event but don't forget to shop around for the best deals.

● **Get insured** A bit of money spent on insurance will give you the cover you need if things go wrong – from the best

Talented wedding photographers are hard to come by, so you are probably going to have to spend a little more

man losing the rings to the venue burning down the night before the ceremony. Given the vagaries of the British climate, be sure that you're fully covered for any damage that could be caused by bad weather. For extra peace of mind, check with your credit-card company to see if any payments you make in preparation for the event might be covered against such disasters.

● **Pay for the best photographer**
No matter how fabulous your friend is at shooting arty landscapes, do not hire him to save a few pounds on your wedding photos. If you go to someone who isn't an experienced wedding photographer, they are sure to miss 50 per cent of the highlights. Think about it this way: would you rather have 20 beautiful photos of the happiest day of your life or 200 blurry ones? You also need someone who is separate from the wedding party and can view every aspect with an objective eye. Talented wedding photographers are hard to come by, so you are probably going to have to spend a little more than you planned to get a good one. It's also worth paying extra to have the photographer on hand early in the day, to get those unique informal shots of the bride and bridegroom, bridesmaids and parents preparing for the ceremony. If you are having a video made at a church wedding, contact the vicar or churchwarden beforehand to check what is and isn't allowed.

● **Print your own invitations** Your guests will probably never notice the deckle edges and silver printing for which the printers charged an extra £1 per card. Instead of having your cards custom made, use invitation software such as that from www.smartdraw.com which, like similar software packages, offers a free trial before you commit, includes modern fonts and graphics and is easy to use. Save money, too, by omitting reply cards. If your friends and family are worth inviting to the wedding they will not mind writing their own replies.

● **Book budding musical talent** If you have always dreamed of having a live string quartet or even a rock band at your wedding reception but can't afford their fees, hire music students. A local school (perhaps one that specialises in the performing arts), university or music college will be able to recommend some students. To avoid disaster, hold a brief audition for your musicians before you hire them, or ask if you can hear them perform at a concert or gig.

A WEEKEND COURSE

Before you start your wedding planning, learn from the experts by going on a weekend course. Although these courses are designed for people embarking on wedding planning as a career, you'll pick up huge amounts of inside information. You could also treat the chief bridesmaid to a hair and make-up course. She may then be able to take care of the bride and other bridesmaids, as well as the bride's mother, and perhaps save you pounds on your bill.

● **Use local expertise** Ask around and you'll quickly discover bargain talent in your area, whether you want a wedding dress or outfit stitched, a cake baked, special ties or cravats made for the bridegroom and his party, or flowers arranged for your church and reception. Before you commission someone to do any one of these jobs, be very clear what you want and what you are asking them to do. Collect pictures and recipes torn from magazines, visit wedding shows and try on dresses you can't afford. If suppliers won't give you illustrated brochures, make careful notes and sketches just after your visit.

● **Focus your flowers** The flowers that will forever be in your photographs are those in the bride's bouquet and those worn by her mother, father, bridesmaids and other relatives, as well as the flowers on your top table, so that's where you want to invest. For the other tables, replace flowers with something you can make yourself: put candles in glass bowls and surround them with glass pebbles, or float tea lights in water (but check the safety clauses in your venue contract and insurance policy).

● **Cut to the cake** Plan to cut your cake and toss your bouquet early in the night: your photographer and video camera operator can then leave early, so cutting down on your costs per hour. After the professionals leave, your guests will also be more likely to start snapping pictures with the throwaway cameras on their tables (if you provide them). Remind them to distribute the best ones after you return from your honeymoon.

CATERER CONFIDENTIAL
8 CLASSY WAYS to cope with a crowd for less

● **Taste before you pay** Even if you have found a catering service you like and are ready to book it for a big event, there may still be some lingering doubts in the back of your mind. If so, ask if they will put on a tasting for you. If they refuse then you may want to think again. Alternatively, ask them to arrange for you to visit another function they are handling so that you can observe how they and their staff perform. If you do this, be sure to dress properly for the occasion, as if you were an invited guest, and don't overstay your welcome. You can pretty much gauge how well the caterer is doing in a half-hour or so.

● **Read the small print** Caterers bank on the fact that most clients won't read their contracts carefully. Read yours, and then read it again, because contracts often include 'hidden' charges. For instance, the company might charge for a set number of guests (that is, you will be charged for 100 people even if only 75 come), corkage on wine you have bought yourself, or overtime for waiting staff who stay late, whether you ask them to or not, so get a breakdown of all extra costs before the big day.

● **Sit and save** Some caterers give their clients the impression that buffets are cheaper than sit-down meals, but that is not true: a buffet actually requires more food and labour. When you have a sit-down meal, chefs control the portions of everything, allowing, for instance, exactly 200g of meat or fish, 150g of potatoes and 125g of vegetables on each plate. With a buffet they have to make much more food, to allow for guests returning for more. And buffets require constant maintenance – servers have to be there to replenish the dishes, and to keep the area tidy. People are also needed to clear plates from the tables, to serve drinks and so on, which requires hiring nearly twice the number of staff.

The cheapest plan is to have a sit-down meal – packaged. Every hotel and club, many restaurants and even some gastropubs offer set-priced meals that include everything from your starter to your champagne toast. Of course, they vary in price, but undoubtedly offer the best value for money.

● **Pick a bargain space** If you are planning a reunion, ask your school or college if you can use their space as a venue for your event for a nominal or bargain fee. They may even be prepared to do the catering for you at a knock-down rate. Or it may be that one of your former classmates runs a pub or restaurant you can use for free – if so

they will be glad of the income you'll be putting their way. For a summer event, plan a big picnic in a free space such as a park or a large garden belonging to a neighbour who will be on your guest list. Remember, though, that if you want a marquee, this in itself is never going to be cheap: one big enough to seat 150 people will cost upwards of £5,000.

● **Get a licence** Whatever venue you choose for your party, and even if you are putting up a marquee, you need a licence if you are asking guests to pay for their drinks (but not if they bring their own). You can ask the owner of the venue to arrange for a licence for you if they haven't got one (they will almost certainly charge extra for the service) or apply for a special licence yourself to your local licensing authority (ask for details at your town hall).

HIDDEN TRUTHS What your **CATERER** doesn't want you to know about meal planning

Don't let your caterer talk you into courses you don't need. If you are serving substantial canapés with drinks, there is no need to serve a starter as well. At a wedding, a dessert before the wedding cake is also unnecessary. Skipping these extra courses could save you a mint. Spend some of this on upgrading the wedding cake. Splurge on a super-rich fruit cake with marzipan and fondant icing, a tier of chocolate cake, beautifully 'iced' in white chocolate and served with a raspberry coulis or a tower of profiteroles. Later, as an extra treat, you could lay on a chocolate fountain with strawberries, cherries and soft dried apricots. Talk to the caterer and, if necessary, lay on the extras yourself.

HIDDEN TRUTHS

● **Employ extra bartenders** Most catering companies will assign one bartender to every 75 guests, but this will almost certainly result in huge queues. Wedding planners in the know say that you should specify in your contract that you want one bartender for every 50 guests at the start of the reception (when canapés are being served and guests will do most of their drinking), and then one bartender for every 75 guests during the meal.

● **Buy drinks by the head, not by the drink** Even if some of your guests are non-drinkers, don't let the caterer talk you into paying by the drink. Many teetotallers break their own rules when the alcohol is free – and what's free for them can cost you £3 or more per drink. Paying by the head will also avoid nasty surprises when it comes to paying the bill. If you are using outside caterers for your event, it is cheaper still to buy the drinks yourself, either at home or on a 'booze cruise' to France, even if you have to hire a small van to transport your bargains home.

● **Splash out on fizz** Champagne, or failing that a good, dry sparkling wine, makes any occasion really special, and many great-value prize-winning vintages can be bought at supermarkets and wine warehouses at home and in France. Buy some single bottles beforehand to test them for taste, or ask for a tasting before you make your choice. By buying in bulk you may also be eligible for significant discounts. Remember to ask your caterers to supply extra fridges or ice and buckets for keeping your fizz nice and cool.

DINNER PARTIES
5 SECRET INGREDIENTS for a great evening

● **Bring your host a thoughtful gift** The key to choosing the perfect gift for your host is to select something that will not disrupt the flow of the party and their last-minute preparations. If you want to give flowers, take the time to make a portable ready-arranged display (small plain plastic pots filled with florists' foam or jam jars decorated with ribbon make excellent 'vases'); if you bring a fresh bouquet the host will have to leave the guests and go searching for a vase. Alternatively, bring a gift such as homemade marmalade, chutney, jam or truffles, good biscuits or pretty napkins. By all means take wine as a gift, but do not expect your hosts to serve it in place of the wines they have chosen to accompany the meal. Polite hosts will assure their guests that the bottle will be greatly enjoyed on another occasion.

● **Penny-pinch with pasta** A pasta dish will stretch a dinner like no other food, and will be economical even if you splash out on one luxury ingredient such as fresh prawns. A dish such as a really well-made lasagne also takes time and trouble that guests will truly appreciate. Pasta is a great way of coping with vegetarian guests, too. To hide the fact that you have chosen pasta to cut costs, give your dinner party an Italian theme. Serve Italian wine and bread (with small dishes of Italian olive oil to dip it into), and throw red-and-white-checked cloths on your tables. To start the meal, prepare plates of antipasto from which guests can help themselves. To top it off, serve a tiramisu, cassata or other Italian dessert.

● **Mix and match** You may think that a few neighbourhood guests with similar interests equals one successful dinner party. Not so. The secret of the liveliest, most memorable evenings is usually a quirky collection of opposites. Mix it up a bit: invite both your conservative neighbour and your bohemian ex-college friend, sit them opposite each other and see what happens. If it all goes horribly wrong you can get people to change places before you serve the dessert.

● **Pets and children should not be seen, or heard** Keep your pets away from your guests unless you know for certain that they will be well received – not everyone likes a bounding, barking dog or cuddly cat. Equally, while casual barbecues are fine for whole families, even good friends will be put out if you spend the evening dealing with screaming infants. Much better to hire a babysitter, who may even be able to help you with some cooking and serving. And unless you have checked with your hosts in advance, never arrive at a dinner party with your children in tow.

EXPERT ADVICE
GREAT TIPS FROM THE PROFESSIONALS

A guide to impeccable table manners

The way you eat and behave at the table is still important, says Nicholas Clayton of The Guild of Professional English Butlers. His guidelines:
• Never talk with your mouth full.
• Don't hold your knife poised as if ready to sign a cheque, and don't point with any of your cutlery.
• Let your food cool of its own accord – don't blow on it.
• A napkin is there to protect your clothes; use it to dab the corners of your mouth but never to polish your teeth.
• Never cut bread or bread rolls. Break the bread with your fingers and butter a small piece at a time. Breakfast toast is the only exception.
• Don't spit unwanted food into your napkin – remove it with your fork and place it on the side of your plate.
• Be careful not to insult your host by adding salt before you have tasted your food.
• When you've finished eating, place your knife and fork or spoon and fork together, vertically. Leave your plate where it is – never push it away from you.
• Don't get drunk; you'll look absurd.

● **Learn to spot an 'empty invitation'** Few people would admit to giving one, but there are some invitations that are offered purely out of social grace, not out of a genuine desire to see someone again. These 'empty invitations' are particularly prevalent at the close of social events such as dinner parties when people have had plenty to drink. If, for instance, you have just met someone at a dinner party and they say 'Let's have lunch' or 'I'll call you', the invitation is only 'real' if you do something positive such as exchange phone numbers or email addresses, and even then it is not guaranteed. To avoid confusion, if you are the one making a parting comment, say something more general such as 'It was good to meet you'.

BEATING THE
CHRISTMAS CONSPIRACY

6 TIPS to prevent the festive season becoming a wasteful spending spree

● **Shop from home** The flurry of catalogues through the letterbox starts as soon as the summer holidays are over, and that's the time to begin looking for affordable gifts that will hit the spot, not least because the best bargains and most popular items quickly go out of stock. The internet is great for gift shopping but you need to be wary of promises of last-minute deliveries that often don't materialise, leaving you obliged to rush around on Christmas Eve looking for a substitute. To be certain of getting gifts in time, try to make your Christmas orders four weeks ahead and, if possible, telephone before you order to double-check on availability.

As well as presents, order all the heavy and bulky supermarket items online and get them delivered – including wine and other drinks, toilet and kitchen paper, cat litter, washing powder, plus tins of tomatoes and sweetcorn, bottles of olive oil, mayonnaise, pasta, rice and other store-cupboard basics.

● **Keep your tree small** You don't need a huge, costly Christmas tree to make a festive statement. A small tree set on a table is just as good as a massive one, though it will look best if you cover the table with a decorative, floor-length cloth. Or dispense with a tree altogether and hang your baubles on twigs you've coated with metallic spray. Pine cones sprayed in the same way, with coloured ribbon attached, make attractive, economy decorations. Prevent bauble breakages and save money, by storing them in used egg cartons.

● **Scout around for postal bargains** Save money on card postage, and help the Boy Scouts, by looking for their Christmas delivery services. The usual (voluntary) charge is around 10p per card for very local deliveries, 15–20p for deliveries further afield. Postboxes are set up in strategic locations around an area. If there is no such service available locally, why not set one up yourself and give the proceeds to your favourite charity? You will need a dedicated group of volunteers for the collection, sorting and deliveries.

For mail you are sending abroad, check out the last dates for sea mail postage, which can be as early as October. Just compare prices: a 500g small packet from the UK to Canada sent airmail costs £10.50, sent surface mail the price is a mere £4.81.

SIMPLY SPECIAL TRIMMINGS

Duck the consumer pressure by starting with something simple and adding your own touches; for instance:
● Buy a ready-made fruitcake, prick holes in the base, dowse with a few tablespoons of brandy and wrap it in foil for a couple of weeks. Then add marzipan and icing. Similarly, you could take the tops off commercial mince pies and add a topping of chopped nuts or marzipan.
● Personalise cheap crackers and slip new gifts into them.
● Make a table centrepiece from cheap shiny baubles piled in a shallow bowl, and tuck in sprigs of sprayed holly.
● Stir a dash of port and some grated orange rind into bought cranberry sauce for a superior flavour.
● Purchase plain cushions and decorate them yourself with sequins, beads or appliqué.

For gift tags, make your own from pieces of card

- **Economise on wrapping** Don't be lured into buying expensive paper. Plain white paper decorated with felt-tip pen or potato prints (fun for children) looks great, and the 'plastic' ribbon sold at the stationers is much more expensive than 'real' ribbon you can buy by the metre from your local haberdashery counter. For a great look, choose one with a metallic edging and simply tie it around a gift wrapped in tissue paper. To wrap small gifts, offcuts of fabric make an unusual and decorative treatment. For gift tags, make your own from pieces of card or wrapping paper – or cut out motifs from cards you have received in previous years. To give a professional finish, make a hole for the ribbon by using one 'arm' of a hole puncher.

- **Shop smart for festive food**
Resist the pressure to stock up for a siege or buy a huge turkey if there are only four of you for dinner. At worst the supermarkets will only be closed for two days over the holiday, so there is no need to buy a lot extra. But to cater for unexpected guests it is wise to have some spare bread in the freezer and a carton of long-life milk in the cupboard.

- **Waste not ...** Don't discard those delicious leftovers. Cooked cold turkey and ham make great sandwiches and, sliced up and well sealed, will keep in the freezer for up to six months. Stock made from boiling up poultry bones with some onions, carrots, mushrooms and herbs makes great soups and freezes well. Oddments of Stilton and hard cheeses also freeze well; defrosted, they can be used as pizza toppings or stuffing for chicken breasts. Save goose fat for cooking the best ever roast potatoes. It will keep for weeks in the fridge.

chapter

16

secrets for
LEISURE TIME

How the professionals plan outings and make reservations with ease

DINING OUT

10 SIMPLE STRATEGIES to ensure that you have a memorable meal and get good value when you eat out

● **Do some research** It would be nice to think we live in a country where you can go to any town or village and be guaranteed good, fresh food. Sadly, despite a growing interest in food and significant increase in the number of good UK restaurants, taking pot luck remains a risky business. From time to time you are still likely to encounter frozen food, sloppily prepared and presented with a limp salad garnish.

But there are excellent restaurants out there and the chances are that you're within striking distance, but you'll have to track them down. The best source of information will be a reliable friend or acquaintance who likes good food. If you are going to a part of the country where you don't know anyone, consult a good guide book. The best on UK restaurants are *The Good Food Guide*, the *Michelin Guide, The AA Restaurant Guide* and Harden's *UK Restaurants*. *Time Out* guides can also be useful if you only want to know about London. All of these publications will give you some excellent suggestions or, at the very least, some safe bets. But new eateries open all the time and there might be a hot new place in town that is yet to be featured in any guide book.

If you're staying in a hotel, ask the reception staff for advice, but don't be surprised if you're recommended a place run by someone's relative or friend.

● **Get a second opinion** If you're trying to book a restaurant for a special occasion, such as a birthday or a major anniversary, it's worth digging a little deeper. Once you have a shortlist, take a look at a few restaurant websites. Most

sites should give you the information you require, including sample menus and possibly a view of the dining area. If you have the time, it might be worth an exploratory visit, maybe for lunch, which is likely to be cheaper than dinner but should give you an idea of whether the place meets your requirements.

● **Know when to keep it simple** If you find yourself in a restaurant that doesn't entirely inspire you with confidence – perhaps there are coffee stains on the menu, or a smell of cooking fat pervades the room, or the staff look bored – then it's best to keep your order simple. Don't go for the 'fish special' or anything too complex. Stick to plain, straightforward dishes, such as steak and chips. And, as overcooking is common in such places, it might be a good idea to order your steak cooked to at least one level below the way you like it – if, for example, you like it medium, ask for it rare. If you are in a pizza restaurant, order the pizza; it's likely to be a better bet than the token pasta dish.

● **Learn what's in season** Given the fact that supermarkets have a range of soft summer berries on their shelves all year, it's not surprising that many people are confused about seasonality. You may have also wondered why even native English strawberries seem to be in the shops earlier than when you were younger. It's not just global warming, but because growers are increasingly using polytunnels to extend the seasons. When a food is truly in season, it's likely to have a fuller flavour and will also be at its cheapest. In-season, home-grown

... in a restaurant that doesn't entirely inspire you with confidence ... it's best to keep your order simple

food is also better for the environment as it hasn't had to be shipped halfway around the world. If you get to know when locally grown fruit and veg is likely to be on the menu, you'll find it easier to spot dishes that must be based on frozen or imported produce, so you can avoid them. Click on a website such as www.bbc.co.uk/food to help you to identify what's in season when, and make sure you enjoy food which is at its freshest and tastiest when you eat out.

● **Be wary of fancy language** Do not be drawn to a place that describes its food as 'nestling in' or 'resting on a bed of' and don't be impressed by its use of adjectives – as in 'simply stunning sardines'. Top chefs tend to prefer brief descriptions and the best restaurants generally let the food do the talking.

How they do it . . .
getting a good table

State any special requirements when you make the booking, advises Andrew Turvil, editor of *The AA Restaurant Guide* and a former editor of *The Good Food Guide*. Be specific and if you want, for instance, a table on the terrace, just ask for it. Of course, promises made on the phone are not always passed on to the waiting staff. So if you asked for a terrace table and they're all full when you arrive, Turvil suggests that you complain to the manager. You may not get what you requested, but you're more likely to be seated somewhere good or be compensated in some way. And if, when you arrive, you decide you don't like the table you specified, act quickly. Most places are happy to move you, if possible. Once you've been to a restaurant a few times and built up a rapport with the staff, getting the right table may be as simple as just asking for your usual spot.

● **Try for a cancellation** Getting a table at a celebrated restaurant can be difficult. So be flexible when you phone up and have more than one date to suggest. If you want to eat out on a Friday or Saturday, especially at a popular venue, you can expect a very long lead time. But it's always worth ringing up at short notice, as tables do come up as a result of cancellations – if customers have to book so far in advance, it's highly likely that someone has had to change their plans.

● **Don't be intimidated** Never allow overbearing or patronising restaurant staff to make you feel uncomfortable. They work in the hospitality industry and it's their job to serve you. If you're not happy with their attitude, don't leave a tip, don't go back and tell your friends not to go there. A tip described on the bill as 'optional' or 'discretionary' is just that. You don't have to pay it, if you're not satisfied with the service.

● **Get the best for less** If you're on a tight budget but want to try one of the country's leading restaurants, then consider going there for lunch. It won't be cheap, but it will cost less than going in the evening. Many top restaurants offer lunchtime menus that are almost half the cost of the dinner menu, yet you still get superb cooking and the same wonderful setting. And, although the service will be just as attentive, the atmosphere is likely to be more relaxed. Be warned, though, that a set lunch is likely to offer a more limited choice of dishes than the evening menu.

● **Avoid unnecessary extras** Many restaurants make their dishes seem better value by giving a price on the menu for a main course that only includes a basic garnish. The waiter will then ask you what side dishes you require – and they cost extra. So enquire about what is served with your choice of dish. Perhaps the potato topping will provide enough carbohydrate and you won't need a helping of chips or perhaps the bed of spinach will supply enough greenery. Sharing one side order with your dining companion may also be plenty. If you discuss it with your waiter, he or she is likely to give you an honest response. And if you're still worried about feeling hungry after you've eaten the meal, make sure you take up the offer of bread; it could be ideal for soaking up the sauce from your main course.

● **Order water from the tap** If you ask for some water in many restaurants these days, you're highly likely to be given a fancy bottle containing some costly liquid from a famous spa. But in the UK, tap water is usually perfectly drinkable and most restaurants will be happy to provide you with a glass or jug of it – often chilled with a refreshing slice of lemon – if you ask for it. So don't just tell your waiter that you'd like some water – unless you really do want the bottled kind. Be specific. Request a jug of tap water and there should be no confusion – and you'll end up with a smaller bill to pay.

WINE SECRETS

5 KEY POINTS to consider when you order wine

● **Buy it by the bottle** Drinking wine by the glass is a good option if you and your dinner companion only want a glass each, or if you want different wines. But if you can agree to drink the same thing, it's likely to cost you around the same price to order two glasses each as it is to buy a bottle. The standard 75cl bottle will give you six glasses between you, so it is always better value for money.

● **Serve yourself** Having someone filling up your glass, when you don't want them to, can be frustrating, and it makes it much harder to keep an eye on how much you are drinking. Of course, restaurants want you to drink as much as possible, because they make a lot of their profit from drinks sales. But if you'd prefer to fill your own glasses, let your waiter know. You might have to say it more than once, but the waiter

should get the message eventually. Some restaurants keep the wine off the table, which can work well if the staff are good at their jobs, but can be frustrating if you want a refill and no one has noticed. Ask for the wine to be left on your table, if you'd prefer it.

● **Bring your own** The BYO phenomenon is not as big in the UK as it is, for example, in Australia, where it's very common for customers to turn up with their own wine. If a restaurant advertises itself as BYO, then you can bring your own bottle with impunity and you'll get the benefit of not paying a high mark-up. It's not unusual for restaurants to mark-up wine prices by as much as 300 per cent. They usually argue that they need this income to make their businesses financially viable and many establishments are not keen for customers to bring their own wine –

Order water from the tap ...

restaurants will be happy to provide you with a glass or jug

but it can be done, even if the eatery doesn't advertise the fact. You might have to pay a corkage charge – usually around £5-£10 per bottle but, even with this, you can save money. Just let the restaurant know beforehand that you want to bring your own wine and find out what corkage will be payable.

● **Be wary with champagne** If you want an aperitif, the waiter might suggest a glass of champagne. This may sound very enticing and maybe you want to impress someone. But be careful when ordering champagne by the glass – even the house champagne can be around £10 per glass and some restaurants offer a range, including several that will cost considerably more. Getting the bill, and discovering you've spent as much as £20

on a single drink, can leave a nasty taste in the mouth. If you don't feel happy about asking the waiter about the specifics of their champagne prices, make sure you see the wine list before ordering your aperitif. Or you could just express your confidence in the quality of the house champagne, if you want to avoid anything that's too pricey.

● **Doggie-bag that Merlot** Are you hesitating about ordering that second bottle, because you're not sure whether you'll actually finish it? Don't forget you could always ask to take any remaining wine home. Most places will happily stick a cork in it and let you take it away to drink the next day. It's not something that happens too often, though, so may get the odd funny look.

CINEMA VISITS

7 SECRETS for having a great time when you venture out to see a film on the 'big' screen

● **Buy tickets in advance** On a typical Friday or Saturday night, hundreds of people will be queuing outside cinemas across the land to buy tickets for some huge Hollywood blockbuster that everybody is talking about. They'll all want to be among the first to see it and up to half of them are likely to be disappointed, as tickets will be sold out well before they reach the box office. And while they're standing there, they'll see others walk up to one of the machines near the entrance, swipe their credit card, grab the tickets that pop out and walk straight in – missing all the queues. These people aren't simply lucky, they're ones who were

wise enough to buy their tickets in advance, online or over the phone. Many people don't yet realise that in some cases it makes no more sense to wander ticketless into a cinema than it does to show up at a rare performance by the Bolshoi Ballet and hope to get in. You might, but you'll more likely find yourself all dressed up with nowhere to go. Visiting your local cinema has changed and a planned outing, complete with pre-booked tickets, can often be essential. But remember that although most cinemas now offer advanced booking, it isn't usually for numbered seats, so you still need to get there at a reasonable time to get a decent place.

HOW TO ORDER WINE
WITHOUT WORRY

IT IS NOW ACCEPTED THAT SOME OF THE FUNDAMENTAL RULES about wine were meant to be broken. Some white wines go well with meat and some of the lighter reds are good with poultry and fish dishes. Food and wine matching can be difficult, especially if everyone at the table is eating different things. Here are some tips on handling the ritual of wine ordering.

MAKE USE OF THE WINE WAITER Many good restaurants have specialist wine waiters – known as sommeliers – who will take your wine order. They are usually highly trained and are responsible for putting the wine list together – and therefore know the contents better than anyone else. They appreciate it when you ask for advice, as they are usually passionate about the subject. The key is to give them a price range. Armed with this, and an indication of the style of wine that you're after, they will be able to give you some choices that you're unlikely to select yourself. A good wine waiter can actually help you to save money, as well as ensure that you drink something really good. Just decide beforehand what style of wine you're after and what food you want it to go with – and don't forget to be clear about the approximate price that you're happy to pay.

DON'T WORRY ABOUT MISPRONOUNCING THE NAME
An experienced waiter will have heard the name of a particular wine pronounced in more than a hundred different ways and is probably far too busy to worry about such things. And it's usually a good idea to point at the wine that you'd like on the list, anyway, so that you can be certain that your waiter knows exactly which bottle you want.

CHECK THE VINTAGE
Make sure that the year – or vintage – on the wine list matches the one on the bottle that is presented to you, before opening it. Different vintages of the same wine can vary in quality and you don't want to be given an inferior year. You never know, you might be given a better one, but do query any difference and don't accept it unless you're entirely happy.

DON'T BE INTIMIDATED BY THE RITUAL OF TASTING It's not a test that you can fail. It's simply an opportunity for you to check that the wine is not oxidised (vinegary) or that the cork hasn't started to rot (a musty taste). It will usually be fairly obvious if something is wrong – and you can ask the waiter to taste it, too. The restaurant will happily replace any bottle that is spoiled. And don't feel under pressure to swill the wine around the glass before you try it, unless you are confident about doing so. Let your waiter know when you're happy with a wine that he or she has recommended; a 'thank you' always goes down well.

secret weapon

FILM SOCIETIES

If you're fed up with the mainstream offerings at your local Odeon or Vue, or live in a remote spot which means that every cinema visit involves a long and tiring journey, why not start a local film society. You'll be able to devise your own programmes and hopefully enjoy the films you choose to show in a more relaxing, club-like atmosphere.

Of course, acquiring the necessary equipment, along with films to view and somewhere to show them, is going to demand time, energy and money. It's not something you're likely to be able to do successfully without help. So start by logging on to the website of the British Federation of Film Societies (www.bffs.org.uk). It will immediately give you access to the wisdom of a community of seasoned film buffs. You can also download the BFFS's advice leaflet on starting a film society, which contains all the basic information you'll need at the outset.

A good way to find out what's currently on ... is to log on to the websites of the three main UK cinema chains

● **Use the internet** A good way to find out what's currently on, and where to see it, is to log on to the websites of the three main UK cinema chains – www.cineworld.co.uk, www.odeon.co.uk and www.myvue.com Click on the film you want to see and check where it's on. Then, when you've found a venue that suits you, buy your tickets online. You'll pay the same as at the cinema box office, plus a small handling fee, but that's always worth it if you want to go on an opening weekend or early in the run of a major release. Tickets can even be booked several weeks in advance.

Another way to locate a cinema or find out where a film is showing is to go to http://users.aber.ac.uk/jwp/cinemas This site lists all UK cinemas, along with details of their size, number of screens, websites and phone numbers. Or for details and reviews of the latest releases, try http://movies.uk.msn.com

● **If it's good, bookmark it** When you find a cinema that's convenient and that you really like – maybe it has helpful staff or generally screens a good range of films or has particularly comfortable seating with good sightlines – you should bookmark it on your internet browser. You will then be able to go straight back to its website in just one click, whenever you want to check what's on and when. Or, you may be able to register with a particular venue, so that they can send you regular emails with details of future programmes.

● **Side-step the pre-show ads** You may hate them, but an audience of mostly young adults, with spare cash in their pockets and nothing to do but stare at the screen, makes an ideal target for advertisers. But you can cheat the system. You could time your arrival to within a minute or two of the start of what you've actually come to see. Cinemas rarely announce when the main feature starts, so you'll have to ask and even then you may not get a clear answer. But politely persist – if you're only going to be sitting there chomping on popcorn, you might as well be enjoying a pre-show drink in a nearby bar or café . You can reckon on there being about 15 to 20 minutes of trailers and advertisements before the main film begins. But there's a danger in taking your seats at the last minute, if they're not numbered. You could find that the best ones have gone and that if you're in a group, you have to split up.

A more rebellious approach is to flout the no-talking rule that's sacred inside a cinema. In fact, it doesn't really kick in until the lights go out completely and advertising often runs with some lighting still on. So chat away until darkness descends. You could talk about how much you hate ads being screened.

● Eat before or after the show

The food they sell you at the cinema is messy, unhealthy and over-priced. And getting hold of it usually means joining a long queue. Cinemas are constantly coming up with new tricks to keep us spending £5-£10 for junk that we'd probably never dream of buying anywhere else. So why not stop buying and eating the stuff. Have a good meal before or after the show instead. Most of us eat the popcorn simply because we associate it with watching a film. But this link is fairly new in the UK. It was only really with the arrival, in the 1980s, of the multiplex cinemas from America that the popcorn-and-cola craze started. Before that an usherette would offer drinks from a tray carried around her neck during an interval between screenings. And going further back still, to before the Second World War, there was no food at all in cinemas, because the owners of the grand 'picture palaces' didn't want their carpets and upholstery ruined by chocolate and spilled drinks. So boycott those trashy snacks as an act of nostalgia for the golden age of film.

● Enjoy the credits

Credits at the end of a film last about 7 or 8 minutes and most cinemas put the house-lights partly up to help people to leave safely. But don't feel you have to rush out. If you want to sit and collect your thoughts after a good film, enjoy the closing music, or find out which locations were used, that's all part of the show and the staff should respect your wishes.

● Try open-air viewing

Why not try something a little different. Pack your deckchair and head for an open-air cinema. Sit back under the stars with a drink in your hand and enjoy a favourite classic – or, in a few, rare cases, one of the latest releases. Click on www.skylightcinema.co.uk for information about open-air screenings currently taking place across the UK and enjoy a unique and exciting experience.

But do be aware of potential pitfalls before you go. You may have to travel some distance for this treat. Only a handful of outdoor cinemas still operate and those that do often rely on subsidies in order to continue. Equipment may be outdated, so if you're a serious film buff, looking to capture every second of what's up there on the silver screen, you could be disappointed. The sound may be drowned at times by passing traffic or have to be kept low to avoid disturbing any neighbours. In the summer months, the evening's screening may have to begin before its dark enough to see the picture clearly. But it's different and fun.

HIDDEN TRUTHS What the major cinema distribution chains don't want you to know about **DVDS**

The hype surrounding the release of the latest blockbuster is designed to get you to rush out to your local multi-screen cinema as soon as possible. But unless you absolutely have to be one of the first to see the latest Hollywood offering, it pays to be a little patient. The time between a film's release in the cinema and its release on DVD is growing shorter. It used to be at least six months, but can now be a matter of weeks. Some companies are even talking about simultaneous releases, since film makers often now make most of their money from DVD sales and rentals. If a film is really good, it will be just as enjoyable to watch at home. This is especially true if you have a large-screen TV, which can show spectacular special effects as well as the smaller screens at the multiplex.

LIVE EVENTS

19 SMART WAYS to track down tickets for key events and get the best value

● **Book at the venue** These days, many tickets – whether they are for sports, music or theatre events – are sold online, usually via a central ticketing service, either owned by the venue or run by their appointed ticket agent. But you should always try the official number or website of the venue first to see if you can buy directly, as that way, you'll cut out the agency's booking fee, which can be considerable. If you don't mind making a little extra effort – and, of course, if it's convenient – it could pay to visit the venue in person to get your tickets. You may find that because of the savings you make, you can afford better seats – and you're likely to get a better choice of where you sit, too.

● **Compare ticket agencies** Even if you can't buy directly from the venue, it still may be possible to shave some money off the total price, as the fees charged by ticket agents tend to vary widely. As a rule of thumb, compare at least three ticket agencies, asking for a breakdown of how much they're charging in fees and postage. Agents generally charge a booking fee on top of the ticket price and there may also be a small transaction fee. Always check what the extras are before committing to buy. The main agencies to check are Ticketmaster, Seetickets, Ticket Web (owned by Ticketmaster). Only buy from legitimate agents. Most are members of the Society of Ticket Agents and Retailers (STAR) and are required to comply with an agreed code of practice. So always enquire if an agent is a STAR member when booking or look out for the STAR logo. For more information about STAR members or their code of practice go to www.s-t-a-r.org.uk, or call their helpline on 0870 603 9011.

● **Go to the fan club** Whenever you're looking for tickets to any type of concert – classical, pop, rock, grunge or folk – it's always worth checking the website of the artists themselves or that of their fan club. It may be possible, by paying a small joining fee, to buy tickets before they're on general sale, and you may get them at a discounted price too.

● **Join a mailing List** Subsidised theatre companies, such as the Royal National Theatre, the Royal Shakespeare Company and the Royal Court, and many music venues charge a small fee to have performance schedules posted to your home. You'll also get priority booking, usually several weeks before tickets are on sale to the general public, and discounted special offers. Often you'll be given the chance to attend a preview performance at very low cost.

There are also a number of free mailing lists. A good one to get onto can be found at www.seetickets.com This site runs exclusive online offers, that can offer extraordinary value.

● **Be emailed in advance** Join an email service that gives you early notice of events. You'll also get priority internet booking from approximately two weeks before tickets are put on sale elsewhere.

Register your contact details on websites such as www.seetickets.com and www.whatsonstage.com and you'll receive vital information on concerts and other events at regular intervals via your email. Registering with these sites is free and they will not sell any of your details on. Additionally www.ticketmaster.co.uk runs a useful 'priority' membership scheme, which you can join by paying a small subscription.

● **Buy single seats** If actually being at an event is what's really important to you – rather than simply enjoying a night out as part of a group – then be prepared to sit separately and ask the box office or ticket agent to check their computer to see if there are any odd seats still available dotted around the auditorium. There often are. Most people are after tickets for two seats or more, so you'll almost certainly find it easier to get into a very popular event if you're prepared to split up your party.

● **Get tickets for 'sold-out' events** Never take it literally when it's announced that there are no more tickets left for a major concert, show or sporting event. In the initial rush for tickets, 'sold out in 20 minutes' is a popular press quote. Events don't usually stay that way, though – it's only the start of a process. Generally an 'extra date' for a big concert will be added within hours of booking opening. Later that day – and for some time after – single tickets will appear on the official website, as booking systems synchronise following the initial rush. A few days, or even a few weeks before the event, advertisements for 'extra tickets just released' often appear. These are tickets that have been returned by tour operators, the press and PR agencies and also seats that have either

been added – around a runway stage, for example – or previously held back by the venue, pending confirmation that sightlines are going to be okay. Some booking agents may have access to really excellent seats at extremely short notice.

● **Look out for special offers** Many newspapers, including *The Times*, *The Sunday Times*, *The Evening Standard* and *The Daily Telegraph*, carry adverts offering discounts on major shows at quieter times of the year; in London, that's generally from midwinter to late spring, excluding Bank Holiday periods. If you are happy to look online, you'll always find plenty of special deals at www.lastminute.com/theatrenow – and possibly at www.theatremonkey.com

● **Try Google or the show website** You may manage to grab a bargain by using a search engine. It can pay dividends to visit Google, enter a search, such as the name of the show or event or where it's being held, and see what appears, both in the results list and the sponsored advertisements at the side of the page. Sometimes exclusive discounts may be hidden on official event websites. So take a look at them and search around a little – the offers are not always easy to find and may be hidden behind 'latest news' or 'booking information' links.

● **Use a discount website** Sign up with a site such as www.showsavers.co.uk and you'll have constant access to a vast range of bargains. If you don't let on where you're getting all your information from, friends may think you have special secret links with the 'glamorous' world of show business.

Buy single seats ... to get into a very popular event

continued on page 308 ➤➤

FREE – OR ALMOST FREE – LIVE PERFORMANCES

A LOT OF LIVE ENTERTAINMENT THESE DAYS is outrageously expensive. But if you can accept the idea that you can enjoy something that doesn't feature premiership football teams, renowned actors, world-famous artists or stadium rock stars, you can live it up for free. Here are some ideas:

FREE CONCERTS IN THE PARK Instead of walking past these events, as people usually do, sit down on the grass as close to the performers as possible, and immerse yourself in the music. The players are usually pretty good, or the town or city wouldn't allow them to play.

LOCAL THEATRE People travel many miles and spend a lot of money to see a West End play. Why not try driving a few miles – or walking if the venue is near enough – to see a local amateur dramatic society's production. Tickets are usually very cheap, and if you volunteer to help to sell some of them, you may even be offered free admission.

OPEN-MIC (PRONOUNCED 'MIKE') NIGHTS These are events where anyone can get up on stage and do a turn and smaller venues often hold them on weekday nights. Many well-known artists have begun their careers like this – performers that people now pay £100 to see from a distance in a football stadium. Even a really awful performance can make you laugh. Try keying 'open-mic night' into Google and see what comes up in your area.

EXHIBITION OPENINGS This is the best entertainment bargain on the planet: free admission, free wine, free canapés, free people-watching and free mingling with the artist – who's bound to be nice to you. You might even discover that you actually like the paintings, sculptures, photographs or whatever else is on display.

FREE LUNCHTIME CONCERTS Many arts centres, churches and cathedrals put on free concerts that fill a lunch hour perfectly. They are usually advertised on posters pinned to the door of the venue, as well as in local freebie newspapers and online. Just turn up and enjoy them. If you've never experienced classical music, hearing it live is a great introduction. Just go with an open mind.

PROCESSIONS AND PARADES From bonfire night to carnivals, from religious festivals to Chinese New Year – there are lots of good reasons for staging a procession. A parade is hard to beat if you like noise, colour and variety. Fancy-dress floats, marching bands, 'twirlers' in bright, short

YOU'LL REALLY ENJOY

dresses with spinning batons, beauty queens and crowds of people make for great free entertainment. Just get there early enough to choose a good vantage point.

AUTHOR READINGS
You've read the book; now listen to the writer. Many well-known and not-so-well-known authors do a circuit of local bookshops to read from their latest publication, sign books and mix with their readers – and they seldom put on a dull performance. Look for notices of forthcoming author readings in your nearest bookshop's window or pick up a leaflet from the counter.

LOCAL TEAM SPORTS
True lovers of cricket, rugby or football can get just as much fun supporting a local village, town or school team as one from the big league. Pick a team to root for, go and watch them a few times – and you'll find yourself experiencing the thrills and emotions that you'd pay two days' wages for at a major British stadium or ground. It may not be Wasps or Manchester United, but at the end of the day, cheering players in a live game can't be beaten.

PUB SESSIONS
One or two nights a week, local pubs may have live music. It might be a new student band trying to make a go of it, or some greying rockers whose hearts are lost in the 1970s. Or you might find an eclectic mixture of 'folkies' with fiddles, accordions and guitars. Give it a go – you could find yourself learning to love a new musical genre.

CITY PERFORMANCES
If you live in a city, then finding free entertainment couldn't be easier. There are concerts in churches, plenty of sporting fixtures, galleries and gigs, lectures and museum tours. Most cities have listings of what's on for free on the internet; all you have to do is search. Here are two examples:

- **Edinburgh** www.theoracle.co.uk is a website that covers 'what's on' in Edinburgh. Its menu includes music, comedy and children's events and there's also a link to free things to do in and around the city. In any one month, you'll find a range of musical offerings, exhibitions, lectures and walks. Information on this user-friendly site is regularly updated, and you can search by time frame (this week or month), event name or venue.

- **London** If you live in or near London and have access to the internet, you'll discover a bewildering choice of free entertainment. The website www.londonfreelist.com lists by category events and attractions that are free or cost £3 at the most. Categories include clubs and bars, comedy, dance, poetry, politics and theatre. The list is updated every day – so what are you waiting for? *Time Out*'s website (www.timeout.com/london) also has lots of information about free fun in the lively capital.

'ENTHUSIASTIC APPLAUSE, PLEASE'
Have you ever considered being in a studio audience? Tickets for the recording sessions of some BBC TV and radio programmes are free and give you the opportunity to see what goes on behind the scenes of your favourite comedy, quiz or current affairs programme. The only restriction is that some shows have a minimum age limit. The BBC does its utmost to make all venues accessible to people with disabilities and will provide sign-language interpreters, if given advance notice. Remember that a show is being recorded in order to broadcast it – so the audience effectively becomes a participant in the show. The BBC can also ask you to leave if you interrupt or spoil the recording process. Go to www.bbc.co.uk/whatson/tickets/apply.shtml and then to the relevant page for the programme you're interested in for tickets. Alternatively phone 0870 9011227. Most BBC studios are based in or near Belfast, Cardiff, Glasgow or London.

● **Buy at a half-price booth** To snap up a last-minute bargain visit London's half-price ticket booth, which has stood in Leicester Square, in the heart of theatreland, since 1980 (a second booth at Canary Wharf closed in autumn 2007). It offers a broad selection of tickets for West End shows at half the official price, plus a booking fee of £2.50. Tickets are only for that day's performance – no advance booking is available and the service is for personal callers only. Before you set out, log on to www.officiallondontheatre.co.uk/tkts/today to find out what's available.

● **Form a group** Put together a group of ten or more people and you could get savings of up to 50 per cent on your tickets. The bigger the group, the lower the price. Extra special rates for midweek matinees often apply for parties of schoolchildren and senior citizens. Always compare the prices of the various group-booking specialists, as both rates and seat locations on offer do vary. If you become a regular group booker, you may also find that you are invited to 'agency evenings' – to see the latest shows for free.

> Put together a group of ten or more and you could get savings of up to 50 per cent on your tickets

● **Book a coach trip** If you can't manage to put your own group together, join an existing one instead, perhaps by signing up for one of the many coach trips that combine transport with a ticket for the show or event that you want to see. Some of these packages include accommodation, where appropriate. These can be excellent value for money as often the all-in price is almost the same or less than the tickets alone would have been, if you had bought them separately.

● **Get a standby ticket** Many venues have a special standby price for tickets that remain unsold an hour before a show or event starts. Savings as high as 70 per cent may be offered to personal callers at the box office. You can get some very good seats this way, as even top shows regularly have to fill their front row with standby users. It's also worth visiting the box office earlier in the day, as standby tickets sometimes go on sale in the morning, when the box office opens. If the venue is sticking to a one-hour-before rule, try to be there about 2 hours before the curtain goes up. You may be able to buy your standbys straightaway, or if, as is likely, you have to wait, at least you'll be near the front of the queue. Remember also, that although standby tickets are usually available to anyone, some are only offered to special groups, such as students and OAPs, who will need to bring ID and evidence of their status with them. These special groups may also be able to book tickets at concessionary rates in advance

● **Go to a preview** Before the official opening night of a play, there are usually a handful of preview performances for which tickets are sold at a greatly reduced rate. But be warned – these early performances are sometimes cancelled at short notice and, if they go ahead, can be a little lacking in polish.

● **Restrict your view** Many venues have a clutch of seats going cheaply in areas of the auditorium that normally command a much higher price. This is because the view from these seats is restricted in some way. The reduction is usually roughly proportional to how limited the view actually is. These seats may only be sold from the venue's box office, so that staff can make any problems involved clear, allowing customers to make an informed choice before they buy. Quite often the viewing restrictions are minor and you can get good seats for a modest sum.

● **Try the upper-circle trick** Buy the cheapest ticket in the upper circle or balcony. On a very quiet night, a theatre or concert hall may close these areas – and you will be promoted to the costlier seats downstairs. Of course, this only works on the less popular shows. And do make sure, if you are moved, that your new seat has at least as good a view as the one you had originally.

● **Move forward** If the show or event is popular and the upper circle or balcony is likely to be kept open, buy the cheapest seats in the stalls or dress circle and then try to move forward into

an unoccupied seat. Remember, though, that moving forward is often frowned upon by other ticket holders and the management may well ask you to move back, if it has not given you permission to change your seat. So it's always best to legitimise your action by asking an usher first if you can move a couple of minutes before curtain-up. Moving forwards is usually less frowned upon after the interval, but it is still better to ask the management if it's okay.

● **Know your venue** However you book your tickets, it always helps to find out about the venue you're planning to visit. Many theatre, stadium and agency websites help their customers to select their seats by displaying all kinds of information about the events for which they're selling tickets. For example, they'll have seating charts, maps and details of transport links and car parks. Just type the venue name into Google, then click on to a website with the details that you're seeking. You'll be better placed to get the best value, as well as something that really suits you.

GAMBLING

6 **INSIDER TIPS** to maximise the fun and increase your chances of winning

● **Develop an eye for a winner**
Horse races are a popular source of entertainment and there's nothing quite like the thrill of picking a horse, placing a bet with a bookie and watching the race unfold. But, to increase your odds of backing a winner, it will pay you to get to know a little about the sport. Log

on to www.britishhorseracing.com or cast your eye over a reputable racing paper, such at the *Racing Post*. Find out the favourites for the races that interest you and learn a little about their past performances or 'form'. Based on this knowledge, pick a few horses to watch out for at the track and try to get there early. Lucy Watson from the British Horseracing Board advises casting an eye over the horses when they parade before a race. The sort of signs you should be seeking in a potential winner are good muscle tone, a shiny coat, bright eyes, forward-pointing ears and an alert manner. Also check how a horse moves. A relaxed fluid gait is ideal but watch out for signs of agitation or nervousness, such as profuse sweating – although this is normal in some animals. And don't be put off by blinkers or visors, which are worn to help the horse to concentrate on the job at hand.

● **Beware of fraudsters** There are unscrupulous people around who may offer you a commission for placing bets on their behalf. You may be asked to pay for the bets and then offered a reimbursement plus a generous commission on any winnings after the race. But you're highly unlikely to receive any money at all. Fraudsters are quite common in the betting business. Usually, if the horse wins they send a courier to collect 90 per cent of the winnings and leave the remainder for the person who placed the bet to pick up. But it if loses, then the gambler hears nothing – and forfeits the stake money. So if someone offers you a 'risk-free' way of betting, they're lying.

● **Play poker** If you're a whiz at cards, then you might like to join a poker-playing circle. There are lots of websites that will teach you the basics of the game along with tips on how to be a winner – just type 'learning poker' into your favourite search engine. Using one of the sites that pops up to get yourself started also means that you can learn online, without having to go 'live' and risk your precious cash, until you've acquired some degree of proficiency.

● **Have a night out at a casino** A visit to a casino can be a fun way to spend an evening, but always remember that casinos are in business to take your money, not hand it out. So the odds of you winning, especially a large sum, are very much stacked against you, but there are ways to increase the likelihood of going home a little richer. For a start, a firm grasp of what you're playing will help, so don't jump into any game too eagerly, unless you've mastered the basics first. Also, avoid drinking too much of the alcohol that will certainly be on offer all around you. You'll need to keep a clear head if you aim to win. Be cautious, too. If you're lucky enough to get an early win, don't become too confident. It may be wiser to pocket the cash and move on, rather than risk gambling away any gains. And if you win a large sum, don't advertise the fact. There will be plenty of shady characters hanging around, who will be happy to

Beware of fraudsters ... if someone offers you a 'risk-free' way of betting, they're lying

take advantage of you. Ask the casino cashier to hold your money until you're ready to leave – and then go quietly.

● **Play online** You don't even have to leave home these days to enjoy the thrill of placing a bet, but be wary. There are fraudsters online too, eager to grab your money. For advice and tips on betting, together with links to reliable online bookmakers, casinos and poker rooms, log onto www.online-betting-guide.co.uk If you do encounter problems with any online site, you may find the help you need to deal with them on the website of the government's Gambling Commission (www.gamblingcommission.gov.uk).

● **Set a limit and stick to it** The golden rule to follow whenever you bet is never to gamble any more than you can afford to lose. It may also be useful to regard the money that you plan to use for betting – at a race meeting, for example – as part of the cost of your outing. Then, any winnings that come your way will be a bonus.

But gambling can become addictive. If you do find that your gambling habit is getting out of hand and that you're having trouble cutting back or stopping altogether, you'll find advice online at www.gamcare.org.uk This website also offers a helpline (0845 600 0133), if you prefer to talk to someone.

FAMILY OUTINGS

8 WISE WAYS to make a day out with the children fun for the adults too

Be prepared ... there are too many opportunities for children to get bored and bad tempered

● **Be prepared** Taking the family to an amusement park, country fair, sports gala or carnival can be a nightmare. There are too many opportunities for the children to get bored and bad-tempered, while your wallet will be emptying all too rapidly. Advance preparation can make all the difference:

✽ **Book ahead** Check if you can do this online or by phone. That way you'll avoid queuing and walk straight in.

✽ **Get a map of the venue** Then you'll be able to timetable events in advance. Work out where to park and a route through the attractions. Make a note of where toilets, food stalls and bars are.

✽ **Pack the day before** Prepare any food, lay out everyone's clothes, pack your essentials bag and charge mobile phones and camera batteries. Then you

can have a leisurely start to your day and set off relaxed.

✽ **Plan your route** Bring a map and download and print directions. Take the phone number for wherever you're going, in case you get lost.

● **Make every minute count** Make the journey to the venue part of your outing – with lots of singing and games (see page 313) to help you along. If you arrive at an amusement park just as it's opening, make a beeline for a favourite ride in an area of the park farthest from the main entrance. That way, you can get the day off to a great start by taking everyone's favourite ride several times, before the queues begin to build up.

Lunchtime queues for food and drink at festivals and amusement parks are

How they do it . . .

eating out with children

Children can feel intimidated in some restaurants – there's too much cutlery or too many glasses on the table, as well as a terrifyingly white tablecloth. So choose your venue carefully. Ask other families for recommendations or go to places such as Pizza Express, that not only serve the type of food that your youngsters are likely to enjoy, but also offer highchairs and wax crayons with tablemats to colour in, while they wait for food to arrive or for adults to finish eating. In fact, it's always a good idea to take your own kit of crayons, Lego or activity books on any family outing. Sit in a booth, if you can. Such partially enclosed spaces are more likely to contain the potential mayhem of family meals. And finally, offer a reward for good behaviour – promise your little ones an ice cream, if they eat all of their main course.

often long, so bring a picnic. You'll avoid a long and tedious wait to be served and probably save some money.

Bring books or games to entertain the children during any waiting time that does arise, such as when five-year-old Jake needs occupying while ten-year-old Ruby rides the roller coaster.

● **Be prepared** Bring a buggy, even if your child is four or five years old. It's surprising how tired little legs can get during a day out and it'll save the strain of endless piggy-back demands. When the buggy isn't occupied, you can use it to carry all your clobber. Survival items worth bringing include hats, sunglasses, sunscreen, disposable wipes, insect-bite cream, plasters and a change of clothes. If the weather looks unpredictable, take lightweight waterproofs, too.

● **Avoid car-sickness** Children seem to be particularly prone to car-sickness, but you can lessen the likelihood of it by keeping children off fizzy drinks and fatty foods before a long drive. Encourage them to take frequent sips of cold, still water to prevent dehydration and don't let them read in the car – instead get them to focus on things

Relax and enjoy yourself ...Try and see the day through your children's eyes and you'll have a lovely time

outside – perhaps by playing some of the games suggested in the box (right). And open the car windows whenever possible to let fresh air in.

● Travel with Harry Potter

Whenever a family trip requires an hour or more in the car, you're confronted with the quandary of how to keep your children entertained. Games help (see right), but may only take you so far. Reading can make them feel sick, as can time on the Game Boy or PSP, which also tends to get them over-excited. And just letting them scream and shout will distract the driver and give you a migraine. One of the best solutions is audiobooks. Listening to an engaging story can keep children quiet for hours. Best of all, your local library will have stacks of audiobooks to borrow, from Winnie the Pooh to Harry Potter.

● Make it interesting

There's no better way to hold children's attention – and educate them at the same time – than to plan adventurous trips or visits to sites of particular interest or beauty. For ideas, click on the websites of organisations such as the National Trust (www.nationaltrust.org.uk). Or visit a zoo or animal park; a listing can be found on www.aboutbritain.com/AnimalsAllRegions. Theme parks can also be fun; www.aboutbritain.com has details of these, too. And many museums and galleries now welcome children and often have exhibitions catering especially for them. Key 'museums and art galleries (in your local area)' into your favourite search engine and see what comes up.

● Let them plan

If the choice of family activities is a source of regular dissent among your children, let them plan a family outing once in a while. You can set broad parameters – budget,

GAMES TO PLAY IN THE CAR

Here are some ideas for making the journey to your venue as enjoyable as the rest of your day out:

Guess the animal Someone thinks of an animal, while others ask questions about it, to which the person can only answer 'yes' or 'no'. Or one person describes the animal and everyone else has to guess what it is.

I-spy This is a classic in-car game and tots can use phonics instead of letters of the alphabet. Beware, though, of the mispronounced phonic 'R'. One parent remembers hours of fun trying to get something beginning with 'W' (phonic). The answer turned out to be 'wain' – and it was indeed 'waining'.

Can't say 'yes' or 'no' One person asks the others questions, in turn, to which they mustn't answer 'yes' or 'no' – anyone who does is 'out' and the questioner moves on to the next person. The last person 'in' is the winner.

'Sausages' One person is 'it' and has to answer other people's questions, using only the word 'sausages'. The questions should be chosen to make a reply of 'sausages' seem so silly that the person designated as 'it' laughs or giggles. The questioner then takes over the role of 'it'.

Pub signs This game only works when you're travelling on roads where you're likely to pass pub signs – not on motorways. Look out for them on your side of the car and count the number of legs, arms and heads on the sign picture or linked to the pub's name – 'The Fox', for example, would give you one head and four legs; 'The Punch and Judy', two heads and four legs. The first to collect five heads, ten arms and twenty legs is the winner.

distance and time frame – and leave the rest for them to organise. This type of planning is a useful life lesson; if your children don't have a great time, they'll have only themselves to blame.

● Remember, it's your day, too

Relax and enjoy yourself. Parents spend so much time being responsible that they almost forget how to have fun. Try to see the day through your children's eyes and you'll have a lovely time. And don't think about cooking supper when you get home – have a takeaway instead.

secrets of
TRAVELLING

Clever corner-cutting tricks of
veteran globetrotters

PLANNING YOUR TRIP

5 THINGS to bear in mind when you're trying to get the best travel bargains

● **Book well in advance – or at the last minute** If you want the best deals, book flights and accommodation months rather than weeks ahead. After this, prices begin to climb and popular flights or destinations start to sell out.

But prices begin to drop two or three days before departure. So, if you're flexible, wait for the last-minute seats that airlines are desperate to fill, or last-minute unbooked package holidays, and you could get a substantial discount.

● **Time your travel for the best deals** You can get much better rates for air fares if you fly at unpopular times. Fares are cheaper off season and what's called the 'shoulder season' – the time between the high and low seasons. Going 'shoulder' means you avoid the disadvantages of total off-peak (it's called 'low season' for a reason – maybe the resort is deserted and all the amenities are closed, or it's freezing, ridiculously hot or the peak time for hurricanes, monsoons or other local nasties).

Other ways to get cheaper fares are:
✈ Travel midweek – fares are usually cheaper on Tuesdays, Wednesdays and Thursdays.
✈ Fly late at night or early in the morning (but think about the implications for accommodation, eating and transport at both ends).
✈ Stay over a Saturday night.
✈ Avoid school holidays and half-term breaks if you're going to popular family destinations.

● **Scour the internet for bargains** There are some great deals to be had, but you will need to shop around. No one site always offers the best bargains – so be prepared to do some legwork, and keep checking for better deals. Try these popular sites:
www.opodo.co.uk
www.expedia.co.uk
www.lastminute.com
www.cheapflights.co.uk
www.tripadvisor.co.uk
www.travelocity.co.uk
www.travelsupermarket.com

● **Check airline prices** Don't assume that the internet will always offer you a better deal than booking directly with the airline. Since the internet revolutionised the travel world, airline pricing has become a much more competitive game. Prices on internet travel sites can offer some pretty great deals, but now the airlines are fighting back and sometimes can meet or beat the rates on the most popular websites. Always check those airline websites or give them a call to compare prices before you book – you may be surprised.

secret weapon

DEAL WITH A HUMAN, NOT A COMPUTER

Who hasn't been infuriated by an electronic switchboard which makes you hang on for ages, or by the countless buttons you have to push to reach a real person when you're trying to book tickets or plan a holiday? Find out the quickest way to talk to a real live human, when calling top airlines, travel companies and hotel chains, on www.cheapflights.co.uk/travel-tips/cheatsheet.html

WARNING

Travelling with no-frills airlines can be a great bargain when everything goes right. But, if delays, cancelled flights and missed connections do occur, they may not offer you as much assistance and support as regular airlines. If, for some reason one of their flights does not leave, their liability is usually limited to giving you a refund or putting you on the next available flight, which may not be until the next day, leaving you to sort out food and accommodation.

● **Go somewhere popular** The amount you pay for a particular flight is determined by how popular the route is, not by the distance. So it's possible to pay a lot less to get from, say, London to Florida, than to some more obscure European destinations. And sometimes you can do better by taking a detour through a major 'hub' airport rather than trying to get direct from one less popular place to another.

USING **THE WEB**

5 WAYS to 'net' a great trip by making the most of travel websites

● **For discount airlines, go beyond the big travel sites** Low-cost airlines such as easyJet and Ryanair never release their inventory to online travel superstores. So, for popular destinations, check their prices against those you've found elsewhere before you buy. You can search for budget airlines routes on www.low-cost-airline-guide.com

● **Check out this website for travel pros** If you've checked the airlines for price quotes, done the requisite internet searches at Expedia, Travelocity and the rest, but still remain unsatisfied with the selection and price, check out www.itasoftware.com – a website used by travel agents, travel websites and the airlines themselves. While you can't book your own tickets through this site, you can sign in as a guest – just change the sales city from BOS for Boston to LON for London if you need UK tickets and prices. The site enables you to perform complex searches, such as the cheapest weekend to travel in any 30 day period, or the lowest prices in any month, with the option to search for multi-segment trips and alternative airports up to 300 miles away. You also get warnings about the hazards of particular routes, such as a long stopover or tight connection. Once you've found the right dates and routes, just click the 'details' icon, which gives you the flight numbers, booking codes and fare codes for each flight on your itinerary. Then, quote these to your travel agent, or to the airline directly.

● **Find Disney savings online** The easiest way to save money on your trip to Disneyland (California) or Disney World (Florida) is to trim the cost of those full-price park passes. Before you plan your trip, it's worth visiting a few Disney discount websites, such as www.themouseforless.com and www.mousesavers.com These and other sites list discount coupons and codes for the Disney theme parks, hotels, cruises, and anything else Mickey-centric.

● **Sit where you want to** Don't let the airline put you in the middle seat of a three-seat row. You want to know where the good more-legroom, exit-row seats are? SeatGuru.com lists virtually all planes and their seating charts, and you can check in-seat power-port locations, too. Most airlines also allow you to check in online from 24 to 2 hours before departure, and you can then view your seat allocation and change it if you wish.

● **Use the web to cut airport parking costs** Don't just turn up and park at the airport. You can reduce car parking costs by well over half if you book even a few days in advance. Try these websites:
www.airparks.co.uk
www.simplyparking.co.uk

www.airport-parking-shop.co.uk
www.holidayextras.co.uk
www.parking4less.co.uk
www.airport-parking-discounts.co.uk
 Or if you're planning on getting to the airport by taxi, book a cab well in advance. Many local companies offer special rates for airport transfers. While you're at it, book one for the return journey too. The taxi driver will meet the flight and check for delays. It's much cheaper than hailing a taxi at the airport. And if you can, search for taxi companies, public transport or car-hire options from your destination airport too.

Sit where you want to... Don't let the airline put you in the middle seat of a three-seat row

GLOBETROTTER
CONFIDENTIAL

10 EXPERT HINTS for a smoother, cheaper trip

● **Always pay by credit card** Under UK law, if you pay by credit card for goods or services worth between £100 and £30,000, the card company is jointly liable, together with the retailer, for any faults or failures. This can be invaluable if, say, your holiday company or airline goes out of business before you travel – a situation in which you may not otherwise get your money back. The protection does not apply if you pay by debit or charge card, cash or cheque – but it does apply to purchases abroad using a UK credit card. It's much easier to resolve a problem with your UK card company than trying to pursue a foreign trader.

se**cret** weapon

ETHERNET CABLE
Most hotels today offer internet access either through a wireless connection in public areas or at a business centre (though this can be costly). Some also claim to have direct internet access in every room. But the quality and reliability of wireless connections vary widely from one hotel to another, and in-room connections often require Ethernet cables that disappear from hotel rooms as quickly as those little shampoo bottles. So always pack a standard modem lead and an Ethernet cable in your laptop case.

EXPERT ADVICE
GREAT TIPS FROM THE PROFESSIONALS

Car-hire tactics for globetrotting drivers

Read the small print very carefully. Terms and conditions will vary according to country.

• **Make sure your pre-booked deal includes 'collision damage waiver'** Some operators will add a charge when you collect the car to waive the insurance excess (the sometimes considerable costs you would have to contribute if there were an accident, theft or other calamity, even if you have 'full' insurance) and not all make this clear in the headline rates. If you frequently hire cars in Europe, you can take out an annual policy to waive these excess charges; contact www.insurance4carhire.com, 020 7372 4538.

• **Never upgrade at the airport** Operators might try to get you to 'upgrade' (at a price) when you pick up a pre-booked car. But if you did your research properly, you paid the best rate for the car you wanted, which won't be the case for the so-called 'bargain' upgrade.

• **Always fill up the car before you return it** Most operators start you off with a full tank and expect you to return the car in the same state. Their rates for filling up can be significantly higher than local petrol prices.

● **Talk the hotel manager's prices down** Here's something the big hotel chains will never advertise: you can negotiate with them. There's always someone in the hotel who is authorised to make a deal, and doing so is easy. Just tell them you'd love to stay there, but their prices are high so you'll probably end up staying somewhere else. If there are empty rooms in the hotel, you can bet you'll get a deal. Another surefire way to get a better rate is to ask, 'Is there a lower rate I qualify for?' The hotel manager could, on the sly, give you the friends and family rate, or any other 'special' rate he has. In the end, hotel managers generally prefer to sell you a heavily discounted room rather than leave it empty. Or try searching for a bargain on www.laterooms.com – the hotel industry's late-availability database. You can get savings of up to 70 per cent if you're prepared to book at the last minute.

● **Double-bag your luggage** If you're planning to take advantage of bargain shopping at your destination, think about packing one suitcase inside a slightly bigger one for the outward journey, so that you have an extra case to stash all your goodies for the return journey. But be sure to check your airline's baggage allowance, and remember not to buy so much that you spend the savings you've made on customs duties on the way back.

● **Go self-catering** It's much cheaper to prepare at least some of your own meals than to pay hotel or restaurant prices for eating out the whole time. Plus you can snack when you like, prepare picnics and cater for picky eaters or children who get impatient sitting waiting for food to arrive in a restaurant.

● **Club together** If you're planning to hire a villa or holiday cottage, think about getting a group of friends or relatives to share your holiday. A place that sleeps eight will cost you more than one that only sleeps four – but not twice as much. This trick can also work brilliantly if you want a free cruise. On virtually all major cruise ships, if you can get eight other cabins booked, the ninth one is free. You don't even need to know the other people in your group. Put up an ad in your place of work, at the local gym, your church or anywhere people congregate. Maybe you'll be lucky and get a group together. At worst, perhaps you'll make a friend or two.

● **Beware mobile phone charges abroad** Did you know you can be charged just for receiving a mobile call while abroad? And even though the European Commission recently asked mobile networks to reduce their charges for overseas calls, using your mobile when away can be far more expensive than in the UK. Prices vary significantly between providers, so check before you go. Also, ask friends to text you rather than leaving voicemail messages, which will cost you money to collect.

Another trick is to buy a new Sim card for the country you are visiting, so you pay the overseas provider direct, rather than having calls routed through your UK provider. This doesn't work everywhere, but it can save you a packet. If you need to keep the same telephone number, you can pre-buy a Sim card for the country you're going to, though it won't be as cheap. Try 0044 (www.0044.co.uk, 0870 950 0044) or UK2Abroad (www.uk2abroad.com, 0870 922 0825).

Warning Most British phones work in Europe, but not necessarily in the USA or South America. Check with your provider before you go if telephone contact is important to you.

● **Pack a change of clothes for a long flight** Aren't you tired of getting off an airplane after several hours and realising that your business suit or smart dress look as though you've slept in them – because you did sleep in them? The solution is to pack a simple, light, crease-proof outfit in your carry-on luggage. After you've settled into the plane, change into these informal clothes and put your smart clothes on a hanger. Towards the end of the flight, change back again – you will arrive looking crisp and clean instead of crumpled and sloppy.

● **Find fault and improve your cabin experience** If you're allocated a bad seat on a plane – for instance, next to the toilet, a screaming baby or a particularly chatty person, how can you escape? Complain about something – anything – that is wrong with your seat. Maybe something's been spilled on the seat, or the headphone jack is loose, or the tray table is shaky. Complain nicely and the flight staff will do their best to move you, as long as there's another free seat somewhere on the plane. If you're dissatisfied with another aspect of your flight, inform the chief purser. This is the person running all aspects of the flight apart from actually piloting the plane, and it's his or her job to make sure you're happy. So explain what's wrong, politely, and you could get a free drink, or food from the first-class menu – or even an upgrade to a better seat.

HIDDEN TRUTHS What airlines don't want you to know about **FREQUENT-FLIER MILES**

• You won't be able to use your air miles on all flights – don't even bother trying to redeem miles to top destinations during the high season. Some airlines are now listing these 'blackout' days on their websites.

• Book early for the best chance of getting the flight you want. Airlines often release their booking schedules 330 days in advance.

• It's easier to use your miles for upgrades on tickets you've already purchased than on free tickets.

• If an airline has already said you can't use your miles on a particular flight, call again as the flight draws nearer; if the plane isn't near capacity, they may let you cash in your miles.

EXPERT ADVICE
GREAT TIPS FROM THE PROFESSIONALS

Use regional airports

It is often worth trying to find an alternative to the busy main airports. Your local airport might have a more limited choice of departure dates and destinations than major airports, such as Heathrow or Gatwick, but you can often find good deals. Airlines are becoming increasingly aware of the cost savings to be made from flying out of smaller airports and there's now a wide choice of both scheduled and charter flights to major European destinations from airports such as Bristol, Cardiff, Exeter, Liverpool, Newcastle, Nottingham, Prestwick, Southampton and Teesside. Contact your nearest airport to find out which airlines operate from there. You could save a lot of money, not just on the flight itself but also on all the associated charges that go with flying from a major airport – such as parking fees, taxi or train fares, or airport hotels if you live far away. You could save yourself a lot of hassle, too.

● **Change your ticket penalty-free**
Airline employees would probably never admit it, but the fees you're often charged if you have to change your airline ticket are negotiable. When changing the ticket, simply ask the agent if it's possible the fees can be waived. The agent's first response will usually be 'no'. Ask to speak to the supervisor, and once you do, make your story a good one: your mum's sick, your boss has called you back urgently or your child's missing you. Ask, be nice, and you might just get those tacked-on fees waived.

● **Ask for a free lunch** If you've been bumped from a flight, or your departure's delayed by hours, you can usually get a meal out of the carrier. If you're not offered food vouchers, ask the gate agent to give you and your party some. They will be honoured at any restaurant in the airport. It's better than just kicking your heels in frustration at the gate.

INSIDER INSURANCE INFO
6 TRAVEL INSURANCE TIPS – experts let you in on the secrets of getting the right cover at the best price

● **Don't book travel insurance with a travel agent or tour operator**
They'll try to sell you a policy along with your travel package, but steer clear. You'll pay premium prices (up to ten times as much as the cheapest providers). Indeed, according to journalist and money-saving expert Martin Lewis, travel agents can make more money from selling you insurance than from the holiday it comes with. Plus, your cover may be inferior compared with policies obtained through an insurance company, broker or other financial intermediary, and you will have less consumer protection. That's because while most organisations selling insurance are tightly regulated by the Financial Services Authority, travel agents and tour operators aren't – they simply have to abide by the industry's own self-regulation (though the UK government is planning to change this).

● **Think about an annual policy** If you're likely to travel abroad more than once a year, buying annual travel insurance could save you money. This will cover multiple trips at little more than the cost of a single trip policy – and depending on the destination, it could be cheaper. Some banks offer such policies along with their accounts, and there are some good deals on the internet (see www.moneysavingexpert.com/insurance/cheap-travel-insurance).

● Get the right medical cover

Medical insurance is an absolute must when you travel abroad, or you could be faced with a vast bill if you have an accident or fall ill. The policy should cover transport home by air ambulance if necessary – you don't want to be stranded abroad if a serious problem occurs. Always declare all pre-existing conditions, even if you think they're unlikely to flare up while you're away, or your entire policy could be invalidated. Which is bad news if you break a leg and the insurer asks for a report from your GP that mentions recent bypass surgery or angina medicines that you didn't declare.

● **Get an EHIC** The European Health Insurance Card (EHIC) replaced the previous E111 form you needed to get medical cover in Europe. It entitles you to the same medical treatment as locals throughout the European Union countries plus Iceland, Liechtenstein, Norway and Switzerland, so that medical treatment that becomes necessary will be provided free or at reduced cost. It's available from www.ehic.org.uk, by phoning 0845 606 2030, and from post offices.

Most insurers require you to obtain an EHIC for European travel, so why bother with medical insurance in Europe? Don't forget that the definition of 'emergency treatment' may vary, as may the standard of care, and reciprocal arrangements won't cover any changes or delays to travel arrangements as a result of accidents or illness – which may be considerable if you are forced to find additional accommodation until you are judged fit to fly. Insurance will also cover medical repatriation, and will often pay if the illness of a close relative compels you to return early.

● **Don't over-insure** Before getting travel insurance, check your house contents insurance – it may cover you for personal property abroad as well. And don't forget that sometimes your bank or card company will throw in travel insurance if you pay for your holiday with a credit card – but check that it includes full medical cover.

● **Carry the details with you** You'll need your insurance details to hand if you have an accident and require emergency treatment. Remember also that insurers often insist that any losses or thefts are reported within a set time, often 24 hours.

> Medical insurance is an absolute must ... or you could be landed with a vast bill if you have an accident

CRUISE CONTROL

3 STEPS to an inexpensive, hassle-free sail on a cruise liner

Don't get
overcharged
for drinks

- **Stick to one cruise line** All cruise lines have loyalty programmes – perks could be anything from £50 cruise vouchers to private cocktail parties or free bottles of wine. And once you prove that you're a loyal customer, many of the big lines will allow you to skip from brand to brand within the same company and still retain your standing in their frequent-cruiser programme.

- **Be clear what's included in the price** Some cruises are 'all in', others charge separately for items such as tips, drinks, port charges and excursions, so it

can be difficult to work out which is really the cheaper deal. See the website www.discover-cruises.co.uk for general information about cruises. To shop for the best prices, try www.cruisedeals.co.uk

- **If there's a problem, simply tell someone** Cruise ships have the best customer service you'll find anywhere in the travel industry, according to one veteran of the business. There is plenty of competition, and bad word of mouth can sink a ship. So if you don't like the people at your table or your cabin's too close to the disco, speak up.

RESORTS AND HOTELS

4 SAVVY WAYS to make your visit less costly and more enjoyable

- **Watch those 'resort fees'** You shopped around for your holiday hotel and got the best deal. But when you get to the registration desk, you find out that there's an extra daily charge as a 'resort fee', supposedly to cover such amenities as the swimming pool and fitness club. The hotel knows that by the time you arrive, worn out by the journey, with luggage and children in tow, you're unlikely to refuse your hotel room because of an add-on fee. So, at the time of booking, scan the fine print and ask the hotel about any fees that are not included in the quote. If you're surprised by such fees at the registration desk, call your credit card company after you've checked in and ask the company to get the fee waived.

- **Skip resort-area crowds** If you're planning a trip to a popular resort area, schedule your holiday for less popular times of the year. For instance, in central Florida skip the popular summer season, and the Christmas and Easter holidays and half-term breaks. Instead, go some time between the end of August and mid December, or from January to mid February. You'll find the traffic, crowds, and queues markedly reduced, and save a lot of money with the off-season rates.

- **Don't get overcharged for drinks** Never assume that prices will be within some range that you have fixed in your mind. Don't fall for the waiter's 'helpful' suggestions to order cocktails by the pitcher or try a special bottle of wine – you could be landed with a much higher bill than you expect. When asking for water, make it clear that you're looking for tap water (free) rather than a bottle of water – always provided that the tap water is safe and drinkable.

● Get your government briefing

Before you book that idyllic break, check the Foreign & Commonwealth Office's travel advice. Call 0845 850 2829 or go to www.fco.gov.uk/travel for a list of places which the government would advise against visiting, and why.

se**cret** weapon

WRINKLE SPRAY

Hotels are more than willing to charge guests an arm and a leg for the dry-cleaning service to revive suitcase-squashed clothing. A relatively new product called X Crease, an anti-wrinkle clothes spray, is an inexpensive solution to hotel laundering. You just hang up your clothing, spray it, smooth out the wrinkles with your hands, and let it air-dry. Available from specialist outlets or on the internet (for instance, at www.livingiseasy.co.uk).

MONEY ON THE ROAD

3 STRATEGIES for dealing with money abroad

● Forewarn your bank and credit-card company Many countries have not yet adopted the more secure CHIP and PIN system, and card fraud is a real risk. So tell your bank or card supplier roughly when and where you will be travelling, otherwise if their computer detects an unusual foreign transaction your account may be frozen just when you're trying to settle your hotel bill.

● Get your travel money at the lowest cost Taking a wadge of foreign currency on your holiday is a theft risk, and bureau de change exchange rates and commission charges can amount to a very poor deal. So limit your foreign currency to what you'll need immediately on arrival. Travellers' cheques are safer than cash, but may also come with a hefty price tag. Using debit and credit cards abroad can offer the best value, because card exchange rates are based on the MasterCard and Visa 'bulk buy' wholesale rates. But bear

in mind that some card providers 'load' exchange rates, some banks charge a set fee each time you use your debit card abroad, ATM cash providers might charge a cash withdrawal fee on top, and if you use a credit card and don't pay it off in full on your return the charges on cash or travellers' cheques will be cheaper than the card interest payments. So choose your cards with care (see www.moneysavingexpert.com/cards/cheaper-spending-overseas), and spend any savings on an extra meal or two in that nice restaurant.

● Pay in the local currency Many outlets in popular tourist destinations will charge you in pounds or dollars instead of the local currency. Don't let them. The catch for this 'convenience' is that they will do the conversion less favourably for you than the going exchange rate. So always pay in the local currency, either with cash or on your credit card.

secrets of
EDUCATION

Getting the best out of school
and university years

EARLY **SCHOOLING**

5 WAYS to help your child to develop the skills to succeed at school – and beyond

● **Start good habits early** How often have you heard the parents of secondary school children saying that they still have to nag their teenagers to do their homework? At that rate they'll be accompanying their student offspring to university. Primary school is the time to start embedding the habits that will stay with your children throughout their education. When children come home from school, have a routine established that rarely varies – a cuddle, a chat about their day at school, a snack or hot meal (if they're hungry), then homework. When the homework is finished, encourage them to play outside when it's fine, riding their bikes or doing whatever else they enjoy.

● **Create the right work space** If possible, give your children a quiet, warm corner away from the TV and computer games to do their homework. They'll need a table, a chair, a decent lamp and perhaps a pinboard.

● **Keep a file of achievements** As soon as your child starts school, buy a box file and label it with his or her name. Use it to keep good work safe (projects, essays, artwork), and to record special awards for extracurricular activities, such as swimming or dance.

● **Help them to do well in tests** You can't take tests for your children, but you can give them the best chances of passing them.
≈ Keep a test calendar. Whenever your child is told about a test, write it on a wall chart. Then you can avoid that last minute panic on the morning of the test.

≈ Never show your anxiety. The more relaxed you seem about your child's tests, the better. Reiterate that it isn't the mark that's important – it's knowing they've done their best.
≈ Send your child to bed an hour early the night before a test. Sleep is vital for a good memory.
≈ Make a proper breakfast on the morning of the test. Go for wholemeal toast and a boiled egg or bacon and a piece of fruit. The fibre in the fruit and

5 WAYS TO MAKE MORNINGS EASIER

Children worry about going to school unprepared. The night before, get everything organised by checking schoolbags, packing PE bags, making sure that they have any special extra things such as project materials or money for a school trip, and keeping an eye on homework.

• Stick to a sensible bedtime. Tired children tend to be late for school and can't concentrate properly. Make sure your child has a sensible bedtime and, for younger children, don't forget that all important bedtime story.

• Set the alarm. Help children to establish a regular morning routine by setting the alarm and getting up at the same time every schoolday morning.

• Eat breakfast. Get up early enough to have a proper breakfast. You don't want a child spending dinner money on snacks at the corner shop on the way to school.

• Leave on time. Some children arrive breathlessly late, after the bell has gone, every day. Children usually hate going into school late and without their friends. Make sure you're up early enough to get them there in time to meet their friends in the playground before the bell goes.

• Don't forget. Put up a memo board near the front door that your child can check for special trips, clubs and activities. Get your children into the habit of using the board to remind them what's happening and to ask you for anything they need.

CHOOSING A PRIMARY SCHOOL

The Education Act makes education 'at school or otherwise' compulsory but it is you, who will need to apply for a school place for your child. Apply in good time for the best chance of getting the school of your choice.

Find a school Start by looking online for schools in your area. If you go to the government website www.direct.gov.uk and click on 'Education and learning', you can then follow the links to finding schools and their Ofsted reports in your postcode catchment. Or contact the local authority, who will send a list of schools in your area.

Learn about the school Once you know which schools are near you, you can find out more by reading prospectuses, exploring schools' websites and visiting schools – as often as you feel you need to. It's also worth chatting to parents of children already at the school. Take advantage of open days or evenings, which will give you the chance to ask questions and look around.

Ask questions Different parents have different priorities when it comes to choosing a school – be it academic achievement, ethos or simply a happy and relaxed environment. Think about what you want to ask about before your visit – and write a list to refer to.

bread, along with the protein and fat in the egg or bacon will help to maintain steady blood sugar levels.

If your child brings the marked paper home, go through it together so you can both see where he or she did well – and where things went wrong.

● **Be alert to subtle warning signs** Sometimes it's hard to tell how well your child is doing at school, especially at a new school or at the beginning of the academic year. But do try to get children into the habit of discussing their day. And, if children say they hate a certain teacher or subject, or that the teacher goes too fast or gives homework that's too hard, it may mean that they're having trouble with the subject and need help. Try to talk this through with your child and don't dive in and talk to the teacher without asking permission – a child might find that acutely embarrassing and end up hating the teacher and subject even more.

BROADENING HORIZONS

9 TIPS – for parents and youngsters on making the most of the pre-teen and teenage years

● **Set aside a study area** A lot of homework is now done on the PC or laptop so your children will probably need a writing/computer table and chair in a relatively quiet, well-lit and warm corner where they can concentrate and work. Make trips to the library a regular feature of your children's lives from an early age. Then you can encourage your school-age child to do some homework there if younger siblings make it difficult to find a quiet space at home.

● **Don't do their homework** Your child may be someone who likes to get homework done as soon as possible. Others need a break before tackling it. Let children organise their own time and try not to interfere unless the work isn't getting done. Remember, your role as a parent is to facilitate and support.

● **Keep up with your child** Research shows that parental involvement is key to children's achievements. We all remember some of what we learnt at school, but many subjects have changed. Get your child to talk about their work and ask them for ideas of how they feel you could help.

● **Subject choices** As children move through secondary school they'll be faced with decisions about what subjects to keep on and what to drop. If they ask for advice, then give it. But don't try to make a child conform to your ideals and expectations.

● **Teenager – be a rebel!** Don't let parents push you into taking subjects that you're not interested in. It's your life and the important business of making decisions about your education is yours.

● **Look to the future** Start building up a portfolio of references and recommendations – you never know when they could come in useful. If, for example, you've starred brilliantly in the school play, then get the drama teacher to write you a report then and there. Then, if you later apply for drama school, you've got a great reference.

● **Get a job** When you're old enough to do some form of paid work, start looking – if you have time. Shop work, waiting at tables, or leaflet delivery all help you to get into the habit of earning, and will stand you in good stead whether you decide to pursue a degree after leaving school (in which case you'll still need a job) or to go straight into the world of work. But never let a job get in the way of studying.

● **Check out universities** 'Your first year in the sixth form isn't too soon to start exploring universities or colleges', says Darren Barker from UCAS, the central organisation that processes applications for full-time undergraduate courses at UK universities and colleges. 'You can access all the universities' and colleges' websites from www.ucas.com' So be sure to start looking early, speak to your careers adviser and, if possible, take a look at universities that appeal and go to some open days.

● **Get in there** Visiting colleges is fun, but to get a real sense of what student life is like, a number of universities and colleges around the UK offer short 'taster' courses, giving you the chance to experience academic and social life on their campuses. Most of these courses are free, and they vary in length from one day to a full week. They're designed to be as realistic as possible, with lectures and tutorials, and will give you the chance to meet lecturers and other students who share your academic interests. These courses are popular. You will need to book early via your chosen college's website to reserve a place.

3 WAYS TO AVOID BEING BULLIED

Being bullied is never your child's fault, but there are some things youngsters can do to make it less likely that they'll be victimised by bullies.

• **Act as if they feel confident** Encourage children not to cower but to 'walk tall' and look people in the eye rather than turning away. This might be hard to begin with, but it will get easier.

• **Make friends** Join sports or other clubs where your child will meet others who share similar interests. Have other youngsters over to do fun things at your house – this will possibly involve internet networking or cooking, video games or football. Make sure there's some popular food in the house, too.

• **Stick with friends** During school break times and when walking to the bus stop, station or home, stay with a group of others. Children on their own are much more likely to be picked on than those with a group.

YOUR PERSONAL STATEMENT

THE ONE PART OF THE UCAS FORM over which you have most control is your personal statement. And because many universities don't interview applicants, this may be the only chance you get to persuade the admissions tutors that you're the person they want. A well-written personal statement can even help you to gain a place if you don't achieve the required grades at A level.

The UCAS *How to apply guide* says that 'the personal statement is your opportunity to tell universities and colleges about your suitability for the course(s) that you hope to study'. It adds, 'You need to demonstrate your enthusiasm and commitment, and above all, ensure that you stand out from the crowd ... Remember that the person reading your statement is an expert in your chosen area of interest so they will want to know the reasons why you have chosen the subject.'

Here are some pointers to writing yours. Remember, though, that there is no magic formula.

Why do you want to take this subject? This
area is the most important one to focus on. You'll be studying the subject for at least the next three years and you need to convince the tutors of your commitment.

Can you show a wider interest? Building on the
first section, you now want to prove your enthusiasm for the subject by describing your involvement in any related extracurricular activities or hobbies.

Talk about your life This final section is the one that
applicants often agonise over – but it should not occupy more than about a third of your statement. It's here that you can be more individual and talk about what excites you, along with any achievements that are not exam related – travel at home or abroad, involvement in the Duke of Edinburgh's Award Scheme, voluntary and paid work, the band or orchestra you play in, the sport you love.

Don't go overboard It's all too easy for positive self-
presentation to sound boastful. Don't.

Keep it simple A writing style that attempts to impress
can sound horribly pretentious. And conversely, writing in note form may only serve to suggest you can't string a sentence, let alone a paragraph, together.

Show your teacher Once you've written a rough
version, ask your teacher to read it and give you some feedback.

But be yourself Admissions tutors say that it's an all too
rare pleasure to read a statement in which the candidate's own voice comes over clearly.

Don't format it The UCAS application is an online form.
There is no word count – instead you have a character limit (4,000 characters including spaces) and a line limit (47). Formatting disappears when you submit it, so avoid bold, underline or italic; and tabs, indents or multiple spaces.

GETTING INTO COLLEGE

6 TIPS for improving your chances of doing the course you want where you want

● **Do a few extracurricular activities well** If you're an A-level school student interested in lining up a good CV for your application, limit your extracurricular activities. That's right – limit them. Admissions tutors would rather see you specialising in two or three outside activities, doing them well and showing commitment – or even leadership – so focus your efforts or what you do best and enjoy most.

● **Work towards your future**
Work experience, placements, summer schools and other courses are all useful preparation for life after uni. If you already know what you want to do after your degree, then get a head start during your sixth form years. Planning to become an architect, for instance? Then make sure the college admissions officers know that you spent your summers working in construction, learning how to build a house from inside out.

● **Consider volunteering** Top of your class, president of the student council association and founder of the French club are all impressive extracurricular activities to be able to quote. But volunteer working experience is another worthwhile string to your bow. Try volunteering at a homeless shelter, offering a few hours a week at a charity shop or shopping or gardening for an elderly neighbour. This will show you to be an active and responsible citizen, and you'll learn about another side of life in your community. Seeing how others live can be a real eye-opener.

● **Set yourself some deadlines** Many school leavers move slowly when it comes to completing their online application. Instead, plan ahead and start your application as early as possible. 'Give yourself the best chance and apply well before the recommended deadline of January 15', says Darren Barker of UCAS. 'Research your choices carefully and don't wait for your exam results before applying'. If you want to take a gap year before starting your course, check that the college will accept a deferred entry application.

● **Send your application on time**
You will need to fill in an online form from the University and College Admissions Service (UCAS), which organises and regulates the entry procedure for most higher education institutions in the UK. Their website www.ucas.com is packed with advice and explains the process of application. You can apply for up to five courses. Some courses and institutions have different entry dates and deadlines for applications – Oxford and Cambridge, for instance, have earlier closing dates – so check which deadline applies to you.

● **Don't get 'googled'** Did you know that 20 per cent of employers look at websites such as Facebook and nearly 70 per cent use search engines to check up on job applicants. There's nothing to stop university admissions officers from doing the same thing – so look carefully at your online profile and erase anything that could let you down.

PAYING FOR COLLEGE

11 TIPS for getting ahead and getting help with the costs of being a student for three or more years

● **Get a head-start** If you want to, take a gap year or some time out to earn money before going to university. Best all round is if you can find a job that has some relevance to your course.

● **Look out for bursaries and scholarships** Universities offer various non-repayable bursaries (depending on income). These range from very little to a maximum of around £3,000 and may come in the form of cash, books or help with accommodation costs. Some even throw in a bicycle. For a list of bursaries go to: http://bursarymap.direct.gov.uk/

Many colleges and universities also offer scholarships, which can be based on your A-level results.

● **Trusts and charities** Once all statutory funding has been applied for, some students may be able to secure additional funding from educational trusts and charities. You can:

☙ **Search on the web** Various websites – such as scholarship-search.org.uk – offer assistance for undergraduate funding. Your student support services will also be able to advise on available grants and scholarships.

☙ **Search beyond the web** Every prospective student knows to scour the internet for scholarships, so there's enormous competition. While the masses are fighting it out, you'll scoop up funds more quickly if you mine sources that aren't so well publicised. Libraries, your Local Education Authority and your Student Support Office may have details of local trusts and charities for the area in which you normally live or where you attended school. And look for reference volumes, such as *The Directory of Grant Making Trusts* in academic libraries.

● **Apply for a loan early** 'You know the old saying about the early bird… Well, it's especially true when it comes to financial aid,' says Ian McLaren Thomson from the Student Loan Company. 'Don't wait until you have a confirmed place on a course before you apply. Simply name the course you are

---

EXPERT ADVICE
GREAT TIPS FROM THE PROFESSIONALS

Make that loan go farther

Irene Donaldson, Head of Student Advisory Service and Equality and Diversity Officer for Students at the University of Dundee, suggests these money-saving tips.

• Don't shop on an empty stomach – you'll fill the trolley with all sorts of goodies you don't really need.

• Shop around for the best mobile phone deals to suit your needs.

• Always ask for student discounts in shops, bars, restaurants, clubs, hair salons and theatres.

• Have friends over for a drink and supper instead of going to pubs and clubs.

• Buy clothes in the sales and from charity shops.

• Visit supermarkets at the end of the day for marked-down fresh food.

• Shop with a friend for 'buy one get one free' deals.

• Save on books by using the university library to its full advantage.

• Spend less on transport. Most bus companies offer special student prices for travel cards and, if you don't have far to go, why not walk or try cycling?

most likely to take. If this changes, then notify your Local Authority at once.'

● **Take a part-time job** This can really ease the financial strain, though it mustn't distract from your studies. A number of employers have student jobs, including the universities themselves. Many have schemes where students can volunteer – and get paid – as lab assistants, campus helpers, fund raisers and mentors; a part-time job doesn't necessarily have to be off-campus.

● **Don't get a credit card** 'That iPod and summer-ball dress can wait,' says Richard Brown from financial comparison website moneynet.co.uk. 'Keep it simple with a current account, savings account and your student loan. If you really find yourself considering a credit card, seek advice first and ensure you know when you can pay it back. As a student, credit cards should always be your last resort.'

● **Check your spending** Budget if you can and keep track of your spending by using cash and checking your balance regularly. Check your current account over the internet with online banking.

● **Learn to budget** Don't just budget on the essentials – rent, food, bills and books. The costs of those coffees between lectures will mount up, not to mention mobile phone bills, printing, transport, and

How they do it . . .
survive on a student loan

Jon Mount graduated last summer from a four-year course at Edinburgh University. 'The first year was pretty straight-forward' he says. 'I got a place in halls and paid termly in advance for my room, breakfast and evening meals, so all I really had to budget for was my social life and my car.'

Unfortunately, the car was a luxury he couldn't afford. 'You end up giving lifts to everyone, so you're the one who can't drink. I had to buy parking permits and still got parking tickets. And then there was insurance. Eventually I had to sell the car and use the proceeds to pay off my debts.'

From then on, in term time and every summer, Jon worked part time to supplement his loan. 'I did the usual shop and bar work, but the best was working for an events crew (moving staging and seating for shows and sporting fixtures). This was a perfect student job – all shift work and I could fit it in around lectures, rugby training and matches – and it was never a problem if you said no. I wish I'd done it in my first year.'

With hindsight, Jon says 'Don't fall into the trap I did, of thinking "I've got an interest-free overdraft" and spending it all in year one. You won't have anything to fall back on in year two. And get yourself a job as soon as you can.'

Take a part-time job. This can really ease the financial strain, though it mustn't distract from your studies

14 TIPS FOR STUDENT SAFETY

A STAGGERING ONE-IN-THREE students becomes the victim of a crime each year. Students these days have computers, laptops, mobile phones, iPods and all sorts of other gadgetry that is easy to steal and, equally, easy to sell. **Here are some steps you can take to avoid becoming another crime statistic.**

Did you know that, statistically, students are one of the most likely groups to fall victim to crime? This is largely because they own more expensive consumer goods per head than the rest of us.

If you are a student, the crimes mostly likely to affect you are mugging, car or bike theft and burglary. Being aware of your vulnerability, and taking some simple preventative measures can help you to avoid becoming a victim.

Living in a hall of residence? Be careful who you let in or who follows you into the building. Lock your bedroom door even if you are only going to the loo.

In a student house or flat? Lock up at night and whenever you go out.

Hole in the wall Never write down your PIN; only use cash machines during the day; and put your card and cash away immediately.

Know the numbers Keep a note of your card details so you can cancel them quickly if they do get stolen.

Don't advertise it If you buy a new piece of kit – a flat screen for your computer or a new iPod, say – then don't leave its empty box outside your flat for burglars to see.

Look after the car Always lock your car and put valuables out of sight; never leave keys in the ignition.

Don't be doped To prevent someone spiking your drink, hold on to it; don't leave it on a table or the bar; or fit a Spikey® – a cheap bottle stopper available at supermarkets.

Take care when using your mobile If your phone is stolen, call the network straightaway to immobilise it.

Don't be an easy target At night walk in groups, and after a night out travel home by pre-booked taxi or stay with trusted friends.

Get insurance Keep receipts and note down the make, model and serial numbers of all your electronic goods in case they are stolen.

Mark your property Use an indelible marking kit to put your student ID number and the initials of your university (such as NU if you're at Newcastle) on your belongings. This makes stolen goods harder to sell and makes it more likely that they'll be returned to you.

Safe storage In the holidays take valuable items home, or ask your university if they have any secure storage facilities you can use.

Hide valuables If you have to leave larger items such as your computer or hifi equipment behind when go home for the holidays, make sure they can't be seen through the windows.

Buy timer switches If the flat will be empty during the break, set timer switches (as little as £2 each) to turn on lamps and radios, so the place looks occupied.

membership fees for student clubs, gyms and societies. And shop around for your insurance. Check with price comparison websites such as www. moneynet.co.uk for the best deals. 'Budgeting is a skill learned over time,' says Irene Donaldson Head of the Student Advisory Service at the University of Dundee, 'but with honesty and patience it can become a tool for managing your life'. You may find it easier to deduct rent, utility bills and books from your loan when you first get it and survive on what's left.

● **Use your student card** 'Exploit your student card where possible,' says Moneynet's Richard Brown, 'and always ask if there's a student rate or discount'.

● **Keep track of your bills** Do you pay the bills in your household? Check out money comparison site: www.uswitch.com to see if you are with the cheapest supplier for your domestic

bills – but always ask your landlord before changing suppliers.

● **Other dos and don'ts** Moneynet's student finance guide offers these tips:
꙰ Don't lend money to other students; you may not get it back.
꙰ Don't borrow money from other students. If you have to borrow then you can't afford it.
꙰ Do beware of putting your name on the gas, electricity or phone bill in a shared house. If you do, insist everyone sets up standing orders so that you get paid automatically, without fail.
꙰ Do look beyond freshers' week when it comes to spending your student loan.
꙰ Don't try to keep up with unrealistic spending habits. There will always be students richer than you. If you have to borrow money for 'good times', remember it is your name on the credit card, your name on the overdraft and, ultimately, your credit record.

SUCCEEDING ON CAMPUS

6 WAYS to make a success of your new life away from all the comforts of home

● **Check out accommodation in person** Before you request a place in a specific hall of residence, visit it. Talk to students currently living there about the pros and cons of the hall and the sorts of students who live there. Would you hate having to share a bathroom? How would you feel about sharing a room with a stranger? In fact, many halls of residence offer single en-suite rooms, so you get all the privacy you need. Some accommodation officers do their best to put people doing similar courses on one

floor, and you can usually choose single sex or mixed accommodation. Think about feeding yourself too. Some halls offer breakfast and evening meal. You usually pay termly in advance, so it's one less thing to think about budgeting for, and a great option in your first year.

● **Meals on a budget** Hungry students need bulky foods. A bowl of spaghetti with a dollop of sauce and some grated cheese is ready in minutes and is filling, satisfying and cheap. Get

UNIVERSITY LIFE

5 THOUGHTS for new students starting university life.

Christopher Butler, head of the Student Counselling Service at Royal Holloway, University of London, offers the following down-to-earth advice for new undergraduates.

1 DON'T PANIC University is a big undertaking and you are going to be there for three years, so you don't have to sort everything out in the first week. Give it a month or so to find your feet.

2 BUILD A ROUTINE FOR YOURSELF At school they timetable the day for you but at uni you have to work to your own. Most people thrive if they have a work and a social routine – get the balance right and don't be afraid to organise it for yourself.

3 DON'T GET OBSESSED Try not to worry about what everyone else is doing. Some people are just incredibly sociable and some drink like fish. You don't have to compete – find a pace and way of life that suits you.

4 NERVES ARE NORMAL Most people find starting at uni a challenge and everyone else might look supercool – but you don't know what is going on underneath.

5 USE THE HELP THAT IS OFFERED All universities have support systems for students. Most students try to manage on their own and only ask for help once they have got into a muddle. Don't let this be you – seek help early.

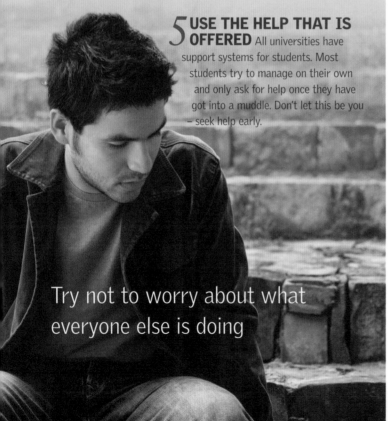

Try not to worry about what everyone else is doing

your vitamin C with an apple or an easy-peel tangerine for pudding. Stock up on potatoes, red lentils (great in thick, filling soups, curries and stews) and eat porridge for breakfast. If you want inspiration and simple how-to explanations, see www.deliaonline.com.

● **Cook together, eat together** One of the best ways to save money, beat loneliness and feel part of a community is to share meals. If you want ideas, try www.studentrecipes.com – an easy-to-use website packed with delicious food at sensible prices. And while you're cooking, you could put on some music and crack open a bottle.

● **Avoiding flatmate fall-outs**
The same disputes come up time and time again with flat sharers. Here are the big ones to look out for – and avoid.
 Money Make sure you split all bills fairly. Avoid phone-bill rows by getting a broadband deal that includes free phone calls, or have your own mobiles.
 Cleaning Clear up your own kitchen mess – quickly – and work out a rota for the bins, loo and sitting room.
 Food Students hate it when someone nicks their milk or cornflakes. Don't.
 Noise Agree a night-time deadline for loud music. If it's late, use headphones.
 Personalities Sometimes you'll have to agree you hate each other, and reach an agreement about who should go.

● **And then there's the degree to think about** The whole business of living is hard enough without worrying about lectures, essays, assignments and exams. But that's why you're there isn't it? Here are some clues to help you to make the grade.
 Don't miss out on lectures. Attending them saves you having to catch up later and makes exams much easier to pass.

Do the reading. Don't leave it to the last minute or, worse, forego it and try to bluff your way through tutorials.

Before an exam, go through old papers and talk to your tutor about timing, so you understand the format and know how long to spend on each section.

Give priority to the questions you know you can answer and those that will earn you the most marks.

Be sure to leave 10 minutes at the end to read through your paper. It's easy to lose marks on sentences that don't make sense because you were rushing.

PARENTS,
LEARN TO LET GO

9 TIPS for parents of students about to go to university

Here are some words of wisdom for you mums and dads from Jane Bidder, author of *What Every Parent Should Know Before Their Child Goes To University* (White Ladder Press, 2005).

● **Teach them budgeting skills** – how much have they got for the term and how can they make it last?

● **Give them a crash course in cooking** as well as operating the washing machine and so forth, if they don't already know how to do it.

● **Give them a book with vital addresses** (yours, Granny's) and important information such as their bank account number in case they lose their credit card.

● **Persuade them not to take too much** (it won't fit in the tiny student room) and pack the car the night before. Be prepared for moods. They're nervous.

● **Don't hang around for too long after dropping them off.** They stand less chance of making friends if you're still clinging to their arm.

● **When you get home, don't go straight into the child's room** Leave it for a few days while you allow yourself to feel sad. Then think of all the things you can do with that free time – once you've cleared out the junk under his or her bed. You could do a class or join a gym. You'll soon get used to it.

● **Keep in touch but not every day** Text instead of ringing because then they can answer when it's convenient. On the other hand, they want to know you're there for them. So send postcards and the odd parcel of goodies. Limit visits to once or twice (max) a term.

● **Ask how work is going** but accept that you can't sit on their shoulders now and check they're up to date with essay deadlines. On the other hand, if they hate their course, suggest they see their tutor immediately. Courses can be changed if it's organised soon enough.

● **Prepare yourself for a changed 'child'** when they come home in the holidays. They'll probably want to go to bed when you get up and get up when you go to bed.

Y,Z

For Reader's Digest

Editor **Rachel Warren Chadd**
Art editor **Jane McKenna**
Assistant editors **Cécile Landau, Marion Moisy**
Researcher **Angelika Romacker**
Proofreader **Barry Gage**
Index **Marie Lorimer**

Editorial director **Julian Browne**
Art director **Anne-Marie Bulat**
Managing editor **Nina Hathway**
Head of book development **Sarah Bloxham**
Picture resource manager **Sarah Stewart Richardson**
Pre-press account manager **Dean Russell**
Product production manager **Claudette Bramble**
Senior production controller **Katherine Tibbals**

Colour origination **Colour Systems Limited, London**
Printed and bound in China

Secrets the Experts Won't Tell You was published
by The Reader's Digest Association Limited, London

First edition copyright © 2009
The Reader's Digest Association Limited,
11 Westferry Circus, Canary Wharf, London E14 4HE

Also available as a hardback under the title *Forbidden
Advice,* adapted from *Forbidden Advice* published by
The Reader's Digest Association, Inc, USA
Copyright © 2007

Front cover iStockphoto.com/Norman Chan; Back cover TL iStockphoto.com/Cristian Lupu, TCL iStockphoto.com/Alex Kotlor, TCR iStockphoto.com/Andrei Tchernov, TR iStockphoto.com/ dra_schwartz; BL iStockphoto.com/Christine Balderas, BCL ShutterStock, Inc/David W Hughes, BCR iStockphoto.com/Katarzyna Macecka, BR iStockphoto.com/Jason Nemeth; 10 Punchstock/ Image Source; 11 L iStockphoto.com/Kateryna Govorushchenko, R iStockphoto.com/Emilia Stasiak; 12 Punchstock/Image Source; 15 iStockphoto.com/Valentin Casarsa; 18 iStockphoto.com/ Philip Lange; 20 iStockphoto.com/Jason Lugo; 23 iStockphoto.com/ Justin Horrocks; 24 iStockphoto.com/Stefan Klein; 27 iStockphoto.com/Cat London; 29 iStockphoto.com/ Robert Kohlhuber; 32-33 iStockphoto.com/Dodeskaden; 36 iStockphoto.com; 38 iStockphoto.com/ Paul Turner; 40 Punchstock; 41 © Reader's Digest; 42 iStockphoto.com/Kateryna Govorushchenko; 45 iStockphoto.com/Roberto A Sanchez; 46-47 iStockphoto.com/Ashok Rodrigues; 49 iStockphoto.com/Chris Cousins; 51 iStockphoto.com/Paulus Rusyanto; 52 iStockphoto.com/Erick Nguyen; 53 iStockphoto.com/ Steve Lovegrove; 55 iStockphoto.com/ Bjorn Heller; 56 iStockphoto.com; 59 iStockphoto.com/ Anatoly Vartanov; 61 © Reader's Digest; 63 iStockphoto.com/Kledge; 64 iStockphoto.com/ Bojan Tezak; 67 iStockphoto.com/ Evgeny Kuklev; 69 iStockphoto.com; 70 iStockphoto.com/ Emilia Stasiak; 72 iStockphoto.com/ Olga Shelego; 75 iStockphoto.com/Emilia Stasiak; 76 iStockphoto.com/Matjaz Boncina; 78 iStockphoto.com; 79 iStockphoto.com/Loic Bernard; 80 iStockphoto.com/Julie de Leseleuc; 84 iStockphoto.com/Lukasz Fus; 86 iStockphoto.com/ Dan Tero, 88 L iStockphoto.com/Olga Shelego, CL iStockphoto.com/Suzannah Skelton, CR iStockphoto.com/Olga Shelego, R iStockphoto.com/Suzannah Skelton; 92-93 iStockphoto.com/ Suzannah Skelton; 94 T iStockphoto.com/Koksharol Dimitry, B iStockphoto.com/Dan Wilton; 95 L iStockphoto.com, R iStockphoto.com/Arpad Nagy-Bagoly; 96 iStockphoto.com/ Koksharol Dimitry; 99 iStockphoto.com/Jill Fromer; 103 iStockphoto.com/Alain Juteau; 106-107 iStockphoto.com/ Maartjie Van Caspel; 110 iStockphoto.com/Kateryna Govorushchenko; 111 iStockphoto.com/ Skip Odonnell; 112 iStockphoto.com/Alex Kotlor; 115 iStockphoto.com/Marie-France Belanger; 116 iStockphoto.com/Marek Tihelka; 118 iStockphoto.com/Eric Delmar; 119 iStockphoto.com; 120 iStockphoto.com/Skip Odonnell; 127 iStockphoto.com/Alex Slobodkin; 128 iStockphoto.com; 130 iStockphoto.com; 133 Getty Images Ltd; 136 iStockphoto.com; 137 iStockphoto.com/ Simon Askham, TR iStockphoto.com; 138 iStockphoto.com; 140 © Reader's Digest; 142 iStockphoto.com/Nancy Kennedy; 143 iStockphoto.com; 144 iStockphoto.com/Dieter Spears; 146 iStockphoto.com/ Maartje Van Caspel; 148 iStockphoto.com/Jiri Vaclavek; 150 iStockphoto.com/Valentin Casarsa; 152 © Reader's Digest; 153 iStockphoto.com/Mark Evans; 154 iStockphoto.com/ Arpad Nagy-Bagoly; 155 iStockphoto.com; 156 iStockphoto.com/ Adam Gryko; 157 iStockphoto.com; 158 iStockphoto.com/Jdiane Diederich; 160 iStock photo.com; 161 iStockphoto.com; 162 iStockphoto.com/Stefan Klein; 164 iStockphoto.com/ Robert Lerich; 165 iStockphoto.com/ Soren Pilman; 166 iStockphoto.com/Dan Wilton; 168 iStockphoto.com/Agita Leimane; 169 iStockphoto.com/Chad Truemper; 171 iStockphoto.com; 172 iStockphoto.com; 173 iStockphoto.com/ Satu Knapes; 174 iStockphoto.com/Yanik Chauvin; 176 iStockphoto.com/Nick Nschlax; 177 iStockphoto.com; 179 iStockphoto.com; 180 iStockphoto.com, T iStockphoto.com; 181 iStockphoto.com/Dave Pilibosian, TL iStockphoto.com/Andrei Tchernov, TR iStockphoto.com/Andrei Tchernov, BR iStockphoto.com/Christine Balderas; 182 iStockphoto.com/Cristian Lupu; 185 iStockphoto.com/Jeff Giniewicz; 186 iStockphoto.com; 191 iStockphoto.com; 193 iStockphoto.com/Hedda Gjerpen; 194 iStockphoto.com/Andrei Tchernov; 196 iStockphoto.com/Oleg Ivanov; 201 iStockphoto.com/Roberto Adrian; 203 iStockphoto.com; 205 iStockphoto.com; 210 iStockphoto.com/Sascha Burkard; 212 iStockphoto.com/Andrei Tchernov; 217 iStockphoto.com/Anne Dove; 219 iStockphoto.com; 223 iStockphoto.com/Liv Friis-Larsen; 226 iStockphoto.com/Maartje van Caspel; 229 iStockphoto.com/Ljupco; 230 iStockphoto.com; 232 iStockphoto.com/Dan Wilton; 237 iStockphoto.com/Michael Tupy; 243 iStockphoto.com/Rene Mansi; 245 iStockphoto.com/ Paul W Brain; 246 iStockphoto.com/ Dave Pilibosian; 248 iStockphoto.com/Eric Isselee; 251 iStockphoto.com/Rene Mansi; 255 iStockphoto.com/ Andreea Manciu; 257 iStockphoto.com/ Alex Hinds; 258 iStockphoto.com/ Christine Balderas; 260 iStockphoto.com/Clayton Hansen; 263 iStockphoto.com; 266 iStockphoto.com/Monika Adamezyk; 270 T iStockphoto.com/ Cindy Minear, B iStockphoto.com/Katarzyna Macecka; 271 TL iStockphoto.com/Willie B Thomas, TR iStockphoto.com/Christine Balderas, BL iStockphoto.com/Trista Weibell; 272 iStockphoto.com/Cindy Minear; 273 iStockphoto.com; 274-275 iStockphoto.com/Lisa Eastman; 276 iStockphoto.com; 278 iStockphoto.com/Galina Barskaya; 280 iStockphoto.com/ Michael Chen; 281 iStockphoto.com; 283 iStockphoto.com/Sascha Burkard; 284 iStockphoto.com/Willie B Thomas; 285 iStockphoto.com; 286 iStockphoto.com/Jose Carlos Pires Pereira; 289 iStockphoto.com, (inset) iStockphoto.com/Elianet Ortiz; 290 iStockphoto.com; 291 iStockphoto.com; 295 iStockphoto.com/ Garett Mosher; 296 iStockphoto.com/Christine Balderas; 297 iStockphoto.com/Marie-France Belanger; 298 iStockphoto.com; 299 iStockphoto.com; 301 iStockphoto.com/Timur Suleymanov; 302 iStockphoto.com; 303 iStockphoto.com; 304 iStockphoto.com/Dane Wirtzfeld; 306-307 iStockphoto.com; 308 iStockphoto.com/Diane Diederich; 310 iStockphoto.com/ Kasia Biel; 312 iStockphoto.com/ Slawomir Jastrzebski; 314 iStockphoto.com/Katarzyna Macecka; 315 iStockphoto.com; 317 iStockphoto.com/Stephen Strathdee, BR iStockphoto.com; 318 iStockphoto.com; 319 iStockphoto.com; 320 iStockphoto.com; 321 iStockphoto.com; 322 iStockphoto.com/ Rebecca Ellis; 323 iStockphoto.com; 324 iStockphoto.com/Trista Weibell; 325 iStockphoto.com/Dragasanu Mihai Octavian; 328 iStockphoto.com/ Dmitriy Shironosov; 330 iStockphoto.com; 331 iStockphoto.com/Sharon Dominick, TR iStockphoto.com; 332 iStockphoto.com/Quavondo Nguyen; 334 iStockphoto.com/Aldo Murillo

Oracle code 250010501S.00.24
Concept code US 4971/IC
Book code 400-439 UP0000-1
ISBN 978 0 276 44558 3